T0331158

Operational Excellence

Operational Excellence

Second Edition

Breakthrough Strategies for Improving Customer Experience and Productivity

James William Martin

Routledge
Taylor & Francis Group

A PRODUCTIVITY PRESS BOOK

Routledge

Second Edition published 2021

First Edition published 2007

by Routledge

600 Broken Sound Parkway #300, Boca Raton FL, 33487

and by Routledge

2 Park Square, Milton Park, Abingdon, Oxon, OX14 4RN

Routledge is an imprint of the Taylor & Francis Group, an informa business

© 2021 James William Martin

ISBN: 978-0-367-49173-4 (hbk)
ISBN: 978-1-003-04525-0 (ebk)

Typeset in Computer Modern font
by KnowledgeWorks Global Ltd.

Contents

About the Author

James William Martin is a Lean Six Sigma consultant and Master Black Belt. For twenty years, Martin has trained and mentored several thousand executives, champions, Black Belts, and Green Belts in process improvement methods including manufacturing, service, and supply chain applications. He has led successful Lean Six Sigma assessments in Japan, China, Korea, Singapore, Malaysia, Thailand, Australia, North America, and Europe. This work included organizations in hardware, software, computer security, retail sales, banking, insurance, financial services, measurement systems, automotive, electronics, aerospace component manufacturing, electronic manufacturing, controls, building products, industrial equipment, and consumer products. He served as an instructor at the Providence College Graduate School of Business for twenty years. Martin holds an MS in Mechanical Engineering from Northeastern University, an MBA from Providence College, and a BS in Industrial Engineering from University of Rhode Island. He also holds several patents and has written numerous articles on quality and process improvement.

Introduction

Supply chains continue to undergo rapid evolution. Operational capabilities are increasing in ways that were not possible only a few years ago. Some organizations now deliver products or services on the same day they are ordered based on digitization and advanced inventory models. Energy efficiency and sustainability are now a focus of ethical supply chains. Global supply chains also have unique information technology (IT) platforms and applications that integrate with the supply chain participants through cloud infrastructure. Trends such as customer experience, Big Data, and the other initiatives directly impact global supply chains. Robotic process automation (RPA) and the Internet of Things (IoT) have applications everywhere. Machine learning and artificial intelligence are being applied across supply chains, just as they are in manufacturing and services. Cybersecurity has never been more important because of remote access to sensitive data.

Globalization has also forced organizations to rethink operational strategy and capabilities. This book shows how to align operational strategy to execute business goals, to design systems to meet customer experience expectations, and to improve performance to increase competitiveness. The emphasis is improving operational efficiency, customer experience, process excellence and productivity. Practical examples and applications are presented for manufacturing, service, and supporting operational systems.

Competitive organizations focus on the usefulness of actions and their beneficial impact. Adaptable organizations do not resist change, rather they embrace it with a willingness to learn and to apply new thinking to solve problems, old and new. They have strong motivation to change behaviors because experience teaches that competitiveness comes from leading rather than following. Change is about relationships and consensus from collaborative teams empowered to apply best practices to improve operational performance.

Customers have high expectations for what constitutes great customer experience. Customer satisfaction is now highly dependent on the interfaces they use to buy, sell, and use products and services. Customer expectations are set based on prior personalized experiences with other organizations when products and services are purchased. Customers now expect seamless personal interactions with organizations as more types of information are exchanged between customers and sellers. From an operational perspective, a balance can be maintained between efficiency and personalization. Digitization is enabling this balance as well as customer personalization.

Product and service design have a direct impact on an organization's operations as well as the products and services that they produce. Understanding the tools, methods, and concepts of design enables process-improvement experts to improve operational efficiency significantly. Design drives a large portion of cost over a product's life cycle. Design impacts on operations include the amounts of direct labor, materials, capital equipment purchases, inventory investment, and others. The deployment of good design practices will reduce total life cycle cost and time to market and will increase quality and promote a better customer experience. Building a core design competency helps organizations compete more effectively through simplified operations

Digitization is now at the core of process excellence. Applications include master data management, modeling of different data types, RPA, data analytics, as well as classic methods such as Lean, Six Sigma, and other initiatives to be discussed in the following chapters. Digitization enables analysis and modifications to local processes without creating large and expensive IT projects. It also supports the basic process characterization skills associated with process improvement initiatives relative to data collection, analysis and solutions.

Twenty years ago, data accuracy focused on metadata moving across one or a few IT platforms, and applications and analytics were local. Metadata is information about data. Sales and invoicing metadata include account name, company name, first and last name, e-mail address, phone number, billing address, shipping address, city, state, zip code, country, province, postal code, DUNS Legal ID, DUNS Site ID, payment terms, sales representative, territory ID, credit limit, and so on. There are literally thousands of metadata fields across IT systems in large organizations. Actual data are created, reviewed, updated, and deleted in metadata fields. We will discuss metadata data and how it is used to improve end to end operations.

Big Data is driving global transformation relative to the ways we learn, work, and produce products and services. First, the IoT consists of devices and sensors that are connected to provide information on status, to predict performance, and to control connected devices. Currently there are more than twenty billion of these connections controlling global production and services across supply chains. They also offer through automation opportunities to improve efficiency while meeting customer expectations. Second, there is virtualization in the design of almost anything today. This enables physical objects to be created using models and algorithms. These models can also be tested in a virtual environment to identify design flaws that can be corrected prior to production. Service systems can also be simulated to analyze their response to incoming demand and capacity changes or if systems are disrupted. Data virtualization promotes the use of Big Data because it can be organized and presented in easily consumable formats that provide insights to relationships and status for operational decision making and to provide a single source of trusted truth.

Although operational changes are being pushed by digital transformations, but the basis for supply chain operations and improvement remain the same: meeting service-level agreements with enough capacity and reducing lead times and operational cost. Supply chains are becoming more complicated with different transportation modes, changes in laws and regulations, and competition from different directions. In addition to technology, the focus is on enabling the workforce. Team virtualization and diversity are competitive advantages. Understanding where value is created and reconfiguring supply chain design will be the key differentiators in an era of global supply chain digitization and competition.

The concept of value helps identify work aligned with customer experience and important to the business versus work that should be eliminated now or when feasible to do so. Even if a process was optimally designed in the past, customer and business needs change. Over time, organizations may add unnecessary operations for a variety of reasons. These situations require processes be redesigned or discarded. Aligning the things that customers value into a process is a powerful way to confirm we are working on the right things and to identify ways to improve the customer's experience. We discuss the concept of customer value and how to enhance it by applying Lean tools and methods to simply, standardize, and mistake-proof processes.

Shareholder value and productivity are higher in organizations that have the right strategic alignment and can execute operational strategy at a tactical level. Effectiveness and efficiency contribute to higher organizational productivity by allocating and utilizing resources to produce products and services efficiently. They do this by using financial metrics that measure year-over-year productivity improvements, shareholder economic value added, and other financial and operational measures.

Quality is enhanced by application of Six Sigma. The Six Sigma improvement model is designed to dramatically improve performance in existing processes. It was originally conceived at Motorola using a "breakthrough improvement" model and is considered one of the most successful process improvement models ever conceived because it enables a systematic analysis of current process performance and provides a detailed roadmap to identify root causes and eliminate them to improve process capability. It aligns to the voice of the customer and voice of the business to increase quality and productivity and to sustain higher performance. Chapter 9 discusses Six Sigma and how it is applied in practice.

Operational assessments are used to identify projects to improve productivity and competitiveness. They contribute to process excellence. Although they require a commitment of time and resources, a well-done assessment documents potential business benefits and shows how to integrate improvement projects and strategically align them. Assessments also help identify where gaps occur and their impact to key processes. Alternatively, they can be focused on a few functional areas such as manufacturing or distribution and workstreams

The last chapter discusses standards as a basis for evaluation criteria that competitive organizations jointly use, as an industry, to regulate public products and services. They also impact suppliers, customers, and society. Global and local standards exist for almost every product and service sold today. An advantage of industry standards is that they are well written by participants in a competitive environment based on extensive experience. They are a consensus of the best practices for designing, producing, and testing. Depending on how they are written, they promote or inhibit competition. No proprietary information will be included in industry standards, and internal standards will normally exceed industry standards to provide competive performance advantages relative to competitors. Highly adaptable organizations will also be able to meet variations of a standard to satisfy localized preferences. It is important that organizations support the creation and updating of their industry's standards for the benefit of everyone. Standards are continually updated to keep pace with the rapid changes occurring in operations.

This book is written for process-improvement experts, consultants, and other people interested in improving global operations. It discusses useful tools and methods that are proven to improve customer satisfaction and productivity. It incorporates practical information to integrate the tools, methods, and concepts necessary to improve productivity from the "voice-of" back into an organization's front office, sales, and back-end fulfillment operations. It brings together leading-edge tools, methods, and concepts that provide process-improvement experts and others a reference to improve their organization's quality, productivity, customer service, and other operations.

Its major topics include alignment of strategy to the design of supporting systems to meet customer expectations, manage capacity, and improve performance. The fourteen chapters have been carefully designed to show relationships between innovative tools and methods for deploying programs of continued excellence, including Lean and Six Sigma. It takes a fresh approach to building improvement teams, both collocated and virtual. It introduces and integrates from an operational perspective several leading-edge topics. These include customer experience, design thinking, Big Data, IT ecosystems, and others in the context of global supply chains.

The interrelationships between Big Data and classic data gathering methods are discussed within the context of IT ecosystems. Supporting systems in most industries are now virtual and data move through many platforms and applications to support manufacturing and service processes. Understanding the ways that virtual work is done also requires an understanding of how metadata is defined, traced through applications, and governed. Operations are now digitized and rely on automation, artificial intelligence, and related methods such as RPA to do work efficiently and cost effectively. Work teams have also evolved. Global virtual teams are the common way to work, especially for supporting back-office operations. All the important topics from the first edition have been refreshed.

Chapters 1, 2, and 3 are organized from a strategic and customer experience perspective. In Chapter 1, the discussion focuses on increasing productivity to compete in the global economy. It explains why organizations that are admittedly inefficient locally can survive in protective environments but, when exposed to external competitive forces, they fail. This reinforces the thought that organizations must promote and augment their core competencies. Chapter 1 also brings together several important concepts relevant for strategic deployment of operations and effective execution.

Chapter 2 discusses change initiatives. It focuses on defining organizational change and executing it in diverse organizations through initiatives such as virtual teams, Lean, Six Sigma, design excellence, supply chain excellence, IT excellence, and others. The major success and failure characteristics of change programs will be discussed relative to these initiatives.

Understanding customer experience enhances operational competitiveness. This is the focus of Chapter 3. The ability to mass-customize products and services that satisfy local needs and value expectations is a competitive strength. Customization for customer segments enables, through technology, enables smaller organizations to dominate their niche and compete effectively with larger and more established organizations. In these competitive scenarios, current investment and infrastructure may no longer be a significant barrier to market entry or have competitive relevance. Chapter 3 provides a firm foundation from which to discuss the more technical aspects of operational excellence that translate the customer experience expectations of the voice of the customer to create new products and services and produce them efficiently for local consumption.

Chapters 4, 5, 6, and 7 discuss tools and methods for enhancing productivity by translating the voice of the customer into high-value products and services. Chapter 4 discusses the translation of the voice of the customer from the external customer perspective back into the design of products and services using useful design methods. These include linking "voice of" with design thinking, concurrent engineering, and design for manufacturing methods to create, design, prototype, pilot, and launch products. The concept of risk and product life cycle issues are also discussed in this chapter. Expanding on these concepts, mass customization is discussed from the perspective of increasing operational flexibility for higher productivity and quality. Additional topics include Design for Six Sigma, design standards, and reducing product proliferation through design-simplification strategies.

The fifth chapter discusses process excellence. Once a product or service is designed, a process must be also designed to produce it. This chapter discusses process modeling, simulation, queuing analysis, linear programming, and work simplification and standardization. Chapter 6 discusses value stream mapping, operational analysis, bottleneck management, and operation balancing, as well as supporting Lean tools and methods. Chapter 7 shows how to calculate productivity, economic value added, and other metrics to measure operational effectiveness and efficiency.

Chapter 8 has been added to this second edition to discuss IT ecosystems prevalent in large organizations, which have hundreds of applications and many platforms to deploy them. These ecosystems use hundreds and thousands of metadata fields to capture customer, supplier, production, financial, and other information needed to produce goods and services and maintain their supporting processes. The impact of the IT ecosystem is discussed in the context of the design of workflow management systems, in design, and in production. These include business process management, business process modeling and analysis, business intelligence, business activity monitoring, and enterprise application integration. Agile project management is also discussed at the end of the chapter.

Chapter 9 discusses the integration of Six Sigma methods to enhance quality, increase productivity and promote operational strategy. The tools and methods range from basic to advanced. Some advanced regression methods were added to this chapter, but the proven approach for executing the Six Sigma initiative remain the same.

Chapter 10 has also been added to discuss Big Data. Big Data requires new data collection and analytical strategies. The growth of data is exponential. The differing types of data (e.g., numbers, text, pictures, videos, voice, etc.) require enormous amounts of electronic storage and specialized analytics. This includes special data conditioning, transformations, and statistical methods for the large databases. Instead of taking small samples from a larger population, we now analyze the entire population (i.e., the entire database).There are challenges, however, in the storage, searching, transfer, and visualization of large databases. At an analytical level, the challenge is to incorporate views of structured data (e.g., organized structure and defined formatting), semi-structured data in which patterns and models are created with analytical effort (e.g., numbers and parsing text), and unstructured data with no definable structure and diverse formats (e.g., text, pictures, voice, video, etc.). New analytical methods are being used to analyze the latter category.

Operational assessments are discussed in Chapter 11 relative to collecting and analyzing information to increase productivity and quality. The management of virtual teams is discussed in Chapter 12 with basic project management methods such as Gantt charts, the program evaluation and review technique (PERT), risk analysis, and other topics. Chapter 13 discusses supply chain excellence and incorporates topics from previous chapter. Finally, Chapter 14 discusses sustaining strategies including standardization and auditing. These include the Supply Chain Operations Reference (SCOR) model, the International Standards Organization (ISO), the Financial Accounting Standards Board (FASB), the Occupational Safety and Health Administration (OSHA), the Federal Drug Administration (FDA), the Automotive Industry Action Group (AIAG), and the Malcolm

Baldrige Award. Metric dashboards are also discussed to help implement effective controls.

I want to thank Michael Sinocchi, my publisher at Taylor & Francis, for providing me an opportunity to update the original operational excellence topics to include the many disruptive technologies that are impacting the translation of customer value through global supply chains. I also want to thank Neelu Sahu who managed the editing and production of this book.

1

Operational Excellence

OVERVIEW

In the last few decades, several accelerating trends changed the way in which we view the management of production. Digitization has been a large transformational force connecting information technology (IT) systems and devices across the world. Work is done virtually for most supporting back-end operations. Work products are to a large extent more informational than material in form. Teams collaborate globally though video conferencing of various types. Productivity and quality are higher. Expectation around customer experience are becoming increasingly personal and seamless. Enhanced operational capabilities support these disruptive changes. The expansion of the Internet in increasingly large bandwidths makes information readily available to much of the world. Operations are focused on enabling innovative ways to do work and offer highly customized products and services globally to customers. These trends contribute to the creation of new production systems that enable organizations to dominate not necessarily by virtual of their size, but on core competencies in niche or newly created markets.

There are definitive steps that organizations take to become more competitive. Our focus is on operational capability that is aligned to strategy. One goal of this book is to integrate customer experience, design, process, and important initiatives such as Lean and Six Sigma into a logical approach for increasing productivity and customer experience. Organizations increase their relative competitive positions by successfully applying and integrating tools, methods, and concepts with available technology as well as human systems. Part of this application is developing competitive strategies by carefully considering customer expectations for how they value products and services. Value is relative to customer expectations around the dimensions of cost, time, availability, and how customers use the things they buy. Different customer segments value things differently. Operational excellence is evolving through breakthroughs in technology such as digitalization, automation, RPA, virtualization, big data, and other disruptive technologies as well as ways to manage people and resources to provide an exceptional customer experience. New trends evolve and old paradigms disappear.

Worker demographics are also changing. This trend directly impacts operational design. Some workers prefer to be on-site to interact with other employees, whereas remote working is preferred by other workers. There are several generations of workers in many organizations, and each has different working preferences, beliefs, and approaches for working. Developing a flexible, diverse, and easily trainable workforce is a strategic imperative. Customers are global, and therefore supporting services must also be global from perspectives of culture, language, and availability at any time and place. The new strategic focus is leveraging worker knowledge and skills to match new operational designs as work changes. The degree of social interaction, both in person and via social media platforms, is also influencing work. This experience is facilitating the ability of workers and customers to customize products and services. Virtual teams are globally enabled as technology provides remote information sharing. Cultural assimilation, training, diversity enablement, and virtualization are key factors for promoting effective teams in multicultural workplaces.

New technologies require continual worker training to support operations across global supply chains. Some technologies are disruptive, and others evolve from changing customer expectations for buying and using products and services. Skilled workers are needed to provide a seamless and exceptional customer experience, whether it be purchasing industrial equipment, receiving materials, or receiving services of various types. Products and services have supporting processes that should be aligned with customer expectations but also have high productivity. In addition, skills change with expectations and technology that influence operational design. Continual worker training of various types is always needed. To complicate matters, it is difficult to find and retain talent. Internal virtual learning universities are being created by organizations to enable workers to train themselves using self-paced virtual learning paths. This enables workers to develop their skills and to match them with available work, which is constantly evolving. But it also requires workers who can be trained and retrained as conditions change. Adaptable and educated workers are always in demand. To be successful, global supply chains must onboard talent around the world.

Virtualization enables employees to work from anywhere and anytime. This is advantageous for both workers and employers from perspectives of convenience, low cost, and high skills availability. As an example, one organization located their customer support center in Egypt because the population is multilingual. This makes it easier to answer questions and provide services to their European customers, who speak many different languages. Virtualization provides organizations with expanded options for how best to manage their workforce. Strategies vary from offshoring to training local workers or a combination of approaches, such as retraining current employees and hiring new ones. Regardless of the choice, if properly executed, productivity is favorably impacted because of stronger and more adaptable skills.

A potentially negative impact from global operations and virtualization is worker burnout. Causes include working on different schedules, continual changes in the types of work and how it is done, as well as team formation. It is not unusual to work with several teams in a short time. To counteract these negative impacts, organizations create wellness programs to promote exercise, good eating habits, and other ways to maintain physical and mental health. Teams are facilitated using technology and provided with tools, policies, and process to do work in standardized ways to reduce stress. Organizational benefits are greater worker satisfaction and longer retention compared to organizations that do not support teams in these ways. There are also laws and regulations implemented especially in the European Union to restrict access to employees when not at work.

Operational excellence integrates customer experience, product, and service design with processes to increase customer satisfaction and worker productivity. Highly competitive global supply chains produce materials and information more efficiently than competitors if the organizational strategy is aligned to operational strategy and executed using the right measurements, initiatives, and projects. Highly innovative solutions become more apparent when operations are defined from a customer experience perspective. Innovation influences operational design to make it competitive. One useful approach is considering the customer experience from purchase and use over the useful life of a product or service (i.e., its life cycle). The proliferation of IT platforms and applications enables a single source of truth for operational control and reporting. They also provide deep insights from data extraction to apply analytics to create and report relationships. Big data provides new capabilities for global supply chains to understand customer and operational transactions in complicated and interactive processes. Operational excellence is focused on adapting to changing customer preferences while maintaining productive operations.

Automation is also being introduced through the IoT and other applications to increase productivity. The IoT is composed of smart devices and sensors that are interconnected. These can be accessed to aid information exchange and support operational management. Operations are also being positively impacted by the use of artificial intelligence (AI) to aid decision making and reduce mundane work tasks, such as building reports or searching for information. In addition to AI, RPA is a growing field that automates routine work. The robots are virtual people efficiently doing repetitive work without error. In contrast with AI, which uses intelligent algorithms to build and use models to recommend decisions based on changing inputs, RPA provides advanced analytics to support people or to supplant people with chat bots and other automation, depending on the application.

COMPETITIVE OPERATIONS

Understanding the voice of the customer helps design and production teams focus product development efforts, deploy technology to align operations, and improve productivity through the efficient use of labor, materials, and capital. Product and service designs determine the operational design, including its supporting processes. Operational design should be considered from a global perspective but with customization at a local or regional level to satisfy cultural preferences as well as economic, political, and other constraints. Aligning with customer experience expectations improves designs of any kind. As an example, when customers want a product faster, this encourages a supplier to think of ways to meet this customer's need. Once a viable solution is found, other customers benefit and the supplier becomes relatively more competitive. Similarly, if customers request new features and functions to a current a product or service, opportunities arise to make designs less costly or more reliable and to incorporate other improvements for competitive differentiation. Differentiation is also created if suppliers work directly with customers and at their locations. Observing how customers use or don't use products and services affords views for creating additional solutions. Customers do not always know what will help them until they are offered a unique solution.

Operational strategy for most industries was relatively simple prior to digitalization and globalization, which disrupted competitive ecosystems. Competitiveness was determined by available technology, design, and operational systems at a regional or at most a national level. Customer preferences and the technology used to design, produce, and mange products and services changed very slowly for most industries. The product life cycle in consumer appliances used to be measured in years or decades, although there were updates and modest increases in performance every few years. Today, many product and services life cycles are measured in years or months. As an example, consumer appliance features and functions proliferate because of both innovation in understanding customer preferences and experiences as well as the evolution in software application, sensor technology, and other digitalization capabilities. Proliferation of products and services is supported by flexible design, production, and fulfillment systems. Also, whereas several decades ago operational strategy changed infrequently, in some industries today it changes more frequently to match global customer preferences that are differentiated at a local level. Disruptions require effectively translating business and operational strategy to match changing customer preferences and expectations.

As an example, the operational strategies of Burger King and McDonald's fast food restaurants are different by design, based on marketing strategies designed to service specific types of customers. An operational comparison shows Burger King uses a customization strategy based on its marketing promise of "You can have it your way." Its operational design enables customers to customize their orders. Burger King also processes burger patties through a "flame broiler," which is its second marketing promise. The process for customer orders is a classic "batch and queue," and the flame broiler constrains the throughput batch by batch. When customers arrive at a Burger King restaurant, they expect (based on the marketing promise) to wait for customized food for a longer period than when they order at a McDonald's restaurant. There is also more wait time variation in Burger King's batch and queue system compared to a more standardized system like that used at McDonald's restaurants. Several of the Burger King supporting processes, like fries and drinks, are standardized. The key concept is that marketing promises influence operational design because customers are promised products and services of specific types.

In contrast to the operational strategy of Burger King, the McDonald's process provides fast and standardized products and service. Customers arriving at a McDonald's restaurant find food products designed in a standardized way to improve process efficiency. McDonald's also maintains a small inventory of food (i.e., still very fresh and made only minutes ago) and is ready to build a meal to satisfy customer demand. The types and quantities of food in inventory were determined by historical customer demand patterns by the minute of the day. Depending on the restaurant, when we purchase meals our expectations will be different. But because we receive products and services as promised, the experience will be great. McDonald's and Burger King target different market segments but are very successful businesses.

In summary, an organization's operational strategy should be aligned with its marketing strategy relative to the expected customer preferences for products and services so that expectations are met at every encounter (i.e., the moment of truth). If products, services, or supporting processes are misaligned with customer expectations, dissatisfaction occurs with negative consequences. Examples include returns and warranty issues, complaints needing resolution, higher transactional cost, and lost revenue. Productivity deteriorates.

Strategic operational linkage is achieved by translating customer requirements into the design of products, services, and supporting processes. The line of sight between business benefits such as productivity and shareholder economic valued added and resource allocations should be clear. Strategic alignment is especially important for larger and more complex systems having interrelated processes impacted by several active initiatives. Table 1.1 provides an example of how two enabler initiatives (e.g., Lean and Six Sigma) are aligned to improve operational productivity. If process yields are low, Six Sigma methods may be useful for identifying the root causes of low yield and creating solutions to eliminate them. Perhaps the problem is a machine creating rework because it cannot maintain a dimensional tolerance. Experiments may be useful for building a regression model to show relationships between the tolerance and several machine settings. Higher process yields correlate to lower scrap

TABLE 1.1

Enabler Initiative Examples

Measurable Improvement	Enabler	Productivity Opportunity	Productivity Linkage to Finance
Reduce scrap percentage	Use Six Sigma methods to increase yield	Reduce scrap expense	Reduce direct labor and materials
Increase inventory turnover	Apply Lean methods to reduce forecasting error and lead time	Lower inventory investment	Increase cash flow and reduce inventory holding costs

and rework percentages, which can save material and direct labor as well as reduce lead time.

In the second example, an inventory turnover ratio is increased by applying Lean tools and methods to reduce the lead time for a hypothetical product. Inventory turnover is a ratio of the annual cost of goods sold (COGS) divided by the average on-hand monthly inventory investment. As an example, if COGS is $12 million annually and the average inventory investment necessary to maintain this level of COGS monthly is $1 million, then the inventory turnover ratio is 12. The benefits realized with a reduction of inventory investment are increases in cash flow because money is available for other uses and a reduction of interest expense needed to maintain the inventory investment using financing.

The concept is that, when selecting projects either at an operational level from management reports or from operational assessments focused on gaps such as scrap, rework, or other issues, it is key that these decisions are linked to an enabler initiative with its tools and methods prior to project execution. All linkages must be measurable. As an example, operational improvements associated with a project should be linked to a financial statement such as profit and loss (P/L), balance sheet, cash flow statement, or others, and to project metrics to calculate their impact on productivity. This is important because project benefits offset the costs needed to create a team and to provide resources. In Chapter 7 we will show how linkage is done using hypothetical financial statements and operational reports.

Operational flexibility, decentralization, and integration have been accelerated through technology improvements and increasingly sophisticated operations management tools, methods, and concepts. Information available to organizations through the Internet has leveled the playing field relative to the ability of organizations to learn and adapt design and operations to align with customers. This has enabled disparate organizations to compete around the world based on the value components of price, speed, utility, and functionality, as well as mass customization of products and services. Mass customization is focused on efficiently satisfying customers' local or personal needs and relies on several supporting structures, such as efficient design and production.

Global supply chain collaboration between participants evolved to reduce end-to-end time from quote to delivery. Collaboration is enhanced by supply chain aggregation or disaggregation of processes. As an example, marketing processes could be done in several countries to meet localization needs. Products could be designed and then manufactured in other countries for worldwide distribution. Back office support operations may be distributed from anywhere. This requires virtual teams, which are now commonplace. These teams, which are usually diverse, also resemble the customer they serve in that they are increasingly multilingual, culturally savvy, technically proficient, and collaborative by training.

Properly facilitated, collaboration within a diverse team increases because team members tend to ask questions from different perspectives rather than immediately moving to a predetermined and perhaps non-optimal solution. Questions are important. Several years ago, I joined a forecasting improvement team. The team comprised twenty people at management and director levels. It had been meeting for two years to discuss forecasting accuracy improvement. During the preceding two years, however, they had only mapped the forecasting process. They did not execute process improvements or improve accuracy. The problem was that the team had focused its scope only on improving forecasting accuracy. The scope ensured no other investigations would occur. After consulting with experts, after two years, the team was told the product forecasting accuracy was consistent with similar industries and benchmark accuracy. The reason this team had made little improvement in its demand process was that it had asked the wrong question. A better questions would have been, "How can we better estimate product demand?" Focusing attention on estimating customer demand would have provided the team with a larger scope for improvement options in addition to forecasting model improvement. Questions are important.

Approximately 50% of this organization's product revenues were from ten large retailers. Several of these collected point-of-sale information as products were scanned in their stores. This demand could be timed with

100% accuracy. The balance of the organization's customers were approximately 1,500 smaller warehouse distributors. Their demand needed to be aggregated by product group and forecasted. Using 100% known demand and the current accuracies over a smaller revenue base ensured overall forecasting accuracy would be immediately improved. If product promotions were offered, demand was simply additive to the already improved forecasts. In summary, organizations with diversity are more innovative because information gathered is more complete and is analyzed from different perspectives. More questions are asked and answered. Problems are better stated, leading to the following observation from Charles Kettering: "A problem well stated is half solved."

It has been shown that when organizations align strategy with design and operations, they consistently outperform global competitors. Competing organizations may even use the same labor, materials, capital, and infrastructure; but they can exhibit different levels of productivity because of differing strategies and execution. Toyota is an example. It efficiently integrates customer feedback, design, and operations as opposed to some of its competitors. The results are vehicles that are lower cost and more reliable, as well as a greater market share. Its success shows that low cost is not the only differentiating factor for gaining market share in the automotive industry. Organizations need to successfully integrate state-of-the art technology and operational methods to compete successfully.

ENHANCING OPERATIONAL CAPABILITY

The strategies and tactics that an organization uses to compete globally have radically changed. At one time, organizational size and available capital would ensure market share and allowed organizations to adapt slowly to changing market conditions. In these older bureaucratic systems, even if newly developed technologies were deployed by competitors, organizations often had enough time to reverse-engineer the new systems, independently develop similar versions, or buy out the competitive organization to remain dominant. Consumer preferences were also relatively stable and geographically isolated to regions. This allowed organizations to easily manage customer value expectations and meet needs. The customer experience was very simple and stable in these relatively static environments, so operational strategies could also remain static. But as globalization and technological advances evolved, customer expectations also evolved. They expected lower cost, high quality, and fast response times. Consider the home appliance industry. In response to competitive pressures, this industry rapidly moved from being a slow innovator to adopting leading-edge approaches to product and services design as well as supporting processes such as logistics, customer service, invoicing, and others. Most industries have reduced product and service development time and cost while offering more differentiated products and higher quality. Market dominance used to be determined by the ability of large organizations to set industry standards and deploy capital intensive barriers that prevented new entrants. Today, smaller organizations may dominate niche markets by neutralizing larger and historically more entrenched organizations. This is because of better customer knowledge, technology for scale, and the creation of flexible operations, including virtual operations.

In John Kotter's book, "Leading Change," he puts forth an eight-stage process to create major change within an organization. These characteristics of effective change include "establishing a sense of urgency," "creating a guiding coalition," "developing a vision and strategy," "communicating the change vision," "empowering a broad-based action," "generating short-term wins," "consolidating gains and producing more change," and "anchoring new approaches in the culture." The ability of an organization to adapt its organization, systems, and people to meet competitive threats is dependent on the organization's culture and is the driving force behind an organization's competitiveness. Organizations will not change without a strong reason. Behaviors that made them successful are not easily abandoned without justification. At times and for differing reasons, some organizations are in crisis. The crisis could be a new disruptive technology, a new competitor, or some other reason threat to the organization. Employees will try a new approach when they have few other choices.

A guiding coalition is also important. These are also called governance councils, and they consist of roles and responsibilities organized to promote an initiative. The leadership council reviews the initiative status through its workstreams and ensures strategy guidelines are followed and resources are made available. There are also workstream teams logically organized by geography, function, work type, or other logical groupings. Each workstream has a charter, a schedule, deliverables, a leader, team members, and associated information. The workstream periodically reports progress to the leadership council.

The leadership council also creates the initiative's vision and strategy, which should be aligned to the larger business strategy. The strategy helps identify the initiative's goals. Examples of goals would be achieving 2% year-over-year productivity improvement, increasing market share by 10%, reducing operating expense by $1 billion. An initiative would include several types of goals, such as those related to higher customer satisfaction, reduced lead time and cost, and higher quality. The leadership council ensures the vision, strategy, and goals align with those of the workstream teams and projects to ensure realization of estimated benefits.

Organizations cannot change without practicing new behaviors. Communicating the vision and strategy as well as the enabling tools and methods help employees see how to align with and contribute to an initiative. There are different types of communication that need to be adjusted depending on the audience, the message, and the format. The broad-based coalition includes both the workstream teams and other employees supporting the team's projects. The goal is to empower a large percentage of more than 30% of an organization to support an initiative by actively practicing the new behaviors. As projects are closed and benefits are realized, these need to be communicated to the organization. An initiative's success depends on communicating the benefits that were gained by practicing the new behaviors. Seeing benefits helps convince people to try different things. As an initiative matures, lessons learned are summarized, changes are made to the strategy, and resources are reallocated to provide additional benefits.

LINKING STRATEGY TO OPERATIONS

Effective execution requires doing the right things efficiently to achieve strategic and tactical goals. Organizations ensure alignment by identifying strategic goals such as sales, cash flow, operating income, sustainability, diversity, and other important goals represented as measurable targets (i.e., metrics). These are set by leadership consensus and based on the general business environment that is impacting the organization. Ideally, the goals set this year will be improvements from the previous year's goals. A good overall operational measure of how well financial goals are met is a year-over-year productivity index. These concepts are

Voice of the Customer (VOC)

Voice of the Business (VOB)

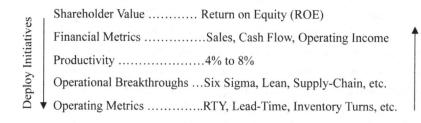

Deploy Initiatives

Shareholder Value .... Return on Equity (ROE)

Financial Metrics ....Sales, Cash Flow, Operating Income

Productivity ....4% to 8%

Operational Breakthroughs ...Six Sigma, Lean, Supply-Chain, etc.

Operating Metrics ....RTY, Lead-Time, Inventory Turns, etc.

Execute Initiatives

Voice of the Process (VOP)

FIGURE 1.1
Strategic execution of business goals.

shown in Figure 1.1, in which the voice of the customer is integrated with the voice of the business through a return on equity (ROE) metric and eventually with the voice of the process through enabler initiatives and their operational metrics. Enabler initiatives are also described in Table 1.1.

Figure 1.1 shows the top-down planning process that ensures alignment throughout an organization. Top-down alignment ensures that projects created in the organization will improve financial as well as operational metrics. This approach is critical for being able to measure overall organization performance according to the financial goals of sales cash flow, operating income, etc. The project execution activities occur down at a process level and they are aligned to and integrated with the higher goals. This strategic flow-down methodology demonstrates the translation of strategy goals (e.g., financial, productivity) into initiatives and then into projects. It helps ensure linkage to operational strategy and execution to ensure the right things are done.

The voice of the business identifies the shareholder value represented as a ROE target. This metric measures the shareholder return on investment.

In non-profit organizations, similar metrics can be inserted in lieu of ROE. As an example, there is a social return on investment (SROI) metric. It measures the impact of a non-profit's intervention on the community when money is invested into a social program. The output benefits included better health and longer life, less pollution, enabling students and others. SROI measures benefits to investment needed to attain them. Non-profits also use investment analyses for financial driven processes such as fund raising. In these scenarios, the question is, "How resources should be invested to generate additional donations?"

A ROE target is cascaded down into an organization using the strategic financial and operational metric goals. In Figure 1.1, the metrics just below the ROE target are sales, cash flow, and operating income. Other financial metrics can be related to these three. The year-over-year productivity target is the bridge from financial metrics to operational metrics. It measures the effectiveness of the total organizational resource allocation and use for increasing sales and cash flow while reducing operating income. The numerator is revenue minus adjustments for pricing exchange rates, and the denominator is total cost minus adjustments. Projects are created that increase sales while minimizing adjustments such as pricing concessions and decreasing operating costs of many types.

Productivity calculations are made at all organizational levels. A complete example will be discussed in Chapter 7. To improve productivity, it is necessary to deploy enabling initiatives such as Lean, Six Sigma, preventive maintenance programs, supply chain excellence, IT deployments, and others. Initiatives and their projects are aligned to improve productivity while balancing resource allocations between initiatives and their projects. Organizational teams have specific assigned goals that will increase total organizational productivity with minimal friction. Process improvement experts focus on areas and projects that have the highest productivity leverage. When projects are completed, lead time and expenses are reduced, and productivity is increased in a measurable way.

It is interesting that different organizational cultures, even within the same industry, sometimes approach strategic goal deployment and execution strategies differently, but the approaches work for them. One reason for this is because they leverage core competencies of different types and to varying degrees. As an example, the culture of a major financial services organization was consensus-based and employee-centric. Improvement projects needed to be executed based on consensus. In contrast, another major financial services organization had a more business- and execution-focused culture. Improvement projects were assigned without consensus and expected to be completed to schedule. Although there were differences in execution style between the organizations, both successfully deployed the Six Sigma initiative, closed projects, and realized benefits. The common factor was effective execution despite differing approaches for employee engagement. Execution is critical to compete successfully.

Not all organizations have an effective execution strategy. As a result, organizational productivity levels vary among similar companies. ROE is higher for organizations that have effectively linked strategies and execution with initiatives that help develop core competencies. Core competencies are highly competitive best practices in finance, marketing, sales, customer service, design, operations, supply chain other processes. These enable organizations to dominate their markets relative to competitors.

Interestingly, most organizations are successful through a few core competencies rather than being excellent in all areas. It is not unusual for an organization to be excellent in sales, marketing, and design but have inefficient production and supply chain processes. Other organizations may have good operations management, but overall organizational performance may be nonoptimal because the wrong products are marketed or products and processes are poorly designed. Few organizations are truly excellent for most core competencies. In contrast, industry leaders are usually those organizations having several core competencies that successfully link strategy to execution.

Although strategy may serve an organization well for a period, competitive environments change because of disruptive technology, laws and regulations, consumer preferences, and other factors. Competitors leave little room for poor strategic execution. As an example, one large international organization was well known for its superior new product development and marketing processes, and it dominated its market for twenty years through design breakthroughs. But, unknown to most people, it had one of the poorest supply chain systems in its industry. Customers complained about poor quality and delivery times. Its strategic focus was on being first to market with innovative designs, and the supporting processes suffered from a lack of investment. It is unwise to rely on only one or a few core competencies. Such organizations are not protected from global competitors. Effective execution is critical for survival. The best strategy for long-term survival is higher productivity and customer satisfaction. These depend on creating core competencies.

Another way to think about productivity is to consider how it is measured apart from an organization. At a macroeconomic level, a country's standard of living is measured as per-capita productivity. Per-capita productivity is composed of labor, capital, and factor productivity components. Factor productivity is the efficient utilization of capital and labor. Countries have different levels of these components. In countries with a high standard of living, the labor and capital bases are large and factor productivity is also high. This implies labor and capital are efficiently utilized through experience, education, and advanced skills. Excessive regulations and laws, poor infrastructure, and other conditions will lower factor productivity by causing friction in the production of good and services. Other countries may have differing levels of these components. Developing countries may have many people but little capital (i.e., money and machines or little education and skills). Their per-capita productivity (or standard of living) will be low. In contrast, some countries may have high capital and labor bases but low factor productivity. They can produce much but cannot efficiently distribute it to improve per-capital productivity.

Factor productivity is a different way to think about an organization's productivity. Initiatives help increase organizational factor productivity through projects that efficiently utilize capital and labor. Several years ago, smaller organizations were not usually competitive with larger competitors. They lagged in capital, labor, and factor productivity. Because of digitalization, however, smaller, and geographically dispersed organizations can now project their presence with little labor or capital but with higher efficiency, such as through software applications on the Internet. Higher productivity is gained because all three components—capital, labor, and factor productivity—are small relative to competitive organizations with expensive fixed assets.

Through digitalization and automation, the relative importance of capital and labor has been reduced because the competitive playing field between organizations of differing size is leveled by technology and innovative ways to conceptualize and produce products and services. As an example, many of these newer products and services are virtual and do not physically exist, although they are accessed using physical objects. Highly productive organizations will increasingly be less capital- and labor-dependent. This is true for products and services with high customer contact as well as back-office operations that are rapidly changing to automate work through RPA to reduce labor and capital utilization.

METRICS

Metrics are used to identify, define, measure, and control performance gaps for improvement as well as to describe operational performance. They should be aligned with higher-level metrics in ways discussed in the previous section and linked to others as needed to measure performance. An example is organizational or corporate warranty expense. It should be clearly defined, measured, and calculated by location. Warranty is an aggregated expense rolled up from lower levels and locations in the organization to ensure linkage as shown in Figure 1.2. This ensures alignment of warranty expenses to one organizational number. Alignment is also

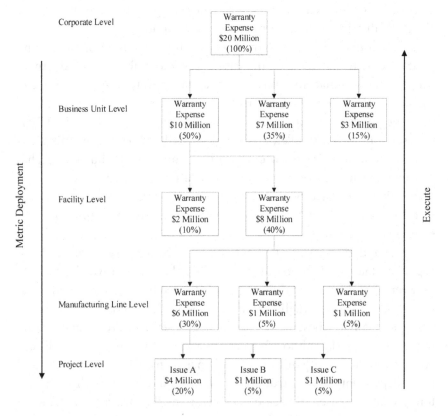

FIGURE 1.2
Strategically aligning metrics.

important to ensure resource allocations are made to those areas where warranty expense is highest. Once reduced, these will provide the most productivity opportunity and ROE.

Warranty expense as shown in Figure 1.2 is linearly additive because its unit of measure is defined in monetary units (i.e., dollars). At an operational level, there are other metrics that must be measured and improved to reduce warranty expense. These are at a project level and they need to be correlated with higher-level metrics, either financial or operational. A second important consideration is the ease of data collection, analysis, and presentation. This is an important consideration for displaying metrics using automated and visual displays to show their status. As an example, for operations centers, process status is displayed using visual display boards. These show the current transaction volume, waiting time, and other measures for managing the operations center.

It is important that metrics be actionable by the people responsible for them. If a material planner is assigned the responsibility for controlling inventory, this person must also be able to see product lead times, demand, inventory status, and other relevant information to determine where inventory should be placed to meet service targets. Because lead times are set by other organizations and demand variation cannot be controlled by material planners, the inventory investment targets must be clearly defined so they coincide within the expected range of lead time and demand variation. Once the inventory investment metric is defined, reasonable, and actionable, it is very difficult to manipulate or to distort it in practice.

Metrics are classified for their organizational impact and specific format. These include the dimensions of time, cost, and quality. Within these dimensions, teams create metrics to measure, analyze, control, and continuously improve process performance. Service centers may use the average time to answer a call, and production may use lead time. Table 1.2 shows a partial listing of common metrics used to measure and control processes across a global supply chain. These can be classified into the dimensions of time, cost, and quality. They are all also linear or volume adjustable.

Metrics can also be classified into the four categories of business, financial, operational, and compensating. Business metrics are used to linearly deploy metrics throughout an organization. They are aggregated at an organizational level, a local business unit level, or a local process level. Business metrics are typically measured on a percentage-of-total basis.

TABLE 1.2

Commonly Used Metrics

Financial	Quality	Customers
• Sales	• First-pass yield	• Customer satisfaction
• Income	• Process capability	• % New customers
• Cash flow	• % Warranty	• % Customer retention
• Productivity	• % Returned goods	• % International sales
		• % Export sales

Research & Development	Process	People
• % New products in last 3 years	• Lead-time	• % Employee diversity
• Product development life cycle	• % On-time delivery	• Training hours per employee
• % Engineering change requests	• % Schedule attainment	• % Employee turnover
• % Cost of sales	• % Machine uptime	• % Employee satisfaction

Materials	Suppliers	Environmental
• % Forecasting accuracy	• % On-time delivery	% Energy costs to sales
• % Schedule changes	• % Supplier satisfaction	
• % Overdue backlog	• Number improvement suggestions	
• % Data accuracy	• Total business benefits	
• % Material available		

Examples include percent recordable accidents, percent of equipment uptime, percent forecasting accuracy, percent on-time delivery, warranty cost as a percent of sales, and scrap and rework as a percent of cost. Financial metrics are directly correlated to business metrics and measure financial performance and productivity. Referencing Figure 1.2, the financial metric warranty expense is correlated to the business metric warranty expense as a percent of sales. Figure 1.2 also shows warranty expense on a percent basis at several organizational levels and its monetary impact.

At a local process level, a third metric type—operational—is defined based on the project type. Operational metrics are used to measure, analyze, improve, and control operations within a process. As an example, warranty expense at a facility level could be caused by three different types of defects. These defects might include a dimensioning problem, an off-color product, or damaged packaging. The corresponding operational metrics would be defined in units of inches, color coordinate using an instrument to measure color, and the tear strength of the packaging. These operational metrics must align with and be translatable into the financial metric of warranty expense and the business metric of percent of total sales.

The fourth metric is a compensating measure because it is used to balance the impact of the other metrics. As an example, reducing process lead time to lower inventory investment requires a compensating metric such as a customer service target so that, when inventory investment is lowered at a constant sales level, customers still receive products. Reducing internal scrap and rework without increasing external warranty expense is another example of a compensating metric.

Metrics definitions are important because they require resources to develop, deploy, and use every day. Important decisions are made based on metrics. Good metrics are differentiated by a focus on both customer value and actions that improve productivity. Good metrics help speed product introductions, improve on-time delivery, optimize capacity, foster continuous process improvement, increase productivity, and align operational performance with strategic goals. These attributes enhance relative competitiveness.

Table 1.3 lists some competitive metrics that enable organizations and global supply chains to compete effectively. These are only a few examples, and different organizations may use others that better reflect their strategy. Net promoter score, which measures the likelihood customers will repurchase products and services, will be discussed in Chapter 3. Other metrics in Table 1.3 measure how well sales and market share are growing. Customer retention is useful for determining whether customers continue to purchase. This does not imply, however, that they are satisfied. There may not be competitive alternatives. Sales from new products and services are good predictors for future sales. Employee-related metrics are an important group for measuring employee satisfaction. The operations-related metrics measure lead times, yields, productivity, and various costs. To summarize, there are many potential metrics that organizations can use to measure their performance. But measurement is only the first step. Analysis of trends and other patterns in the metrics will yield insights for process improvements and creation of aligned projects. Organizations should use a minimum number of metrics to cost effectively focus on the important performance predictors.

Productivity at an organizational level is calculated as outputs divided by inputs. It is useful because it calculates throughput relative to the

TABLE 1.3

Some Competitive Metrics

---

1. Customer net promoter score
2. Percent new customers
3. Percent customer retention
4. Percent international sales
5. Percent new products
6. Sales growth by market segment
7. Employee net promoter score
8. Employee cultural and global diversity
9. Year-over-year productivity
10. Quote to cash lead time
11. First-pass yields
12. Safety indexes
13. Order fill rates
14. Deliver to requests
15. Delivery to promises
16. Sales, General, and Administrative (SG&A)
17. Delivery costs
18. Operations costs
19. Working capital
20. Income from operations

---

resources needed for the throughput. At an operational level, it is similarly calculated but at a cost-center level. Productivity also varies by industry and is used to estimate relative organizational competitiveness within an industry. At an individual organizational level, year-over-year productivity measures how well an organization performs. Table 1.4 shows relative organizational competitiveness. It is a qualitative representation which suggests that industries move from left to right relative to the removal of competitive barriers. The question for a specific organization is how to increase productivity to offset competitive pressures. These pressures may or may not be fair, depending on geographical, technical, political, and cultural barriers to market entry. The productivity numbers do not represent all industries and organizations. The thought is that organizations with low productivity are protected if isolated from competitors. If competition is high, then higher productivity will be needed to compete. Barriers to market entry (e.g., geographical, technical, political, and cultural barriers) can isolate an organization for a time. Productivity can

TABLE 1.4

Competitive Evaluation

		High (>4%)	Highly Competitive Regionally	Highly Competitive Nationally	Highly Competitive Internationally
Operational Efficiency–Productivity		Medium (0–4%)	Erosion of Regional Market Share	Erosion of National Market Share	Loss of National Markets
		Low (<0)	Erosion of Regional Market Share	Loss of National Markets	Not Competitive Nationally or Internationally
			High	Medium	Low

Geographical/Technical/Political/Cultural Barriers to Market Entry

be set at convenient levels (e.g., low, medium, and high) using industry benchmarks of productivity performance data.

Productivity levels vary by industry and organization. The important concept is how well a specific organization compares to its competitors. But being competitive with current competitors may be enough if disruptions such as unexpected new market entrants, market collapse, technology advances, customer preference changes, or other conditions occur. This situation is in contrast to organizations that have comparatively low productivity levels that are noncompetitive. Organizations make choices when they create strategies, enable initiatives, design products and services, and create supporting processes. Making the correct choices reduces organizational friction and increases effectiveness, efficiency, and productivity. This increases competitiveness. In the absence of artificial competitive barriers to market entry, it will always be true that competitors have advantages. But these need to be offset by creating competitive solutions. In contrast, noncompetitive organizations will not be able to satisfy demands with lower costs, faster service, and higher quality and variety. The competitive landscape in the automotive and consumer electronic industries provide useful case studies for the importance of creating operational excellence.

BENCHMARKING

An important goal of benchmarking is to provide information useful for developing solutions to improve performance. There are right ways and wrong ways to undertake an external benchmarking study. These are applicable to benchmarking done either internally or externally. Benchmarking studies identify the goals and objectives as part of the planning phase. The first step in the process is to clearly establish the goals, including the information that must be collected to answer the relevant benchmarking questions. The plan will include a schedule, the resources, and the specific activities that need to be completed to accomplish the deliverables. A second important question is where the benchmarking information will be collected and from whom. A third consideration is who will collect the information and in what form. After the benchmarking information has been collected, it is important to determine the analytical tools and methods required to answer questions. The team must also consider how the benchmarking information will be communicated and how it will be incorporated to improve internal operations. It is important to bring together a cross-functional team to undertake the benchmarking activities that have the required analytical skills to successfully quantify their analysis.

The team should align the benchmarking process to the project's goals and objectives in the project charter. The project charter acts as a guide as to where the benchmarking study will begin and end. After the team has aligned to the project charter and its key milestones, which should be broken down into key activities and work tasks that form the basis for the benchmarking plan. Assignments are made to complete the planned work tasks. The team should be trained to collect the benchmarking data in a standardized manner to ensure the analysis can be accurately extrapolated across the various internal processes that are part of the study.

Internal benchmarking is done with similar organizational functions in the same organization. An example would be comparing key performance metrics across several distribution centers in a logistics network, such as inventory turnover by distribution center. If the distribution centers have similar operations, products, and sales volumes, then comparison of turnover ratios would be useful if poorer performing distribution centers could learn from the higher performing ones. But if some have different operational designs or serve differ market segments, then an internal benchmarking comparison might not be useful.

If this is a process analysis, then a process map is also needed. It should include metrics related to time, cost, and quality within the benchmarking scope. This will create a clear understanding of work tasks, operational definitions, work sequences, and methods as well as inspection procedures. It is also important to walk through the process to ensure the required information has been accurately collected for analysis from the people doing the work. It is important that the correct analysis is conducted to reach unambiguous conclusions. As an example, when we find one distribution center is better than the others relative to inventory turnover, we need to support this statement with why it is better. What is operationally different between the best and the others? To summarize, internal and external benchmarking are useful methods to identify solutions for effectively improving products, processes, and other systems.

As a first step, organizations should internally benchmark themselves against the best of the processes. The best process may be defined by the distribution center with the highest turnover ratio. This best performance is an entitlement level. Entitlement is a concept used to understand how much a process can be improved without major redesign. It is not unreasonable to ask why all distribution centers do not have similarly high turnover ratios. What is the best distribution center doing that the others are not? An internal benchmarking study should be designed to gain information for how to move poorly performing processes to better performing ones. In other words, what can be reasonably accomplished through internal improvements given current constraints (i.e., design limitations relative to products, process, and other systems)?

External benchmarking compares organizations in the same industry sector (i.e., direct competitors or competitors in completely different sectors but doing similar functions). Competitive benchmarking is conducted through industry associations or third-party research organizations. In these studies, it is important to ensure an "apples-to-apples" comparison between the products, services, and other systems being compared to each other. This requires that the organizations being benchmarked have similar processes.

When benchmarking is conducted with organizations outside an industry, the benchmarking organization may be able to gain insights into how radical changes to their product, services, or supporting processes might improve internal operating performance. As an example, Federal Express Corporation (FedEx) evaluated the Internet technology explosion of the mid-1990s and began to offer transfer of information through e-mail. They partially redefined themselves as an information courier. Also, United Parcel Service (UPS) and FedEx have formed associations with other organizations to create seamlessly integrated processes. Examples include Kinko's, Staples, and other consumer sales outlets where customers can drop off packages or send documents via e-mail with electronic signatures. External benchmarking enabled UPS and FedEx to expand market share beyond their original service offerings. In summary, the important elements of a benchmarking study are to ensure relevant information is collected, analyzed, and will be useful for making improvements.

SUMMARY

Several accelerating trends have changed the way in which we view the management of production. Digitization has been a large transformational force connecting IT systems and devices across the world. Work is done virtually for most supporting back-end operations. Work products are, to a large extent, more informational than material in form. Teams collaborate globally though video conferencing and remote connectivity of various types. Productivity and quality are higher. Expectations for customer experience are becoming increasingly personal and seamless. Automation is also being introduced through the IoT and other applications to increase productivity. The IoT is composed of smart devices and sensors that are interconnected. These can be accessed to aid information exchange and operational management. Operations are also being positively impacted with the use of AI to aid decision making and to reduce mundane work task such as building reports or searching for information. In addition to AI, RPA is a growing field that automates routine work. Enhanced operational capabilities support these disruptive changes.

At one time, organizational size and available capital could ensure market share and enable an organization to adapt slowly to changing market conditions. Market dominance used to be determined by the ability of large organizations to set industry standards and deploy capital-intensive barriers that prevented new entrants. Prior to the advent of globalization, an organization's operational strategy was relatively simple in that it was determined by the organization's available technology, its logistical systems, and competitive threats on a regional or national level.

Today, competition is fierce. In fact, in some situations, smaller organizations dominate their market by neutralizing larger and historically more entrenched organizations. Effective execution requires doing the right things efficiently and according to schedule to achieve strategic and tactical goals. Competition leaves little room for poor strategic execution. The ability of an organization to adapt its organization, systems, and people to meet competitive threats is dependent on the organization's culture, which is the driving force behind the organization's competitiveness. Organizations will not change without a strong reason, and behaviors that made them successful are not easily abandoned without justification.

We have also changed the way we think about product and process design and their management. Understanding the voice of the customer and customer experience expectations are now an important basis from which to design products and processes and to more clearly focus development, deploy technology to align operations, and improve productivity through an efficient use of labor, materials, and capital. Operational linkage is also now carefully incorporated into strategic and operational planning. A clear line of sight between anticipated business benefits in terms of organizational productivity and ROE to the allocation of resources is an integral component of operational execution to improve financial and operational metrics. These are used to identify, define, measure, and control performance gaps. In addition to the dimensions of time, cost, and quality, metrics can be classified into dimensions of business, financial, operational, and compensating. Best-in-class metrics are differentiated by a focus on customer value and an ability to help focus attention on activities that help improve operational efficiency and organizational productivity.

2

Organizational Change

OVERVIEW

In this era of digitization and automation, change is difficult to avoid. It is about adapting an organization to embrace continuing change based on opportunities to improve operational effectiveness and efficiency as well as customer satisfaction to increase competitiveness. The mindset of we always did it this way never worked. In today's environment, this fallacy is exposed very quickly by global competitors. Change is about changing people's attitudes in an environment where opportunities evolve, and solutions depend on organizational creativity.

Organizations need to adapt and change to satisfy new customer preferences, and to utilize new technology and other disruptive trends that change the competitive landscape. Organizations change to embrace new attitudes and behaviors by employees and other stakeholders. As an example, a culture might be focused on activities that helped drive the organization's past success but have little current value. At one time, these activities were valued from customer and organizational perspectives. These were competitive strengths that now are no longer aligned with the organization's strategic direction needed to meet customer expectations and increase productivity. Competitive organizations focus on the usefulness of their actions and their beneficial impact to productivity. Adaptable organizations do not resist change, rather they embrace it with a willingness to learn and apply new thinking to solve old problems. They have a motivation to change behaviors because experience has taught them that competitiveness comes from leading rather than following. Change is all about relationships and consensus building by collaborative teams empowered to apply best practices for improved operational performance. Improved operational performance drives business benefits that increase productivity by increasing sales, cash flow, and reducing operating income. Higher customer satisfaction results from a more seamless experience. There also fewer product returns and other customer dissatisfaction expenses.

Change initiatives should be especially focused on those parts of the organization that need refreshing relative to people, process, policy, or technology. The tools and methods that are applied need to be integrated into a framework with the right sponsorship, goals and resources. Sustaining the long-term effectiveness of change initiatives requires incorporating new behaviors into an organization. These must become the way people work. To be widely adopted, they must be built on a firm basis and be impactful to be sustainable. Relationship building is also important. Real change that is impactful and sustainable helps build collaboration and relationships between stakeholders.

Change is also about expectations, so employees know the purpose for the change. Asking people to change habits must make sense and be important for them, their organization, customers, or other groups. To be purposeful, changes should directly impact current operations and improve them. They should be based on a deep understanding of the underlying process relative to how it works, including its inputs and the outputs it supplies to the successive operations. Change recommendations need to be based on a current baseline assessment as well as the desired state. The desired state should be achievable with available resources and knowledge. This implies an organization's work must be transparent and embrace factual discussion and informed action.

Corporate culture significantly impacts an organization's operational performance, either positively or negatively. Culture is difficult to change for various reasons. A problem with asking organizations to change the way they do things is that they achieved success based on current paradigms and culture. Unless an organization can see value in changing its "way of doing things," they will not undertake a major change initiative. To complicate matters, the most successful people in an organization are often the most isolated from information showing the necessity of change. Sometimes those who control the organizational power structure and resources stand to lose the most from a dramatic change within their organization. This situation, if it exists, may place the proponents of change on the defensive. As Machiavelli stated in 1513, "The innovator has for enemies all who have done well under the old and lukewarm defenders in those who may do well under the new." Unfortunately, this observation is remains true today.

Reactive and slow-to-change organizational cultures may fail to achieve their full potential, and, in today's competitive environment, problems with launching new products, getting to market late, and other aspects of poor strategy and strategic execution can put an organization out of business. Change is difficult to implement in any organization, but success can be measured. There are common metrics used to manage and evaluate the effectiveness of change initiatives. The first is the percentage of people using the new tools and methods. But this simple conversion percentage needs additional context to accurately measure the effectiveness of an improvement initiative. If the conversion percentage is low, an analysis needs to be made to identify which tools and methods are being used and which ones are not. Deployed initiatives that do not create observable business benefits usually fall into general disuse. For this reason, it is important to also measure the cumulative net business benefits of an initiative by benefit type, project type, and location across an organization. An initiative should also produce benefits greater than its cost.

Business benefits include revenue enhancement, cost reduction, asset conversion, cost avoidance, and increases in customer, suppler, or employee satisfaction. They should be measured at a project level and aggregated up through an organization to demonstrate where the initiative is successful in achieving its goals and objectives. Another useful approach when measuring the effectiveness of an initiative is to identify key success factors specific for the organization to reinforce these success factors in subsequent projects. Barriers that prevent a successful deployment should also be identified with plans to remove them. It is important to obtain periodic feedback from key stakeholders to identify ways to improve and accelerate projects. Finally, to the extent senior management takes a hands-off approach to an initiative, it will fail. A stakeholder analysis should be done after completing the initial project charter to enable the team to obtain approvals, periodic feedback, sponsorship, information, resources, or other help.

Academic studies show that one of the most important characteristics of successful organizations is an ability to develop and execute their strategic vision at a tactical level through core competencies. This was discussed in the previous chapter as a strategic flow down. Integration of operational capability across an organization is enhanced with an empowered and diverse workforce. This helps create an "execution culture." Important characteristics of execution culture are an ability to set and achieve year-over-year strategic goals and increase productivity. Proper strategic execution enables organizations to dominate their markets. In contrast, unsuccessful organizations fail to effectively articulate or align operational systems behind their strategic vision. These organizations become less competitive unless protected by barriers to market entry such as favorable laws and regulations, geographical isolation, or other advantages or by possessing unique advantages such as intellectual property.

In summary, competitive organizations align operational strategy with core competencies. If new competences are needed to execute competitive strategy, then plans are made to deploy initiatives to develop new ways to work. These are learning organizations that embrace diversity and empower their workforce to effect change. These changes require some risk, but it is managed based on the organization's risk tolerance. The goal is to leverage disruptive technologies, digitization, automation, and other new methods to accelerate productivity growth and improve customer experience.

WHAT IS ORGANIZATIONAL CHANGE?

Organizational change is successful when most people in an organization consistently practice a new behavior. But, to practice new behaviors, individuals must be convinced they provide value. There are usually different types of cultural changes taking place within organizations at all times. Sometimes the change is rapid and dramatic. These situations often occur because of internal or external conditions that threaten an organization. Examples include bankruptcy, a forced merger with another organization, downsizing of a product line, or a loss of productive capacity.

Most of the time, however, cultural change is incremental and unfolds over time. A transition period may last between five and twenty years or even longer, depending on the specific organization and industry. In situations where successful change occurred, the changes evolved either through the execution of myriad strategically linked tactical projects or a major shift in strategic direction. In either situation, execution cultures tend to be more successful than those which have difficulty executing strategy because they align strategy throughout their organization in measurable ways using linked metrics targets and frequent reviews of performance under the direction of a leadership council.

There is a saying: "What gets rewarded gets measured, and what gets measured gets done." Execution cultures effectively align rewards and punishments with strategic and tactical goals. There is accountability for effective and efficient project execution. In an execution culture, accountability is the normative behavior and gets rewarded. These organizations are more adaptable to changing global competitive conditions. They also closely align strategy and execution to prevent situations where the wrong initiatives and projects are supported.

CHANGE READINESS

In the first chapter, we discussed Kotter's eight attributes for successful change as well as the need for core competencies. Organizations differ in their readiness for change, even when there is an urgent reason. Adaptable organizations embrace initiatives. They learn to use the new tools, methods, and concepts and look for beneficial ways to integrate them into operational strategy in a manner that is aligned with the organization's overall strategy. The attitude is proactive. Opportunities to improve operational performance and customer experience are embraced on a continual basis. This provides another core competence, i.e., the ability to adapt to disruptive events and increase competitiveness. External challenges become opportunities for these organizations. These organizations do not need a burning platform and do not need to be forced to change if there are significant benefits.

Adaptable organizations can change more easily because their culture also embraces facilitation tools that enable efficient change. Because change is normal, the adaptable organization is highly trained in methods to understand plan and execute new ways to work. Facilitation brings people together to develop broad consensus on the best ways to investigate opportunities, quantify benefits, and develop competitive solutions. These are learning organizations. Although any organization may have some barriers to change, facilitation helps to overcome or even remove these barriers. Typical barriers are associated with current success, lack of time and resources, and other factors.

After a supporting leadership council establishes a framework for change, readiness depends on several common change-management facilitation methods. Some of these will also be discussed in Chapter 14 in the context of sustaining initiatives and projects. Deployment planning starts after a leadership council is formed and key stakeholders are identified to support it. The planning was discussed in Chapter 1. It included integrating the initiative into the organization's strategic planning with additional goals that can be achieved through various change initiatives (e.g., Lean, Six Sigma, and others). Organizational strategy is executed using applied projects. Over time, solutions from numerous projects slowly change an organization's products, services, and process workflows and create a culture that embraces the right types of changes. Part of the planning process is assessing where each initiative is likely to create benefits based on its tools, methods, and purpose. Practical projects are also identified, and people assigned to move them to completion. These people or change agents will be trained and supported to practice the new tools and methods. This is the beginning of change readiness. The successful completion of projects or short-term wins will change organizational behaviors and how people work.

Project scoping is an important tool that is used to structure a problem for solution using a formal project. It is discussed several times in this book from differing perspectives. Project planning helps clarify a project's objectives, metrics, customers, stakeholders, and team members. A useful approach is asking what is or is not in the project's scope. Is the project focused on consumers or retail operations? Is it focused on one region or another? Similar questions are asked until the scope of the project is clearly defined. Project scope also helps identify where a team will work.

A team's authority is described though a project charter, which is built from its scope. Project charters are also discussed throughout this book from different perspectives of application. The charter is a communication tool that reiterates the scope, goals, and deliverables of a project (i.e., the metrics for success and targets), the schedule for work, estimated benefits, team members, resources requirements, and other information as needed. Once the charter is drafted, the team can engage with stakeholders and customers.

A formal stakeholder analysis is needed to identify internal or external people who could be impacted by a project, need to approve work, or may provide resource or support. An example is shown in Figure 2.1.

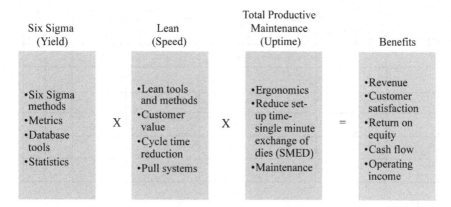

FIGURE 2.1
Operational initiatives increase productivity.

Stakeholders represent the project's scope. The broader the scope, the more stakeholders who will need to be included in the project. A stakeholder analysis is a useful tool to help understand initial stakeholder positions to gain support. The second question is, "What do they need from us?" Will they need project updates, inclusion of their feedback into the project charter or other types of work? After this, the stakeholders are rated on a scale between strongly against the project to strongly supportive of it.

Stakeholders provide support based on their best interests. Stakeholders who directly benefit from a project's solutions will be more supportive of a project. In contrast, those who may lose power or must provide scarce resources may resist a project or modify its scope. The goal of a stakeholder analysis is to identify the important stakeholders and understand what is needed for approvals, resources, and team members to successfully complete the project. Properly constructed, a stakeholder analysis moves stakeholders from their current level of support to a higher level and further clarifies the project's charter.

A resistance analysis, shown in Figure 2.2, is also a useful method for evaluating potential organizational barriers to expected change. A resistance analysis reduces organizational friction that occurs because of poor communication or execution by a project team, cultural differences across an organization, an unwillingness to share available resources, or concerns about a potential loss of organizational power due to changes in policy, roles and responsibilities, processes, and other changes. This tool categorizes elements of the project into change promoters and inhibitors.

| Stakeholder Name | Level of Stakeholder Attitude / Support | | | | | What do we need from them? | What do they need from us? | Communication Method | How Often | Who |
	Strongly Against	Moderately Against	Neutral	Moderately Supportive	Strongly Supportive					
		X ———→								
	X ———→									
			X ——→							
				X —→						
					X					
					X					

FIGURE 2.2
Stakeholder analysis.

Promoters include project alignment, effective communication, empowerment, training as required, rewards and recognition, and clearly defined roles and responsibilities as well as team facilitation. Barriers to change include conflicting stakeholder priorities, fear of the unknown, bureaucracy (ie, the need for extensive and sometime irrelevant information before allowing project movement), limited training, little rewards and recognition, and poorly defined roles and responsibilities. The goals are to understand the organizational environment and create a plan to overcome obstacles that impede a project's success.

An infrastructure analysis evaluates the resource ecosystem and supporting processes to look for constraints that may impeded a project's progress. Infrastructure includes materials, facilities, equipment, people, training systems, reward and recognition systems, as well as information technology (IT) systems that impact a project. The project impact varies and includes lack of resources for data collection, analysis, or implementing improvements. An infrastructure analysis is useful to identify barriers that, if not overcome, can stall a project. If there are several projects all competing for common resources, it may be better to phase their execution or initiate other projects that require different resources.

As a team works through the project stakeholder and resistance analyses, it should also identify project risk with a view toward eliminating it from the project or mitigating its impact. There are several types of project risk: resource constraints, stakeholder support, technology (especially if it is new and untried), cultural aspects that impact the adoption of new behaviors, and external micro and macroeconomic risks. Once identified, risks can be prioritized for elimination or mitigation.

Another important analysis for change is a RACI analysis, which is used to define team roles and responsibilities. RACI is an acronym for roles, accountability, consulted, and informed. People who do the work are the ones responsible for the work product. Work is assigned by managers who are accountable to the organization that it is completed on time and accurately within budget. Projects have subject matter experts who provide consultative advice during a project. Others need to be informed of a project's status. These are the stakeholders that provide approvals, resources, and other forms of assistance to a team. Many process issues that are associated with process complexity, outdated policies, poor communication are caused by poor RACI analysis. An example is shown in Figure 2.3.

Communications of different types are needed throughout any project. A team must know its stakeholders, the messaging, and the best communication format to deliver the message. An example is shown in Figure 2.4. An organization will need to know the project's scope, benefits, resource needs, and other information that should be included in the team charter. The messaging will be updated to include what the eventual changes will be and how best to implement them. Effective communication throughout a project is important because it helps a team obtain resources and organizational support for its project activities and the changes that will eventually need to be implemented. An organization's communications team should be consulted for how best to communicate the project for different

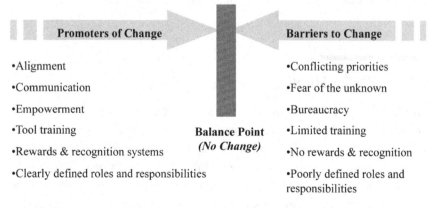

FIGURE 2.3
Resistance analysis.

What	Organization	Responsible	Accountable	Consulted	Informed

- **Responsible:** Do work tasks

- **Accountable:** Assign and approve work

- **Consulted:** Subject matter experts who provide information

- **Informed:** Communication received when work tasks are complete

FIGURE 2.4
RACI analysis.

audiences and messaging formats. It is important that messages be consistent throughout an organization and easy to understand based on the audience. Effective communication is an important characteristic to show people what needs to be changed, how to change it, and the benefits the proposed changes will deliver. People have a greater tendency to agree on what the problems are and what needs to be changed if unbiased facts and analyses are used to show why they are necessary. Change initiatives also require other soft skills, including the basics for building diverse teams, developing team consensus, and presenting analyses and recommendations to stakeholders in formats that are easy to understand.

MANAGING CHANGE

Simply asking people to change a behavior without providing the vision, training, and other resources necessary to successfully implement the required change causes frustration and demoralization. In contrast, developing a coherent vision and strategy and a deployment plan that is well resourced and supported helps enable effective change. An initiative is an enabler that ensures relevant strategic goals and objectives are executed at every level of an organization. It provides tools, methods, and concepts that help people define problems, measure their extent, analyze root causes, and implement effective solutions to change products, processes, and supporting processes.

There are four key conditions that must exist for an organization to successfully change: strategic vision, relevant core competencies that can execute the strategy, initiatives that reinforce or create new core competencies, and an ability to execute projects with the initiative. Initiatives evolve to link an organization's strategy to an ability to execute projects at an operational level. In other words, some initiatives should be deployed before others for success. As an example, a Lean initiative should be deployed before a Six Sigma initiative, so that processes are well defined and standardized prior to the investigation of root causes; otherwise, any statistical models that are developed might not be stable. The exception would be a recognized need for focused improvements. Sometimes several initiatives are operative at one time and resources must be prioritized. In summary, initiatives are important to enable strategic execution at an operational level. They also help change organizational behaviors as projects are completed using tools and methods integral to the initiative.

Managing change is easier when the strategy is clearly focused on the need for change and provides a vehicle for implementation. Linkage between strategy and initiatives will help focus projects to improve key metrics. If new product development lead times are too long, then this chronic problem can be investigated and solutions can be created to reduce lead time. If machines break down unexpectedly and cause missed production schedules, preventive maintenance projects can be deployed to reduce or eliminate future maintenance issues. An organization's operational competency or ability to execute strategy will increase over time as it completes hundreds or even thousands of improvement projects. Properly aligned and executed projects will increase productivity in a sustainable way. Over time, the repetitive cycles of project identification and execution will change an organization's culture.

At any time, an organization may have several major initiatives in progress to improve core competencies or create new ones. Initiatives could be deployed to improve the process performance of functions such as marketing, sales, finance, engineering, manufacturing, and supply chains. Initiatives have tools, methods, and concepts that organizations use to improve skills and capabilities across their organization. Resources are

Message Element	Stakeholder A	Stakeholder B	Stakeholder C
Stakeholder Group			
What information do they need?			
What information do we need?			
In person?			
Telephone?			
Email?			
Other			
Date			
Responsible			

Communications of different types are needed throughout any project. A team must know its stakeholders, the messaging and the best communication format to deliver the message. It is important to engage with your organization's communications experts.

FIGURE 2.5
Communication planning.

aligned to the benefits offered by each initiative. This requires a correct prioritization of resources to ensure they are effectively utilized to execute strategic goals for each initiative.

Figure 2.5 shows the three operational initiatives known as Six Sigma, Lean, and Total Productive Maintenance (TPM). When properly defined, prioritized, and deployed, these initiatives work synergistically to increase an organization's productivity. This directly impacts long-term competitiveness. With resource prioritization in mind, it is important that a governing body (i.e., the leadership council) coordinate initiatives that compete for resources. Governance aligns resources relative to strategy and benefits.

Communication of the initiatives being deployed should use a simple and consistent message. These should describe why an initiative is important to the organization and how it is different from other initiatives. In addition to ensuring effective communication, the people who will become part of the new imitative must be trained in its tools and methods because these are necessary to work on the projects supporting the benefits. Tracking metrics are also needed to integrate projects and benefits across an organization. Organizational learning and competence help initiatives become successful. New skills are gained through the practical application of tools and methods in project teams. Applied projects are critical to ensuring an initiative meets its benefit targets. But not all projects can be completed with the same tools and methods, hence the need for more than one operational initiative.

The types of projects follow from potential benefits. This means projects may be assigned to one initiative and then moved to another as benefit opportunities and resource availability change. Using Lean, Six Sigma, and TPM as an example, resources may be shifted across the initiatives depending on potential benefit. There may also be a sequence for implementation. As an example, Lean is typically applied before Six Sigma to simplify and standardize a process before gathering data for analysis. Performance gaps also help identify the types of projects required to close the gaps.

There are different types of projects. Some have known solutions and are called "just-do-it" projects. These do not need in-depth analysis. Capital expenditure projects are a second type in which requirements need to be carefully documented, but a known solution can be applied with investment. Lean projects are focused on understanding customer value and squeezing out wasteful process steps, then standardizing and mistake-proofing the remaining process steps and their operations. Six Sigma projects are focused on data collection, analysis, and model building to modify variable settings. Six Sigma tools and methods require applied statistics and model-building training using regression and other statistical analyses. As organizations automate and expand IT ecosystems, large data sets with different data formats have pushed analytics to extract large amounts of data (i.e., Big Data), condition it, and apply appropriate analytical methods different than those required for analyzing small samples typical of Six Sigma. TPM also has specialized tools and methods. Reengineering projects dramatically change significant portions of an organization These programs require major changes to organizational hierarchies and policies and the addition or elimination of products, processes, and other organizational structures. Each initiative also has unique tools, methods, and concepts that are used to identify and execute applied projects.

Figure 2.5 shows that Six Sigma, Lean, and TPM have unique tools and methods. Six Sigma increases operational yields though root-cause identification and analysis using simple or complex analytical tools. Lean maps customer value through an end-to-end process to identify ways to simplify, standardize, and mistake-proof operations. The goal is to pull value through the improved process in synchronization with customer demand (i.e., the takt time). There are also overlaps of tools and methods between these initiatives. Each uses process mapping, brainstorming, and simple analytical tools and methods. Some Lean tools and methods are also used to ensure effective and sustainable process control in Six Sigma initiatives.

TPM ensures tools and machines are available as needed to sustain a process, as well as process standardization. In TPM, availability is analogous to ergonomic tools and methods that help ensure people are available for work and work is performed safely without injury over time. TPM enables an operation to produce "more and more" by increasing resource "uptime." Six Sigma enables an organization to increase yield, i.e., to make an operational output "better and better." Lean enables a process to produce "faster and "faster." The combined result is greater organizational productivity. These initiatives work synergistically to increase productivity, reduce lead time, reduce process cost, and improve quality.

There is a sequence of steps that is needed to effectively deploy an initiative. First, an initiative must have tools and methods useful to an organization. At any point in time, an organization has many performance gaps that need to be closed by projects. But the specific tools and methods vary by project. Organizations should ensure proper alignment of productivity opportunities with tools and methods required to identify root causes of performance gaps and execute solutions for successful project closure. An important part of an evaluation process is assessing where to focus initiatives. Applying relevant financial and operating models build a business justification for certain projects and initiatives having a higher probability of obtaining senior leadership support.

If approved for deployment by senior leadership, a leadership council is formed to guide an initiative's deployment. This council should be representative of the major organizational functions that will be impacted by the initiative. Its purpose is to coordinate communication, project selection, resource allocation, and benefit reporting. This improves the likelihood that goals are met on schedule. The leadership council and supporting teams are trained on the specifics of the initiative and how to deploy it. After the leadership council approves the deployment plan, middle management is trained to identify improvement opportunities using formal operational assessment methods. Managers are also trained to use tools and methods that enable project closure and reporting as well as the teams. After processes have been analyzed and the project has been identified through the operational assessments, the people who will execute the projects are selected and trained. The deployment goals and schedule are finalized at this point because projects, resources, and benefits are estimated and on a deployment roadmap. Deployment modifications are made when necessary to increase its effectiveness.

BUILDING TEAMS

High-performance teams are no accident. There is a proven methodology to build these teams. The team building process includes ensuring a team has a defined project objective and deliverables and the resources to achieve its deliverables. The people comprising a team should represent the process under investigation (i.e., the scope). Ideally, the team should be diverse for effective problem solving and have a range of relevant skills. Facilitation is important. Proper facilitation ensures team members contribute and reach agreements using agreed-upon ground rules. Teams move through a maturation process that increases trust and understanding of each other's perspectives when moving projects to closure.

Developing a high-performance work team is a process. The first step is to develop the team's project charter. The project charter embodies the business justification for the project, including its benefits and its required resources. It also communicates to the organization where the team will work, what problems will be investigated, and the beneficial business outcomes expected from achieving the goals by solving the problem. Project charters also contain team members and information relevant for project coordination.

Project charters contain the four previously discussed metrics. These include the business and financial metrics showing leadership the positive impact expected from the project, as well as balancing metrics to ensure the team does not drive the other metrics to an extreme. As an example, if a team is reducing process rework expense, it should also measure returns and customer satisfaction to ensure one metric is not optimized at the expense of another one. Inventory turnover was previously provided as another example in which we discussed increasing the turnover ratio while maintaining customer service levels. As the project team works through root causes, they likely will also create project-focused metrics. As an example, inventory is usually increased by long lead times. Long lead times may have several causes, such as large lot sizes, scheduling misses, poor quality, maintenance issues, and other operational issues.

In these situations, the project charter will be updated to reflect changes in direction as the team works though its root-cause analysis. The project team must always ensure there is direct alignment between all four metrics as the root-cause analysis and solutioning proceeds so that different organizational levels can see the interrelationships. When the project team improves lower-level project metrics, leadership and stakeholders should clearly see direct improvements in higher-level financial and business metrics as well as operational changes without a deterioration of compensating metrics.

High-performance work teams should be selected to align with the project's end-to-end scope as well as the processes immediately before or after the process being investigated. Team members should also have direct knowledge of their portion of the process to ensure full contribution. Once the team is organized, its dynamics will need to be facilitated. Teams mature through four stages: forming, storming, norming, and performing. In the formation stage, the team members start discussions of their project's scope and objectives. During this first stage, there usually are no significant disagreements regarding how best to proceed with the work. However, as the team moves through the second maturation stage (i.e., storming), disagreements are likely to arise because of differing interpretations and perspectives of information and the best way to proceed with the project work. Facilitation can usually move the team past the storming stage through to the norming and performing stages to work together effectively and to efficiently coordinate the project's work.

Initiatives provide a proven structured methodology useful to identify the root causes for issues and analyze them to identify solutions. The identification of root causes requires tools and methods specific to the investigation. These vary across industries and functions. Manufacturing systems may require statistical models based on experimentation, and logistical issues may require the application of operations research tools and methods; for service systems, other specialized tools such as automated data collection across several IT platforms and applications may be needed. Regardless of the initiative, a root-cause analysis carefully defines the problem and eventually arrives at its solution. Common methodologies include Six Sigma's Define, Measure, Analyze, Improve, and Control (DMAIC), Deming's Wheel (i.e., Plan, Do, Check, Act), and Lean's "understand value, create a value stream map, eliminate process waste, etc." Most problem-solving methodologies use scoping, problem identification, data collection, data analysis, creating solutions, and controlling or sustaining the solutions.

Initiatives need to be periodically evaluated to maintain their effectiveness. A potential problem occurs if they are deployed independently of other initiatives and compete for scarce resources. There may also be overlapping tools and methods that create confusion. To avoid competition and confusion between initiatives, it is common to link them under an umbrella initiative as discussed earlier, i.e., operational excellence (OPEX), which is used to coordinate and prioritize projects and resources.

DEPLOYING CONTINUOUS IMPROVEMENT TEAMS

Organizations that deploy advanced initiatives such as Lean and Six Sigma usually have some initial infrastructure including people trained to use basic quality improvement and operational tools and methods. A continuous improvement initiative provides a common language from which to start advanced initiatives. As an early initiative evolves, it creates core competencies for quality improvement as well as other benefits. In time, the available projects that benefit from using continuous improvement tools and methods will become saturated and the benefits will plateau. At this point, additional tools and methods will be needed to increase productivity (i.e., a second initiative). The prior initiative will already have identified opportunities that need different strategies for root cause identification and solutioning.

High-performance work teams enable a continuous improvement initiative. They are dispersed across an organization as quality circles composed of workers trained to use basic quality improvement methods. They improve quality within their work area with the help of a facilitator. The initial continuous improvement teams in the 1980s were seldom aligned with an organization's strategic goals; the project benefits were often low relative to the required investment of employee time and other resources. This is because the projects of non-aligned teams will not be supported due to other priorities that are strategically aligned to produce benefits. Non-alignment also contributes to poor project selection and execution. This causes a continuous improvement initiative to fall into disuse. Other reasons for the failure of an initiative are poor training, lack of leadership support, poorly documented benefits (or none), and poor project execution.

In contrast, other organizations in the 1980s significantly increased productivity using continuous improvement by ensuring alignment to strategy and effective execution. This accelerated the deployment of subsequent initiatives. By the late 1990s, many organizations that had difficulty with continuous improvement started using Lean and Six Sigma. Continuous improvement programs were invigorated when the success factors inherent in Lean and Six Sigma were reapplied to them. Using additional tools and methods with strategic alignment, the productivity gains became impressive. Interestingly, Lean and Six Sigma training are typically offered to a small fraction of an organization to improve the performance of entire work teams in a process (e.g., accounting) or between several processes (e.g., a portion of a supply chain). As part of these deployments, other employees are trained to apply continuous improvement within their own work teams. In this context, these initiatives are compatible.

Deploying a continuous improvement team requires using success factors common to any business engagement: creation of the leadership council, deployment plan and schedule, performance goals, project charters, consistent messaging, and training team members. Continuous improvement initiatives help lay the foundation for Lean and Six Sigma deployments by disseminating the terminology, basic tools, and methods that will accelerate these and subsequent initiatives.

DEPLOYING LEAN

The automotive industry was under competitive pressure from Toyota to improve quality performance and reduce cost. The industry initially emulated some of Toyota's operational systems embodied under the general term "Lean" and implemented the balance of them in 1990s. Lean systems optimize a process by matching its throughput to incoming customer demand using a takt time, and they simplify, standardize, and mistake-proof processes by eliminating non-value-add activities or waste, such as that associated with defects, unnecessary motion, unnecessary movement of materials, waiting, and other types of process waste. The result is an adaptable system with flexible cross-trained workers, reduced order-to-cash lead times, and reduced cost with higher quality.

Lean is effective for process improvement because people from the front office to the factory floor can use its simple but effective methods of work simplification, standardization, 5-S, cleaning local work areas, throwing out unneeded materials, value flow mapping, mistake-proofing, and others to analyze and improve their processes. 5-S is a particularly useful method. It is an acronym for sorting, simplifying, sweeping (i.e., cleaning the work area), standardization, and sustaining process improvements. 5-S and other Lean methods will be discussed in Chapter 6. The value of Lean for process improvement and significant productivity improvement is well documented after more than 50 years.

An integrated Lean system has several attributes. The first is problem-solving groups or continuous improvement teams. These enable organizations to improve quality by training workers to efficiently operate machines and other resources. Second, workers are trained to use simple tools to identify improvement opportunities. Performance measures and visual reporting are also key characteristics. Process simplification, standardization, and mistake-proofing help stabilize a process. Schedule stability is needed to match external customer demand to production using the takt time. A takt time calculation is done as follows: if daily external demand is 100 units and 500 minutes is available per day to produce the 100 units, the calculation would be 1 unit is produced every 5 minutes each day.

A process workflow is analyzed using value flow mapping (VFM). A VFM shows the interrelationships of operations within a process including its rework loops and wasteful work operations. Examples include the unnecessary movement of materials, setting up of jobs, processing of the work, inspection of work, storage of information or materials, and similar activities that do not add value. Value-add operations are those required by a customer, those that physically transform an object (physical or informational), and those that are done right the first time. In contrast, non-value-add operations are missing one of more of these characteristics. Note that processes transforming information rather than physical objects are analogous.

After the VFM is analyzed relative to value, the non-value-add operations are eliminated. A VFM has the practical effect of helping simplify a process the right way to reduce its complexity, cost, and lead time. It also shows ways to reorganize the physical layout of a process to further lower cost and lead time. Bringing operations in closer proximity and in a logical sequence reduces unnecessary movement between workstations and helps communication. As an example, using a U-shaped work cell enables easy balancing of production because workers can move within the cell to complete work tasks. If the volume coming into the work cell fluctuates (with the takt time recalculated in these situations), it is easier to expand or contract the number of workers.

Design modifications are successively applied as a process is simplified, standardized, and mistake-proofed. Mistake-proofing ensures high process quality using inexpensive error warning and control systems. Depending on the process, TPM and single-minute exchange of dies (SMED) methods are implemented to further ensure process stabilization to maintain the takt time. External demand on a system can also be level-loaded to reduce its variability. Mixed-model scheduling will reduce lead time when product and process designs are simplified. Once a process is simplified and has a stable takt time, pull systems are implemented using Kanban quantities and standard transfer containers to control the flow of work. Kanban systems also help maintain stable inventory levels and aid in identifying process issues that impact the flow of a process. Finally, incorporating suppliers into the customer's process helps reduce the variation of work flowing through the system, and such networks are integral to the long-term success of a Lean system.

DEPLOYING SIX SIGMA

The Six Sigma initiative focuses on breakthrough process improvements as opposed to more gradual improvements typical of a continuous improvement initiative. Both are needed to improve quality. The Six Sigma quality initiative began at Motorola during the 1980s in response to competitive threats from Japan and other countries to its consumer electronics business. During the 1980s, quality improvement strategies evolved. An important improvement was the recognition that although every employee should be trained in basic quality methods, a dedicated group of internal quality consultants is needed to focus on difficult process issues. These became known as breakthrough change agents or Black Belts.

In the mid to late 1990s, the Six Sigma, Lean, and TPM programs quickly became the top productivity programs at many organizations. They contributed significant annual productivity improvements with other initiatives such as supply chain, product design, reengineering, and others. The three operational initiatives of Six Sigma, Lean, and TPM were usually folded into the concept of OPEX.

Business models change and disruptive technologies always appear that require initiative modifications.

The effectiveness of OPEX approach is indisputable to those who helped drive its many successful deployments. Effective deployments require certain success factors, but not all organizations properly implement OPEX and its supporting initiatives. The result is that benefits are mixed and the program falls into disuse. Key success factors for any initiative requiring resources are alignment to organizational strategy and support of leadership. Six Sigma has two success factors that made it popular. These are project selection and execution, using effective tools and methods by highly skilled internal consultants (i.e., Black Belts).

A Lean Six Sigma deployment using both Lean and Six Sigma methods should provide productivity increases in the range of 1–4% for organizations with revenues exceeding one billion dollars, depending on the industry. If your organization is not driving productivity at this level, then the deployment strategy and project execution methods should be reviewed for improvement. The tools and methods incorporated into the deployment strategies, tactics, and project execution are well known and proven, so adjustments to a deployment can be easily made to get on track.

Six Sigma has five sequential phases described by the acronym DMAIC. The DMAIC methodology was applied by Black Belts to complete beneficial projects. But, some organizations utilize DMAIC to enhance employee skills. The DMAIC phases are define the project; measure the process key metric, also called the key process output variable (KPOV); analyze collected data, improve the KPOV by changing one or more key process input variables (KPIVs); and place the process into control. The initial Six Sigma deployment had followed a MAIC methodology, which resulted in false starts relative to project identification. The define phase was inserted, as was the concept of the voice-of-the-customer (VOC), to ensure that projects were selected and defined carefully before work started and that they were focused on customer satisfaction as well as the voice-of-the-business (VOB) to effectively align to strategy.

The initiative is deployed after leaders are trained in its basic concepts and the deployment plan is created with executive stakeholders. The deployment planning is usually facilitated by external consultants. After leadership engagement, the project champions are trained to select projects, the belts, estimate benefits, and guide the program's deployment. Belts are assigned to projects to apply the DMAIC methodology to investigate the root causes for process breakdowns and develop solutions to eliminate them.

There are several success attributes for deploying a Six Sigma initiative. The first and most important one is to execute actions for organizational alignment, leadership engagement, and deployment. After alignment, the Six Sigma initiative is deployed at successively lower levels of an organization. Once the leadership council or executive steering committee is selected and is operative, champions are selected and trained to guide the tactical aspects of the Six Sigma deployment. Deployment champions guide the initiative at a divisional level, ensuring the project selection process (through the project champions) and remains on target. Project champions provide organizational support to the belts to ensure projects are closed on schedule and benefits are properly assigned to the initiative. Project selection is documented using charters, which provide a good foundation for success. The business opportunities (i.e., the projects) also help determine the belts assignment to specific projects.

After belts are assigned to projects, the project team refines the project's problem statement, goals or objectives, and other information. This requires reviewing the project's KPOVs that will be baselined and improved. These are aligned to the VOC and the VOB. Integral to this evaluation process is the creation of a high-level map of the process showing its scope (i.e., its inputs, outputs, and many process steps or operations). As the team starts the measure phase, a second important task is to accurately measure the performance gaps of the KPOVs using DMAIC process capability methods. The project's benefits are verified based on the KPOV performance baselines and targets. When the team begins the analysis of the root causes for poor KPOV performance, other quality tools and methods are employed to analyze potential causes for the poor KPOV performance. Brainstorming methods are also used to identify potential causes for poor performance. These are the many input variables (X). Through subsequent data collection and analysis, one or more of these input variables will be found to impact the project's KPOVs. Effective data collection and measurement are critical to continue an analysis of root causes to identify the KPIVs.

In the analysis phase of the project, analytical tools and methods are used to identify the major root causes for the process breakdowns. The tools and methods vary between industries and within an organization (e.g., manufacturing versus accounting). But the goal of any DMAIC analysis is a consistent mapping between KPIVs (root causes) and a project's

KPOVs, which are the project metrics to be improved. These are used to build the Six Sigma model: $Y = f(X)$. This formula describes the change of a KPOV (Y) in terms of changes of the process KPIV (X).

In the improve phase of a project, the team changes the levels of the KPIVs to evaluate their combined impact on one or more KPOVs under controlled conditions. Once the relationship is understood, a process pilot is conducted. In the pilot, solutions to the root causes are applied; when performance to target is confirmed, the changes to the KPIVs are integrated into a control plan. Many of these controls are Lean tools and methods such as 5-S, modified work instructions, training, mistake-proofing, elimination of unnecessary operations, and others. In the control phase, a complete cost-benefit analysis is made to verify the benefits of the project. When the project is completed, the team identifies the lessons learned and communicates them across the organization.

DEPLOYING DESIGN EXCELLENCE

Product and process design drive an organization's cost structure and long-term productivity. A simple design will take less time to build and will have higher quality and lower cost than a more complicated one. This will make it more competitive. As an example, I worked for a European manufacturer of direct current motors that turned the read-write head of computer disc drives. Our competitors were in Japan and the United States. Each competitor developed a different design solution to meet customer requirements. The European manufacturer's motor had a plastic cooling fan glued to one end. The U.S. version had the fan screwed onto the end of the motor. In contrast, the Japanese left the fan off the motor entirely as it was not needed. A braking mechanism was also applied to the motor housing to reduce its speed. The braking effectiveness relied on the housing's surface finish or roughness. The European manufacturer's design could not consistently match the surface finish (surface roughness) requirements. Their solution was to polish the motor housing. This rework process contributed to rusting of the housing. The U.S. and Japanese manufacturers met the surface finish requirements of the customer, and their housing did not require refinishing. The relative quality was highest for the Japanese motor, and the European manufacturer had the poorest quality. The Japanese also had the lowest cost, whereas the

European manufacturer had the highest. Over time, the European manufacturer was forced out of the market, and the Japanese firm dominated it. The problem was poor communication within the European manufacturer's organization. As an example, there were three versions of the motor design. The European manufacturer had the most recent design drawings, our U.S. assembly operation had an older version, and the customer had an even older version of the motor design. This situation was completely unnecessary because the European manufacturer was first to market with their motor.

Design simplicity enables process simplicity and easier communication between customers, producers, and suppliers. Effective product and service design is important because most of a product's total life cycle cost is committed at the design stage. In addition to cost, time to market is critical for success in many industries. As an example, in electronic manufacturing, the first company to market achieves approximately 70% of the market share for the life of the product, with the other 30% of the market share going to competitors arriving later. The early entrant then can scale production and reduce costs more efficiently than latter entrants, resulting in higher profits.

I was also involved in a design project to develop the high-volume manufacturing application of a specialty adhesive. This adhesive eliminated several manufacturing operations and components. It also introduced a unique and exciting modification to the product design with a potential to increase market share. But the technology was so revolutionary and expensive that, by the time manufacturing prototypes were produced, it was found that the product performance of laboratory samples in the field were marginal and solutions would require higher materials costs. The design simplicity was offset by high process complexity. Groupthink pushed the project forward and its manufacturing process was deployed to several facilities. The project came to a halt only when it was found that, under higher heat manufacturing conditions, the adhesive and component could not be removed from their mold. This situation necessitated the older process be immediately implemented and the new design be halted.

The tools and methods of Design Excellence bring customers and project teams together to prevent poor design practices and behaviors such as that one. Failing to employ best-in-class design principles will result in a non-competitive position. Organizations need to create effective design strategies and execute them for efficient operations.

There are several steps organizations should also take to improve design practices. The first is to incorporate a customer's requirements early in the design process. Quality function deployment (QFD) helps capture the VOC and align it with the VOB. QFD incorporates key design features and functions related to features and functions. These impact a design's reliability, maintainability, serviceability, ease of assembly and disassembly, customer usability, how well it can be installed at a customer's location, its upgradeability, availability, disposability at the end of its life cycle, and the ability to recycle it if necessary. In the second step, a design team is assembled and managed using concurrent engineering methods. The team's performance is measured using appropriate criteria. These enable the team to meet customer performance requirements and other requirements on schedule and on budget. In the fourth step, design alternatives are selected using effective brainstorming and prioritization methods such as analytical hierarchy process and Pugh matrix methods. These prioritization tools will be discussed in Chapter 4. The final design alternative is the one that embodies the best features and functions of the initial designs.

Integral to the development of design alternatives is consideration of how the production process will be impacted by the final design. Design-for-Manufacturing (DFM) tools and methods are used to simplify and mistake-proof product designs. It is important to consider costs and performance over the total life cycle (i.e., from the time of manufacture, use by customers, service by field technicians, and eventual disposal). DFM will be discussed with examples in Chapter 4.

The final design is tested under expected customer use conditions. Some important analytical tools used for these evaluations are statistically based experiments that help build models to describe the effects of changing levels of KPIVs on the KPOVs to find the best combination of variable levels that meet performance targets. This design strategy helps ensure the final design configuration will optimally perform under all expected environmental and customer use conditions.

In subsequent steps, the design is progressively fine-tuned and evaluated for failure and risk using a failure mode and effects analysis (FMEA), reliability testing, and other evaluative methods. FMEA is a structured brainstorming method to help analyze the ways in which products or services can fail. In an FMEA analysis, KPOVs (outputs or customer performance measures), failure modes, and the causes for failure are methodically evaluated, scored, and prioritized to reduce risk. Countermeasures are placed against each failure mode to reduce its occurrence and to improve the ability of the measurement system to detect the failure mode if it should occur. Reliability testing is also used to predict the likelihood of a design to continue performing over an extend time. After full performance evaluations, the original design is modified to ensure it meets requirements. After the capability of a design is verified, it is formally transferred to production. During the design phase, the concurrent engineering team will have been communicating to the production team to ensure alignment.

DEPLOYING IT EXCELLENCE

IT is integral to any organization. IT evolved to dominate most organizational operations as they evolved toward service and information applications as opposed to producing physical objects. This brought many products, services, and supporting operations into an IT ecosystem. This ecosystem consists of numerous IT platforms and applications that manage and report global transactions through various processes (e.g., design, production, finance, and others). As process complexity increases, IT becomes increasingly important for improving productivity. In nonmanufacturing organizations, IT is the principal process design focus that coordinates and controls processes. In industries having major supply chain functions, IT integrates the entire business enterprise through digitalization. It is also the major differentiator for productivity and competitiveness.

IT design and development activities begin with the VOC and VOB to ensure alignment with organizational strategy. They require integration using a QFD matrix (or similar tool specialized for gathering IT requirements) to gather the VOC and the VOB and translate these into features and functions. The second step is use of Agile Project Management (APM) methods. APM methods parallel those of Lean and concurrent engineering, but they are applied to software development using short development cycles called sprints.

Sprints enable customers and stakeholders to provide feedback for newly created features and functions so improvements can be made immediately. This feedback provides for several software iterations and better design. It also requires prioritization of features and functions using the customer and stakeholder feedback. This helps focus the team on design revisions required by the customer. Software development is faster using APM. The team is self-organizing around customer requirements and work tasks. The work tasks are shared by using an activity backlog board, which lists the required work. Team members pull work tasks from the backlog in such a way that new features or functions are created during each sprint. At the end of a sprint, customers and stakeholders review and approve the new features and functions. Collaboration is high throughout the project, and customer and stakeholder feedback are frequent.

DEPLOYING CUSTOMER EXCELLENCE

Customer excellence gathers customer feedback using different forms of listening posts, which can include surveys, interviews, social media, and collecting information at customer touch points. This information is incorporated into modifications to products and services as well as operations to increase customer satisfaction. The specific ways in which customers should be engaged are integrated into an organization's customer experience strategy. This strategy varies by industry and market segment.

The first step for deployment is for leadership to develop a customer strategy. It is also important to proactively gather information on customer needs, value elements by market segment, and translate these into requirements with prioritization. Customer needs can be described as basic, performance, and value. Basic needs are specific to the industry in that all competitors provide them to customers. Performance needs differentiate competitors relative to price, quality, or time. Value elements vary by market segment and describe how customers value price, speed, utility, functionality, and the relative importance of products and services. This information is translated into the design of products, services, and supporting processes to increase customer satisfaction.

SUMMARY

Organizational change requires embracing change based on opportunities to improve operational effectiveness and efficiency as well as customer satisfaction to increase competitiveness. Change is difficult to implement in any organization. To change an organization, new behaviors need to be practiced until they become daily routines. The goal is to increase the percentage of people using the new tools and methods that are introduced by programs or initiatives. Initiatives need to be strategically aligned and provide benefits relative to the committed resources. Initiatives that do not create observable business benefits fall into disuse. For this reason, it is important to measure the cumulative benefits of an initiative by type, impact, and other relevant criteria against goals.

Corporate culture significantly impacts an organization's operational performance, positively or negatively. Culture is difficult to change for various reasons. A problem with asking organizations to change the way they do things is that they achieved success based on current paradigms and culture. Unless an organization can see the value in changing its way of doing things, they will not undertake a major change initiative. Operational improvements change processes to close performance gaps. This provides benefits from new technology, tools, and methods that change the way work is performed. Numerous cultural studies show successful change initiatives have key success factors. John P. Kotter and similar researchers have described them. Adaptable organizations can more easily change because their culture also embraces facilitation tools that enable efficient change. Because change is normal, the adaptable organization is highly trained in methods to understand, plan, and execute new ways to work. Facilitation brings people together to develop broad consensus on the best ways to investigate opportunities, quantify benefits, and develop competitive solutions. These are learning organizations. Although any organization may have some barriers to change, facilitation removes these. Barriers are associated with current success, lack of time and resources, and other factors. Initiatives need to be periodically evaluated to maintain their effectiveness. A potential problem occurs if they are deployed independently of other initiatives and compete for scarce resources. There may also be overlapping tools and methods that can create confusion. To avoid competition and confusion between initiatives, it is common to link them under an umbrella initiative known as operational excellence (OPEX), which is used to coordinate and prioritize projects and resources.

3

Customer Experience

OVERVIEW

Customer experience is rapidly evolving. There was time when market research was the only way to gather the voice of the customer (VOC). In today's environment, many forms of listening posts have been created to gather the VOC from different perspectives. In addition, customers are not waiting to tell organizations what they think. They are becoming increasingly comfortable with self-service using automation to obtain goods and services rather than relying on others. Self-service provides more user control of the experience. Not all customers want this ability, but many do. Automation can also provide a very deep customer experience because it uses previous purchase decisions to build predictive models to mimic the customer's purchasing behavior. The result is that they are presented with information, products, and services that coincide with historical preferences. This promotes customer satisfaction.

We as customers have a perception of great customer service or product design as well as the interfaces that customers access for transactions. Customer satisfaction is now highly dependent on these interfaces because expectations have been previously set based on prior personalized experiences. The expectation also carries over to personal interactions. When customers receive good service from automated bots, they then expect no less from personal interactions where more types of information are available for transmission between customers and sellers. In both situations, a balance must be set between efficiency and personalization.

Other expectations now routine for customer experience are transparency for information collected and products and services provided. It is unlikely today to fail to meet customer expectations without reports showing up on social networks calling out an organization for poor services or products. Transactions are increasingly transparent. In this context, it is also important that personal privacy be respected when personal information is exchanged. Data that are requested should be needed only for the transaction and encrypted for security. The General Data Protection Regulation (GDPR) requirements discussed in Chapter 10 and Table 10.7 are applicable. Customer satisfaction will not be high for organizations that mishandle personal information or have had data breaches.

Employee training is always relevant regardless of the level of automation applied by an organization. Customers will always interact with employees to some degree. These encounters influence their perceptions of an organization based on previous experiences with other organizations. Employee skills should always be updated and expanded. Soft skills related to listening, negotiation, subject matter expertise, and an ability to resolve issues quickly and effectively will always enhance the customer experience. Relationship building, to the extent possible given the nature of the interaction and transaction, is also important.

Leading-edge organizations do not just listen to customers but ask them about needs requiring solutions. Sometimes customers do not know what is needed until suppliers go on-site and see their products and services being used by the customer's employees. Customers are also evolving their own products, services, and supporting operations. Suppliers need to understand industry trends to continue providing value to their customers. They need to enhance the customer experience by proactively managing the back-end of their customer-facing process. To do this customer transactions are analyzed for ways to enhance customer satisfaction while maintaining operational efficiencies. As an example, customers increasingly do not like waiting. The tolerance for waiting varies from person to person and by use case. Models are being built to ensure minimum waiting time and high customer satisfaction while lowering operational cost. Data management enables the application of analytics and modeling to develop predictions of customer behavior based on correlated factors to enhance the customer experience.

As a result, analysts must continually learn new analytical skills. This information is incorporated into success measures and dashboards for reporting, operational management, and continuous improvement. Two useful metrics are customer satisfaction (CSAT) and the net promoter score (NPS), in addition to industry-specific metrics such as active users of a service or customers who opt into software applications after free trials. In this chapter, we will discuss ways to gather and analyze the VOC. Then in Chapter 4 we will discuss translating the VOC into the design of products and services.

Gathering "voice of" information is a general phrase for all methods used to collect information from suppliers, employees, partners, and customers. It involves both active and passive collection. Active methods include visiting customers, partners, and other groups to conduct focused interviews that involve customers in meetings to understand moments of truth. These are points in the supplier–customer interactions where expectations are met or are not met. In contrast, passive methods rely on collecting information from analyses of complaints, warranty reports, and similar sources, often without contacting those providing the information. Once "voice of" information is gathered, it is conditioned, categorized, and analyzed by modeling relationships between inputs (e.g., demographic or stratification variables) and outputs of interest (e.g., measures of satisfaction, loyalty, or performance).

Creating a consensus with stakeholders and other respondent groups requires that survey questions be unambiguously framed to ensure consistent interpretation and delivered using a standardized process across interviewers. In this context, well-documented procedures, a standardized process, and reliable survey tools and methods are needed to define, gather, and summarize the "voice of" information. Otherwise, there will be misunderstandings. People have different perspectives, and they take actions reflecting their unique understanding of the relevant information. As an example, a classic "voice of" exercise is to ask participants what information will be important for controlling operations. The situation could be a movie theater, restaurant, or anything else. The list of recommendations might include operational productivity drivers such as employee attendance, sales, inventory levels, complaints, and similar items. The customer-centric metrics will be missing. In contrast, when the participants are asked to assume the role of customer, a different list of recommendations is made. This list is likely focused on ease of use, such as parking, access to products or services, safety, price, and similar needs. Combining the two lists provides a holistic basis for a comprehensive array of "voice of" information. Process improvement planning will be more balanced using this approach.

Understanding customer needs and sentiment are the basis for product design and service improvement. Listening to customers provides unique opportunities for improving products and services or to design entirely new ones that excite customers. Process improvement programs rely on planning and on gathering and analyzing the VOC to identify gaps and project opportunities. The "voice of" focus has been expanded to include other stakeholder groups, such as employees, suppliers, and others, to improve products and services. In this context, an interesting application is "voice of" the field, which includes sales staff and service people. Their recommendations help augment information to better describe the customer experience.

The "voice of" information is gathered from diverse sources, using efficient methods. These sources are called listening posts. A survey may rely on one or more listening posts having differing costs, time commitments, and information content. Examples include social media (e.g., Twitter, Facebook, or LinkedIn), complaint logs from customer calls, voice transcripts, information contained in published articles or similar published sources. The data from these sources are unstructured, meaning the data are not simply numbers in tables. These data are used to augment traditional data sources such as customer concessions for poor service, warranty expenses, and similar types of information that are available in a structured format (e.g., numbers representing expenses, times, and the number and types of complaints). Figure 3.1 describes listening posts (or modes) and data collection strategies. There are basic considerations when planning to gather "voice of" information. The first considerations are the purpose for the data gathering and the needed information. It is important to consider how the information will be used, i.e., for process improvement to increase customer service satisfaction and or to reduce the time between product order and delivery to improve the customer's purchasing experience. Initial planning considers data type, the target audience (including segments and respondents), the type of survey (e.g., transactional, relationship, in-person, etc.), the timing, and resource availability.

Who uses the product or service? **Why? What? Where? When? How?**

Types	Listening Mode	Questions	Topics	Tips
• Individual • Group	• Phone interviews (active) • Email and written surveys (passive); transactional and relationship surveys • Focus groups (active) • Kano Analysis (active) • Warranty, returned goods and complaint analysis, sales and customer service (passive) • Customer dashboards • Social media (Twitter, Facebook, Linked-in) • Industry events (trade shows, conferences) • Organizational and competitive news (Gartner, industry news)	• Open-ended • Top 3 to 5 issue list • Follow-up • Quantitative	• Describe their process • What is working well? • What are the issues? • Who should be contacted for more detail (reports, analysis, process mapping, etc.)? • Are there operational, financial and customer issue reports, organizational charts, etc.?	• Eye contact • Listen! • Take notes verbatim • Review notes after the meeting, provide draft to interviewee for corrections, follow-up if needed

FIGURE 3.1
Ways to obtain "voice of" information.

SURVEYS

The purpose of the survey, including the information required to act, needs to be established and agreed upon by stakeholders. In other words, why is the survey being done? This leads to the proposed specific combination of survey elements needed for success, as shown in Figure 3.1. Second, there must be sponsorship to ensure resource commitments, the team, and the schedule. Once the team is formed, the survey is carefully designed to identify the target audience (i.e., segments and respondents), the segments by product, distribution channel, industry, revenue, geographical region, and the level of organization (e.g., account, business unit, etc.).

Successful surveys are usually personal and brief, with advance notification for participants and a standard process for conducting and managing them. They have the right frequency, the right language, include incentives (if useful), and provide closed-loop feedback to respondents. It is important that respondents see demonstrative continuous improvement based on the information they provide in a survey. This latter attribute is often neglected because of technological barriers and cost. This limitation has been recently removed through active data monitoring enabled by digitization of the emerging listening posts. These include text mining of social media, complaint logs and transcripts, telephone calls, industry forums, publicly available customer news, customer-facing stakeholders, blogs, etc., as well as mobile app development, virtualization, shared calendars and applications like Microsoft Outlook and SalesForce.com, and predictive analytics. Predictive analytics are used to show which variables (e.g., demographic information, cost, or perceived quality) most positively impacts customer experience represented by output variables such as loyalty metrics and higher customer-retention rates. Statistical models are created to explain relationships between various data points.

Organizations use surveys for various reasons. Examples include obtaining customer, employee, or supplier feedback to enhance the total customer experience, benchmarking competitive products and services, reducing complaints, and enhancing revenue. Surveys must be aligned to an organization's goals regardless of their intent. Identifying a survey's goals is like building a house: the foundation must be built correctly. So, we start a survey by ensuring the questions to be answered are aligned with stakeholder expectations, are unambiguous, and will provide enough information for analysis and subsequent operational improvement projects. This requires that stakeholders must be consulted when designing and deploying a survey. A "voice of" team works to integrate stakeholder needs into a survey by framing questions of increasing specificity, i.e. by starting with higher-level questions and working down to specific questions. Survey questions should be designed in a way that provides information for operational improvements. Some questions and formats are better than others.

Let us use a generic use case focused on automotive replacement parts. Consider the questions that might be relevant to this organization's goals. How do we increase sales to automotive parts customers? Which customers purchase which products and why? What are the customers' common demographics? Which customers leave us? What is similar between them? Based on a customer's previous purchases, which type of promotion would appeal to them? What are the credit risk profiles for customers who default on loans? How can we determine when a vehicle needs maintenance? The team also needs to visualize how the responses to these questions will be used by the organization; this will inform how the responses will be reported

How will each question be analyzed? What are the follow-up questions? Which customers? Which product? Where and when did customers make purchases? How were last year's sales stratified by various demographics? This approach naturally leads to identifying participants and the methodology needed for obtaining useful information. Methodology is important because there are several different types of data obtained in surveys, and the analytics to understand these data differ as well. Data conditioning is also required to prepare the data for analysis because surveys are collected into databases that may contain thousands or millions of transaction records. Depending on type and size of the databases, advanced tools may be needed to bring data together for analysis, such as analytical sandboxes and advanced database management and analysis software associated with Big Data applications. Establishing goals and answering questions requires thinking through the types of data needed for analysis (e.g., numbers, text, pictures, sound, or other types).

There are different formats for survey questions. These must be carefully considered when creating a survey. The first format is contingency questions. These questions are answered if a respondent provides a particular response to a previous question. This avoids asking participants questions that do not apply to them. Matrix questions are a second type, in which identical response categories are assigned to multiple questions. These questions are placed one under the other, forming a matrix with response categories along the top and a list of questions down the side. This is an efficient use of page space and respondents' time. Closed-ended questions constrain respondents' answers to a fixed set of responses. Most scales are closed-ended. Other types of closed-ended questions include yes/no questions, multiple-choice questions where a respondent has several options from which to choose, and scaled questions where responses are graded on a continuum. An example would be rating a product on a scale from 1 to 10, with 10 being the most preferred. Methods include the Likert scale, semantic differential scale, and rank-order scale.

There are other types of questions that are less structured. Open-ended questions enable respondents to provide answers without predefined options or categories. The respondent supplies an answer without being constrained by a fixed set of possible responses. Examples include completely unstructured responses (e.g., "What is your opinion on questionnaires?"); word association, where words are presented and the respondent mentions the first word that comes to mind; and sentence completion, where respondents complete an incomplete sentence (e.g., "The most important consideration in my decision to buy a new house is...").

Other questions require respondents to do work. Using story completion, respondents add information to continue a story based on a given prompt. For picture completion, respondents fill in an empty conversation balloon. And for a thematic apperception test, respondents review a picture to create a story for what they think is happening in it. Some survey questions create more information than others, but regardless of the type of survey question being asked, a chronic problem with surveys is that the questions do not provide enough quantification or specificity for effective action. Understanding how information will eventually be used will help format useful questions. Asking questions in different ways will provide information around market segments, competitors, and current performance.

Customer interviews are another important method to actively obtain VOC information. These can be done automatically using e-mails and mailings, or they can be conducted in person. In either situation, questions should be relevant to the VOC information that must be collected for analysis and structured to prevent biased information. It is important to plan interviews carefully prior to collecting customer information to ensure team members understand common definitions and the interviewing methodology. This is particularly important when framing questions for written or e-mail surveys. If e-mails and mailings are used to obtain information through a survey, then they should be tested using a small sample to validate questions for clarity and relevance.

E-mails and written surveys typically have a very low response rate, but they are relatively inexpensive to conduct and analyze. In contrast, personal interviews will provide more information but are more expensive. The general format for effective personal interviewing is to probe the customer with relevant and very clearly phrased questions, which are followed with clarifying statements. At the end of an interview, validation questions should be asked to confirm the customer's responses to prior questions. In-person interviews can be conducted one-on-one or with a focus group of several individuals. Focus group interviews have an advantage over one-on-one interviews in that group dynamics may increase the number of new ideas. Focus group interviews, however, must be facilitated properly to be effective. If on-site interviews are used, it will be useful to gather customer information relative to how a product or service is used, including who is using it, where they use it, why they use it, when they use it, how they use it, and other relevant information to identity opportunities that increase performance and excitement features and functions.

Each interviewing strategy has advantages and disadvantages with respect to the types of information gathered and cost. As a rule, the greater the interpersonal interaction between the interviewer and interviewee, the more relevant information will be obtained. In fact, this is the major advantage of actively obtaining VOC information. However, for building quantitative models requiring large amounts of data, surveys may be a better choice because larger samples can be statistically analyzed.

A second consideration focuses on sample representation and size, response rates, business rules regarding nonresponse, do-not-contact requests, survey fatigue, data cleanup (i.e., contact lists) before and after the survey and before or during reporting. The planning goals are to prevent biased sampling, poor sampling representation, nonresponse, and variation between interviewers or responses to a given question.

Nonresponse bias occurs if respondents differ in meaningful ways from non-respondents. In the 1936 American presidential election, when Alfred Landon ran against Franklin D. Roosevelt, the sampling was biased because of the survey method used to estimate which candidate was preferred for president. The survey respondents tended to be Landon supporters, and non-respondents were Roosevelt supporters. A low percentage of the sampled voters completed the mail-in survey, which overestimated voter support for Alfred Landon and led the *Literary Digest* voter survey to predict that Alfred Landon would beat Franklin D. Roosevelt in the 1936 presidential election. But the survey suffered from undercoverage of low-income voters, who tended to be Democrats. If some members of the population to be surveyed are not fully represented in the sample this is under-coverage. Nonresponse bias must be controlled when using surveys. Another form of bias is voluntary response bias, which occurs when survey respondents are self-selected volunteers. An example is a radio show that asks for call-in participation in surveys on controversial topics (e.g., abortion, affirmative action, gun control, etc.). The resulting sample tends to overrepresent individuals who have strong opinions on these issues or those whose opinions align with the source of the survey (e.g., a conservative radio show has conservative listeners, so the call-in responses are likely to be similar to that presented by the radio show).

Cognitive issues may also cause survey errors in the interviewer or respondent. The survey planning process needs to consider these potential situations as well. These include forgetfulness from not concentrating, misunderstanding that leads to flawed assumptions, sensory errors that cause misidentification, inadvertent errors caused by distraction and fatigue, delay in task execution due to slow information processing, an inability to adapt to changing environments, and intentional errors for various reasons.

Surveys must also conform to laws and restrictions on using personal information and non-contact requests. This requires informed consent by opting into a survey. There are two ways to opt into a survey. The first is explicit consent, in which a person must actively select the survey. The second is implicit consent, in which the organization conducting the survey simply posts a notice to the respondent. Many countries have enacted privacy laws that protect personal information. In Chapter 10, we will discuss these privacy requirements in the section titled Data Security.

Once the survey is planned and reviewed, the team will conduct the survey. It is crucial that the people doing the survey are well trained. Some teams practice by asking each other questions and doing mock surveys. It is important that the people doing the survey remain neutral, understand the survey questions, and follow the agreed-upon process. If the questions are asked in person, each question should be presented to the respondents in order and verbatim. The answers should be recorded accurately and verbatim with no summarization or adjustment by the interviewer. Inconsistencies in answers should be managed. If questions are not fully answered, then follow-up questions may be needed. These should already be part of the survey plan. All survey information should be kept confidential.

Once the survey is completed, the responses will need to be verified for accuracy and consistency, and corrections will be made by the interviewer. Business rules are needed to address nonresponse, do-not-contact requests, survey fatigue, and data cleanup (i.e., contact lists) before and after a survey. These rules should be integrated with the survey methods, whether e-mail, phone, site visits, and others. All corrections need to be available for auditability. Problems may arise regarding incorrect process (e.g., the flow of questioning was interrupted) or mathematical errors such as incorrect or transposed numbers. There could also be typographical errors or illegible writing. Information may also be missing. After the reviewer makes corrections, the responses are conditioned for either manual analysis or machine summarization. The team should have procedures for handling incorrect data, sampling issues, and other problems.

Analytical methods have been developed to extract useful "voice of" information from diverse listening posts. Examples include visualization of data patterns, text mining of unstructured data, application of descriptive statistics, cross-tabulation, correlations, and predictive models. Models show relationships between input (predictor) variables (e.g., demographic and other information) and one or more output variables. Output variables (i.e., key process output variables, or KPOVs) measure customer experience. Examples include percentage of respondents who are satisfied with a product or service, how much they spent, or their intent to repurchase in the future. Accurate models help increase service performance by showing what inputs need to be adjusted and to which level. In other words, this analysis can indicate how improvements in customer satisfaction through operational improvements will increase revenue, profitability, and customer retention.

TABLE 3.1

Identify Survey Types and Respondents

Customer Interaction	How	Who
Transactional	At time of service	Anyone
Loyalty	Removed from transaction	Key stakeholders
Alerts	Unusual events and significant complaints	Key stakeholders
Advocacy	Face-to-face meetings with major customer and stakeholders	Key stakeholders
Major interactions on the customer experience map	Purchase, deliver, setup and install, use, and service (moments of truth)	Key stakeholders
Industry panels	Industry meetings and action groups	Industry experts, consultants, competitors, and customers through open forums
Benchmarking	See best practice's list	Key stakeholders
Internal interaction	How	Who
Partner and supplier surveys	Transactional and loyalty surveys, meetings, etc.	Partner and supplier stakeholders
Field sales	Transactional and loyalty surveys, meetings, etc.	Sales management
Other employee surveys	Online surveys of employee satisfaction or opinions, meetings, etc.	Partner with employees

An important goal is increasing the actionable information from "voice of" surveys and related data collection activities so the analysis will be quantitative. As an example, we are often asked by different organizations to take a survey when purchasing a product. A typical question focusing on the time to checkout is, "Were you satisfied with the time for check-out?" The response from this question is either yes or no, which creates a percentage satisfied statistic. A more efficient way of asking this and similar questions would be, "How long did it take to check out?" "How long did you expect to check out?" and "Were you satisfied with the time to check out?" This series of questions helps create central location (mean, median) and dispersion (variance) statistics over many transactions. Table 3.2 shows that quantitative information enables more effective questioning.

Recently, I visited a major retailer and took the post-purchase survey. Table 3.3 list the types of questions I was asked. Some are inputs (independent variables) and others are outputs (dependent variables). Comments have been added to the questions from a process improvement perspective. The variables are inputs or outputs and represent different types of data, each having a differing informational content, either nominal (e.g., a label) or ordinal (e.g., its sequence contains information). Note that none of the questions are continuous, which has a maximum information content for a given sample size. From an analytical perspective, these questions are weak. It will be difficult to build a robust predictor model for

TABLE 3.2

Maximize Information Content

Question	Answer	Data Type	Comment
Were you satisfied with the wait time at checkout?	Yes	Discrete	Limited information; large sample sizes are needed.
How long did you wait at checkout? (*in seconds*)	2 minutes	Continuous	This provides the actual time waited.
How long did you expect to wait at checkout? (*in seconds*)	1 minute	Continuous	This is a gap to be closed (but it is associated with a certain customer demographic).
How long do you wait at our competitors?	1 minute	Continuous	This is a competitive gap that may need to be closed.
Gather demographic data		Discrete or continuous	These are the independent variables (also named input variables).

TABLE 3.3

Retail Survey Example

Question	Variable
How likely are you to recommend this store to others?	**Dependent ordinal (model using analysis of variance) with transformations, or ordinal logistics regression (i.e., on a scale of 1–10, with 10 being most likely).**
Please copy your Store#, ID#, date of visit, time of visit, and products purchased exactly as they appear on your receipt. Please note the letters are case sensitive.	**Independent variable, nominal:** day and time of day are continuous; needed a magnifying glass to type in Store#, ID#, and the date, time, and products purchased information.
What is your gender? (Male or Female)	**Independent, nominal**
Which of the following best captures your total household income last year before taxes? Please include income from all sources. (various amounts from $7,500 to $20,000, or prefer not to answer)	**Independent, ordinal if in categories or continuous if an amount is entered**
(Getting what you needed quickly): Specifically, how satisfied were you with the following areas? (list of store sections): 1 = Extremely dissatisfied… 10 = Extremely satisfied, and NA	**Dependent, ordinal**
(This store's employees): Specifically, how satisfied were you with the following areas? (list 1 = Extremely dissatisfied… 10 = Extremely satisfied, and NA	**Dependent, ordinal**
(Availability of the products you were looking for): Specifically, how satisfied were you with the following areas? 1 = Extremely dissatisfied… 10 = Extremely satisfied, and NA	**Dependent ordinal:**
(Quality of products): Specifically, how satisfied were you with the following areas? 1 = Extremely dissatisfied… 10 = Extremely satisfied, and NA	**Dependent ordinal**
(Appearance of the store): Specifically, how satisfied were you with the following areas? 1 = Extremely dissatisfied… 10 = Extremely satisfied, and NA	**Dependent ordinal**
(Ability to save money): Specifically, how satisfied were you with the following areas? 1 = Extremely dissatisfied… 10 = Extremely satisfied, and NA	**Dependent ordinal**

them. If the variables had been continuous, the analytics would be more useful, the sample sizes would be smaller, and the ability to predict future outputs would be more accurate and precise. Table 3.4 shows how these variables could be modified to provide more information and how the predictor models could be made more efficient.

There is a correlation between the NPS and repurchase—namely sales. The NPS is between 0 and 10. A zero implies no recommendation and low satisfaction, whereas a 10 implies a high recommendation and high satisfaction. The scale is categorized as net detractors between 0 and 6, neutral between 7 and 8, and promoters between 9 and 10. The net promoter statistic is calculated as percentage promoters minus percentage detractors. As an example, if 100 people were surveyed with 30 detractors, 20 neutral, and 50 promoters, the net promoter score would be calculated as 50% – 30% = 20%, or 20. Benchmarks are available for different industries. Organizations need a NPS that is higher than competitors. Because customer satisfaction depends on the overall customer experience, improvement projects should be carefully selected and aligned to solve several related customer issues. As an example, improvements in product availability, pricing accuracy, location, and other areas may be needed to improve an NPS rather than a single issue.

Competition occurs within increasingly narrowly defined market segments where organizational size often becomes irrelevant. Narrow market segments enable smaller organizations to successfully compete against larger ones by arriving to market earlier with competitive products or services that exceed customer expectations. Translating the VOC enables an organization to develop exciting new solutions to old problems or to completely redefine older problems in terms of new paradigms and solutions. As an example, understanding key customer value elements such as time, price, utility, and function facilitates improvements to processes by eliminating nonessential or inefficient operations using value flow mapping. Understanding customer needs and value perceptions also drives organizations to identify and align its resources behind core competencies focusing attention on necessary improvements to process design. Failure to effectively translate the VOC into products and processes results in lost customers and higher costs caused by breakdowns at the customer interface. These appear as high warranty expenses, returned goods, customer credits, poor customer retention, and other issues; in the most severe situations, customers are lost.

TABLE 3.4

Analytical Options

Current Survey Format	Current Models	Improved (Actionable) Format	Additional Models (More Efficient)
Dependent Ordinal: How likely are you to recommend this store to others? 1 = Not likely at all... 10 = Extremely likely	ANOVA (with transformation) or ordinal logistics regression (or could also be used as an independent variable to predict another dependent variable, such as sales or net promoter score).	Transformation of Y	Multiple linear or logistics regression
Independent Ordinal: Which of the following best captures your total household income last year before taxes? Please include income from all sources. (various amounts from $7,500 to $20,000, or prefer not to answer)	ANOVA (with transformations) if all independent variables are discrete, otherwise ordinal logistics regression	Ask actual income	Multiple linear or logistics regression
Dependent Ordinal (Getting what you needed quickly): Specifically, how satisfied were you with the following areas? (list of store sections): 1 = Extremely dissatisfied... 10 = Extremely satisfied, and NA	ANOVA (with transformations)	Ask satisfaction on a scale of 0% to 100%	Multiple linear or logistics regression
Dependent Ordinal (This store's employees): Specifically, how satisfied were you with the following areas? (list 1 = Extremely dissatisfied... 10 = Extremely satisfied, and NA	ANOVA (with transformations)	Ask satisfaction on a scale of 0% to 100%	Multiple linear or logistics regression

Efficient: Produces a smaller variance of the parameter estimate and a smaller sample size is required to reject the null hypothesis: parameter = 0.
Consistent: The estimated values of the parameter will correspond to the true value.
ANOVA = *analysis of variance*

How does an organization know it is meeting the VOC? Several metrics are used to measure and improve VOC performance. These include market share percentage, revenue growth, margin percentage, percentage customer retention, customer returns as a percentage of sales, warranty expenses as a percentage of revenue, customer acquisition costs, and customer satisfaction as measured by NPS. There are other metrics, used by specific industries, to ensure effective VOC measurement. These metrics can be summarized as follows: if an organization is increasing its market share in a profitable way and customer satisfaction is high, then the organization is performing well in its market. But there should be plans to meet competitive threats by strategic planning to increase market share and margins from year to year.

MARKETING TRANSLATION

Marketing strategy influences the design of products and services as well as internal processes. Competitive organizations evaluate how, when, why, and where customers use their products and services and align operations to those details. Customer requirements, once gathered, are translated through the supply chain to ensure alignment. In today's global competitive environment, many industries have to customize products and services to satisfy local customer preferences. Organizations that do this effectively have a competitive advantage.

Marketing brings customer requirements into the organization. These may be for individual customers or for market segments, and the requirements may be enhancements to current products or services, or they may be requests for innovative solutions to new needs. In parallel, marketing actively works with design engineering to translate the major themes obtained from the VOC analysis into customer critical-to-satisfaction (CTS) characteristics, which are more detailed but not quantified. These CTS characteristics are then broken down in high-level metrics related to critical-to-time (CTT), critical-to-cost (CTC), critical-to-quality (CTQ), critical-to-safety (CTSF), and so on, depending on the industry, and each of these has initial performance targets. Design engineering continues the internal translation process by further breaking down the CTS, CTT, CTC, CTQ, and CTSF metrics into internal specifications by mapping them to the sub-systems that will satisfy customer requirements. These provide functional, dimensional, and aesthetic characteristics as well as other product or service attributes identified through the VOC translation process. Integral to these translation tasks are testing of various design iterations though focus groups and test marketing prior to full-scale commercialization. At this step of the translation process, design engineering is a gatekeeper to ensure that customer requirements will be met and that the product or service can be produced efficiently. Competitive benchmarking is another important activity between marketing and designers. It helps identify needed feature and functions that competitors may be implementing but may be missed by other VOC programs.

Marketing strategy begins with the goal of executing an organization's high-level strategic goals and objectives to meet sales and revenue projections. Integral to these activities is the design of marketing research studies to gauge customer satisfaction levels and identify customer preferences and needs for new products and services. Effective marketing research requires stratifying markets by demographic factors to build models to forecast sales. After the initial sales models are built, test marketing plans are developed to improve the accuracy of the initial sales forecasts. Estimating new product demand is a methodological process. Information related to desired features and functions, the range of prices that customer are willing to pay, and other information is carefully collected from targeted market segments using structured plans. The marketing team identifies potential customers by market segment and their preferences for features, functions, price, and other attributes. Marketing models are developed using this information. Relevant information may include real disposable income, age, education level, and other descriptive information. Ideally, an organization will have a history of sales for similar products and services to these customers.

The market research methodology is quantitatively based on experimental design strategies and statistical analysis. The goal is to capture customer buying preferences using demographic factors that are statistically relevant to the targeted customers' purchase intent. Data collection is conducted through test markets and analyzed to estimate the expected market share for a product or service. In the test marketing phase, some factors such as pricing are varied to analyze the impact on customer purchase intentions. Pricing evaluations are made on the basis of several considerations, with design attributes or features by market segment being the most critical. Therefore, the market research must be carefully planned and structured to provide useful information.

Another consideration is anticipated life cycle, which is an estimate of the length of maturation stages through which a product or service will move. This analysis is made based on similar products or services currently sold in similar markets. Depending on the specific industry, products and services have different useful lives. As an example, an automobile has an economically useful life of six to ten years, depending on the type of automobile, its expected type of use, and the recommended level of maintenance. In contrast, other products are seasonal fads. These latter products and services may have useful lives measured in months or weeks. Life cycle is important to consider how features, functions, pricing, and other attributes need to change to maintain competitiveness. As a result, design is heavily influenced by anticipated life cycles.

Marketing helps refine initial the estimates of market potential and penetration rate to forecast market share. This concept is shown in Figure 3.2. The shape of the growth curves depends on a specific product or service and the industry. Market penetration is estimated as a percentage of market potential. The shape of the market penetration rate curve is based on the concept of cumulative adoption. It takes time for a new product or service to be adopted or purchased by customers. This time lag is dependent on the ability to inform customers of the availability of the product or service as well as the purchasing preferences and behaviors of customers.

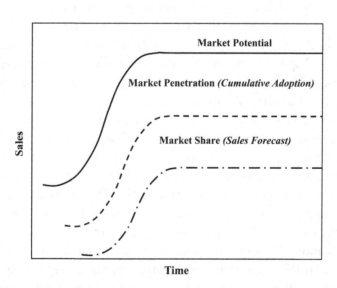

FIGURE 3.2
Forecasting sales.

Some customers are early adopters, and others are later adopters. Early adopters purchase products as they are released to a market to begin using features and functions. Early adopters are also likely to pay more than later adopters.

The initial market penetration estimates are also modified based on the market share and sales of similar product and services. It is important to estimate market potential, market penetration rate, and market share of new products or services correctly because sales forecasts are built using this information. Sales forecast that are higher than actual sales will lead to inefficient operations, including excess capacity or not enough capacity. Excess capacity is seen in too many people, excess or obsolete inventory, and other issues, whereas insufficient capacity causes delays to deliver the product or service to customers. The first situation results in higher operational costs. The latter situation results in lower sales and customer satisfaction. Sales forecasts lower than actual market demand results in lost revenue. Market penetration rates are estimated from field testing. Projected penetration levels, if not high enough, can be increased by changes to features, functions, pricing, and other attributes as well as using advertising and promotional programs. Final sales projections are developed based on these marketing research planning activities. Over time, demand forecasts are improved using feedback of actual to predicted sales by market segment.

Market segment demand is estimated based on the best available information. In this estimation process, the market share of similar products and services can be very useful in estimating the market share demand for a new product or service. Second, market segments are stratified by demographic factors and their levels. Stratification is especially important for global organizations competing in a market segment within different regions and countries. As an example, teenage students who purchase computers is a market segment. But it may be useful to further stratify this segment based on local culture and personal preferences and provide variations of the basic product design or service. Computers could be offered in different colors; different languages may need to be added, and with differentiated features and functions. In this context, it is important to consider the ability of local culture to use and purchase the new product or service. Laws and regulations are also important considerations. Significant modifications to a product or service design may be required to sell within a country or region. This is especially true for products or services that may impact safety. There may also be country-specific tariffs and taxes, which would increase total customer cost and make products or services less competitive in a local market, potentially even pricing the organization out of that market. As part of marketing analysis, price elasticity must also be estimated. This evaluates how much customers of different market segments will pay for features and functions as well as competitive pressures. Finally, customer feedback is needed to ensure things stay on track. Feedback is gathered using carefully designed studies, including focus groups and surveys. Statistical methods enable extrapolation from the analysis and limited samples to estimates of market share and forecasting models. This information is fed to design engineering and operations.

Figure 3.3 shows the steps to create a sales forecast for new products and services. It is calculated using market potential, penetration rate, the estimated number of customers who will purchase the product or service, the number of customers who either are aware of or could be made aware of the product or service, the sales success, and the anticipated usage rates

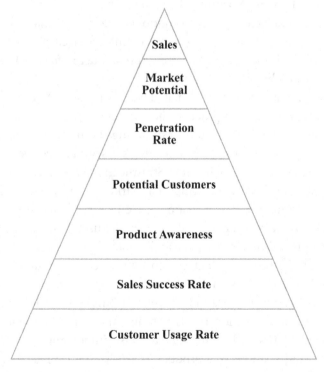

FIGURE 3.3
New product sales forecasts.

for the product or service. Market potential is estimated using the size of the current customer base, the likelihood a customer will use a product or service, the awareness and the availability of a product or service (i.e., the ability of the organization to effectively distribute the product or service to the customer at a local level), and, finally, the intention of a customer to actually make a purchase. This is shown in Figure 3.4.

Figure 3.5 shows market penetration patterns that depend on specific products or services. These penetration patterns are impacted by advertising, local laws and regulations, available distribution networks, product, or service pricing levels, as well as the relative importance of the product or service to the customer. The market penetration rate can be described in terms of a diffusion model based on the concept of early and late adopters and the uniqueness of the product or service relative to those products and services that can be substituted for the new product or service. These concepts are shown in Figures 3.5 and 3.6. The model shown in Figure 3.6 is the basis for the market penetration graph shown in Figure 3.5.

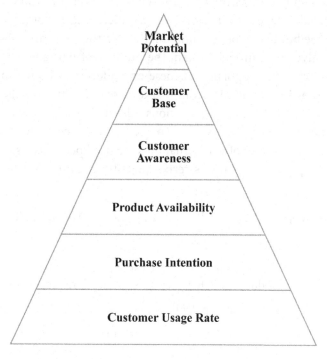

FIGURE 3.4
Estimating market potential.

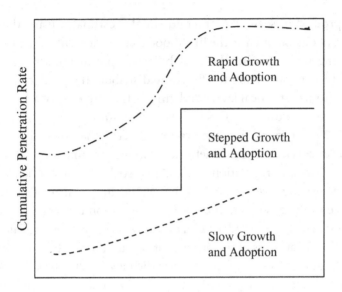

FIGURE 3.5
Market penetration patterns.

Table 3.5 shows an estimate of the sales potential for a new residential valve. Sales depends on several factors, including the number of new houses to be built and the potential market for the new valve. Assuming the new valve has a unique design, the number of new adopters is estimated as 20%. The proportion of these new adopters who will purchase the valve is estimated at 80% from market research. Customer awareness is estimated at 80% based on previous advertising of valves of similar design. The sales effectiveness is 50% based on the success rate of previous proposals. The number of valves that must be used per house is estimated as 10. Multiplying the various terms together provides a total annual

$$\text{Adoption}_t = C_{\text{innovation}}(MP\text{-}TA_t) + C_{\text{imitation}}(TA_t / MP)(MP\text{-}TA_t)$$

1. $C_{\text{innovation}}$ and $C_{\text{imitation}}$ are estimated from similar products (product analogies) using regression analysis.

2. MP = market potential.

3. TA_t = cumulative adopters at time.

FIGURE 3.6
How to estimate a market penetration rate.

TABLE 3.5

Estimating Product Demand

Number of new houses to be built	100,000
Number of new adopters	20%
Proportion to buy	80%
Awareness	80%
Sales effectiveness	50%
Use per customer	10
Annual sales (units)	64,000

Sales of a new commercial valve must be estimated for the next year.
The valve is sold in residential housing in groups of 10.

demand of 64,000 valves at the current sales price. However, sales could be increased by lowering the sales price, increasing advertising, and taking other actions. The strategy needs to be balanced relative to its impact on gross margin and profitability.

Marketing plays a very important role in helping design engineering obtain the VOC, and in turn helping operations estimate production demand. Marketing also has a direct impact on operations because operational capacity depends on demand. Figure 3.7 shows that demand for a product or service moves through four stages during its life cycle: introduction, growth, maturity, and decline. Figure 3.7 associates a modeling method for estimating demand by stage. Prior to introduction of a

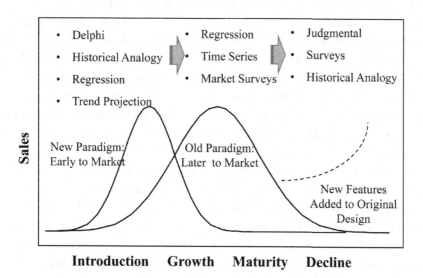

Introduction   Growth   Maturity   Decline

FIGURE 3.7
Forecasting methods by product life cycle.

new product or service to the market, estimates of demand depend on the available and quantified information. Information comes from several sources, including customer and sales feedback and historical sales of similar product and services. In the absence of historical or firm estimates, an organization relies on mathematical methods. If there are no available marketing data, organizations must rely on best judgment. This may create inaccurate forecasts that have negative operational impacts. In addition to the long-term product life stages, products and services may also have localized demand patterns based on seasonality, economic cycle, and other related factors. In summary, marketing's demand forecasts for new products and services must be quantified on both a long-term and a short-term basis. Longer-range demand estimates are important when they require significant capacity expansions rather than a simple extension of current product or service offerings.

KANO NEEDS AND VALUE

Dr. Noriaki Kano, Dean of Engineering of Tokyo University, wrote a book describing a method to gather and analyze customer needs. Its basis was from work with Konica Camera during the 1970s. Konica wanted to differentiate its cameras from competitors. Initially, it sought advice from its product designers. However, the information gathered by the design engineers was not useful for creating cost-effective features and functions customer would purchase. Dr. Kano took a different approach. He asked customers and laboratories that developed pictures what they would like to see for camera improvements. Based on customer interviews and on-site visits, Dr. Kano found unspoken customer needs. Konica developed several design improvements based on Kano's analysis. Three customer-need categories were identified (Figure 3.8): basic, performance, and excitement.

Basic needs are unspoken by the customer. The expectation is that a product or service will satisfy these needs at a basic level. It takes methodical research to extract information from customers because they rarely describe the basic needs in ways that are actionable. In fact, customers do not notice when their basic needs are being met because they are expected. Another characteristic of a basic need is that, when it is absent, the customer will immediately notice and complain about its absence. An example is going to a restaurant and receiving the food cooked properly.

FIGURE 3.8
Kano needs and value elements.

If the restaurant meets this basic need, i.e., cooks the food properly, the customer does not really notice because this is an expectation; if the food is not cooked properly, however, the customer will complain.

Customers differentiate one product or service from another based on performance needs. These are associated with differentiated value elements including cycle time, price, utility, and functions of products or services. Customers will usually be able to state the levels at which performance needs must be met to ensure satisfaction. There are usually competitive alternatives available to customers. This enables comparisons of on-time delivery, product pricing, and other performance characteristics between competitors. Customers will usually pay more for performance features and functions if they are important. Excitement needs delight customers. An example is when a customer says, "Wow! I didn't know I needed this!" These features and functions are unique. Early adopters will pay higher prices than later adopters. Over extended periods of time, excitement needs become performance needs and performance needs become basic needs. Personal computers are an example. Examples of basic needs are the ability to run common operating systems and connect to the Internet. Performance needs might be micro-processor speed or other functions that improve speed or make a computer easier to use. Excitement needs might be completely new microprocessors, software performance, advanced video imaging, and other unique features and functions.

Value is divided into the elements of convenience and price. In certain situations, customers may be willing to pay a higher price for the convenience of obtaining a product or service. As an example, a retail store may have higher prices than competitors because it is open twenty-four hours a day and is conveniently located. Convenience can be further broken down into sub-elements of time and perceived benefits. Some customers may prefer faster service than others and either expect this performance or will pay a higher price to have it. Perceived benefits can be further divided into sub-elements of utility, function, and relative importance to the customer. The relative prioritization of these five value elements varies by market segment. These value elements are used in combination with the three Kano needs to obtain useful information to design products and services or to improve their performance.

Customers with similar needs and value expectations are gathered into a market segment for several reasons, including building analytical models and providing scale for the development of products and services. There are many ways to create market segments, and they vary by industry. Examples include age, income level, location, job function, interests, purchasing habits, direct or indirect sales, and other factors. One segmentation strategy considers direct customers (e.g., a retail store like Lowes) as one segment and indirect customers (e.g., contractors who in turn sell to homeowners, who are the final customers) as another segment. Segmentation helps create focused products and services that have real value to the people using them. Market segmentation proceeds from the general to the specific to create broad market segments that can be successively divided into narrower ones. Asking questions related to who uses the product or service as well as where, when, why, and how they use it helps understand needs and how features and functions are valued by the segment.

Figure 3.8 describes the fifteen combinations of three Kano needs and five value elements. This and additional demographic information can be translated into specially designed products and services. Organizations that understand market segmentation in the context of VOC will be competitive and will be able to focus resources on narrow market segments in ways to compete with other organizations, even if they are larger and more established. Bringing together the information from Tables 3.1 and 3.2 and Figure 3.1 with Figure 3.8 helps initiate the VOC translation process. Translation enables organizations to align the gathering, analysis, and translation of the VOC into meaningful internal metrics and targets to identify performance gaps. New or modified products and services are created to close gaps and thus increase productivity and global competitiveness. This is done in a systematic way using standardized tools and methods.

Figure 3.9 shows that VOC information is organized into major themes after it is collected from listening posts. These correlate to quantitative measures of price, time, and quality (i.e., utility and function). This starts the metric definition phase of translation. The themes are refined into "critical-to" (CT) characteristics. The CT characteristics are

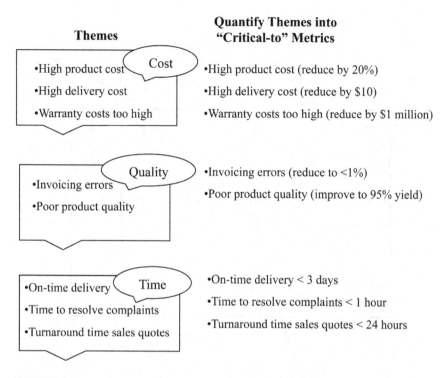

FIGURE 3.9
Organizing "voice-of" information.

evaluated, organized, and prioritized for solution. In Figure 3.9, one CT characteristic is time, and three examples are shown: on-time delivery < 3 days, time to resolve complaints < 1 hour, and turnaround time for sales quotes < 24 hours. Now we have a metric and target. The next steps, which will be discussed in later chapters, are defining the metric, so it is unambiguous, and creating historical baseline from which to start improvement work.

QUALITY FUNCTION DEPLOYMENT (QFD)

Quality function deployment (QFD) is the structured methodology used to map CT characteristics into design specifications, i.e., KPOVs or "Ys." QFD is also used to analyze the performance of KPOVs to targets and current system performance to identify gaps. Information technology

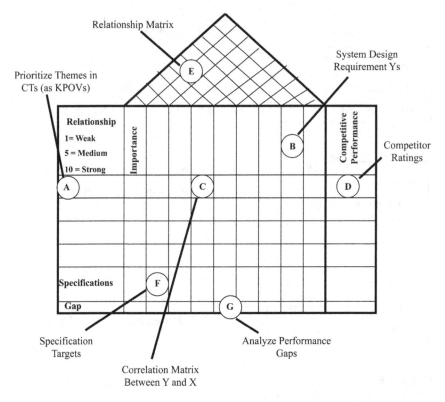

FIGURE 3.10

House of quality. CT = critical-to characteristic; KPOV = key process input variable; Y = outputs; X = inputs.

facilitates internal and external benchmarking. Mapping is useful in coordinating communication between the design team and other organizational functions. This ensures the linkage of the VOC and KPOVs to designs and processes. The QFD methodology is organized as the "house of quality" (HOQ) shown in Figure 3.10. The HOQ is divided into sections or rooms that summarize information relevant for understanding relationships between customer requirements (i.e., KPOVs and system elements of the product or service design).

The CT characteristics drive the internal specifications corresponding to KPOVs. These KPOVs are refinements of a CT characteristic (e.g., delivery time measured in days starting at time A and ending at time B). Recall that these are initially higher-level ideas. The analysis focuses general concepts into quantified metrics. When their performance is compared to targets product or process performance gaps are identified that require that new or modified systems be created.

These KPOVs are further defined as one or more specifications, or Ys that in aggregate satisfy the CT expectations of the customer. They are controlled by key process input variables (KPIVs), i.e., "Xs" that drive the levels of the Ys. This is the Six Sigma model relationship $Y = f(X)$, where we understand how the level of Y changes as inputs (X) change. The goal of mapping the KPOV to specifications is to develop these quantitative relationships or models between the Ys and their associated inputs (or Xs). The HOQ enables a team to see interrelationships between several KPOVs and the variables driving them. In addition, it shows current gaps in the sub-systems producing features and functions (i.e., the Ys as well as the Xs). This relationship information is useful when making design tradeoffs between the sub-systems. As an example, one KPOV may be that an automobile has a fuel economy of 25 miles per gallon as well as a minimum weight for road handling and safety. The HOQ would show interrelationships between sub-systems and their Ys that would provide tradeoffs between mileage and weight.

Section A of Figure 3.10 prioritizes the CT characteristics represented as KPOVs. The relative importance ratings (i.e., the prioritization) are estimated using prioritization tools that will be discussed in Chapter 4. In QFD literature, these CT characteristics are called the whats. In section B of Figure 3.10, the design requirements (i.e., the Ys) are listed as specifications. These Ys are called the hows. Section C of Figure 3.10 shows correlations, if they exist, between each KPOV and the Ys (i.e., correlations between the whats as they relate to the hows). A rating system of 1 to 10 is used to indicate weak (1), medium (5), and strong (10) correlations between the whats and the hows. Competitive benchmarking, shown in section D, is also used to aid the analysis. Section E is used to evaluate relationships between one or more design elements (i.e., the Ys or the hows) because there may be design conflicts, again on a scale of 1 to 10. A rating of 10 implies a high correlation between design elements or Ys. The impact of this correlation could be positive or negative. This information aids tradeoff decisions. Section F lists the performance targets for the Ys. Several Ys may be required to satisfy a specific KPOV or CT characteristic. In section G, specifications are compared to the current design's capability to identify performance gaps. Performance gaps require that one or more projects be deployed to improve system performance. Alternatively, entire new systems may need to be created.

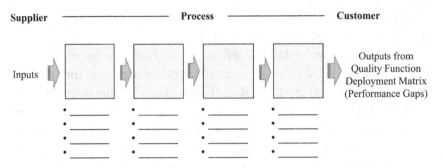

FIGURE 3.11
How to use a SIPOC to translate the VOC. SIPOC = supplier, input boundary, process, output boundary, and customer; QFD = quality function deployment; VOC = voice of the customer.

Service systems can also be designed using the QFD methodology, although process mapping at various levels and of different types is usually more convenient. Mapping a process begins with identifying the project's scope, which in turn helps determine where the process lies and its beginning and end points. Figure 3.11 shows a high-level map or SIPOC, which is an acronym for supplier, input boundary, process, output boundary, and customer. A SIPOC analysis captures the prioritized list of KPOVs or Ys. This information is used to associate them to process steps or operations and the Xs that control the Ys. The SIPOC chart becomes more detailed and quantified until a system model can be created to quantitatively describe the relationships of process inputs and outputs (i.e., $Y = f(X)$). Depending on the project, a high-level description may be adequate or a more detailed process maps be needed. If the quantification is complete, a system model can be created, and simulations can also be developed by varying the input levels.

CUSTOMER EXPERIENCE MAPPING

Obtaining customer feedback is often done through surrogates such as sales and marketing personnel or third parties. Seldom do the people responsible for process improvement have access to direct customer feedback. This resultant information is not actionable.

A problem with surveys (i.e., indirect feedback as opposed to in-person surveys) is that the customer message is diluted. Customers are also inundated with requests for feedback from many sources. A large supplier may use several surveys requesting feedback from the same customers too frequently. There may also be issues with the phrasing of questions, their delivery, or the dilution of sample sizes over products, services, and respondents. The analytical results from poorly designed surveys will not be useful for driving process-improvement actions. As a result, there is a heavy reliance on information gained passively from product returns, warranty issues, and other feedback systems rather than direct customer feedback. But imagine using a method that enables a process-improvement team to work directly with customers to identify key touch points and performance gaps.

Customer experience mapping (CEM) is another translation method wherein customer feedback is translated back through a process to identify improvement opportunities. CEM is a joint supplier-customer workshop in which the key touch points between suppliers and customers are mapped to identify gaps at various touch points. Touch points are embedded within the higher-level steps associated with the sale, purchase, delivery, and use of products and services. A CEM is built with these steps listed in a sequence (Figure 3.12). Then the goals of each step are listed from the customer's perspective. In this context, the "customer" is a persona representing a part of the organization (e.g., purchasing, production, and other functions using the product or service). Goals are the persona's expectations relative to the dimensions of pricing, time, and quality. Beneath each step are operations needed to complete the setup and meet the goal. The team identifies barriers to excellent customer experience for each step and its operations. Then it creates actions to eliminate the barriers to excellent customer experience. The advantage of the CEM approach is that customer needs and expectations (i.e., the goals) are more clearly understood through joint team interactions and consensus.

A CEM can also become a long-term road map or model to continuously improve the customer experience by integrating the information into a supplier's formal "voice of" programs (e.g., VOC, voice of partner, and the voice of field). These "voice of" programs capture metrics that measure customer relationships from perspectives of loyalty and transaction experience using interviews, electronic surveys, and analyses of returns, allowances, warranty information, and other methods discussed earlier. An effective CEM program helps validate information collected through passive data collection methods. Ideally, in aggregate, the information

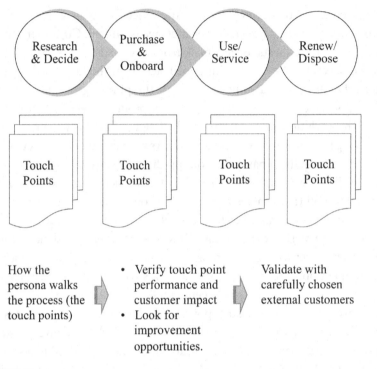

FIGURE 3.12
Customer experience mapping.

will enable an organization effectively focus its continuous-improvement efforts to improve total customer experience.

CEM is a powerful method to bring customers and internal stakeholders together to understand how the customer walks through the process of discovering, purchasing, and using an organization's products and services. The experience is from a customer's perspective. The goal is to understand where a customer's experience touch points match to identify where the customer experience is exceptional and where there are gaps. This allows the organization to create projects to eliminate those gaps, to strategically align with the customer's teams to measurably improve their experiences, and to drive innovative solutions to exceed customer expectations. Innovation solutions enhance an organization's competitiveness. Operations benefits from the unique perspectives identified during the workshop.

The workshop planning process begins by identifying the objectives and deliverables, including the scope (i.e., what the workshop will do and what it will not do). The participant list and logistics are finalized with facilitator. Next, the planning team identifies personas associated with predefined use cases. Personas include the interacting customer and stakeholder roles at touch points throughout a use case process. The personas have different experience expectations. A common use case is the process of purchasing a home and applying for the loan. A second use case would be renting an apartment. You can envision how these use cases would unfold using previous experience. The personas would be easy to identify, too: a real estate agent or landlord, a bank manager, and others. Relative to business processes, some customer personas include a purchasing manager, an accounts payable team, and the people using the product or services. Personas from the supplying organization include the sales team, production and service teams, the invoicing team, and others depending on the use case. The use case in which personas interact is also called a process. An example use case is the sales process, where customers obtain product or service information as solutions to meet the customer's needs. Another use case is invoicing a customer and acknowledging payment. A third use case is servicing a product at the customer's location. Workshops should be focused on use cases and the relevant persona should be invited to build the experience map.

After the use cases and personal are identified, an initial CEM is created for the basic steps of the process. Typical steps are researching the product or service and making a purchase decision. Other steps include onboarding, using, and renewal or disposal/termination of the product or service. Associated with each step are sequential operations that provide measurable outputs that complete the step and move the customer to the next one. In the workshop, the customer or supplier may add operations that exist or delete ones that do not exist. These operations, after discussion, are tagged as meeting requirements, exceeding requirements, or not meeting requirements (i.e., pain points). The supplier's team usually creates the initial map using previous information from the customer's voice of surveys and internal stakeholder feedback. The initial map will not be completely accurate, and it will be updated during the workshop. A word of caution: CEMs must be completed by actual customers and not only by internal stakeholders.

As the joint supplier/customer teams work through the use case, operations that increase friction and customer frustration (i.e., gaps in the process) are identified for action and prioritization. Prioritized actions will be grouped into common root causes or solutions (e.g., policy, automation, communications, training, process simplification, and other categories). Gaps and actions should be measurable and should have benefits for their elimination. Benefit examples include higher revenue, fewer returns, and less wasted time for the personas involved in resolving issues. This is also a good opportunity to challenge assumptions made by both teams, asking, "Do we need to do this operation that way? Where is value best added by each persona for the use case?"

As the workshop proceeds, previously internally focused operations will be refocused to look externally from the customer's perspective to improve their experience. Innovative solutions should be investigated to reduce non-value-adding operations or rework loops. These insights will position the supplier as a strong partner to the customer. Projects will be created internally at the supplier's and customer's operations as well as at their interface. When the workshop and its deliverables are complete, several important post-workshop activities need to be done.

First, all of the gaps, actions, and recommendations should be organized into common groupings, known as workstreams, based on the likely root cause or solutions (e.g., policy, automation, training, etc.). Second, a sponsor, workstream lead, and team members need to be assigned to the workstreams. The lead will meet with the sponsor and team after the workshop to create a project plan. This plan will be reported out in a few weeks to the overall project manager and core team. Reports will periodically reoccur. The workstreams will then be placed on an improvement roadmap with key deliverables and actions measured and tracked to completion.

SUMMARY

Customer interactions are increasingly more personal and engaging. Smart devices and social media enable customers to interact with suppliers to a much higher degree. Many transactions are initiated using mobile devices. The decision to purchase is immediate. And the supporting systems around a purchase need to be immediate (e.g., confirmation of purchase, order status, delivery estimates, and returns, as necessary). Operational systems are being adapted to service remote customers. Examples include automation, self-service inquiries, chat bots, and other software that directly engage customers to immediately answer inquiries. Customers can also access service agents because many work remotely and across the world to provide immediate service for inquiries. This provides real-time customer support. Customers are also being trained to use products and services through videos and self-service training.

Understanding the customer experience helps identify new products and services and improvements to current ones. It focuses on gathering the VOC in ways that facilitate its translation though an organization. VOC information is gathered from many sources, some of which are relatively new (e.g., social media). The plan to gather VOC incorporates combinations of listening modes, questions, and interview topics to create unique and focused surveys. Listening modes have differing costs and time commitments and produce different levels of information. For these reasons, they need to be carefully planned, piloted, and fine-tuned. A chronic problem with surveys is that the questions do not always provide quantification for effective process improvement. The question format limits the information available for analysis and the subsequent models that help identify improvement projects. Improvement projects should be selected and aligned to resolve customer issues. Sometimes several projects may be needed to favorably impact overall customer experience. As an example, improvements in product availability, pricing accuracy, location, and other areas may be needed to improve an NPS rather than a single issue.

Benchmarking best survey practices reveals methods that are critical for economically gaining information. Like building a house, the foundation must be firmly established prior to conducting a survey. The purpose of the survey, including the information required to act, needs to be established and agreed upon by stakeholders. There should also be sponsorship to ensure the team is resourced and supported. Once the team is formed, the survey must be carefully designed to identify the target audience (segments and respondents); the segments by product, distribution channel, industry, revenue, geographical region, or level of organization (e.g., account, business unit, etc.); and the survey questions. The survey questions must be designed in a way that provides information for process-improvement work. Survey practices are part of a larger process that requires business rules for non-response, do-not-contact requests, survey fatigue, and data cleanup (e.g., contact lists) before and after a survey. These rules are integrated with correct survey methods such as e-mail, phone, site visits, etc. Communications are also important. In some applications, external marketing communication to respondents through key stakeholders such as executives, sales, marketing, and others is important to reinforce the importance of the survey as well as internal communications to stakeholder groups.

Translating the VOC through an organization enables the development of exciting new solutions to old problems or the complete redefinition of older problems in terms of new paradigms and solutions. Understanding key customer value elements such as time, price, utility, and function facilitates improvements to processes by eliminating non-essential or inefficient operations using value flow mapping. Marketing strategy helps provide VOC information for the design of products, services, and internal processes. Competitive organizations create formal systems and organizations to learn how, when, why, and where customers use their products and services. Translation also enables organizations to align the gathering, analysis, and translation of the VOC into meaningful internal metrics and targets to identify performance gaps. New or modified products and services are created to close gaps to increase productivity and global competitiveness. This is done in a systematic way using standardized tools and methods. Then they align this information to production, supply chain, and other processes using translation tools and methods.

The Kano method is used to identify basic, performance, and excitement needs. There are others, but these are the common ones. Basic needs are expected offerings. Performance needs differentiate one supplier from another based on price, timeliness, and performance. Excitement needs are initially unknown but, once known, are very desirable. Different market segments have differing needs perspectives. Value expectations are a second dimension useful for capturing "voice of" information. Customers place different values at different times for products and services. Value is composed of price and convenience. Customers will pay a higher price for convenience, which is a combination of timeliness and benefits. Benefits include functionality, utility, and relative importance to a customer. Utility is a measure of preferences over some set of goods and services. We differentiate customers in fifteen ways using the three Kano needs and the five value elements. This differentiation helps when translating the "voice of" information in the design of product and services.

An important translation tool is the QFD methodology. This is the structured methodology used to map "critical-to"-customer requirements into design specifications (i.e., KPOVs or Ys). QFD is used to analyze the relative performance of KPOVs to targets and current performance to identify gaps. QFD also facilitates internal and external benchmarking. Mapping is useful in coordinating communication between the design team and other organizational functions.

CEM is a powerful method to bring customers and internal stakeholders together to understand how the customer walks through the process of discovering, purchasing, and using an organization's products and services. The experience is described from a customer's perspective. The goal is to understand where a customer's experience touch points match to identify places where the customer experience is exceptional and where there are gaps. This is a different approach from obtaining customer feedback through surrogates such as sales and marketing personnel or third parties, which be unactionable.

This chapter's topics form the basis for upcoming discussions on increasing design and operational efficiencies. Our goal will be to present and discuss the tools, methods, and concepts of operations management, including product and service design, Lean, Six Sigma, productivity analysis, and other important operational concepts in an integrative manner to demonstrate how they can be effectively used to increase an organization's operational efficiency in today's world.

4

Designing for Customer Value

OVERVIEW

Design engineering has been revolutionized through the application of new digital technology. Some major trends are virtualization and three-dimensional printing. Virtualization enables design concepts to be created, inspected, and tested using computers without actually creating a physical object. Prototypes can then be built using three-dimensional printing technology with the appropriate materials. Algorithms based on data models virtually test design concepts to find flaws or better solutions. Artificial intelligence is used to aid designers by identifying relationships and patterns to quickly solve complicated problems, and artificial intelligence communicates with engineers through speech technology to make designs easier to use. Virtualization also provides numerous potential solutions to engineering problems represented by creating mathematical models and algorithms, which is known as generative design.

Design engineering is also focused on connecting machines, people, resources, and computers into expanded networks utilizing global 5G bandwidth with connections to multiple types of devices and sensors, i.e., the IoT. There are now more than 20 billion devices connected to networks. This ecosystem enables machine-to-machine and machine-to-human connections. In conjunction with artificial intelligence, all systems are becoming "smart," including cities, homes, cars, manufacturing, and distribution networks of all types.

Artificial intelligence can also be programed into robots having the manual dexterity to build products or to deliver services, as well as to assist design activities by building complicated, precision prototypes or testing them under adverse conditions. This reduces engineering lead time and risk during laboratory and field trials. These also have practical applications to manufacturing, services, and supply chains. Modern design engineering is blurring the lines between physical machines, people, and digitalization through virtualization and artificial intelligence. The world has now begun a fourth industrial revolution.

Product and service design has a direct impact on an organization's operations. Understanding the tools, methods, and concepts of design will enable process-improvement experts to significantly improve operational efficiency. Design drives a major part of cost over the life cycle of products and services. These costs include direct labor, materials, capital equipment purchases, inventory investment, and other costs. The deployment of best-in-class design practices reduces total life cycle cost and time to market and results in higher quality. Building a core competency in the design of products and services helps organizations compete more effectively. Best-in-class design practices are also available to competitors for the efficient design of products and services. The purpose of this chapter is to present basic and well-accepted design concepts for immediate use by your organization. The discussion will be focused on applications to products and services.

How does an organization measure the effectiveness and efficiency of its design activities? Table 4.1 lists ten common metrics organizations use to measure key attributes of its design process. The first metric is time from concept to market. The ability to bring a new concept quickly and efficiently to market or to commercialize it greatly increases an organization's

TABLE 4.1

Competitive Product and Service Design

Metric
1. Time from concept to market.
2. Number of changes to final design.
3. Percentage of warranty cost to revenue.
4. Percentage of maintenance cost to revenue.
5. Total customer life cycle cost.
6. Market share percentage of new products introduced within the past five years.
7. Actual standard cost versus target cost.
8. Percentage excess and obsolete inventory caused by design changes.
9. Design costs as a percentage of total revenue.
10. Function and feature cost ratio compared to competitors.

market share. This is important for some industries where an organization's market share significantly increases if it is the first to market with a new product or service. A second metric is the number of changes to the final design after it is released to operations. Getting to market first is important, but, if a product or service contains defects, then its life cycle cost will increase, and there will be process issues and customer complaints resulting in refunds for defective products or services. The metric of the percentage of warranty cost to revenue measures defects found by customers, whereas percentage of maintenance cost to revenue evaluates high maintenance costs that impact customers.

At a higher level, designs are measured using total customer life cycle cost. This is a major competitive differentiator. As an example, the total ownership costs of an automobile depends on several factors, including fuel costs. Higher miles-per-gallon fuel economy will attract customers, although the selling price may be a little higher if ownership costs are lower over its life cycle. The ratio of new products to old should be higher in a best-in-class organization. Market share should also be higher as measured by market share percentage of new products.

Metrics that evaluate cost efficiency include the actual standard cost versus target cost, percentage excess and obsolete inventory caused by design changes, and design cost as a percentage of total revenue. Finally, function and feature cost ratio compared to competitors is a measure of the value of features and functions from a customer perspective and relative to competitors.

A common model for design consists of the five phases shown in Figure 4.1 These include concept creation and approval, development of alternative designs, prototype development and testing, pilot tests of the new design under actual operating conditions, and the commercial launch. This model forms a basis for managing design deliverables across multifunctional groups and to provide feedback for improvement. Figure 4.1 shows that the design phases overlap. This implies that communication occurs between teams such as marketing, production, and others. It facilitates a collaborative project management approach in which cross-functional teams work with together through the five design phases.

The design process has common activities. These are listed in Table 4.2. The first is the identification and translation of customer requirements into design elements to meet specifications. Specifications are "calibrated" to the voice of the customer (VOC). Typical tools used to execute these activities include marketing research tools and methods, quality function

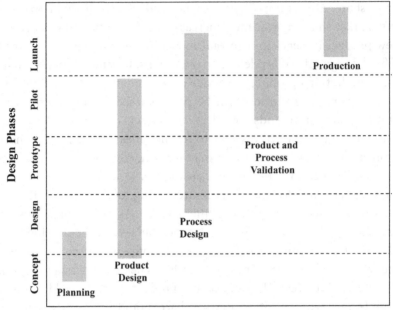

Product Development Cycle

FIGURE 4.1
Design phases.

TABLE 4.2

Common Design Activities

Activity	Tool
Translation of voice of the customer into design specifications	Marketing research tools and methods, quality function deployment, competitive analysis and benchmarking, target costing, etc.
Gathering information relevant to constructing the design	Concurrent engineering, design reviews, historical performance data, manufacturing and supplier data
Continuous improvement of design process to reduce cycle time, reduce costs, and improve quality	Computer-aided design, computer-aided engineering, etc.
Leveraging technology to increase analytical efficiency	Monte Carlo simulation, finite element analysis, experimental design, statistical tolerances
Project inceptions and management	Design reviews, Gantt charts, etc.

deployment (QFD), competitive analysis and benchmarking, target cost-ing, and others. Marketing research and QFD were discussed in Chapter 3 as integrated qualitative and quantitative methods that help identify cus-tomer preferences and value expectations. The "target cost" for the prod-uct or service is based on marketing research and competitive analysis. Setting a target cost is important to ensure cost effective and profitable design. A design team uses target costing component by component, including associated services such as delivery, setup or installation, and maintenance support across the life cycle.

The next activity is to bring together the information needed to start creating design alternatives or solutions. Information from prior or simi-lar designs is very useful in the evaluation process. New technology such as computer-aided design, rapid prototyping, simulation algorithms, com-puter-aided manufacturing, statistical tolerance testing, and others accel-erate the design process. Effective project management and team building are critical for project success as the design project proceeds through the five phases of concept, design, prototyping, piloting, and launch.

Design practices vary by industry and with specific products or services. Creativity is very high when there is little required structure for the design (i.e., few customer or marketing requirements) and design constraints are low (i.e., when there are fewer requirements specified in advance). As the design constraints increase or have been determined in advance, then available solutions are less. If the constraints are minor, the design requirements are less limiting and teams can efficiently work to identify solutions. There are also several ways that a design process can fail. One of the most obvious is designing at the very edge of technical feasibility or organizational capability. Other risks include designing products and services that require large capital investment, are subject to changes in customer requirements or demand, or fail to efficiently use the necessary design tools and methods. Organizational and team dysfunctions also increase risk.

DESIGN OBJECTIVES

Successful organizations ensure their processes meet customer needs in ways that make them more competitive vis-à-vis competitive products or services. Table 4.3 lists ten key objectives that ensure cost-effective designs.

The first ease of assembly. If a design has numerous components or complex assembly procedures, then more work is required to produce it than a simpler design. There will also be a greater likelihood that errors occur when handling and assembling components or when customers use it. The first objective is to simplify a design from a manufacturing perspective. Service systems use Lean methods for process simplification. A simplified product or process is easier to produce and has lower cost and higher quality. Designs should also be easy to disassemble and modify or highly configurable as in software applications. Examples for product design include designing components to snap-fit together rather than requiring the use of an adhesive or mechanical fastening to make disassembly easier and less expensive.

Designs should function over their useful life based on reliability and availability estimates. If an automobile is maintained according to the manufacturer's service recommendations, it should be available for use. Its mechanical and electrical functions should perform according to initial reliability estimates. The easier and less costly a product is to install and maintain, the greater its perceived value to the customer. For service systems, the easier a new service system is to deploy, use, and maintain, the more likely it will be used by customers. Customer satisfaction increases when products or services are easy to use. When customers have problems using a product or service, they complain or return them. In some situations, failure to use them correctly causes breakage or injury to a customer. An example would be the purchase of an electronic device having too many features and functions, requiring customers to invest time to learn them. These may even be confusing and prevent use. In contrast, products such as software that can self-install, repair themselves, and initiate upgrades without customer intervention are preferred. Products and services should also be easy to dispose of or recycle.

In Figure 4.2, a qualitative representation of the rework aspect of a new design is shown. Best-in-class organizations ensure the design process has the necessary resources and is executed using tools and methods to achieve the ten design objectives listed in Table 4.3. If design flaws can be identified and eliminated during the concept and design phases, then the overall life cycle costs will be lower than if a new design is released and its flaws are found by external customers during commercialization. Studies show a cost multiplier effect when going from the design to other phases and then to customers. In other words, if a design flaw is found by an external customer, the results will be costly product returns, high

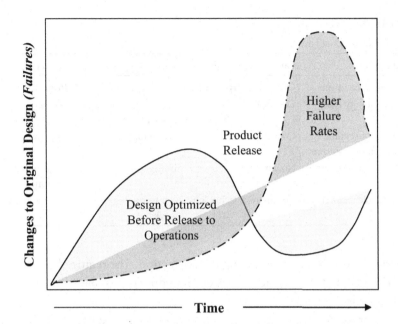

FIGURE 4.2
Engineering changes and rework.

TABLE 4.3

Key Design Objectives

Objective
1. Ease of manufacturability and service deployment
2. Design for manufacturing or Lean systems for services
3. Design for assembly/ disassembly or configuration flexibility
4. Product or service reliability
5. Ability to install or deploy
6. Ability to use
7. Ability to service or ensure operational stability
8. Ability to maintain or use every day
9. Ability to upgrade the product or service
10. Ease of disposal, recycling or phase-out of the system

TABLE 4.4

Contributing Cost Factors

Category	Current Capability	Edge of Capability	Not Feasible
1. Design lead time	Cycle time targets met	Some targets not met	Project failure
2. Technology risk	Low risk	Some technology not available	Project failure
3. Available capital and labor resources	Cost targets met	Over budget	Cost overruns
4. Performance gaps	No gaps	Some gaps	Requirements not met
5. Available technology	Commercial technology	New technology available	Project failure

warranty costs, and lower customer satisfaction. The required changes to the design and their impact on production operations may also cause significant cost increases.

New product or service project costs depend on the five major factors listed in Table 4.4. These include design lead time, the degree of technological risk the available capital and labor resources, the types and magnitude of the performance gaps that must be closed, and the technology available to produce the design. The longer the design phase lead time, the longer it takes to get to market. In some industries, the first to market receives 70% of the market share for the entire life cycle. In these industries, design lead times have dramatic impact on the profitability. The second factor is technological risk. Technological risk occurs when a design relies on leading-edge technology that has not been widely used for similar applications. In extreme situations, the technology is co-developed with the design itself. A new design poses high risk to an organization if it depends on the development of new technology. For this reason, technological risk needs to be estimated and managed to maintain planned schedules and cost. Projects not requiring leading-edge technology or having simple modifications and extensions to current products or services with proven solutions have less risk than unknown technology. Poor planning or long lead times also increase the risk of a design project because of increases in costs, whether that is materials, labor, tooling, or capital expenditures. Long lead times impact market share and future revenue.

If the performance targets exceed those seen by an organization during previous design iterations, there will be risk. Design risk increases when competencies cannot match new performance targets. If required technology is not available, then the design will fail or its profitability will be marginal over its life cycle.

CONCURRENT ENGINEERING

Developing design speed and agility enhances the simultaneous execution of parallel processes with coordination. Using concurrent engineering (CE), team members from different functions are brought together to form high-performance project teams. This facilitates communication and collaboration between team members. The application of CE methods helps design teams identify a variety of design solutions. This reduces time to market as well as cost. The focus is on development of customer solutions and satisfying requirements rather than only specifications.

CE benefits are well documented and listed in Table 4.5. Improved communication is one benefit that stems from forming cross-disciplinary teams to focus on new product development. This results in fewer misunderstandings across organizational functions and shorter lead times to develop and commercialize new products or services. Reductions in lead time between 5% and 50% are common. The person-hours to complete a project is often 20% less than projects not managed using CE. There are also fewer mistakes and design changes because the new design is transferred to production with several design reviews already completed during development. CE reduces tooling and capital expenditures because fewer tooling modifications are needed during the production phase.

TABLE 4.5

Ten Concurrent Engineering Benefits

Benefits
1. Improved communication
2. Fewer misunderstandings between organizational functions
3. Reduced cycle time to commercialization
4. Increased productivity
5. Reduced tooling and other capital expenditures
6. Fewer mistakes and higher quality in the design phase
7. Fewer engineering changes after the design phase
8. Greater organizational competitiveness
9. Best practice sharing and leveraging new knowledge
10. Improved organizational profitability

TABLE 4.6

Concurrent Engineering Implementation

Implementation Actions
1. Create a multidisciplinary CE team.
2. Develop a detailed project plan.
3. Assign project tasks based on project plan.
4. Develop product and process data based on VOC information.
5. Develop design goals, a preliminary BOM, a preliminary process flow chart, and a preliminary list of special characteristics.
6. Evaluate required technology to create and manufacture the product design.
7. Develop the product assurance plan with operations and quality assurance.
8. Validate the new product design through testing and evaluation under controlled conditions (i.e., pilot tests).
9. Scale-up for product commercialization.
10. Feedback and lessons learned by the team.

CE = concurrent engineering; VOC = voice of the customer; BOM = bill of material.

Table 4.6 lists ten steps to move through the CE deployment process. The first is to create the initial CE team. If this is the organization's first CE project, it is a good idea to retain consultants or send people to workshops to learn the information needed to kick off the CE process. The CE team should be facilitated to ensure proper meeting practices are followed. The team should also create a project charter describing its assigned work plan, with a Gantt chart to schedule project work tasks, see interrelationships, work task time duration, and required resources. The charter should also contain the specific goals and deliverables for the new design and its sub-systems, including required features, functions, dimensions, and aesthetic features. Project planning is best done using software, such as Microsoft Excel-based templates or Microsoft Project, to facilitate the flow of information and changes to project status. This enables project activities and resources to be adjusted easily as conditions change during the project. Project activities and associated work tasks are assigned based on team member expertise.

Once the CE team is organized and starts its planning, gathering data relevant to the project's scope is a top priority. This information will enable the team to identify gaps by deliverable. Identification of performance gaps shows how modifications should be made to the current design or requirements for new sub-systems to close the gaps. Additional actions include creating a preliminary bill of material (BOM), process flow charts, and a list of special characteristics and unique features and functions of the new design. In parallel, the CE team evaluates the technology that will be required to develop, test, and produce the new design candidates or alternatives. Eventually, a final optimized design will be selected that blends the best features and functions from all the design alternatives that have been evaluated.

In parallel with designing the product or service, the production team will develop the new production process to ensure quality levels are high, target costs are met, and lead time is to target, as well as other requirements. Quality assurance also develops a quality control plan and works with other teams to develop supporting documentation. This includes inspection, audit, and other procedures that reflect the voice of the customer (VOC) and the voice of the business. Finally, as the final design is validated though testing under controlled conditions (i.e., pilot tests), it is scaled for commercialization. Throughout the CE process, the design team incorporates lessons learned and best practices into their project work.

DESIGN FOR MANUFACTURING

Product and process simplification are probably the two most useful concepts for designing. Simple systems are faster and cost less than more complicated ones. The lead times are shorter than that of more complicated systems because unnecessarily complex products or processes are more difficult to understand, modify, and control. The cumulative impact of complexity may not be seen until an extended period has passed and failures begin to occur in the field. There are two initiatives or programs useful for reducing complexity. Design for manufacturing (DFM) is used to reduce product design complexity, and Lean methods are used to simplify process complexity. There are strong analogies between the two initiatives.

In the mid-1980s, DFM was popularized through the work of Dewhurst and Boothroyd, two resident professors at the University of Rhode Island. Their work was a modification of classic value engineering. In value engineering, a product design is broken into its components, their assembly operations, and the elemental work tasks of each operation. Using value engineering, the standard cost of all components and the standard work tasks needed to produce a product is estimated. Using this initial analysis,

TABLE 4.7

Ten Steps to Implement Design for Manufacturing

Step
1. Simplify through elimination of unnecessary components.
2. Use standardized materials, components, and procedures where possible.
3. Combine several functions into one component.
4. Eliminate different materials.
5. Eliminate screws, fasteners, adhesives, and secondary operations.
6. Ensure components can be easily aligned to allow vertical assembly.
7. Ensure assembly operations are visible and easy to perform.
8. Mistake-proof assembly operations to prevent misalignment and assembly errors.
9. Ensure products are easy to disassemble, service, maintain, and dispose.
10. Ensure products are easy to test and analyze.

the value engineering team attempts to reduce the product's complexity through the elimination or combination of components to reduce assembly time and materials cost. In this value engineering analysis, design alternatives are compared to the current baseline design relative to features, functions, costs, and time to assemble. The goal is to reduce the number of components and materials, the standard time to assemble one unit, as well as the per-unit cost. Published case studies have consistently shown reductions in component count that exceed 50% using DFM methods. There are also corresponding reductions in standard cost, the number of required suppliers, inventory investment, and time.

Table 4.7 lists ten steps to implement DFM. The first is simplification of a design through the elimination of unnecessary components, which also eliminates their assembly time and cost. Simplification includes the elimination of unnecessary features and functions, combining features and functions or components, and reducing assembly and inspection operations. If several components are combined into fewer components, there will be fewer assembly operations. The number of different materials should also be reduced, if possible, to enable combining product features and functions. An example is molding several components that use the same material (e.g., a type of polymer or plastic) into a single part. Because screws, fasteners, adhesives, and secondary operations increase cost and lead time, they should be eliminated if possible.

The product or service should also be designed for easy assembly. Components should be aligned to allow vertical assembly by robots or machines. Standardized materials, components, and procedures should also be used whenever possible. Standardized components and procedures also enable easier assembly of the product or deployment of the service, resulting in fewer mistakes. Standardization enables multiple sourcing of components by purchasing and lower costs.

Product quality is also improved when assembly operations are visible and easy to perform by workers or machines. As an example, imagine trying to assemble two components without being able to clearly see the assembly operation because it is hidden. Assembly operations that remain after implementing steps one through eight should be mistake-proofed to prevent errors. Products should be easy to disassemble and serviced at remote locations. At the end of their useful life, disposal should be inexpensive and safe. Finally, new products and services should be easy to test and analyze, both during assembly and at a remote location.

The deliverables or milestones from designing products or services are listed in Table 4.8. This is a generic list, and different industries may have more of these deliverables or fewer. These are incorporated into the five phases that were shown in Figure 4.1. These will be discussed in the following sections.

TABLE 4.8

Design Deliverables

Deliverables	
1. Marketing strategy and voice of the customer	11. Prototype build
2. Product/process data	12. Engineering drawings and specifications
3. Product reliability studies	13. Equipment and tooling requirements with manufacturing
4. Design goals	14. Testing requirements
5. Preliminary bill of materials and process flow chart	15. Packaging specifications
6. Preliminary list of special characteristics	16. Process instructions
7. Design failure mode and effects analysis (DFMEA)	17. Measurements systems analysis
8. Design for manufacturability applications	18. Preliminary process capability study plan
9. Design verification	19. Production trial run with manufacturing
10. Design reviews	20. Customer production part approval

CONCEPT PHASE

In Chapter 3 we discussed the steps necessary to identify and translate the VOC into internal design specifications. This translation process began with identification of the VOC by market segment. Using various data collection tools and methods, the CE team organized the VOC into the major themes that were shown in Figure 3.9. A prioritized list of "critical-to" (CT) characteristics was created by aggregating and quantifying the VOC themes. Now we will discuss their prioritization.

In one method, the CE team uses a weighting system called the paired comparison method (PCM), in which each CT characteristic is ranked against several evaluation criteria. The CT characteristic that ranks highest relative to the evaluation criteria would have the highest total ranking. PCM compares CT characteristics in pair-wise combinations, as shown in Figure 4.3 for a software product. The CT characteristics are reduce lead time, improve reliability, easy to maintain, and easy upgrade installation. The four CT characteristics listed in Figure 4.3 create a total of six pair-wise comparisons: $4!/((4-2)! \times 2!) = 6$. This pair-wise analysis asks a simple question, "Which CT characteristic should be ranked higher than the other?" Each CT characteristic is compared to every other. In the example, reduce lead time won in all three comparisons with the other CT characteristics, whereas improve reliability won two out of three comparisons, easy to maintain won none, and easy upgrade installation won one out of three comparisons. The relative success fraction of a CT

Critical-to	Successful Paired Rankings	Add "1"	Success Fraction	Prioritization Ranking
Reduce lead time	3	4	0.4	1
Improve reliability	2	3	0.3	2
Easy to maintain	0	1	0.1	4
Easy upgrade installation	1	2	0.2	3
Total	**6**	**10**	**1.0**	

FIGURE 4.3
Paired-comparison method.

characteristic is calculated by dividing the adjusted ranking of each CT by the total adjusted ranking of 10. The analysis shows that reduce cycle time is the highest priority CT characteristic. This information would be inserted into house-of-quality (HOQ) shown in Figure 3.10 or Figure 4.10 in the Importance column. A paired-comparison test is easy to use, but it has low resolution because there is no numerical scale.

The analytical hierarchy process (AHP) method, shown in Figure 4.4, is another analytical method that can help prioritize CT characteristics. The AHP method was developed by Thomas Saaty and uses a quantitative scale to compare CT characteristics with a higher resolution than a paired-comparison test. In Figure 4.4, the scale has been set as 1, 5, or 9. However, a higher-resolution scale, such as 1, 2, 3, 9, and 10, can also be used for analysis. The AHP ranking comparisons are more complex than a paired-comparison method. Using AHP for the same software example, each of the CT characteristics is ranked against the others using

CTC	Reduce Cycle Time	Improve Reliability	Easy to Maintain	Easy Upgrade Installation	Normalized Rankings	Prioritized Rank	Original Paired Comparison Rank
Reduce cycle time	1.0	5.0	9.1	9.1	2.3	0.6	1
Improve reliability	0.2	1.0	9.1	9.1	1.1	0.3	2
Easy to maintain	0.1	0.1	1.0	0.2	0.1	0.0	4
Easy upgrade installation	0.1	0.2	5.0	1.0	0.4	0.1	3
Total	1.4	6.3	24.2	19.4	4.0	1.0	

(1) Same importance
(5) More important
(9) Much more important

FIGURE 4.4

Analytical hierarchy process (AHP) method. CTC = critical-to-customer characteristic.

the numeric scale of 1, 5, or 9. Reduce cycle time has a ranking of 5 versus improve reliability. In other words, reduce cycle time is more important than improve reliability. Similarly, improve reliability is much more important than easy to maintain because it is ranked 9 compared to easy to maintain. The AHP method is very useful in practice and the calculations can be made by computer. Note that the prioritization is like the paired-comparison test.

DESIGN PHASE

After ranking the CT characteristics, current sub-systems that positively or negatively influence the CT characteristics are rated. A new product or service may be a moderate improvement over the current design or a completely new design. If it is like a current design, existing sub-systems are reviewed for their ability to meet the customer's CT requirements. Performance gaps that require improvements to current capabilities require incremental changes. Completely new designs will rely on the application of available technologies to create new features and functions.

The team gathers relevant requirements, including specifications related to fit, form, function, and production feasibility. Its important that new products and services consistently meet customer requirements. Capability analyses are made using testing and historical performance. Engineering drawings, models, performance testing, and field performance information are evaluated for additional design improvements. This latter information focuses on ease of installation and maintenance, serviceability, and disposability (including recycling).

Design and performance depend on technological maturity within an industry and organization (i.e., state-of-the-art capabilities). Some organizations create more efficient designs than others (i.e., they are more competitive). In Chapter 2, in the section entitled, "Deploy Design Excellence," an example was discussed in which three manufacturers of direct current motors had different motor designs and differing quality and cost positions. Recall that the Japanese company had the simplest and most competitive design. Global competitive advantages depend on setting correct design goals and performance objectives and on following good design principles. Simplicity is very important. Design complexity can be seen in a product's BOM. The number of components and assembly operations grows with complexity. This increases design lead time and costs, and mistakes are easier to make without compensating mistake-proofing strategies and controls.

Organizations need to get new products and service design right the first time. How can an organization do this? It is important to ask the right questions at the start of the design process. The best place to start is with the external customer by gathering the VOC. Second, assembling a cross-functional team and creating an aligned project plan coinciding with release to production is critical for success. Facilitation also helps ensure design teams do not become side-tracked or focus on the wrong requirements and solutions. Through facilitation and brainstorming, alternative design solutions will be more likely to close the performance gaps.

Brainstorming can be used to better manage the project or to identify ways to close performance gaps. It is useful in almost any situation where new ideas are needed to move forward. There are different types of brainstorming, from simple idea generation to the use of highly structured checklists such as those used in the theory of inventive problem solving (TRIZ). The TRIZ acronym is translated from the Russian phrase for the theory of inventive problem solving. TRIZ was invented by Dr. Genrich Altshuller while a political prisoner in a Soviet Union prison camp as a structured approach to identify solutions to solve design problems. During his imprisonment, Dr. Altshuller analyzed the Soviet Union's patent literature for common themes in inventions across diverse industries and applications. His hypothesis was that analogous problems in different industries had similar solutions that could be applied to new and different problems in other industries. He found only a small fraction of inventions required completely new technology. Most problems had been solved more than once, but in different industries.

In recent years, the TRIZ methodology has been reformulated as four steps: identify the problem, formulate the problem, search for a previously solved problem, and look for analogous solutions to the current problem. Dr. Altshuller and his consultants found thirty-nine engineering parameters that can be used to search for a previously solved problem. They also found forty inventive principles to aid in the identification of an analogous solution. These are always under active investigation by TRIZ consultants. There are numerous examples where TRIZ has been successfully applied in practice to the design of products and services.

Table 4.9 shows how the TRIZ methodology that was applied to identify ways to reduce the lead time of a product across a global supply chain.

TABLE 4.9

TRIZ Applied to Reduce Lead Time

TRIZ Principle	Solution
Segmentation (1)	Divide into different product centers, make some things 100% in different countries.
Take out (2)	Lean manufacturing: eliminate steps and operations in the process.
Local quality (3)	Position casting manufacturing close to customers.
Merging (5)	Bring things together; manufacture the product closer to final assembly.
Universality (6)	Design product to perform multiple functions; develop a generic design.
Preliminary action (10)	Complete as many operations in advance as possible.
Beforehand cushioning (11)	Ensure supplier quality and systems are very good to avoid waste.
The other way around (13)	Bring final assembly to China; analyze worst-case supply chain events.
Spheroidality/curvature (14)	Have someone else make the castings and get out of the way.
Partial actions (16)	Complete the product partially, move along faster; forget component cost savings to reduce inventory levels and increase cash flow and customer service (i.e., profitability).
Another dimension (17)	View your organization from the outside in using consultants; don't make the product.
Periodic action (19)	Transfer batches rather than process batches; decrease lot size.
Feedback (23)	Change magnitude of feedback (metric); move from inventory metric to profitability or customer satisfaction.
Intermediary (24)	Merge one object temporarily with another (i.e., hire a consultant to help).
Discarding (34)	Migrate advantages of Chinese manufacturing to another location.
Multiple matching (37)	Ensure supplier teams are diverse to eliminate groupthink.
Boosted interactions (38)	Implement risk- and revenue-sharing partnerships.

The product under analysis was a heavy industrial component manufactured in China and used in the United States. This product had a long lead time between customer order and customer delivery. This caused high inventory investment across the organization's global supply chain. The example shows how TRIZ offers different ways to view this long lead time/inventory problem. Some of the alternative solutions were not manu-facturing the product in China, manufacturing it at other locations, and manufacturing some components in one place and other components at other locations. Although not every solution listed in Table 4.9 is feasible, many alternative solutions were created for consideration using TRIZ. Brainstorming methods such as TRIZ can be very useful for designing products and services.

Once the solution begins to take shape, a preliminary BOM is created for products or a schematic with roles, and responsibilities, work actives, and systems for services is drawn up. The BOM shows the parts list and the hierarchal position of each component, including materials, suppliers, testing requirements, assembly instructions, and workflows. In parallel, process engineering creates the new process workflow for the products as well as the production systems and technology required to produce the new design. At this step in the design process, the design team needs to work closely (i.e., concurrently) with process engineering and production oper-ations to ensure a smooth transition for commercialization. Specifications for performance, dimensional tolerances, and other requirements need to be complete before a final transition to production. Ideally, the new prod-uct will be production-friendly, i.e., able to be produced with high qual-ity and to the target cost and lead time. As an example, small tolerances require highly precise equipment be used by production. This may require the purchase of new equipment at higher cost to avoid rework, scrap, and customer returns. Relative to services, the people must be highly trained, and their tools and equipment should be available to provide the required customer service (i.e., actual capacity must meet demand on the system).

Target standard cost is calculated as sales price minus required profit margin. There are competitive pressures to keep standard cost as low as technically feasible to meet profit margin targets. It makes no sense to design a product or service with a high and noncompetitive standard cost and then add the required profit margin only to see it fail to sell. Best-in-class organizations work through a series of analyses to ensure their products or services are well positioned relative to competitive offerings and have the features and functions that customers need and value at a competitive price. Target costing is shown in Figure 4.5.

Based on competitive pressures and technological maturity, finance, marketing, design, production, and other stakeholders set a target standard cost. Standard cost targets are allocated to every component in the BOM for products or to the list of work tasks in a service system. Each design is

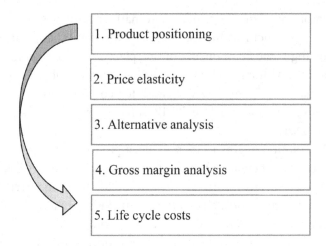

1. Product positioning

2. Price elasticity

3. Alternative analysis

4. Gross margin analysis

5. Life cycle costs

FIGURE 4.5
Target costing.

carefully evaluated for cost-reduction opportunities and competitiveness based on benchmark data. There is an interplay between the stakeholder teams where price elasticity is measured in test markets, design alternatives are evaluated for price reductions, and gross margin targets are modified. This is often done across the design's life cycle because an organization may be noncompetitive in one phase, but in total very competitive. This strategy enables designers to evaluate features and functions across the entire life cycle for cost savings. The CE team coordinates the purchase and manufacturing of materials and components across the supply chain using the BOM, technical specifications, and related information. Figure 4.6 shows a common method for doing this coordination using the HOQ matrix as extrapolated though a supply chain. Each part of a supply chain creates solutions to "what" is required versus "how" it will be done.

PROTOTYPE PHASE

As the CE team works through various design iterations, portions of each design alternative will eventually be incorporated into the final design solution. In this process, sub-systems are tested and evaluated.

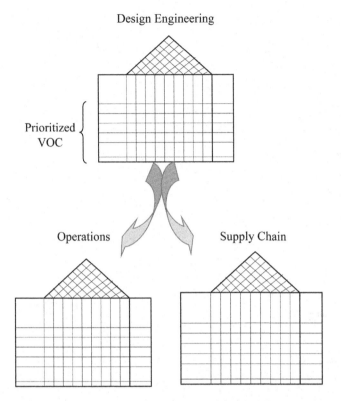

FIGURE 4.6
Translating voice of the customer (VOC) into an organization.

The Pugh matrix shown in Figure 4.7 was developed by Dr. Stuart Pugh to analyze various alternative systems and is a useful tool for this work because it helps to evaluate and prioritize CT characteristics of alternative designs during the prototyping phase. It begins with an evaluation of each alternative against the current baseline design. The best design alternative becomes the CE team's new baseline and is progressively augmented using the features and functions from the other alternatives to develop a final optimized design.

The software application example is again shown in Figure 4.7 with four CT characteristics. Each alternative is evaluated against the prioritized CT characteristics. These CT characteristics were previously prioritized in the chapter using the paired-comparison and AHP methods shown in Figures 4.3 and 4.4. Using the prioritized CT characteristics listing, each alternative is compared against the current baseline design one at a time using

CTC	Importance Ranking (from AHP)	Alternative A	Alternative B	Alternative C (Baseline)	Alternative D	Alternative E
Reduce cycle time	1	−	+	B	+	−
Improve reliability	2	+	+	B	+	−
Easy to maintain	4	−	−	B	+	+
Easy upgrade installation	3	+	S	B	−	+
Total +'s		2	2	0	3	2
Total −'s		2	1	0	1	2
Sum of +'s and −'s		0	1	0	2	0
Weighted Total +'s		5	3	0	7	7
Weighted Total −'s		-5	−4	0	−3	−3
Weighted Total		0	−1	0	4	4

Note: Alternatives D and E are superior to the current baseline design, but the CE team can learn something from each of the alternatives, which can be incorporated into the final design.

FIGURE 4.7
Prioritizing design alternatives using a Pugh matrix. CE = concurrent engineering.

a variety of testing data and other relevant information such as design drawings, process charts, capability studies, and design failure mode and effects analyses (DFMEA). If the alternative design is superior to the current design relative to a CT characteristic, it receives a +. If it is inferior, it receives a minus sign (–). If it is equivalent, it receives an S for similar. Additional +s and –s can also be used in the analysis. Eventually, these +s and –s are weighted using prioritization rankings, and a weighted total is calculated for each design alternative. The design alternative with the highest positive weighted total score is considered superior to the current baseline.

The goal is to incorporate the highest-ranking features and functions into the final design. As the final design emerges from this analysis, actual working models are built and tested to ensure they meet performance specifications. Engineering drawings, the BOM, test and inspection procedures, tooling, and other equipment as well as packaging specifications are almost finalized at this point. There may be minor changes to the final design after it has been evaluated during the pilot phase of the project.

PILOT PHASE

Before the pilot phase, process engineering and production operations have worked together concurrently to develop process layouts, work and test procedures, measurement systems, training procedures and equipment. At this point, the new design assumptions regarding lead time, cost targets, quality levels and performance are almost fixed. A carefully controlled trial of the new product or service is made under actual production or usage conditions to verify whether the assumptions can be met in practice. Analysis of the results from this pilot study help finalize the design.

LAUNCH PHASE

The product launch phase starts commercialization. The technical issues have been solved by this point of the project. Over time, under prolonged customer, use any remaining issues will be found. These will most likely focus on usability, serviceability, maintainability, and reliability. If the CE team effectively identified issues, found solutions, and incorporated these prior to commercialization, the number of engineering changes will be small, and the new product will be successfully commercialized relative to lead time, cost, and quality.

RISK ASSESSMENT

Projects have risks and issues that must be managed. A risk is an uncertainty associated with one or more key project deliverables. These include

	Occurrence Probability			
Impact	<25%	26% to 50%	51% to 75%	>75%
Low = 1		• Capture critical-to characteristics		
Med = 5		• Schedule		
		• Cost targets		
High = 9		• Deploy technology		
		• Meet specifications		

Risk = Impact x Occurrence Probability

FIGURE 4.8
Risk assessment.

accurately capturing customer requirements, meeting the agreed-upon project schedule, meeting cost targets, successfully deploying the required technology, and creating the production process. In addition to risks, there are external factors that may impact a project. Some of these are associated with macroeconomic and microeconomic trends and competitive threats. Although project teams cannot eliminate these external factors, contingency plans can be created to mitigate their impact on a project.

Project risks are also characterized by their impact and occurrence probability as shown in Figure 4.8. The impact rating has a scale from 0 to 9. High risks can be managed. The first risk, Capture CT characteristics, reinforces that these criteria are important for developing a saleable product and earning returns, or that any product must be retrofitted to make it saleable. Focusing on the wrong CT characteristics results in features and functions that need to be modified, poor demand forecasting, missing competitive threats, cost overruns, and schedule misses. Risk can be mitigated if the VOC is correctly captured by the marketing group and other responsible groups. Similarly, when there are limited customers for a new product (i.e., a few major customers), it is important to communicate with these customers throughout the design process.

Late entry into the market (i.e., taking a long time from design to value) enables competitors to gain significant market share. Performance issues that impact cost or customer satisfaction or delay commercialization of a new product or service may make it unattractive to customers when it finally reaches the market. Project schedule risk occurs for a variety of reasons including labor shortages, capital shortfalls, technology gaps, inefficient coordination of resources, as well as others. Contingency plans should be made using a risk-assessment model like the one shown in Figure 4.8 or more sophisticated models depending on the industry. Scheduling risks must be managed throughout a project as it moves through the concept phase to production and commercialization.

The third project risk category is related to cost issues that negatively impact a project. Scheduling issues will usually have a direct impact on a project's cost. These vary for a variety of reasons, such as unexpected increases in the cost of raw materials or increased usage of labor, materials, and components. Other reasons include lower than expected process yields and technical issues with solutions that increase costs. Supply chain issues, such as material scarcity or unavailable materials, labor, or capital, also adversely impact project costs.

Technological risks occur when using leading edge or to-be-developed technology. The further an organization moves from its current technology toward unfamiliar technology, the greater the project risk. New design teams should try to avoid relying on the co-development of new technologies to support their project. These situations almost always cause a schedule delay or higher project costs, and there may also be unexpected quality issues as the new technology is fine-tuned. Leading-edge technology that supports a project should be developed in advance if possible. In some industries, it will need to be co-developed. In these situations, contingency plans need to be created to manage and mitigate technological risks.

The fifth risk is a failure to meet performance requirements. Because a new design has never been fully evaluated as an entire system, it is not surprising that there may be performance gaps once the system is designed and built. The risk is higher for completely new designs as opposed to upgrades to a current system. Use of good design practice and methods will provide the team with its best chance for success in achieving project deliverables. Otherwise there may be an inability to scale the design concept from the laboratory to production while meeting customer requirements. Performance risk can be managed by the team to minimize its impact on the project.

DESIGN FOR SIX SIGMA

Design for Six Sigma (DFSS) and similar methodologies focus on translating the VOC in a meaningful way from concept to commercialization and back to the customer. thereby closing the customer's voice-of feedback on original requests for improvement to a current design or for a new design. This helps avoid a simple internal focus on the voice of the business rather than the VOC. In a traditional design approach, products and services are built component by component, which sometimes causes the higher-level system to be sub-optimized from cost, performance, and lead time perspectives. In contrast, the DFSS approach focuses on optimization of features and functions mapped from customer requirements into design solutions. The mapping starts with the big Ys or customer requirements into smaller ys that are specifications into the xs or design variables that impact these outputs (ys). The DFSS optimization methods quantity the $Y = f(X)$ relationships. The quantification relates changing the average level and variation of the outputs by varying the inputs using statistical models.

The DFSS methodology is characterized by five sequential phases with deliverables. These are shown in Table 4.10. In addition to these deliverables, Table 4.11 lists the key tools and methods used to complete each deliverable. The first phase is identification of the customer requirements using the VOC. The second phase requires translating the VOC requirements into internal specifications and developing design alternatives. In the third phase, the alternative design concepts are coalesced into a final design that is optimized using statistical models. Optimization ensures that reliability, serviceability, and other performance specifications will be met in practice. The fourth phase, validation of a performance against VOC requirements under expected environmental conditions and customer usage, is evaluated using specialized capabilities analyses to demonstrate low failure rates. The fifth phase is incorporation of all lessons learned by the CE team for future development projects.

In the identification phase, customer needs and requirements are gathered using market research tools and methods including quality function deployment (QFD). This is a critical step of the DFSS method because a competitive advantage is created by effective translation of the VOC into cost effective and high-performance products and services. These customer requirements or (CTs) are identified and quantified using market research and QFD methods. This information is used to calculate internal design

TABLE 4.10

Design for Six Sigma Deliverables

Phase	Deliverables
Identify	a. Identify customer needs, expectations, and requirements (CTCs) using marketing research, QFD, and related tools. b. Establish metrics for CTCs. c. Establish acceptable performance levels and operating windows for each output.
Design	a. Evaluate and translate CTCs into functional specifications. b. Evaluate and select concept designs with respect to design specifications and targets using DFMEA, alternative ranking methods, focus groups, and QFD.
Optimize	Select important design concepts for optimization using experimental design methods, reliability analysis, simulation, tolerance design, and related optimization tools.
Validate	a. Pilot/prototype according to design specifications. b. Verify that pilots/prototypes match predictions; mistake-proof the process and establish the process control plan for CTCs using capability analysis, mistake-proofing, control plans, and statistical process control.
Incorporate	Verify manufacturability and CTCs are met over time using design reviews and metrics scorecards.

CTC = critical-to-customer characteristics; QFD = quality function deployment; DFMEA = design failure mode and effects analysis.

specifications and performance targets for the specifications. Scorecards are also created to report CT characteristics and specification current performance (if it exists) and their targets. The DFSS scorecard will be discussed in the validation phase with an example. At the end of this phase, the VOC requirements should be translated into CT characteristics or higher-level requirements and internal specifications. The team also finalizes performance levels for the design's features and functions (i.e., CT characteristics).

In the design phase, solutions are mapped to the CT characteristics and specifications using QFD methods. Several alternative design concepts and prototypes are often created in this phase to evaluate solutions from different perspectives. These design alternatives are evaluated using a variety of analytical tools and methods, including a Pugh matrix. To the extent that solutions already exist and satisfy the required features and functionality, they should be incorporated into the new design, unless better ones have become available. This will enable the team to focus on performance gaps

TABLE 4.11

Design for Six Sigma Tools and Methods

Phase	Tool/Method
Identify	• Market/customer research
	• QFD
	• CTC flow down
Design	• Brainstorming, etc.
	• QFD
	• Robust design
	• Monte Carlo simulation
	• DFMEA
	• Reliability modeling
	• Design for manufacturing
Optimize	• DOE
	• Transfer function $Y = f(X)$
	• Design/process simulation tools
	• Tolerance design
Validate	• Process capability modeling
	• DOE
	• Reliability testing
	• Mistake-proofing
	• Statistical analysis
	• Preliminary quality control plan
	• Updated DFSS scorecard

QFD = qualify function deployment; DFMEA = design failure mode and effects analysis; CTC = critical-to-customer characteristic; DOE = design of experiments; DFSS = design for Six Sigma.

without current solutions. Eventually, combinations of design alternatives may be combined into the final design using a Pugh matrix.

Tools and methods used in this phase include brainstorming, QFD, robust experimental design evaluations using statistical models, Monte Carlo simulation to determine optimum tolerances for variables, DFMEA to analyze how a design might fail and the causes of failure, reliability analysis to predict the useful life of the product or service in the field under actual usage, and DFM. DFM tools and methods integrate and focus design activities.

The DFMEA is used to analyze the ways (i.e., modes) in which a design could fail to meet customer requirements. Countermeasures are developed to prevent or manage the potential failures identified. Figure 4.9 shows a generic DFMEA form, and Tables 4.12 and 4.13 list important attributes of this DFMEA form. The failure mode is a description of a nonconformance

Process or Product Name:					Prepared by:		Page ___ of ___						
Responsible:					FMEA Date (Orig) _____ (Rev) _____								

Process Step/Part Number	Potential Failure Mode	Potential Failure Effects	S E V	Potential Causes	O C C	Current Controls	D E T	R P N	Actions Recommended	Resp.	Actions Taken	S E V	O C C	D E T	R P N

FIGURE 4.9
Design failure mode and effects analysis (DFMEA). SEV = severity; OCC = occurrence probability; DET = detection probability; RPN = risk priority number.

or failure of a sub-system. A failure effect is the impact on the customer from the failure mode if it occurs. Severity is an assessment of the seriousness of the failure mode for the customer. Severity is measured using a scale from 1 to 10, with 1 signifying a minor impact on the external customer and 10 representing a very severe impact on the external customer. The failure cause describes how the failure mode could have occurred.

TABLE 4.12

DFMEA Definitions

Term	Definition
Failure mode	Description of a nonconformance or failure for a system.
Failure effect	Effect of a failure mode on the customer.
Severity	Assessment of the seriousness of the failure mode on the customer using a scale of 1 to 10.
Failure cause	Describes how the failure mode could have occurred.
Occurrence probability	An assessment of the frequency with which the failure cause occurs using a scale of 1 to 10.
Detection probability	An assessment of the likelihood (or probability) that your current controls will detect the failure mode using a scale of 1 to 10.
Risk priority number (RPN)	Risk Priority Number (RPN) = (Severity) × (Occurrence) × (Detection). It is used to prioritize recommended actions. Special consideration should be given to high severity ratings even if occurrence and detection ratings are low.

TABLE 4.13

Twenty Steps to Create a DFMEA

Step
1. Assign a DFMEA number.
2. Assign a title to your DFMEA.
3. List department and person responsible for the DFMEA.
4. List customer and product name.
5. Assign a DFMEA start date.
6. Assign current date.
7. List core team members.
8. List design systems based on hierarchy.
9. List potential failure modes.
10. List potential failure effects.
11. Assign severity to each effect.
12. List potential failure causes.
13. Assign occurrence probability to each cause.
14. List current controls for causes.
15. Assign detection probability to causes.
16. Calculate the RPN.
17. List preventive or corrective actions.
18. Assign responsibility for preventive or corrective actions.
19. Record preventive and corrective actions by date.
20. Recalculate RPNs and reprioritize RPNs.

DFMEA = design failure mode and effects analysis; RPN = risk priority number.

The occurrence probability is an assessment of the frequency with which the failure cause occurs, using a scale from 1 to 10, with 1 representing a minor impact on the external customer and 10 signifying a major impact. The current controls relate to the systems in place to prevent the failure cause from occurring or reaching an external customer. The detection probability is an assessment of the probability that current controls will detect the failure cause, using a scale of 1 to 10. In this inverse scale, 10 means the current controls are not effective, whereas 1 implies that the current controls are very effective in detecting a failure mode. The risk priority number (RPN) is calculated as the RPN = (severity) × (occurrence) × (detection) by failure cause. The RPN ranges from 1 (minor) to 1,000 (major) and is used to prioritize recommended countermeasures for each of the failure causes associated with a failure mode. Special consideration should be given to high severity ratings, even if occurrence and detection ratings are low.

TABLE 4.14

Ten Methods to Increase Product Reliability

Method

1. Develop sample size plans to determine the number of test units required to calculate reliability percentages for units under test with statistical confidence.
2. Develop specification demonstration plans to estimate the maximum number of failures that will occur in a predetermined time duration.
3. Determine accelerated life test plans to calculate the number of test units to be allocated to each experimental condition of the experimental design.
4. Use parametric analysis of repairable systems to estimate the mean number of repairs over time for units under test, assuming a specific distribution.
5. Use nonparametric analysis of a repairable system to estimate the mean number of repairs over time for units under test, without assuming a specific distribution.
6. Use accelerated life testing to build models of failure time versus several independent variables.
7. Use regression-based testing to build models to predict time to failure versus several independent variables, including covariates, nested terms, and interactions.
8. Use probit analysis to estimate survival probabilities of test units exposed to an experimental stress condition.
9. Use distribution analysis to determine the time to failure probabilities for a design characteristic exposed to an experimental condition.
10. Integrate information gained from reliability analyses into the DFMEA.

Reliability analysis uses a variety of statistical methods to evaluate the likelihood of a design meeting performance targets and the occurrence of failure modes under a variety of expected use conditions. These analyses often use accelerated methods. Table 4.14 list ten methods to increase the reliability of a product or service. The first is the development of sampling plans to estimate the number of test units required to calculate reliability percentages for units under test with statistical confidence. The second is the development of demonstration plans to verify a maximum number of allowed failures within a predetermined time. This information is used to create accelerated life test plans to calculate the number of test units to be allocated to each experimental condition of an experiment. Accelerated testing enables a design to be stressed for short periods of time to predict its performance at lower stress levels for longer periods of time. An example would be to heat a component at 100°C for twenty-four hours to develop correlated failure rates at a lower temperature for twelve months. A service example would be to use models to analyze high demand on a service system and its impact on customer service levels and system cost.

Parametric analysis of repairable systems estimates the mean number of expected repairs to a system over time for units under test by assuming a specific probability distribution. In contrast, a nonparametric analysis of a repairable system is used to estimate the mean number of repairs to a system over time for units under test, but without assuming a specific probability distribution. Distribution assumptions are important when building accelerated testing models of time to failure versus several independent variables. The accelerated testing models are based on a model with linear or exponential relationships between time to failure and independent or accelerating variables. However, regression-based testing can also be used to build reliability models to predict time to failure versus several independent variables and covariates, nested variables, and variable interactions. Probit analysis is a method used to estimate survival probabilities of test units exposed to an experimental stress condition. Distribution analysis is used to determine the time-to-failure probabilities for design characteristics exposed to an experimental stress condition. Finally, all information gathered during reliability testing and analyses is incorporated into the DFMEA after several design alternatives have been evaluated using reliability testing the project moves into the optimize phase.

In the optimize phase, important characteristics of one or several alternative designs are incorporated into the final optimized design. Relevant tools and methods include Monte Carlo simulation, tolerance design, computer-aided design, and finite element analysis are used to develop tolerances for the KPIVs that impact the KPOVs (or Ys). Figure 4.10 shows how the HOQ is used to translate CT characteristics into specifications to build and analyze transfer functions, i.e., $Y = f(X)$. The levels of the KPIVs are varied according to an experimental design or model to evaluate their combined impact on the KPOVs. The underlying statistical models are regression-based, hence the relationship $Y = f(X)$.

Once the transfer functions ($Y = f(X)$) have been calculated, the KPIVs are set to levels that ensure the KPOVs (or Ys) are at their optimum levels. This concept is shown in Figure 4.11. Statistical tolerance refers to a methodology specifying the range over which KPIVs can vary while the associated Y remains optimized and on target with minimum variation. A KPOV should exhibit a level of variation small enough such that, when its level changes because of variations of the Xs, it remains within specification. Complicating a tolerance analysis is the fact that measurement error adds to the variation of the measured KPOVs or KPIVs. Capability analysis will be discussed in Chapter 9.

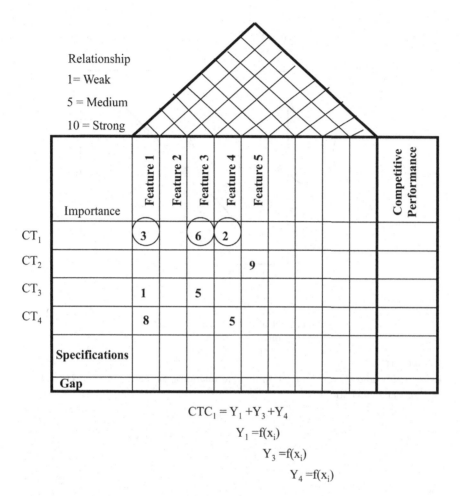

FIGURE 4.10
Building a transfer function: $Y = f(X)$. CTC = critical-to-customer characteristic.

In the validation phase, prototypes are carefully evaluated under controlled production conditions. These evaluations are called pilots. Pilots are needed to evaluate the prototypes against the predicted performance targets. Based on the pilot results, specifications of the KPOVs (Ys) and KPIVs (Xs) are finalized by the CE team. Measurement methodologies and testing requirements are also finalized. The DFMEA is updated with pilot evaluations and is used to implement mistake-proofing strategies and countermeasures to control variations of the KPIVs. This information is incorporated into the preliminary quality control plan, shown in Figure 4.12. Quality assurance will also include a process failure mode and

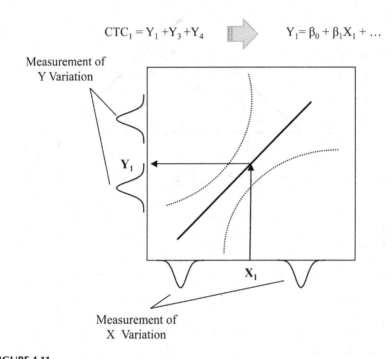

$$CTC_1 = Y_1 + Y_3 + Y_4 \qquad \Rightarrow \qquad Y_1 = \beta_0 + \beta_1 X_1 + \ldots$$

Measurement of
Y Variation

Y_1

X_1

Measurement of
X Variation

FIGURE 4.11

Using design and process simulation tools to tolerance the design. CTC = critical-to-customer characteristic.

Title:											
Process Name:			**Prepared by:**						**Page: 1 of 1**		
Location:			**Revised by:**						**Document #:**		
									Revision: 1.0 Date:		
Process Step	Description	Output (Y) or Input (X)	Specification			Measurement			Who	Where Recorded	Action
			LSL	Target	USL	Method	Size	Frequency			

FIGURE 4.12

Required documentation for the preliminary quality control plan. LSL = lower specification limit; USL = upper specification limit.

Product Scorecard Analysis					
Product Number: Design Engineer: Customer:				Date:	Revision:
Facility: Performance Category	Parts-Per-Million (PPM)	Opportunity Count	Defects-Per-Million Opportunities (DPMO)	Normalized Yield	Sigma Score (Zst)
1. Product Performance:					
2. Process Performance:					
3. Raw Material Performance:					
4. Purchased Parts Performance:					
Product Scorecard Summary:					

FIGURE 4.13
Developing the product's design for Six Sigma (DFSS) scorecard.

effects analysis into the quality control plan and finalize it with the customer and design team.

An integral part of the quality control plan is a scorecard of all variables and their actual performance against targets. The DFSS scorecard is a more recent example, and it is shown in Figure 4.13. This scorecard represents a summarization of several levels of the final product design. These include performance by customer requirement, process performance by operation within each process workflow, raw material performance, and purchased part performance, which are rated using quality metrics. Quality metrics and how to calculate them will be discussed in Chapter 9. These include parts per million (PPM), opportunity counts, defect per million opportunities (DPMO), normalized yield, and the Six Sigma Score (Z_{st}). These capability metrics are directly correlated to defect percentages. DFSS scorecards also can be modified to measure across a supply chain.

In summary, in the validate phase, after working prototypes are built and tested under controlled production conditions, evaluations are used to demonstrate that a new design can be produced under production conditions with high quality. A preliminary quality control plan is created in the validate phase to communicate controls for the design and its supporting process to tie back to the customer requirements. At the end of this phase, the team integrates the lessons learned for use in future design projects.

In the incorporate phase, the team gathers lessons learned from its recent design work to create documentation. This includes detailed drawings of the product or process workflows, specifications and tolerances of each KPOV (or Y), a list of important design features and functions, as well testing requirements. Integral to documentation and transitioning activities is the transfer of design knowledge to the process owner and local work team. At this point in the project, final verification of a design is made by operations and quality to ensure it achieved all cost and performance targets. The DFSS scorecards are also updated to reflect any new information.

DESIGN STANDARDS

An extremely important aspect of a new product or service design is ensuring it meets the design standards for the local market in which it will be sold. As a simple example, in Singapore and Britain, the steering wheel of automobiles is located on the opposite side from those driven in the United States, Canada, or Germany. This is an obvious example of a product that must meet local design standards for local customers. It is critical that a design team have representatives from the appropriate countries and regions in which a new product or service will be sold. But, equally important, the VOC must be gathered at a local level to ensure they will be purchased.

Global and local design standards should be easy to understand by their user community and should facilitate global collaboration on design projects. Ideally, they should be transferable from one region to another without costly and time-consuming requalification. Product and process workflows should facilitate modularization to enable interchangeability of sub-systems and components. This strategy allows local customization to satisfy customer requirements in niche market segments (i.e., mass customization of the new service offering).

Process design should also facilitate movement between regional locations regardless of configuration. Common user interfaces should be developed to allow interaction with different systems across a single organization or between global organizations. Ideally, product and process design will enable scaling to higher performance levels as technology evolves over time. Software is designed this way in that updates are periodically downloaded to users. To the extent designs meet or even exceed global and local standards, overall competitiveness is increased. In other words, an organization's competitiveness is directly related to its global and local design competency.

MASS CUSTOMIZATION

Mass customization of a product or service depends on its design and associated process. Mass customization enables organizations to provide customers with unique styling, features, and functions that meet the needs and value expectations of its diverse customers. It is dependent on an ability to deploy common infrastructures that can support product and process differentiation. An example is efficient production changeovers from one automobile type to another based on dynamic changes of external customer demand. Having a common design platform enables an organization to produce the same base design (e.g., an automotive chassis) and apply customization at the point of production (e.g., a vehicle model). This strategy also contributes to higher quality levels and lower cost while external customers enjoy differentiated products or services.

Creating common designs and processes takes many years of carefully planned capital investment. The first step to build mass customization capability is to analyze product profitability and volume to eliminate unprofitable and low-volume products. Reducing product proliferation is an excellent way to concentrate resources on profitable products and services. A second step is to reduce design complexity by analyzing the BOM or number of process steps and eliminating non-standard materials, components, or operations on a continuing basis. Materials, components, and processes that are hazardous or require specialized training and maintenance are also good candidates for elimination. Remaining components should be modularized when feasible, and their features and functions should be combined into a single sub-system or operation to reduce complexity.

It is also important to understand component dependencies to develop realistic tolerances to reduce cost and lead time while increasing quality. This reduces rework and production inefficiencies. The design of components, sub-systems, and higher-level assemblies or even processes should be based on machine and tooling capability to reduce the number of complexity of job setups for manufacturing or service processes. In combination, these strategies help enable mixed-model production scheduling, which is a basis for mass customization. Mixed-model scheduling systems reduce the lead time to produce products by producing them more frequently. The Additional strategies to facilitate mass customization are to postpone final product customization to latest possible time and to deploy a production scheduling system aligned to real-time customer demand.

Mass customization can also be achieved if an organization can outsource production at lower cost, with reduced lead times and higher quality. Outsourcing is advantageous when a design or process requires expertise outside the normal competence of an organization. This enables an organization to concentrate on core competencies and frees up internal resources. Outsourcing is advantageous if a new technology, including its equipment and work procedures, are hazardous or the necessary equipment is not available within an organization. Finally, joint ventures (a type of outsourcing) may be useful to minimize risk, to access new technologies and markets, and to achieve scale more quickly. Table 4.15 summarizes ten key mass customization steps.

TABLE 4.15

Ten Steps to Mass Customize Products

Step
1. Analyze product profitability and volume and eliminate unprofitable and low-volume products.
2. Analyze the bill of material and eliminate non-standard materials, components, and processes.
3. Eliminate materials, components, and processes that are hazardous or require specialized training and maintenance.
4. Modularize and combine sub-system functions to eliminate components.
5. Understand the dynamic relationships between product materials, components, and sub-systems to develop tolerances to achieve high capability levels.
6. Design components, sub-systems, and products based on machine and tooling capability and to reduce or eliminate job setups.
7. Outsource all processes that are nonproprietary and can be done elsewhere at a lower cost, with a lower cycle time, and with higher quality.
8. Integrate concurrent engineering project management methods and design-for-manufacturing (DFM) methods throughout the product development process.
9. Postpone final product customization to the latest possible assembly time and based on actual customer demand.
10. Deploy a scheduling system based on real-time customer demand.

WHAT IS DESIGN THINKING?

Design thinking approaches the gathering of customer needs and values from a human-centered perspective. This is where any artist or engineer must start to create useful solutions relevant to those who will use them. Human-centered design is the basis for design thinking, and its first step is empathize (i.e., discover the problem). See the design thinking roadmap shown in Table 4.16. The remaining steps include define (i.e., structure the problem for solution), ideate (i.e., develop a solution), prototype (i.e., build the solution), and test (i.e., pilot the solution).

Design solutions are focused on meeting basic customer's needs, improving performance, or creating differentiated products and services. Basic needs are those that are required just to be in a market (e.g., restaurants serve food or rental agencies provide automobiles). The solutions for basic needs are widely known within an industry. In contrast, performance attributes are competitive differentiators across an industry. Organizations compete by creating designs to meet or exceed industry-wide performance by attribute while balancing time, cost, and performance relative to competitors. Differentiated products and services are game-changers that create entirely new markets or establish a dominant player within a market. Organizational design strategies and methods vary by industry (e.g., service, heavy manufacturing, construction, etc.) and by focus (e.g., basic, performance, or differentiation needs). These strategies range from the purely aesthetic to the highly structured in an engineering sense. The associated tools and methods reflect their creation.

Customer experience mapping was discussed in Chapter 3. Recall that customer experience mapping forms a firm basis on which to "discover" the customer's problem relative to the use of products and services. Interviewing and other forms of data collection are also useful with data analytics to obtain customer insights. These approaches to gathering the VOC help empathize a customer's experience through research and deciding, purchase and onboarding, using and servicing, as well as renewing and disposing of a product or service. Figure 3.12 described the process.

Charles Kettering said that, "A problem well stated is a problem half-solved." Defining a problem requires creating a structured problem statement relative to scope, metrics, and improvement goals. Table 4.17 provides examples of a structured approach to problem definition. A problem statement is refined through iterations to refine the scope and

TABLE 4.16

Design Thinking Roadmap

Phase	Deliverables
1. Empathize (Discover the Problem)	• Look at design problems from a customer perspective (create personas and use cases). • Take a Gemba walk with customer to observe the problems firsthand. • Engage the customer through conversation (open and structured, e.g., Kano analysis). • Map the customer experience by persona and use case. • Use feedback such as surveys by persona and use case. • Empathize Review
2. Define (Structure the Problem for Solution)	• Define the problem(s) from the persona and use case perspective (e.g., create problem statement, such as "A problem well defined is half solved"). • Create a design thinking charter with scope and expected outcomes (e.g., what is success?). • Consider stakeholder impact. • Translate expected outcomes into CTC attributes, such as cost to target, functional and feature performances are met, structural form and aesthetics are considered, production ready for cost effectiveness, enabling tools and methods exist (i.e., not theoretical), distribution friendly to customers, maintenance is easy, upgradability is easy, and sustainability roadmap exists (i.e., repurpose, recycle, dispose) and is optimized over the product's life cycle. • Define Review
3. Ideate (Develop a Solution)	• Brainstorm alternative design concepts based on persona and use case. • Prioritize the best design alternative using tools such as a Pugh matrix. • Translate CTCs into preliminary specifications. • Use QFD to evaluate sub-systems for meeting specifications. • Confirm that prototype attributes meet acceptance criteria. • Ideate Review

(continued)

TABLE 4.16 (Continued)

Design Thinking Roadmap

Phase	Deliverables
4. Prototype (Build the Solution)	• Design a prototype (i.e., a physical or conceptual representation of the best design alternative that is sufficient to allow evaluation) on which to base the Test step (i.e., a pilot). • Evaluate the prototype through testing, experimentation, and simulation to confirm specifications, CTCs, and acceptance criteria by persona and use case. • Conduct appropriate risk analysis. • Create Test (Pilot) plan. • Prototype Review
5. Test (Pilot the Solution)	• Begin the Test (Pilot) step; the product pilot evaluation tests a prototype design under limited real-world conditions to verify that its performance meets the original design requirements. • Confirm specifications, CTCs, and acceptance criteria by persona and use case and solution of the customer's problem statement. • Create final design documents and control plan. • Create a scale-up plan (i.e., create an engagement plan and communications strategy). • Testing Review

CTC = critical-to-customer characteristic; QFD = quality function deployment.

quantify associated metrics to create CT outcomes. The first example shown in Table 4.17 is focused on increasing the yields (i.e., the success rate) for hiring new employees. The scope is narrowed to the new applicant hiring process in the Southeastern United States. The associated metrics are used to balance cost, hiring cycle time, and yield. This information is used to refine the problem statement and create improvement outcomes for internal stakeholders and customers. This focus can also be expanded to include applicants by considering their experience with the hiring process. The other two examples involve call center and website design.

Once a customer's problem is well stated (i.e., structured), the design team can begin discussing ways to solve the problem through design. The approach varies by problem type. The solutioning (i.e., ideation) activities can range from simple brainstorming to complicated mapping of requirements to specifications and then into the systems that will provide

TABLE 4.17

Structuring a Problem for Solution

Example	New Hiring Process (Services)	New Call Center (Logistics)	New Website (Software)
Business Case	Employee hiring is a chronic problem within the Southeastern region of the United States. Out of every 100 applicants, only 5 are hired (5% yield), resulting in a per applicant cost of $5,000 versus $2,000 in other regions. **We would like to significantly increase the yield of hiring qualified employees.**	A demand analysis has shown a need for a logistics call center (to receive and ship orders) within the United States to handle increasing demand (more than 50%) over the next 10 years. Current operating costs are 25% higher than industry average. Also, a disaster and recovery analysis recommends a separate facility. **An additional facility is needed with lower costs.**	Profit margins have decreased by 50% in the past 3 years. Although there are likely several reasons for lower profit, one is a 10% decrease in customer transactions per year for the past 3 years. **A new website will help attract new customers.**
Scope	The applicant-to-new employee hiring process within the Southeastern United States.	Finalize exact location, design new call center to handle a 50% increase in capacity.	The website should be designed using the current menu and location information. Key requirements are to display menus, locations, and specials and to take reservations.
Metrics	• Cost per applicant • Time to hire an applicant • % qualified applicants • Yield of new employees to applicants	• Location metrics: cost, infrastructure, available workforce, etc. • Facility: layout, skills, equipment, risk offset, organizational structure, etc.	• Accuracy of information • Load in less than 10 seconds • Must be accessible on different browsers and software versions • Language must be at an 8th-grade level and fonts easy to read for visually impaired people

Problem statement	The yield from applicants to new employees within the Southeast United States is 5% and is 2.5 times more expensive per applicant than other regions.	An additional 50% capacity to receive and ship orders will be needed over the next 10 years in a separate location having at least 25% lower operational costs.	The number of customers has decreased by 30% in the past 3 years.
Critical-to-Customer Outcomes	Within 90 days:	Within 18 months:	Within 30 days:
	• Reduce cost per applicant by 60% or more.	• Increase capacity by 50% or more.	• The goal is to increase customer traffic associated with the website by 25% or more.
	• Reduce the time to hire an applicant by 70%.	• Maintain service levels at 99%.	
	• Improve number of qualified applicant by 70%.	• Reduce operational costs by 25% or more.	
	• Increase the yield from applicant to new hire to 95%.	• Identify a new facility in the United States.	
		• Design and staff the facility.	

• It must include graphics of the restaurant and key dishes
• The website must cost less than $10,000
• It must be finished within 30 days.
• It must be easy to maintain and update

functional performance and useful features. There are many ways to brainstorm; one of the most useful is visualizing the ideal final state. This method describes a solution independent of current constraints or design (e.g., zero time delays, no maintenance, no cost constraints, the problem solves itself, etc.) and then works to achieve these ambitious goals. It is important to include people representing the problem's entire scope from end to end and to carefully describe the project's goals and deliverables. Facilitation is recommended to ensure best practices are followed.

In complicated situations, QFD, also named HOQ, can be used to map (i.e., translate) the problem now framed by goals and metrics with targets into solutions. This approach was discussed in Chapter 3 and 4 and is shown in Figures 3.10 and 4.10. QFD provides a structured framework for translating critical-to-customer outcomes into new features and functions, helps communication across functional teams, identifies design constraints and trade-offs, incorporates competitive benchmarking, and helps visualization of critical-to-customer prioritization.

Several different solutions may come out of the ideate phase. These will need to be evaluated attribute by attribute for their impact on the design goals. A Pugh matrix can be used to move toward a single candidate or perhaps a combination of several ideas into one solution to prototype. Recall that, in using the Pugh method, one solution is chosen as the baseline design and the other solutions (designs) are evaluated attribute by attribute in comparison to this baseline, using a +1 if the attribute is better or –1 if the attribute is worse. The alternative with the highest score is chosen as the prototype candidate and modified if its attributes were ranked lower than other solution alternatives. The result is a superior solution to prototype.

In the fourth phase of design thinking, a prototype is created to demonstrate how the solution (now the best design concept) works. A prototype is a physical, conceptual, or virtual representation of a new design, both aesthetically and functionally, and it is sufficient to enable evaluation for a test by persona and use case under controlled conditions. A prototype demonstrates key process features and is a working model of the new design. It usually has a limited performance range, but it can be tested by customers and stakeholders to provide useful feedback prior to more extensive testing. Testing or piloting a prototype under limited real-world conditions helps verify that performance meets the original goals. It is a small-scale yet complete real-life representation of design performance that is usually limited to a single location or time. Examples include testing a new operational procedure with a few workers, test marketing new financial services with one customer, implementing a new employee-evaluation system with a limited number of managers, or testing new supplier-rating system with a few suppliers. Design thinking is an alternative design methodology and is compatible with DFSS, Agile Product Development, and other recent design methodologies.

SUMMARY

Design is a competitive differentiator that drives demand and most of an organization's costs. The more complex a design, the higher the total organizational costs and resources it requires. Poor design, including high design complexity, increases lead times and reduces overall quality of a product and its supporting systems. Designs should be globally and locally adaptable based on customer preferences. They should be easy to produce and use over their life cycles. They should be transferable from one region to another without a requalification. DFM and mass customization principles should be employed within a framework such as Six Sigma, design thinking, Agile, or another integrating philosophy. Designs should enable systems to be easily and cost effectively scaled to higher performance levels as technology evolves over time.

Best practice designs use concurrent engineering (CE) to manage the design process within a DFSS, design thinking, or Agile framework; use DFM to design products and services that are easily produced for customers; apply QFD methods to minimize variation and effectively translate the VOC into design features and functions; use DFSS methods to understand how components interact to provide functions, dimensions, and other product features; meet global and local standards to expand marketing and sales opportunities; apply mass customization tools, methods and concepts to reduce the order-to-delivery lead time; and outsource work that can be done more efficiently elsewhere.

5

Process Excellence

OVERVIEW

Process design mirrors the products and services that an organization produces. Disruptive trends and technologies directly impact business process design. In response to disruptions, business processes need to rapidly evolve to meet new market dynamics to transform how machines, people, information, and other resources are managed on a global basis. Work is changing. Customer experience is now central to how business processes are designed. Given the mobility of customer demand, which appears anytime and anywhere through mobile devices and other sources, business processes need to be agile to provide the customization and experience customers expect. Workflow automation is a critical enabler for process design and especially for customer facing and supporting processes. Algorithms with artificial intelligence increasingly optimize solutions for customers.

Process improvement also has been positively affected. Customers want solutions faster based on deep insights into well-designed processes using advanced analytics. Unlike previous project-focused efforts where data were manually and slowly gathered for analysis, the new expectation is that discovery and analysis will be completed in hours or days rather than in weeks or months, with effective solutions quickly following that analysis. Projects must be properly framed to focus crisply on the real problems. Solutions need to be focused on updates to information technology or RPA rather than on creating manual interventions. In parallel, continuous improvement projects within work groups are now identified and executed by highly skilled teams having the prerequisite analytical skills, including knowledge of data mining of large databases.

Digitalization is at the core of process excellence. Applications include master data management, modeling of different types, workflow automation through RPA analytics, as well as classic methods such as Lean, Six Sigma, and other initiatives to be discussed in the following chapters. Digitalization enables analysis and modifications to local processes without creating large and expensive information technology projects. It requires the basic process-characterization skills associated with process-improvement initiatives such as Lean and Six Sigma as well as analytics. The application of process improvement in a digitalized environment requires compatable skills associated with process and analytics as well as automation. Process design is increasingly competitive and requires a workforce with advanced skills. Investment in technology is also needed. The alternative is a degradation of operational capabilities.

Customers expect digitalization to provide a seamless experience. Business process excellence is the glue that ties marketing promises into product and service design to enable supporting processes that deliver the marketing promise. Customer service excellence is now the differentiator for competitors. Translating customer requirements into measurable outcomes is highly relevant for success. This implies business excellence requires an ability to gain deep insights in very large and complicated databases with methods to answer relevant questions. Data are difficult and expensive to gather, manage, and analyze. It needs to be used wisely. The proliferation of information technology platforms and applications that can number in the hundreds or thousands do not make process design easy. But organizations need to develop strategies for excellence that meet customer experience expectations while allowing the organization to remain efficient and competitive.

Organizations design products and services to meet customer needs and value expectations. The design of the supporting processes follows this philosophy. Poorly designed supporting processes result in higher costs and process breakdowns, which cause quality and delivery issues. A process design should follow the design of its product or service. This will ensure that the process is aligned with the voice of the customer (VOC) and meets an organization's productivity goals. To do this, the objective of good process design is to create workflows that dynamically meet external demand, within ranges of designed capacity and target service levels, and using a minimum amount of required resources to meet productivity

TABLE 5.1

Competitive Metrics – Process Design

Metric
1. Throughput time
2. Number of changes to final process design
3. Percentage of warranty, scrap, rework to standard cost
4. Actual standard cost versus target cost for the process
5. Process engineering costs as a percentage of total revenue
6. Process capability of new equipment

goals. Several metrics that enable an organization to measure and manage productivity are listed in Table 5.1.

Reducing the lead time of a process helps increase throughput rates to convert investments in labor and materials into sales. This also helps reduce resources such as inventory and makes the process more adaptable to changes in external demand or production schedules. Reducing process design changes is another indicator of how well the process was designed. The percentages of warranty, scrap, rework, and similar failure costs that measure process quality help guide improvement efforts. The goal of process design is to avoid or minimize these costs. Failure costs reflect wasted direct labor and material usage and increase the standard cost of production. It is important to measure process engineering costs as a percentage of total revenue to compare one process to another to look for improvement opportunities and to determine whether the well-designed processes have high process capability relative to meeting design specifications.

The specific processes used will vary by industry, available technology, and internal work procedures and controls. Although the product or service design has a major impact on the process design, there are efficient or best-in-class methods to design a process that significantly increase operational efficiency. As an example, call centers use simulation and queuing models, and transportation companies use transportation network and routing models. Table 5.2 lists ten major steps useful for designing processes efficiently. The first step is to align the productive resources of an organization with the VOC based on its strategic goals and objectives. This is done by accurately translating the VOC into the design into then into the new supporting process. Design engineers should have followed best methods, such as design for manufacturing (DFM), which were discussed

TABLE 5.2

Ten Steps to Design Processes

Step
1. Ensure the VOC has been effectively and accurately translated into the process design.
2. Ensure the product is designed using best-in-class methods, including DFM and DFMEA.
3. Focus on the key outputs of the process related to utility and functionality.
4. Create the simplest possible process design and ensure it has high process capability.
5. Create flexible and virtual transformation systems using best-in-class resources from around the world.
6. Ensure the work is organized so all the information necessary to perform it is localized at its source.
7. Ensure first-pass yields are high and the work is done only once; create a PFMEA for the new process design.
8. Balance the system's throughput using the its takt time and ensure that bottlenecks and capacity-constrained resources meet the takt time requirements.
9. Use visual controls in the process and across the supply chain to ensure everyone has visibility to system status.
10. Continuously improve process performance using Lean, Six Sigma, and similar methodologies.

VOC = voice of the customer; DFM = design for manufacturing; DFMEA = design failure mode and effects analysis; PFMEA = process failure mode and effects analysis.

in Chapter 4. DFM is a critical set of tools for creating designs that are easy to build, carry low cost, and have higher quality.

Another important concept discussed in Chapter 4 was the use of design failure mode and effects analysis (DFMEA). DFMEA is important in translating the VOC into production operations because it provides process engineers with a view into important design attributes and current risks related to fit, form, and function. It also provides recommended countermeasures to prevent product or service failures, both in the production process and when used by customers. Process engineering uses DFMEA and other design and process engineering documentation to design their process workflows. This is done concurrently as the design team does its work. Once all the necessary information has been made available to the process engineering group, they create the supporting process.

A process should be designed in a way that is can be easily scaled and deployed across an organization's global supply chain. It must be flexible and provide enough capacity to meet global and regional demand. Another consideration is that its performance is readily available to those who use and control it. It should also be highly reliable, easy to upgrade and maintain, and easily transportable. This means work tooling, equipment, work instructions, testing procedures, and other documentation needed to produce the product or service should require minimum translation into local languages and be culturally neutral. The documentation should be highly visual and easy to understand without extensive training. Complicated process designs, work instructions, equipment, training requirements, and other supporting resources have higher failure risks. Risks are compounded when a new product or service design relies on new technology.

A process failure mode and effects analysis (PFMEA) is created by process engineering using DFMEA. PFMEA is critical for identifying potential failure points within the new process and where modifications are required to achieve target standard cost, lead times, and quality. Once a process has been designed, its work operations should be balanced based on required takt time. Takt time is calculated by dividing the available production time by the required number of units that must be produced during the available production time. As an example, if there were 480 available minutes in a day and 60 required units, then the takt time would be calculated as one unit every eight minutes. Bottleneck resources will adversely impact a system's takt time if they are not available. Although most balancing analyses focus within a system's facility at one location, balancing of workflows across operations or workstations can also be done across an entire system. In other words, if a process is geographically dispersed, its takt time can still be calculated and controlled virtually across the system. In this scenario, process measurements and controls should allow for easy interpretation of the system's status anywhere in the world at any time. This information should also be readily available to all supply chain participants. To achieve takt time reliability over time, it is also important to deploy continuous improvement initiatives such as Lean, Six Sigma, Total Productive Maintenance, and others to continually improve the new process over time.

The complexity of a process is determined in part by the types of external interfaces with customers and other groups (i.e., the degree of contact). This concept is shown in Figure 5.1, in which a high degree of customer interface requires high level skills to meet operational requirements. High-contact processes, if not properly designed, will be less efficient, less operationally flexible, and more costly than low-contact processes (e.g., back-office transactional operations). Advances in technology, offshoring,

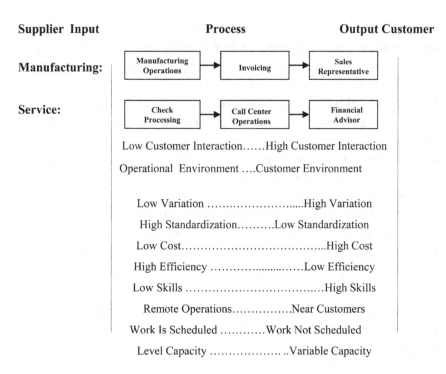

FIGURE 5.1
Process design at the customer interface (*old paradigm*).

changes in the global geopolitical environment, and increasing global competitiveness have expanded global capacity in industries such as software development, design engineering, call center management, financial transactions, and others. They have been enabled by highly skilled labor pools in countries such as India and China and in broader regions such as Southeast Asia and Eastern Europe. Offshoring has also increased product and process standardization. This facilitates the efficient global deployment of work. The resultant business benefits are lower per-unit transaction costs than previously attainable in locations where material and labor costs have been higher. Technological improvements have directly impacted our ability to work anywhere in the world, and most information-generating processes are now virtual.

In conjunction with enabling initiatives such as Lean and Six Sigma, processes should be holistically created and controlled in contrast to those that may depend on isolated operations. Permeable systems should be created using technology to create virtual processes that enable an entire supply chain to interact according to business rules with customers, suppliers, and internal stakeholders both dynamically and virtually. These permeable systems integrate back-office operations with customer-facing operations. As an example, an improvement project was started in a global call center to reduce average handling time (AHT) to answer customer questions. The process had a long AHT and a low customer service level. Service level was defined as the time from the start of a customer call to accurately answering a customer's questions. AHT is the time an agent spends on the phone providing the information to a customer. AHT also includes follow-up activities necessary to close out a customer inquiry. It should be noted that AHT and service level targets vary by customer market segment.

In this situation, operational standards required that agents be assigned to different market segments based on their skill and experience levels. In the more complicated market segments, customers asked in-depth questions about their service package. As a result, the target AHT for that segment was longer than other segments. The project was focused on one market segment. The historical AHT for this market segment, based on historical statistics, showed the AHT was 120 seconds versus the 90-second target. It was found, through data collection and analysis, that the AHT sometimes exceeded 240 seconds for certain agents. Several process issues were identified after mapping and analysis. The major contributor to longer AHT was a lack of standardization, training, and mistake-proofing.

It was found agents did not have standardized scripts to guide their customer interactions. This forced them to answer the customer's questions in a non-standardized manner. AHT increased with the variation of the customer calls. In addition, agents did not have easy access to the information needed to answer customer questions. This resulted in more lost time. Another factor that contributed to the high AHT was poor agent training, which was exacerbated by high turnover within the call center. The solutions included standardizing the process by market segment through implementation of Lean methods, including process improvements (e.g., the 5-S method) and mistake-proofing strategies. After completion of the project, the AHT across 500 agents was reduced by more than 20% with appropriate AHT and service level targets set by market segment.

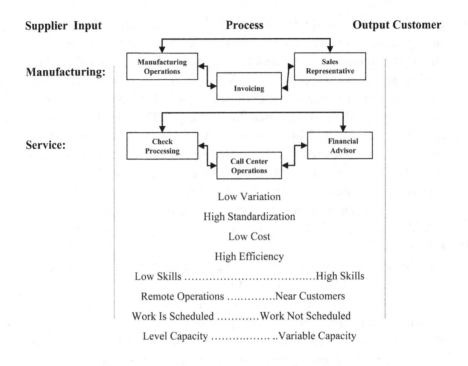

FIGURE 5.2
Process design at the customer interface (*new paradigm*).

Figure 5.2 shows a new paradigm that is evolving, in which process standardization is enabled through technology and initiatives. These systems are characterized by higher operational efficiencies, as well as higher quality and lower per-unit transaction costs. There is continued movement toward automated self-service systems. Many major retailers have customers who shop in clubs or online. These processes are highly efficient and flexible with respect to customer interaction (i.e., purchase and returns).

Complicating process design is the fact that product and services have specific delivery systems. These are based on available technology and cost. Figure 5.3 shows four types of production systems. These are job shops, batch operations, assembly operations, and continuous operations. It classifies these four systems into dimensions of volume, variety, and their operational flexibility. A job shop production system is characterized by operations performed by dedicated machines and highly trained people. Products and services moving through a job shop require unique

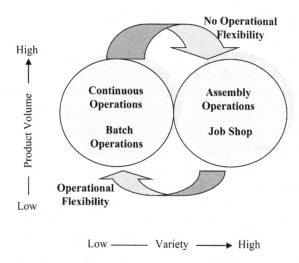

FIGURE 5.3
Operations strategy based on volume versus variety (*old paradigm*).

sequencing and combinations of work operations. Job shops can produce a diverse range of products and services. An example would be visiting a hospital and being moved from department to department based on the type of medical service being received from the system. Another example would be the manufacture of a customized product that requires several machine setups specifically for the work. Unless the underlying product or service design has been highly standardized using DFM and related methods, customized products or services must be produced using a process based on a job shop design.

In batch operations, products or services are produced periodically in batches having similar setups. Examples include short runs of similar products or services. Normally, batching can be done if similar work can be grouped based on similar features and functions by design. Batched work is produced on a periodic basis depending on demand. Lead times depend on the size of the batch and its throughput rate. Chemical mixing and periodic software releases are examples of batch operations.

Assembly operations use a combination of supporting operations, such as job shop, batching, and others, to produce high product variety at high volumes. Their capacity is matched to the required takt time. This implies all system components must be balanced with each other to meet the system's takt time. The manufacture of automobiles, appliances, and similar high-volume standardized products having a variety of model types are examples of assembly operations where similar models are produced at once.

In continuous workflow processes, low-variety products and services are transformed at a high rate on a continuous basis (i.e., a unit flow system). These systems have high design commonality up to a point at which they may become slightly differentiated into different products or services. Examples include petroleum refining and other types of processing industries, or high-volume service transactions such as call centers. These have a common internal process that can produce slightly differentiated products and services based on highly skilled agents assigned to a customer segment.

Figure 5.4 shows how many industries are expanding the technological barriers that have historically constrained operational strategy to a single production system having lower throughput rates and higher per-unit costs (e.g., job shop, batch operations, or assembly operations). These industries are migrating toward mass customization of products or services. DFM and Lean methods help simplify processes and allow the cost-effective production of a variety of products. Greater process and operational flexibility are also enabled through common designs and by reducing lead times through a variety of methods. These include value flow mapping, bottleneck management, mixed-model scheduling systems, transfer batching, and several other tools and methods that increase operational flexibility. These will be discussed in Chapter 6.

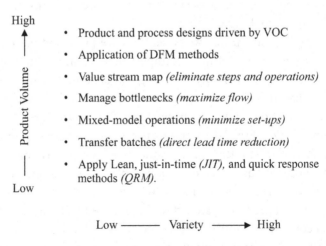

FIGURE 5.4
Operations strategy based on volume versus variety (*new paradigm*).

One way to understand how a process should be designed is to consider the hierarchy of the product or service it will produce. In manufacturing, this is reflected by a bill of material (BOM) hierarchy. A BOM is used with other documentation such as the DFMEA as a basis to design a production system. It shows hierarchal relationships between each level of the design and how it should be built using work instructions and other job aids. As an example, an automobile has four wheels and each tire has five lug nuts. The BOM would include four wheels per automobile and five lug nuts per wheel related in a hierarchal manner. This concept also applies to services. McDonald's builds hamburgers. The BOM of a hamburger would specify one roll split in half, one hamburger patty, tomato, lettuce, pickles, and any other materials placed on it. The engineers designing McDonald's process would build its process to include this BOM as well as those for its other products. As a third example, customers who purchase mutual funds and other financial services have a product and service portfolio (i.e., the BOM) that provides their financial advisor with information useful in managing their investments.

Table 5.3 lists twenty process-related steps that ensure a new product or service can be successfully produced. Several of these require supporting documentation from the design phase of the project, including a preliminary process description based on a BOM or the service description based on use cases by customers or other persona. These are developed by process engineers as part of the CE team during design development. The descriptions should include operational spatial relationships and the key inputs, process operations, and outputs at each step of the process.

A DFMEA and preliminary quality control plan should be available to the process engineers to ensure a new design has been fully evaluated relative to its failure points. Process engineering also works with suppliers to design equipment, tooling, and facilities (if necessary), as well as measurement equipment, testing equipment, and other supporting resources. This information is used to create a PFMEA. The PFMEA is comparable to the DFMEA, except that the process design is aligned to the critical design characteristics or specifications of each operation. If a specification requires a certain surface roughness, process engineering will ensure machines can meet this requirement. For a call center that requires an AHT of less than 60 seconds, the process engineers will ensure the system has the capacity to meet this specification.

The pre-launch control plan is built using information from the DFMEA and PFMEA to communicate important information necessary

TABLE 5.3

Twenty Steps to Create New Product or Service Processes

Step
1. Preliminary process flow chart
2. Product assurance plan
3. DFMEA
4. Preliminary quality control plan
5. New equipment, tooling, and facilities requirements
6. Gages and testing equipment requirements
7. Product and process quality systems review
8. Process flow chart
9. Floor plan layout
10. PFMEA
11. Pre-launch control plan
12. Process instructions
13. Measurements systems analysis
14. Production trial run
15. Preliminary process capability study
16. Production part approval
17. Production validation testing
18. Packaging evaluation
19. Production control plan
20. Quality planning sign-off and management support

DFMEA = design failure mode and effects analysis; PFMEA = process failure mode and effects analysis.

for successful production. Work instructions, training, measurement systems, preliminary process capability studies, and related documentation are also created to support the process. This information is used to plan the production trials to evaluate how well the combined design and process meet the original customer requirements (i.e., critical-to-customer characteristics). Production trials are used to finalize changes needed to commercialize the product. These validation activities ensure that customer requirements are met under actual production conditions. If production validation testing is successful, the new production system will be scaled to full commercialization. In parallel, design components of the packaging are evaluated. Then the quality control plan and related documentation are updated. The deliverables consist of a process flow chart, work and inspection procedures, floor plans, and an updated production schedule. The project schedule includes the balance of the deliverables that are necessary to support the new process.

MODELING PROCESSES

Modeling processes enables experimentation and evaluation of alternative process designs under varying process conditions. The ten steps shown in Table 5.4 help implement process modeling. The first step is to bring together a group of people trained to build and analyze process simulations. They should have skills in engineering or statistics. Training provided by consultants or suppliers may also be useful. The second step is to create a list of use cases or examples of where the model can be applied to create benefits such as reductions in lead time or costs and process simplification. There are modeling methodologies that can be used depending on the type of process and questions that need to be answered in the analysis. Examples include simulation, queuing analysis, linear programming, and customized models and algorithms for specific applications.

Once the team has selected the type of modeling methodology, it selects the software and hardware. Modeling software has been developed for a wide range of applications based on differing assumptions. These assumptions range from simple to complex. It is always more efficient to use

TABLE 5.4

Ten Steps of Process Modeling

Step
1. Organize a group of people who have been trained to build simulation models.
2. Develop a list of areas in which the model's methodology can be realistically focused.
3. Research and select off-the-shelf modeling software and associated hardware to match expected process applications (e.g., manufacturing, service systems, warehousing, logistics, etc.).
4. Develop a library of use cases and applications that can be used as examples of applying the model within your process.
5. Develop the underlying model structure including its goals and objectives, system constraints, and parameter settings.
6. Determine probability distributions of the metrics and time span of the model.
7. Develop decision rules, including initial and final states of the model.
8. Develop plans to obtain the necessary process data to test model accuracy.
9. Analyze the output of the model using statistical tests to determine the significance of the model's output.
10. Document and communicate the model's results and develop plans to implement solutions as practical.

software designed specifically for your application because it will already have relevant models that will be easier to modify and interpret. As an example, there may be specially designed modeling software options for manufacturing, financial services, call centers, warehousing, inventory management, distribution networks, and others. It is easier to use software that has easily configurable system elements and reflects your process rather than having to create new models. It is also a good idea to create a library of use cases and examples. This helps communicate the advantages of process modeling to stakeholder groups by showing them alternate process designs

The team next builds its process model. This involves documenting the process from start to finish, including its serial and parallel operations, decision points, rework loops, constraints, parameter levels, and metrics. In addition, probability distributions are determined for the model's inputs and outputs (i.e., the metrics). The model's structure, time span, and decision rules should mirror the important characteristics of the actual process. After the model is created and run, the process data are collected to test its accuracy. Finally, the analyses are documented in an appropriate format and communicated to stakeholders with recommendations and practical solutions for process optimization and improvement.

Figure 5.5 shows that process models are virtual representations that correspond to a real process. The interrelationships of the operations within a process may initially be unknown or poorly understood. The dynamic or complex performance of integrated processes may not be completely understood without creating models. Operational relationships are usually complicated and not obvious because real systems have ambiguity and time delays between the event occurrences and when their outputs are seen. This makes it difficult to understand relationships between cause and effect within a process. Therefore, mapping of processes along with their parameters and decision rules into a virtual model will be useful for understanding and improving operational performance. The advantages of a using a process model are that its structure and operational components can be easily modified and event frequency can be compressed to enable numerous evaluations of process modifications to identify an optimized final state.

Simulation is useful for modeling diverse types of processes. Within a process, system capacity can be evaluated under various constraints, comparing system performance between several alternative designs and

Process Characteristics

•Unknown process performance and inter-relationships

•Dynamic and complex performance of system components

•Ambiguity and poor resolution of performance

•Time delays between events and their measurement

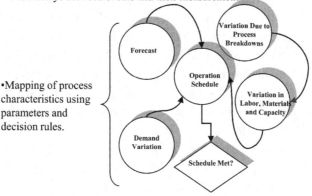

•Mapping of process characteristics using parameters and decision rules.

Virtual World Process Characteristics

•Known model performance

•Specified inter-relationships between system components

•Ability to experiment and resolve inter-relationships

•Ability to compress time between events

FIGURE 5.5
Process complexity.

conducting sensitivity analyses to determine the impact of varying one or more key process input variables (KPIVs) on key process output variables (KPOVs). A simulation model can be flexibly designed to evaluate event probabilities based on their underlying probability distributions. Or, if the goal is maximization or minimization of an objective function (i.e., a KPOV) and the model has clearly defined constraints, then linear programming might be useful for modeling the process. Queuing models provide additional tools and methods to model processes if they satisfy certain assumptions and fit predefined criteria.

The first step for creating a simulation model is asking what the expectations from the analysis are. Other relevant considerations include the project's budget and schedule. Developing simulation models are interactively modified to evaluate performance. The second step is defining the scope of the simulation relative to the operations being modeled. In other words, where does the model begin and end? Then the underlying functional relationships (i.e., $Y = f(X)$, where Y is the KPOV and X is the KPIV) are evaluated. These form the basis of the model. The relationships between the model KPOVs and the KPIVs must be defined in terms of these $Y = f(X)$ transfer functions as well as applicable decision rules and constraints. The fourth step is the collection of process data to help structure and analyze the model. The sources include process maps, historical process data related to throughput rates, yields including rework and scrap, machine and direct labor cycle times, downtimes, lot sizes, inventory levels, floor layouts, and other relevant operational data, depending on the process. The specific data collected and analyzed should correspond to the questions that need to be answered by the analysis.

It will be useful to discuss the simple example shown in Figure 5.6 to demonstrate the basic steps for conducting a simulation. The first step is

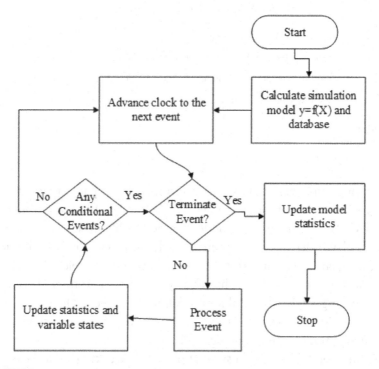

FIGURE 5.6
Simulation.

defining the functional relationships between the output and its inputs as represented by the expression $Y = f(X)$. In step two, the system's clock is set to time $t = 1$, an event is simulated, and the model's statistics are updated by the model's algorithm, which represents the business rules. If the simulation is not at its terminal time, the clock is advanced to the next time period ($t = 2$) and the simulation cycle continues until the terminal time. Statistics are collected based on the functional form of the model, which depends on the probability of the event occurrence at each operation.

We will discuss two simple examples, a single operation and a workflow that consists of three sequential operations. In Figure 5.7, a single operation and independent variable, cycle time, has been assigned probability values over its observed range of cycle times. A specific cycle time of twelve days is used as an example. This simulation model is based on a uniform distribution and generates random numbers with a uniform occurrence having a probability between 0 and 1. These random numbers are transformed using the cumulative density function (cdf) of cycle times of the actual observed distribution. The cdf has a range between 0 and 1 based on the original probability density function (pdf). The relationship of a cdf to an independent variable can be discrete or continuous depending on the pdf, which is based on the distribution assumption. This example uses a uniform distribution. The functional relationship between cycle time and its occurrence probability has been discretely defined in Table 5.5. A random number in the range of greater than 0.539828 and less than 0.617911 is defined as a discrete cycle time of 12 days. Using a continuous "cdf," we also map a one-to-one relationship between the continuous random variable in the range between 0 and 1 to a specific cycle time. This is shown in Figure 5.7.

Figures 5.8, 5.9, and 5.10 show three common probability distributions that are used in simulations. There are others for specific applications that have different distribution assumptions. Once the statistical sampling shows the pattern or distribution of the variable to metric being analyzed, which in this example is cycle time, the empirical data are fit to a standard probability distribution using goodness-of-fit testing methods. Once a match to a specific probability distribution is found, the formula for the calculating events is determined and built into the model at the correct operation. Recall this formula is calculated using the cdf of the pdf.

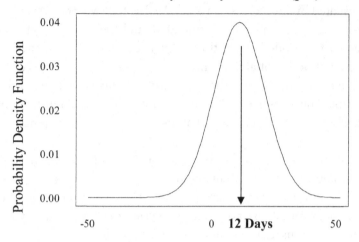

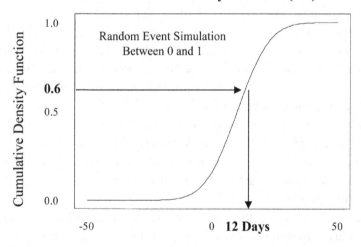

FIGURE 5.7

How simulation works. Every event has a probability. If we know its probability density function (pdf) then we can calculate the cumulative density function (cdf). When we simulate a random event between 0 and 1, we can use the cdf to generate an event from the original pdf. If the random number is less than 0.617911 and higher than 0.539828, then the event is 12 days.

TABLE 5.5

How Simulation Works

If the random number is less than 0.617911 and higher than 0.539828 then the event is "12"		
Value of X	**Probability**	**Cumulative Probability**
17	0.0312254	0.758036
16	0.0333225	0.725747
15	0.0352065	0.691462
14	0.0368270	0.655422
13	0.0381388	0.617911
12	0.0391043	0.579260
11	0.0396953	0.539828
10	0.0398942	0.500000
9	0.0396953	0.460172

Figure 5.11 shows how these concepts are applied in practice. In this example, the cumulative cycle time through the process is calculated by adding the simulated cycle times at each sequential operation. Operation 1 is uniformly distributed, with a lower cycle time of 10 seconds and an upper cycle time of 30 seconds. These two parameters specify a unique uniform distribution for Operation 1. Operation 2 is a normal distribution, with a mean cycle time of 60 seconds and a standard deviation of 10 seconds. Operation 3 is exponentially distributed with a mean cycle time of 90 seconds. The cumulative cycle time, across the process, is the sum of the three operational cycle times. The analysis shows the median cycle time through the process is ~144 seconds with a right-skewed distribution of cycle times. This simple example shows the underlying logic behind a simulation model. This method, however, would be tedious to apply to more complicated processes with several operations, parallel paths, decision points, and rework loops. Off-the-shelf simulation software can be used to simplify and reconfigure the model easily, depending on the objectives of the analysis.

The dynamic performance of certain systems has been studied by mathematicians, statisticians, and operations research professionals. These

Probability Density Function

$$f(x) = \frac{1}{\beta - \alpha} \qquad \alpha \leq X \leq \beta$$

Cumulative Density Function

$$F(X) = \frac{X_i - \alpha}{\beta - \alpha} = r_i \qquad \alpha \leq X \leq \beta$$

Generated Random Number

$$X_i = \alpha + r_i (\beta - \alpha)$$

FIGURE 5.8
Uniform distribution. Assume the uniform distribution had a maximum of 6 and a minimum of 1. If a random number of 0.5 was generated by the computer, the value of X_1 would be 3.5, which is the mean of this distribution.

studies created analytical models called queuing or waiting line models. If certain assumptions can be met, queuing models are useful and easy to apply. The same type of model can often be used in different processes that have common assumptions. Also, in many analytical situations, the same practical problem can be solved using more than one analytical technique. As an example, some processes can be analyzed using simulation, queuing analysis, or linear programming with similar results. Although simulation is useful in almost any analysis, queuing analysis and linear programming are usually more efficient if they fit because they have an an exact analytical solution.

Figure 5.12 shows an example of the various components that characterize a queuing model. This queuing model could be used to describe a process for a bank, a restaurant, or any system in which customers arrive, are serviced, and depart. The specific queuing model depends on

Probability Density Function

$$f(x) = \begin{cases} \dfrac{1}{\sigma\sqrt{2\pi}} \, e^{-(x-\mu)^2/(2\sigma^2)} \\[2em] 0 \end{cases}$$

Generated Random Number

1. Generate U_1 and U_2 as IID(0,1), let $V_i = 2U_i - 1$ for I =1,2, and let $W = V_i^2 + V_2^2$.

2. If W>1, go back to step 1. Otherwise, let Y=SQRT[(-2lnW)/W], $r_1 = V_1 W$ and $r_2 = V_2 Y$.

3. Then r_1 and r_2 are IID N(0,1) random variables.

4. Calculate a specific random variable from actual distribution using it mean and standard deviation as follows:

$$X_i = \mu + \sigma \, r_i$$

FIGURE 5.9
Normal distribution.

Probability Density Function

$$F(X) = \lambda e^{-\lambda X} \qquad X>0; \lambda>0$$

Cumulative Density Function

$$F(X) = 1 - e^{-\lambda X}$$

Generated Random Number

$$X_i = -\lambda \ln(1 - r_i)$$

FIGURE 5.10
Exponential distribution.

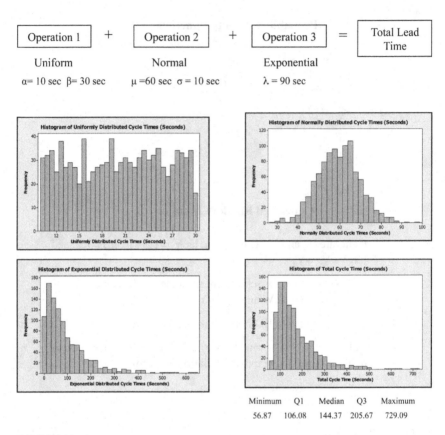

FIGURE 5.11

Estimating lead time across several operations. Simulation is especially useful when the output at every step is not normally distributed and thus cannot be analytically combined into a total. Q1 = first quartile; Q3 = third quartile.

assumptions. These include the arrival distribution of customers into the process as specified by an average arrival rate. A second assumption is the size of the incoming arrival population (calling population). It may be very large (infinite) or small (finite). The analysis varies depending on the answer. Arriving customers may choose not to join the line if the waiting line is too long (i.e., balking), or, once they join the waiting line, they may leave it (i.e., reneging).

A queuing model calculates several statistics, including the average number of people waiting in line, the average wait time, the average number of people waiting within the whole process (i.e., the number waiting in line and the number being serviced), how long customers wait on average

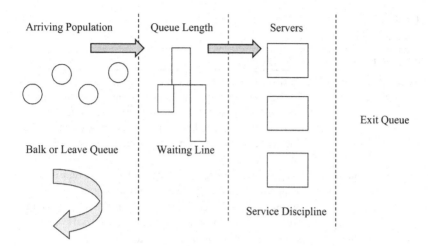

FIGURE 5.12
Common elements of a queuing system.

within the process (i.e., average time waiting in line and being serviced), and the utilization of the processes' servers and other relevant statistics.

Table 5.6 lists common statistics obtained from queuing models. Much information can be gained immediately once the process assumptions are known, but the specific form of the equations providing the information listed in Table 5.6 vary based on the underlying probability distributions, which depend on specific assumptions or characteristics

TABLE 5.6

Questions Answered by Queuing Models

Question
1. Arrival rate into system (λ)
2. Average units serviced (μ)
3. System utilization factor (λ/μ) note: $\lambda/\mu < 1$
4. Average number of units in system (L)
5. Average number of units in queue (L_q)
6. Average time a unit spends in system (W)
7. Average time a unit waits in queue (W_q)
8. Probability of no units in system (P_0)
9. Probability arriving unit waits for service (P_w)
10. Probability of n units in the system (P_n)

TABLE 5.7

Queuing System Characteristics

Characteristic	Description
Arrival distribution:	The arrival distribution is specified by the inter-arrival time or time between successive units entering the system; this is also affected if the unit balks and leaves the line because it is too long (i.e., prior to joining the line) or reneges and leaves the queue because the wait is too long (i.e., after joining the line).
Service distribution:	The pattern of service is specified by the service time or time required by one server to service one unit.
System capacity:	The maximum number of units allowed in the system. In other words, if the system is at capacity, units are turned away.
Service discipline:	There are several rules for a server to provide service to a unit, including first-in-first-out (FIFO), last-in-first-out (LIFO), service-in-random-order (SIRO), prioritization of service (POS) or another general service discipline (GSD).
Channels:	The number of parallel servers in the system.
Phases:	The number of servers in series within a given channel.

Queuing systems are characterized by the arrival distribution of the calling population, the service distribution, the number of services, the number of phases, the service discipline, and system capacity.

of the process. Table 5.7 describes the basic components of a queuing model. The arrival distribution or calling population defines the first characteristic. The second is the probability distribution of service provided to the calling population. The third is the system capacity. Some systems cannot accommodate all arrivals in a specific period. An example is a retail store with limited parking or the drive-through window at a bank that only allows a specific number of automobiles to wait in line. The fourth system characteristic describes the service discipline. Some process systems allow first come, first served prioritization (i.e., first in, first out, or FIFIO), whereas others use a different service discipline. The number of channels in the system refers to the total available parallel servers in the model. An example would be a bank that has several associates who provide service to customers waiting in line. The number of phases refers to the number of subsequent operations past the first sever in a channel.

A concise notation was developed to make their descriptions easy to understand and interpret because there are different types of queuing models and each is specified by the characteristics of the system being

TABLE 5.8

Modified Kendall's Notation (a/b/c): (d/e/f)

Characteristic	Description
Arrival and service distributions:	M = exponentially distributed E_k = Erlang type – k distributed D = deterministic or constant G = any other distribution
Service discipline:	There are several rules for a server to provide service to a unit, including first-in-first-out (FIFO), last-in-first-out (LIFO), service-in-random-order (SIRO), prioritization of service (POS) or another general service discipline (GSD).

Kendall's notation summarizes the modeling characteristics of a queuing system where a = the arrival distribution or pattern, b = the service distribution or pattern, and c = the number of available servers or channels. Other characteristics can also be added to Kendall's original notation, such as those by A.M. Lee: d = the service discipline, and e = the system's capacity; and a final addition by H.A. Taha: f = size of the calling population (i.e., infinite or finite).

modeled. This notation was developed by Kendall and is shown in Table 5.8 along with modifications. Table 5.8 lists common probability distributions used to describe the arrival and service patterns that occur within a system. Table 5.9 summarizes our queuing discussion and lists the important queuing model characteristics. Integral to modeling efforts is building a process map of the workflow according to one of the examples shown in Figure 5.13 or using modified versions of these examples. Once the basic system characteristics have been determined and the process layout has been specified, the team can collect data for the arrival and service rates

TABLE 5.9

Queuing Model Characteristics

Calling Population	Service Discipline
1. Infinite distribution	1. Deterministic (constant) service
2. Finite distribution	2. Distributed pattern of service
3. Deterministic arrivals	3. Service rules (FIFO, LIFO, SIRO, POS, GSD)
4. Distributed arrivals	4. Single phase
5. Balking or reneging allowed?	5. Multiple phases
6. Single channel	
7. Multiple channels	

FIFO = first in, first out; LIFO = last in, first out; SIRO = service in random order; POS = prioritization of service; GSD = general service discipline.

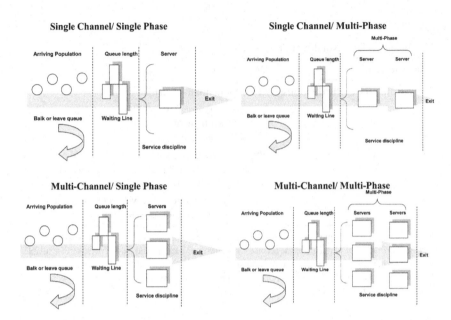

FIGURE 5.13
Common queuing models.

and the other system characteristics to build the model and understand the expected process performance. The characteristics of these models are shown in Table 5.10 using Kendall notation. This notation succinctly represents the key characteristics of each model based on the underlying process. There are other types of queuing models that can be matched your process. A literature search is the best way to find the model that matches your team's requirements.

The (M/M1) model can analyze processes characterized by Poisson arrival and exponential service distributions, a single channel with a first-come-first serve (FIFO) service discipline. An example would be waiting in line at a ticket office where there is one server. The (M/M/k) model is used to analyze processes with several parallel servers. Examples would be waiting lines in supermarkets and banks when there are several associates processing transactions. The (M/G/k) model, if modified with a capacity constraint, is used to analyze processes with a finite number of arrivals allowed into the system. An example would be a website designed to handle a limited number of incoming transactions. The fourth model (M/M/1) is applied to situations where the calling population that requires

TABLE 5.10

Characteristics of the Four Models

Model Type	Process	Arriving Distribution (Calling Population)	Service Distribution	Service Discipline
(M/M1)	Single channel	Poisson arrivals, infinite calling population	Exponential service distribution	FIFO
(M/M/k)	Multiple channel	Poisson arrivals, infinite calling population	Exponential service distribution	FIFO
(M/G/k)	Multiple channel	Poisson arrivals, infinite calling population (capacity constrained)	General service distribution	FIFO
(M/M/1)	Single channel	Poisson arrivals, finite calling population	Exponential service distribution	FIFO

FIFO = first in, first out.

service is small (finite). An example would be a repair shop servicing a limited number of on-site machines.

An example of the (M/M/1) queuing model is shown in Table 5.11. Its formulas are easy to calculate manually, although other models may have more complicated calculations. In this example, customers arrive at an average rate of 20 per hour. The arrival rate fluctuates with customers arriving faster or slower than 20 per hour. The service rate is 25 customers on average per hour. On average there is capacity to provide service. A requirement of queuing models is that the average service rate must exceed the average arrival rate. The variation of arrival rates will require some customers to wait for service sometimes; alternatively, if arrival rates are low, then servers will sometimes be idle.

To build a model, arrival and service rates are estimated empirically with check sheets, automatically by software specialized applications that measure transactions and transformations with business rules between systems or using historical records. Integrating data into a queuing model helps show where capacity should be added and how to set the system's

TABLE 5.11

Example of a Simple Queuing Model (M/M/1)

Description	Calculation
1. Arrival rate into system (λ)	$\lambda = 20$ per hour
2. Average units serviced (μ)	$\mu = 25$ per hour
3. System utilization factor (λ/μ) note: $\lambda/\mu < 1$	$\lambda/\mu = 0.80 = 80\%$
4. Average number of units in system (L)	$L = L_q + (\lambda/\mu) = 4.0$ units
5. Average number of units in queue (L_q)	$L_q = \lambda^2/[\mu(\mu-\lambda)] = 3.2$ units
6. Average time a unit spends in system (W)	$W = W_q + (1/\mu) = 0.20$ hours
7. Average time a unit waits in queue (W_q)	$W_q = L_q/\lambda = 0.16$ hours
8. Probability of no units in system (P_0)	$P_0 = 1-(\lambda/\mu) = 0.20 = 20\%$
9. Probability arriving unit waits for service (P_w)	$P_w = \lambda/\mu = 0.80 = 80\%$
10. Probability of n units in the system (P_n)	$P_n = (\lambda/\mu)^n P_0$

In this example, customers arrive at a repair shop at an average rate of $\lambda = 20$ per hour; the average service rate is 25 customers per hour. Assume a Poisson arrival distribution, an exponential service distribution, a single-channel/FIFO service discipline, no maximum on the number in the system, and an infinite calling population. FIFO = first in, first out.

rules to minimize customer waiting time and system cost while achieving service levels. Queuing models can be combined with marketing research to build competitive service levels and waiting times by segment to ensure high customer satisfaction and high operational efficiency.

Table 5.12 shows another advantage of queuing analysis. The units of measure are in hours. As an example, for the last analysis, 49 customers arrive each hour and the system can service 50 customers. The average

TABLE 5.12

Queuing Analysis Study of Capacity Utilization

Arriving	Service	Average Number Waiting	Average Waiting Time	Average Server Utilization	Average Customer Receiving Service	Average Number in System	Average Time in System
10	50	0.014	0.0014	20%	0.2	0.214	0.0214
20	50	0.075	0.0038	40%	0.4	0.475	0.0238
40	50	0.905	0.0226	80%	0.8	1.705	0.0426
45	50	2.292	0.0509	90%	0.9	3.192	0.0709
49	50	13.586	0.2777	98%	0.98	14.506	0.2973

As the system's capacity utilization approaches 100%, waiting time significantly increases. Assumption include a single-channel queue, a Poisson arrival rate, and an exponential service rate.

waiting time is 0.277 hours or 16.62 minutes. As the utilization of a system increases, the average waiting time for service rapidly increases. In a service pool like a call center, capacity can easily be increased to match demand. This may not be possible if servers are few and highly skilled (i.e., cannot be replaced easily or others quickly trained). But there are operational strategies that efficiently add capacity with high utilization. In manufacturing, one strategy is to use low-cost machines in parallel to each other, with some idle during periods of low demand. These idle machines are activated to meet demand rather than fully utilized regardless of demand. The old paradigm was to use expensive machines and keep them running at all times to attain high utilization or production efficiency. This built excess inventory. An analogous situation would be using low-cost workers to complete smaller and standardized work rather than more complicated work. Another example would be a call center that uses technology to transfer incoming customer calls that exceed local capacity to other call centers that have excess capacity at the time (i.e., level-loading demand across a global system).

Another type of analytical algorithm useful for designing and optimizing a process is linear programming (LP) and its various models. Table 5.13 lists several linear programming models, but there are many others. LP models minimize or maximize an objective function. Maximization or minimization (i.e., optimization) is constrained relative to resource scarcity, minimum service levels, and many other factors. Optimization objectives include maximizing profits, minimizing cost, maximizing service levels, or maximizing production throughput. Table 5.14 shows the basic components of an LP model to build a supply

TABLE 5.13

Linear Programming Applications

Application
1. Maximizing service productivity.
2. Minimizing network routing.
3. Optimizing process control.
4. Minimizing inventory investment.
5. Optimizing allocation of investment.
6. Optimizing product mix profitability.
7. Minimizing scheduling cost.
8. Minimizing transportation costs.
9. Minimizing cost of materials mixtures.

TABLE 5.14

Linear Programming Characteristics

What is Linear Programming?

1. An LP algorithm attempts to find a minimization maximization or solution when decisions are made with constrained resources as well as other system constraints. As an example, supply chain optimization problems require matching demand and supply when supply is limited, and demand must be satisfied. An LP problem is comprised of four major components:

    1. Decision Variables within analyst's control...When and how much to order ...When to manufacture...When and how much of the product to ship.

    2. Constraints placed on the levels or amounts of decision variables which can be used in the final solution...Examples are: Capacity to produce raw materials or components... Production can only run for a specified... number of hours...A worker can only work so much overtime ...A customer's capacity to handle and process receipts.

    3. Problem objective relative to minimization or maximization. Examples include maximizing profits, minimizing cost, maximizing service levels and maximizing production throughput.

    4. Mathematical relationships between the decision variables, constraints, and problem objectives.

When do we have a solution to a linear program?

1. Feasible Solution – Satisfies all the constraints of the problem or objective function.

2. Optimum Solution – The best feasible solution, relative to the decision variables and their levels, that achieves the objective of the optimization problem. Although there may be many feasible solutions, there is usually only one optimum.

chain model. It includes decision variables that can be varied for optimization, including when and how much to order, manufacture, or ship through logistical systems. Constraints are limitations placed on the decision variables such as available capacity, manufacturing scheduling sequence, materials or components, minimum sales level, and others. An LP model is used to evaluate relationships between decision variables and their constraints relative to the model's objective. An optimum solution will be the best feasible solution relative to the levels of the decision variables that achieve the objective of the optimization problem, which is either minimization or maximization without violating the constraints. Although there may be several feasible solutions, there is usually only one optimum solution.

Figure 5.14 shows how an LP model is mathematically constructed. The objective function represents the goal of the optimization. Each decision variable X_i is weighted by an objective coefficient C_i. The optimization

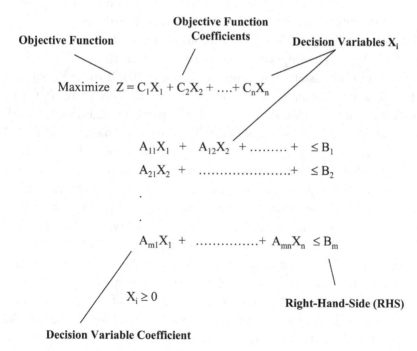

FIGURE 5.14
Basic linear planning model formulation.

of the objective function is constrained by the minimum or maximum amount of resources that can be used in the final solution. Each decision variable in a constraint is weighted by a coefficient showing its relative contribution to optimization. The right-hand side (RHS) of each constraint can be of three types: less than or equal to, equal to, and greater than or equal to. Less than or equal to implies the resources when used in combination cannot exceed a maximum. These are usually applied to limited material and labor resources. Equal to imply the combination of decision variables must exactly equal a number. In greater than or equal to equations, the combination of decision variables cannot fall below minimum value. These are usually associated with minimum demand that must be satisfied. In standard LP models, all decision variables are constrained to be positive (i.e., $X_i > 0$).

The example shown in Figure 5.15 involves a simple transportation network consisting of three manufacturing facilities and four distribution centers. This is special type of LP algorithm called the transportation model. The most common objective of a transportation model is to minimize transportation costs between manufacturing facilities and distribution centers. This example shows two constraints: the maximum available material that can be shipped from a given manufacturing facility, and the demand of each distribution center for the material. If the material supply and required demand do not balance, then "dummy" manufacturing facilities or distribution centers are incorporated into the model to balance supply and demand constraints. The problem shown in Figure 5.15 is analyzed using Excel's "Solver" algorithm, but other software can be used for analysis. The optimum solution is also shown in the "From/To" matrix with the shipment costs of the facility and distribution center (DC) combinations. As an example, the per-unit cost from Facility 1 to DC 1 is $10, and the maximum available supply from Facility 1 is 100 units. The demand of each distribution center is shown as DC 1 = 150 units, DC 2 = 200 units, DC 3 = 50 units, and DC 4 = 200 units. The optimum solution is shown in the Candidate Solution matrix. In this solution, Facility 1 ships 50 units to DC 3 and 50 Units to DC 5. The total cost of the optimum solution is shown in the Cost matrix as $3,750. A general form of the model is shown at the bottom of Figure 5.15. LP models have proven useful in process workflow modeling and analysis in many diverse fields of business and science.

From/To		DC 1	DC 2	DC 3	DC 4	Supply
	Facility 1	10	20	10	5	100
	Facility 2	5	15	20	30	200
	Facility 3	3	5	20	5	300
	Demand	150	200	50	200	

Candidate Solution						Shipped
	Facility 1	0	0	50	50	100
	Facility 2	150	50	0	0	200
	Facility 3	0	150	0	150	300
	Supplied	150	200	50	200	

Cost

Facility 1	$	-	$	-	$	500	$	250	
Facility 2	$	750	$	750	$	-	$	-	
Facility 3	$	-	$	750	$	-	$	750	

Total Cost $ 3,750

$$\text{Min } Z = X_{11}+X_{12}+X_{13}+X_{14}+X_{21}+X_{22}+X_{23}+X_{24}+X_{31}+X_{32}+X_{33}+X_{34}$$

$$X_{11}+X_{12}+X_{13}+X_{14} \leq 100$$
$$X_{21}+X_{22}+X_{23}+X_{24} \leq 200$$
$$X_{31}+X_{32}+X_{33}+X_{34} \leq 300$$
$$X_{11} + X_{21} + X_{31} = 150$$
$$X_{12} + X_{22} + X_{32} = 200$$
$$X_{13} + X_{23} + X_{33} = 50$$
$$X_{14} + X_{24} + X_{34} = 200$$

$X_{ij} \geq 0$ for I =1,2,3; j= 1,2,3,4

FIGURE 5.15

Transportation system example. DC = distribution center.

SCHEDULING ALGORITHMS

Organizations use scheduling systems to optimize production. A mathematical scheduling approach is very useful for the right production applications. Lean systems use pull scheduling systems coordinated by visual or electronic controls. To demonstrate the importance of scheduling rules to reduce lead time, Figure 5.16 shows two scheduling models

Original Job Order	Modified Sequence	Processing Time	Required In Day	FIFO Time	Days Late	
A	A	1	3	1	0	
B	B	3	9	4	0	
C	C	4	12	8	0	
D	D	5	15	13	0	
E	E	2	6	15	9	Late
F	F	3	9	18	9	Late
G	G	4	12	22	10	Late
H	H	1	3	23	20	Late
I	I	1	3	24	21	Late
J	J	4	12	28	16	Late

Total Time:	28	85	
Mean Job Process Time:	2.8		

Original Job Order	Modified Sequence	Processing Time	Days Required	Minimum Time	Days Late	
A	A	1	3	1	0	
B	H	1	3	2	0	
C	I	1	3	3	0	
D	E	2	6	5	0	
E	B	3	9	8	0	
F	F	3	9	11	2	Late
G	C	4	12	15	3	Late
H	G	4	12	19	7	Late
I	J	4	12	23	11	Late
J	D	5	15	28	13	Late

Total Time:	28	36	
Mean Job Process Time:	2.8		

FIGURE 5.16
How scheduling rules impact material flow. FIFO = first in, first out.

that differ only with respect to rules. The first model uses a first come, first served scheduling rule (FIFO), whereas the second uses a minimum processing time rule. The calculations show it is easy to see that, for this example, the minimum processing time scheduling rule reduces both the number of late jobs as well as the lead time for all ten jobs processed through the system (i.e., 156 versus 115 days). The underlying concept is that a transfer batch model reduces lead time over a batch model. In this simple example, the scheduling rules had a large impact on a system's lead time. Prioritization rules have a significant impact on a process efficiency.

The second scheduling algorithm is shown in Figure 5.17. This is an assignment model in which n jobs are assigned to exactly n work cells based on the historical processing time or cost for every combination of job and work cell. The example models an $n \times n$ use case. It should be noted that in more complex situations in which there are n jobs and m work cells, the number of alternative schedules rapidly increases according to the formula $(n!)^m$. In these more complex analyses, a solution requires an analysis using simulation methods. There are three steps in using the assignment algorithm. The first step makes row calculations in which the smallest number (i.e., time or cost) in a row is removed from all other numbers in the same row. The second step requires the same calculations to be made column-wise by removing the smallest number in every column from other numbers in the same column to create a reduced matrix. In the third step, a test is made to see if exactly n lines can cover all the 0s. In the current example, exactly n lines cover all the 0s, showing an optimal assignment of jobs to work cells. This optimum assignment recommends assigning Job 1 to Work Cell 1, Job 2 to Work Cell 3, Job 3 to Work Cell 4, and Job 4 to Work Cell 2. The total processing cost equals $60 + $35 + $45 + $25 = $165, which is the minimum for this example.

In Figure 5.18, a more sophisticated algorithm is used to schedule at least two days off per week per employee. In this algorithm, starting with Worker 1, the days requiring the smallest number of employees (i.e., Wednesday and Friday) are scheduled as days off for Worker 1. In the second iteration, the schedule of Worker 2 is determined by first removing one day from the original daily schedule except for the days off taken by Worker 1. This is because Worker 1 will work these days (i.e., Monday, Tuesday, Thursday, Friday, and Sunday). These five days now require one

Initial Table

	Work Cell 1	Work Cell 2	Work Cell 3	Work Cell 4
Job 1	$ 60	$ 90	$ 45	$ 60
Job 2	$ 45	$ 85	$ 35	$ 50
Job 3	$ 90	$ 45	$ 60	$ 25
Job 4	$ 30	$ 45	$ 90	$ 60

Step 1: Row Reduction (Remove smallest number from each row)

	Work Cell 1	Work Cell 2	Work Cell 3	Work Cell 4
Job 1	$ -	$ 60	$ 15	$ 30
Job 2	$ 10	$ 50	$ -	$ 15
Job 3	$ 65	$ 20	$ 35	$ -
Job 4	$ -	$ 15	$ 60	$ 30

Step 2: Column Reduction (Remove smallest number from each column)

	Work Cell 1	Work Cell 2	Work Cell 3	Work Cell 4
Job 1	$ -	$ 45	$ 15	$ 30
Job 2	$ 10	$ 35	$ -	$ 15
Job 3	$ 65	$ 5	$ 35	$ -
Job 4	$ -	$ -	$ 60	$ 30

Step 3: Line Test (Number of lines required to cover all zeros)

	Work Cell 1	Work Cell 2	Work Cell 3	Work Cell 4
Job 1	$	$ 45	$ 15	$ 30
Job 2	$ 10	$ 35	$ -	$ 15
Job 3	$ 65	$ 5	$ 35	$
Job 4	$	$ -	$ 60	$ 30

Step 4: Optimal Assignment

	Work Cell 1	Work Cell 2	Work Cell 3	Work Cell 4
Job 1	Job 1=$60			
Job 2			Job 2=$35	
Job 3				Job 3=$25
Job 4		Job 4=$45		

FIGURE 5.17

Assignment algorithm (n_{jobs} to $n_{work\ cells}$).

	Monday	Tuesday	Wednesday	Thursday	Friday	Saturday	Sunday
Required Coverage	3	5	2	6	2	4	3
Worker 1	3	5	2	6	2	4	3
Worker 2	2	4	2	5	2	3	2
Worker 3	2	3	2	4	1	2	1
Worker 4	1	2	1	3	1	1	1
Worker 5	0	1	0	2	1	1	0
Worker 6	0	0	0	1	0	0	0

	Monday	Tuesday	Wednesday	Thursday	Friday	Saturday	Sunday
Worker 1	Worker 1	Worker 1		Worker 1		Worker 1	Worker 1
Worker 2		Worker 2		Worker 2	Worker 2	Worker 2	Worker 2
Worker 3	Worker 3	Worker 3	Worker 3	Worker 3		Worker 3	
Worker 4	Worker 4	Worker 4	Worker 4	Worker 4			Worker 4
Worker 5		Worker 5		Worker 5	Worker 5	Worker 5	
Worker 6				Worker 6			
Actual Coverage	3	5	2	6	2	4	3

FIGURE 5.18
Scheduling workers.

less person to meet their schedule. The algorithm continues until each day has been assigned the required number of workers, with each worker having at least two days off from work. In summary, this algorithm demonstrates an efficient method to schedule resources.

Figure 5.19 shows an integer linear programming model applied to a scheduling model. The objective is to satisfy all required schedules with a minimum number of agents per shift and at minimum cost. In this example, the objective function is to minimize monthly salary cost, given each shift has a constraint relative to the minimum number of agents assigned to it. Notice that the schedule is classified into 4-hour time intervals spaced over six periods. This schedule could also have been classified into hours. Because agents work an 8-hour shift, there are multiple shifts working in parallel in any four-hour period. As an example, Period 1 starts at 8 AM and ends at 4 PM. Between 8 AM and 12 PM, 20 agents are needed to answer customer calls. However, during the period of 12 PM to 4 PM, 30 agents are needed. This implies that 10 additional agents must be added between 12 PM and 4 PM. The constraint on the staffing schedule is that an agent cannot work more than 8 hours in a 24-hour day. This means four shifts of workers must be staffed according to the solution provided at the bottom of Figure 5.19. Shift 1 should be staffed using

Period	Time	Agents	Salary
1	8:00 AM to 12:00 PM	20	$ 2,000
2	12:00 PM to 4:00 PM	30	$ 2,000
3	4:00 PM to 8:00 PM	40	$ 2,500
4	8:00 PM to 12:00 AM	30	$ 2,500
5	12:00 AM to 4:00 AM	10	$ 3,000
6	4:00 AM to 8:00 AM	10	$ 3,000

Assumption: Each agent works 8 hours with no breaks

Minimize $Z = 2X_1 + 2X_2 + 2.5X_3 + 2.5X_4 + 3X_5$ **Staffing**

Period 1	$1X_1$	$+1X5 \geq 20$	20
Period 2	$1X_1 + 1X_2$	≥ 30	30
Period 3	$1X_2 + 1X_3$	≥ 40	40
Period 4	$1X_3 + 1X_4$	≥ 30	30
Period 5	$1X_4 + 1X_5$	≥ 10	10
Period 6	$1X_5$	≥ 10	10

Agents Per Shift: 20   10   30   0   10   =   **$ 165,000**

FIGURE 5.19
Linear programming model applied to scheduling.

20 agents, Shift 2 using 10 agents, Shift 3 using 30 agents, and Shift 4 using 10 agents. This optimum solution will require 140 agents for a total monthly salary of $165,000. This is the minimum cost solution obtained using the LP algorithm. LP algorithms provide extreme flexibly to model different scheduling systems and constraints.

Over the past several years, advanced software has been developed to increase the efficiency of a scheduling process. These are based on LP or simulation algorithms with user-friendly interfaces and easy-to-understand decision-making tools that optimize resources to satisfy demand at minimum cost based on capacity and other user-defined system constraints. In fact, sophisticated scheduling software routinely provides detailed staffing schedules based on worker skill levels, function, location, shift, pay rate, restrictions on schedule, and other constraints.

WORKING ENVIRONMENT

It is important that the work environment supports production. Associates who are an integral part of a new process should be well trained in its operations to achieve time, cost, and quality targets. There are actions to ensure an efficient working environment. The first is executive leadership that communicates the organization's vision and especially with respect to operations, in clear and concise terms. This helps prioritize work and allocate resources efficiently. Organizational values should be promoted in a consistent manner. Consistency is important to minimize misunderstood priorities when it comes to project selection, execution, and resource allocation. Second, strategic goals should be aligned throughout an organization to show all associates how their work fits into the vision roadmap. This helps demonstrate how work, at a tactical level, is integrated across an organization. It is necessary to translate higher-level goals and objectives down through successively lower levels of the organization to ensure goal alignment at an initiative and project level. Communications should be simple and consistent with organizational norms and values. Resource alignment is also critical to ensure the workforce has the tools and resources necessary to do their work.

It is important to onboard and train people who have the organization's core values including diversity. Having the right people at the start will minimize organizational barriers to collaboration and success. Employee incentive systems should also be consistent with organizational goals and values to reinforce needed behaviors. Removing other barriers to organizational change ensures it is reinforced at all levels. TIt is also important to efficiently execute strategic goals to meet productivity targets as well as enhance customer, supplier, employee, and shareholder satisfaction. Success breeds success and is a powerful motivator for future process improvement. Finally, it is important to develop learning systems to ensure employees are continuously learning and adapting to changing business conditions. These several actions improve process performance and increase competitiveness.

High-performance work teams are an integral part of process design. It makes no sense to design a competitive process if its workforce does not have proper incentives, training, and willingness to achieve productivity and quality targets. The first key step to develop high-performance work teams is to ensure the team understands its goals along with the work. The second step is to hold team members jointly accountable for the success or failure of their assigned projects. This will tend to increase cooperative behaviors and collaboration. Third is to ensure the team has a diverse and properly facilitated membership. Team members should have the required skills, and it is important to ensure the team has adequate resources. Clear roles and responsibilities are important. Systems should promote sharing information to further promote cooperation. Any team conflicts should be resolved in a positive manner using proper facilitation methods. To remain on schedule, effective project management practices should be used. Ideally a team will remain together for an extended period to mature into a high-performance team.

High-performance work teams mature through a four-stage process. These are the forming, storming, norming, and performing stages. In the forming stage, a team initially meets and starts creating common goals. Productivity is low in this formative stage. Basic facilitation tools and methods should be deployed in the formative stage to accelerate the maturation process. One of the most important facilitation tools, at this point, is a project charter. A charter specifies where the team will work, the resources required for its activities (including data collection and analysis), and eventual process recommendations for improvements. Other charter information includes deliverables for the work, expected business benefits (both financial and operational) and costs as well as the schedule, stakeholders, and other relevant information.

In the storming stage, conflicts often arise between team members because of different perspectives regarding how the work should proceed. Facilitation is especially useful in this stage. Facilitation includes agreement of how the team will govern itself to ensure disagreements are resolved and decisions are effectively made. In the norming stage of the team maturation process, the team's productivity increases as it resolves team conflicts more effectively than in the storming stage. The team begins to achieve its goals and the project's milestones. Finally, in the performing stage, the team works very well together to consistently achieve its goals. An important enabler of high-performance work teams is an organizations' reward and recognition system. It should be aligned to recognize team's contributions to the organization.

Work simplification is based on three concepts: not creating work if it is not needed, efficiently doing the work that should be done, and standardizing the work to be done so it is consistent regardless of the person or machine doing it. Work simplification starts with design. The fewer the components or assembly operations, the less work that is required to produce a product or deliver a service. This concept is embodied in the DFM concepts listed in Table 4.7. Another recommendation is employing simple automation and mistake-proofing of work operations to minimize the percentage of manual activities within a process workflow. This will reduce the direct labor requirements necessary to produce a product or service; it will reduce errors as well. Once the required operational sequences have been determined by process engineering, the flow of work across the system is balanced using the system's takt time. Takt time is the number of units to be produced within an allocated time (e.g., a work shift). A previous example was having a production schedule of 80 units and 8 hours (480 minutes) of available manufacturing time. This requires a takt time of one unit every 6 minutes throughout the 8-hour shift. Once the takt time is calculated, the sequence of work tasks is grouped into workstations consisting of one or more work tasks. The cumulative completion time of all work tasks within a group or workstation must be less than or equal to the system's takt time. In other words, if the takt time is one unit every 6 minutes, then the cycle time for every operation or workstation must be 6 minutes or less.

To achieve this takt time, work tasks are broken down into smaller groups of lower-level work tasks as shown in Figure 5.20. To do this, work tasks are studied to find the best way to complete them. Common methods to analyze work tasks are work sampling, micro-motion studies, and predetermined time standards from tables grouped by type of work task. Work sampling studies a work task over a period of time and determines the best way to accomplish it. Micro-motion studies are like work sampling but are more precise in determining task time duration because the tasks are broken down further into micro-motions. Cameras can be used to record each motion so they can be reviewed several times to achieve accurate calculations. Time duration is also measured at a microsecond level of precision. Predetermined time standards are applied up front to a new process design and later validated through work sampling or micro-motion studies. Time standards are used with similar analyses of machine cycle times to balance the flow of work across a process to achieve the required takt time.

The data collection template shown in Figure 5.21 is useful for collecting process data for analysis to determine how much time is required to

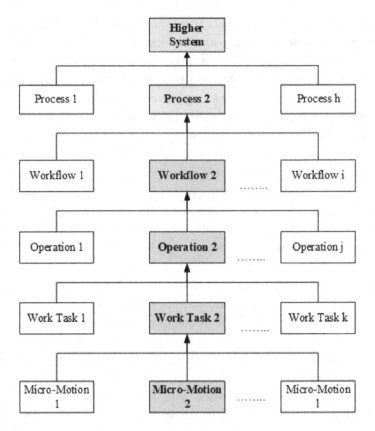

FIGURE 5.20
How to identify lower-level work tasks.

complete a work task. An initial baseline analysis consists of an operation and the time required to complete each work task is recorded. The first analysis looks for wasted or non-value-add time. Next, time standards are calculated for each work task based on the elimination of wasted time and includes labor and the use of tools, materials, and fixtures. The work task is classified as setting up a job, inspection of work, doing the work, moving the work, or waiting for materials or information. As part of this analysis, unnecessary work tasks are eliminated, the remaining work tasks are mistake-proofed, and the time standards are updated. Finally, the employees that do the work are trained to use the new work methods, tools, and inspection and measurement systems. Visual examples of good and poor workmanship are also frequently used to control and improve work methods.

Department:				Date:									
Process:				Operator:									
Workflow:				Takt Time:									
Operation Number:				Required Production:									
Product Identification:													
				Time In Minutes									
Sequential Work Task	1	2	3	4	5	6	7	8	9	10	Etc.	Total	Percent
Set-up													
Inspection													
Process													
Transport													
Waiting													
Etc.													
Total:													

FIGURE 5.21
How to develop time standards.

Employee training is critical to a new process. To build an effective training program, the training is focused and its goals are clear. Goal alignment and clarity ensure training is beneficial to both the organization and its employees. It is also important to measure the training effectiveness as opposed to simply counting the number of trained employees. The training should be designed to appeal to different learning styles (e.g., somatic or touching, auditory, visual, and intellectual) to increase its effectiveness at an individual level and, by extrapolation, to the group level. Blended learning models are particularly helpful for increasing training effectiveness.

Blended learning combines on-line learning, workbooks, and presentation materials using a mix of instructor and participant presentations. Participants study training modules prior to meeting so that the instructor and participants are able to interact for a higher proportion of time during a workshop. Immediate application of training is another important consideration. Participants should immediately practice what they learn through applied projects. Effective training should create benefits that can be measured. To aid in this, post-training materials should be developed to reinforce the training concepts, with coaching and mentoring to clarify and reinforce the concepts. Finally, the training process should be continuously improved using the latest training methods and theories as well as participant feedback.

SUMMARY

The design of a process directly correlates to the product or service that is produced. For this reason, process engineering works closely with the design team using concurrent engineering methods. Once the new process been designed and its operational relationships are documented, it is useful to quantitatively model it to understand dynamic relationships for optimization. The modeling approach will vary depending on the process, ranging from evaluating process layouts using a whiteboard to highly mathematical analyses. The information gained from process modeling helps reduce process variation and ensures the design intent will be realized. This approach reduces time and costs while improving quality. It is also important to create a work environment that reinforces organizational change, learning, and high-performance teams. Operations and their work tasks should be standardized and mistake-proofed. Finally, associates should be trained to use new tools and methods and to follow work and inspection instructions.

6

Lean Process Improvement

OVERVIEW

Mapping the things customers value into a process is a powerful way to confirm we are working on the right things and then to identify ways to improve the customer's experience. The concept of value helps identify work aligned with customers and important to the business versus work that should be eliminated now or when feasible to do so. Even if a process was optimally designed in the past, customer and business needs change. Technology also evolves. Over time, organizations may add unnecessary operations for a variety of reasons. This requires processes to be redesigned or discarded. In this chapter, we discuss how the concept of customer value can be enhanced by applying Lean tools and methods to simplify, standardize, and mistake-proof processes.

The application of Lean tools and methods will enable organizations to consistently realize significant operational benefits through higher material and information throughput. But an integrated approach is required to fully realize all potential benefits. A Lean system has several operational components that function together. Several of these must be implemented before customers can see significant improvement in their experience. The application of process improvements to enhance customer experience requires improving quality, ensuring equipment and machines are properly maintained and available for use, standardizing work, mistake-proofing operations, and applying other tools and methods. These tools and methods must be integrated, and there is a sequence for their

TABLE 6.1

Competitive Metrics – Lean

Metric
1. Lead time and throughput rate
2. Asset utilization
3. Percent of value-add time in total time
4. Unit cost
5. First-pass yield

implementation. As an example, maintenance improvements, work standardization, and mistake-proofing precede takt time stabilization.

Transforming an organization into a Lean enterprise requires a great deal of practical and hands-on learning through the application of Lean tools, methods, and concepts to projects. The effectiveness of a lean transformation can be measured using the key metrics shown in Table 6.1, namely reductions in lead time, higher throughputs, higher asset utilization including inventory reductions for constant sales, increased percentages of value-add time in the total process time, lower unit costs, and higher first-pass yield. In this chapter, we will discuss Lean tools and methods that will improve these metrics.

Lean deployments deliver benefits, several of which are listed in Table 6.2. The first is higher customer on-time delivery (i.e., schedule

TABLE 6.2

Ten Benefits of a Lean Deployment

Benefit
1. Higher customer on-time delivery (schedule attainment)
2. More value-add time
3. Higher throughput rates of materials and information
4. Faster machine or job changeovers (especially at bottlenecks)
5. Greater machine uptimes (available time)
6. Higher quality of work (less scrap/rework/warranty/returns)
7. Less floor space utilized
8. Lower inventory
9. Higher supplier on-time delivery
10. Lower overall system cost

attainment). A simple and standardized system will tend to execute its delivery schedule more consistently than one that is more complex and exhibits high process variation. A value-add operation has three attributes. The operation must create a feature or function requested by the customer, the work object (i.e., material or informational) must be physically transformed, and the work must be done right the first time. Value flow mapping (VFM) at a process level is a useful tool for identifying work that does not add value. This helps reduce the percentage of non-value-add (NVA) work. Elimination of NVA work will increase the relative percentage of value-add work. Note that value stream mapping is done at an enterprise level, whereas VFM occurs at a process level.

VFM is also useful for identifying operations that constrain the flow of materials or information (i.e., bottlenecks). This helps a VFM team focus projects to increase the time available at a system's bottleneck. Lean improvements include faster machine throughputs, less time for job changeovers (especially at the system's bottleneck resource), greater machine uptime (i.e., available time), and higher quality of work (i.e., reduced scrap, rework, warranty, and returns). Additional benefits are less floor space utilized, lower system inventory, and lower overall system cost.

A Lean enterprise consists of the ten operational components listed in Table 6.3. A Lean enterprise will have these components and perhaps some others specific to their industry. If an organization implements just a few components, it will not realize all the advantages of

TABLE 6.3

Ten Components of a Lean System

Component
1. System performance measurements
2. Just-in-time workflow; stable system
3. Standardized work (5-S)
4. Mistake-proofing
5. High quality
6. Total productive maintenance
7. Single-minute exchange of dies
8. Visual workplace
9. Container design (i.e., packaging)
10. Supplier agreements

a Lean enterprise. Performance measurements show where to focus improvements and will help evaluate their effectiveness. Measurements are important because a Lean implementation requires several years. The second key component is just-in-time (JIT) and standardized workflows. JIT implies that raw materials, components, and information are delivered to a process just when they are needed for production. JIT workflows increase system flexibility because raw materials, work-in-process (WIP) inventory, labor, and other resources and capacities can be kept at a low level and made available only when needed for transformation activities. Demand and lead-time variation are also decreased by implementing a JIT workflow.

Lean systems require that work tasks to be standardized and done consistently. Work standardization includes written work and inspection instructions, employee training, and tools and methods. Mistake-proofing is very important for work standardization. It starts early in the design phase using design for manufacturing methods and other design tools. If correctly implemented, only the simplest design that meets customer requirements is released for production. High quality is a prerequisite for standardized operation and JIT workflows.

As a Lean deployment evolves and processes become predictable, more advanced tools and methods are applied. Two are Total Productive Maintenance (TPM) and the single-minute exchange of dies (SMED). TPM is the study and deployment of preventive and corrective maintenance practices. It ensures machines will not unexpectedly break down and disrupt process throughput. SMED is a set of tools and methods that study how jobs are set up. Its goal is to reduce setup time and cost to increase scheduling flexibility as well as quality and reliability of setup. In SMED, a key concept is to separate external from internal setup operations. Internal setup operations must be done on-line whereas external ones can be done off-line. The concept is that if operations can be done off-line, there will be little direct impact on production schedules. Modifications to on-line setup tooling and fixtures and application of mistake-proofing strategies help reduce the time required to complete on-line setups.

Visual controls are integral for status communication within and between processes. In a visual workplace, the operational status can be immediately seen (i.e., they are visible). The key steps necessary to implement a visual control system will be discussed later in this chapter.

TABLE 6.4

Ten Methods to Improve Process Efficiency

Method
1. Use capacity intelligently.
2. Improve quality, maintenance, and training.
3. Create product family processes.
4. Use multifunctional equipment.
5. Measure lead time, quality, and up time.
6. Simplify processes.
7. Use multiskilled workers.
8. Only accept orders you can complete.
9. Make to order with no excess.
10. Partner and share demand data with a few suppliers.

Additional supporting components of a Lean system include rules governing the flow of standardized amounts of material or information (service industries) based on the concept of "Kanban" containers and supplier agreements, which will also be discussed later in this chapter. Long-term cooperative supplier agreements ensure suppliers have real-time access to their customer schedules (i.e., demand) to align their production to the customer's process.

Table 6.4 summarizes ten proven methods to increase process efficiency. The first is intelligent use of capacity within a system to maintain its scheduling flexibility to ensure short lead times. Improvements in quality, maintenance, and training reduce process breakdowns and reduce rework. The creation of product family processes based on similar product or service designs allows the design of common processes. This reduces the number of job setups and increases scheduling flexibility. Other benefits with fewer setups are higher yields from preventing setup scrap and reduced lead time for producing different products. Using multifunctional equipment also increases process flexibility because equipment can be used to produce more than one type of product. The important concept is to not create overly complicated and expensive equipment, rather to have equipment that can be easily modified for different types of work. Design commonality also contributes to designing multifunctional machines.

Metric measurement of lead time, quality, and up time are also important. Process simplification is a major topic of this chapter. Multiskilled workers increase process flexibility because direct labor can be matched more closely to production. An organization should only commit to orders it knows it can efficiently produce on time. Making promises to deliver orders that cannot be made results in scheduling problems because other orders must be reprioritized for production. This practice wastes capacity and other resources. Products should be made with no excess unless this is a strategic decision based on external or internal factors. Making an excessive amount of a product also wastes capacity and resources. Finally, contractual obligations should be consistent across a supply chain and should promote common incentives to ensure an uninterrupted supply of materials and services.

MAPPING VALUE

Value stream mapping (VSM) is a useful and productive method. It is also called "brown paper" mapping because the maps are sometimes created on brown paper taped to a wall during interactive process-improvement workshops. Process operations are represented with individual sticky notes. Visual information, describing metrics, and opportunities for improvement are also attached to the operations in the map. A simple VSM is shown in Figure 6.1 with notes and descriptive information showing metrics. The process mapping symbols are also shown. These vary by application. In manufacturing, symbols depicting factories, trucks, and operations are used, but service industries there are symbols that represent flowing information. Below the VSM, additional information is attached to show how the workflows are managed within a process. This can include inspection and data collection forms, quality reports including scrap and rework, maintenance reports showing setup times, machine breakdowns, and other information useful for analyzing the process. An important attribute of a VSM is that it is visual and built operation-by-operation by the people doing the work. Also, major workflows are studied as needed in detail and are quantified with key operational metrics.

Figure 6.2 shows a VFM of processes within a value stream. The concept and methodology are like the VSM, but a VFM is applied at a lower

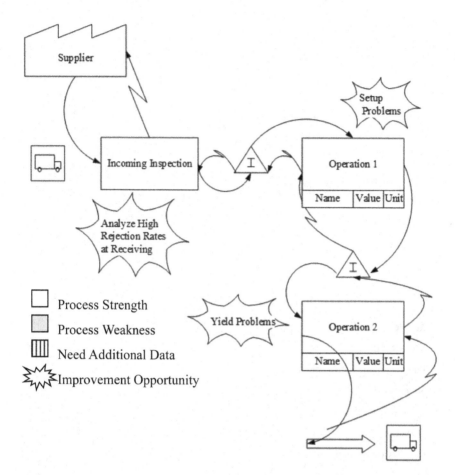

FIGURE 6.1

Value stream or "brown paper" mapping at an enterprise level. Attach information to the value stream map that shows how the process is managed, such as management reports, inspection and data collection forms, quality reports including scrap and rework, maintenance reports showing machine breakdowns, and any other information useful in analyzing the process.

level. The list of operational metrics is gathered for each operation during construction of a VFM. These are used to describe a process, the entire value stream, or other levels such as a facility within a VSM and its processes or just one facility within a supply chain. The mapping becomes more detailed as the VSM team begins to focus on major processes and their workflows.

Value Stream Mapping

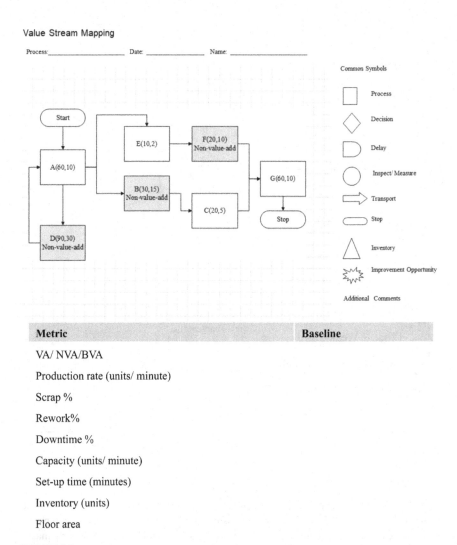

FIGURE 6.2
Analyzing a process. VA = value-add; NVA = non-value-add; BVA = business value add.

BALANCING FLOW

In Figure 6.3, a more detailed process map is shown as a network of connected activities. Each operation is quantified using its average and standard deviation of cycle time measured in seconds, shown in parentheses as (mean, standard deviation). After this type of process description is created, the initial takt time and the key operational metrics listed at the

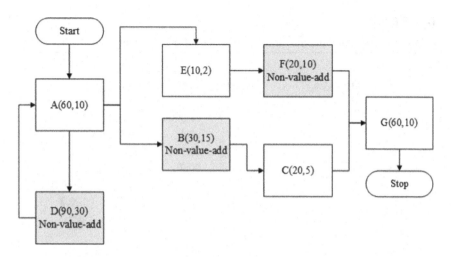

FIGURE 6.3
Process mapping current process.

bottom of Figure 6.2 are estimated from data collected from the process. Figure 6.3 shows three NVA operations located at operations B, D, and F. An initial goal should be to eliminate NVA operations, and then, over time, improve the efficiency of the remaining operations through simplification and standardization. Business value-add operations are needed for regulatory and compliance reasons or technical constraints. Examples include audit, certain types of testing and additional operations that are not value-added but must be done.

The takt time of this network is shown in Table 6.5. It is calculated as the daily demand on the system, which is 1,000 units, divided by the available time, which is 7 hours or 25,200 seconds after breaks have been subtracted from the total time of 8 hours. The takt time for this example is 25.2 seconds per unit. In other words, every 25.2 seconds, one unit is produced and exits the process.

The next step is to add the cycle times at each operation to estimate the total time to complete one unit. In this example, it takes 290 seconds to complete one unit. Dividing the total time to complete one unit by the takt time shows that the process requires 11.5 people or workstations with each producing at the takt rate. Note that the 11.5 must be rounded up to 12 because you can't have half a person or half a workstation. This rule is correct if every operation takes exactly 25.2 seconds to complete. In practice, however, this is not usually true because some operations take longer or

TABLE 6.5

Calculating Takt Time and the Minimum Number of Workstations

Operation	Expected Time	Standard Deviation	Variance
A	60.0	10.0	100.0
B	30.0	15.0	225.0
C	20.0	5.0	25.0
D	90.0	30.0	900.0
E	10.0	2.0	4.0
F	20.0	10.0	100.0
G	60.0	10.0	100.0
Total	290.0		1,454.0

Demand per shift:	1,000.0
Allowed time (breaks):	3,600.0
Available time:	25,200.0
Takt time =	**25.2**
(seconds per unit)	

Theoretical minimum operations or stations:

Time to produce one unit:	290.0
Takt time	25.2
Number of people:	**11.5**
(or a minimum of 12)	

less than exactly 25.2 seconds. Table 6.5 shows that the operational cycle times range between 10 and 90 seconds. This means we must balance the work tasks within each operation across the 12 people so that no person is allocated work with a completion time exceeding 25.2 seconds or too little work. But this may not be possible if the operations are not adjacent. As an example, we must use 14 rather than 12 people because some operations cannot be combined and have idle time.

A situation shown in Figure 6.4 is a more likely scenario where some operations cannot be combined and additional people are assigned to operations, as seen in process D, resulting in idle time. But an initial balancing requires all operations or groups of operations have a takt time of less

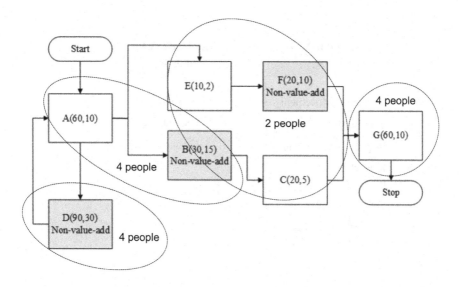

Initial Efficiency% = 1- [(14-12)/12] x100 = 100% - 17% = 83%

Lead time on critical path A-D-B-C-G = 290 seconds

FIGURE 6.4
Operation balancing.

than 25.2 seconds to meet demand. The calculated efficiency of the current operational balance is 83% of the calculated optimum because we must use 14 people versus 12 people. The team would immediately remove all NVA operations (i.e., B, D, and F) and rebalance the process with fewer resources. Over time, various types of process waste would also be eliminated, such as process scrap and rework, maintenance issues, non-standardization, and other waste. Reducing process waste will "lean out" the process to consistently meet the takt time of 25.2 seconds, but with less resource utilization.

Figure 6.5 shows how value adding work is separated from non-value adding work. Value adding work is needed by a customer, is physically changed by an operation and done right the first time. What is value adding in one industry may not be in another. Logistics is an example, where the movement of materials is value adding as a core competency; whereas in most of other industries movement of materials is a form of process waste. unnecessary movement of material and information are minimized. Eliminating the non-value adding components shown in Figure 6.5 helps reduce wasted resources in a process which also helps

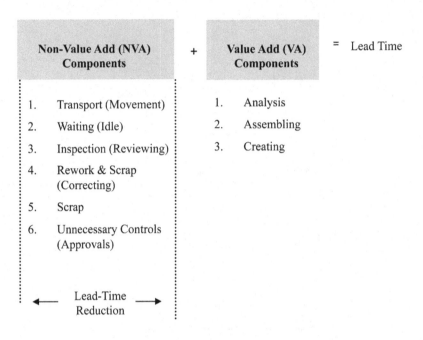

Value Adding Operation = Customer Needs Feature or Function +
Physical Transformation + Done Right the First Time

FIGURE 6.5
Simplifying a process.

stabilize the takt time i.e. fewer operations reduces overall lead time variation.

OPERATIONAL EFFICIENCY

When a process is analyzed, "red flag conditions" may be found. Red flag conditions are frequent changes to a job, overly complex processes, operations lacking work and inspection standards, poor measurement systems, lack of employee training, or long lead times between jobs. If order-to-delivery lead times are long or jobs are infrequently scheduled, special causes of variation may act on a process. Other red flag conditions are poor employee morale or poor working environment related to lighting, cleanliness, visual perception, or noise; in situations in which capacity is constrained, equipment and people may be pushed to their operational limits. Some of these red flag conditions could exist within a process.

At an operational level, the effects of red flag conditions may be longer lead times, high per-unit costs, and lower quality. As an example, high inventory could be caused by waiting for materials or people. Waiting could be caused by poorly trained associates, or cluttered workstations could make it difficult to find the materials. Or there could be unnecessary movement of materials because they do not have an assigned location and associates must search for them. Other effects include creation of NVA operations, batching of work, redundant controls, inefficient machine or job setups, ambiguous goals, poorly designed work and inspection instructions, outdated technology, a lack of useful information to execute work tasks, poor communication between associates, limited or poor coordination of resources, ineffective training especially with respect to cross-functional skills, and higher process complexity.

Red flag conditions contribute to error conditions that in turn contribute to errors. As an example, in noisy and cluttered work environments, people lose focus and may start to work a job but fail to choose the right components because of distractions. This red flag condition has created an error condition. If an associate does not see the error and uses the component, then an error or defect is created. The consideration now becomes how soon will the defect be found. If it reaches a customer, the costs are higher than if it is immediately found. Knowing that red flag conditions exist enables them to be eliminated, along with their associated error conditions. Quality and lead times are immediately improved.

There are many other proven tools and methods to identify the process improvements that help improve operational efficiency. Table 6.6 summarizes these. Capacity planning helps ensure capacity is matched to actual demand. Capacity utilization rates differ by industry. Process-intensive industries such as paper manufacturing or oil and gasoline refining are designed to operate at a 95%+ utilization rate and have products designed for continuous changeovers (e.g., changing the ratios of raw materials in a blend on the fly). These production systems are continuous. Call centers also have high capacity utilization because work can be distributed over many agents by technology. Their capacity utilization rates often exceed 95%. Incoming demand can be balanced by rerouting the volume to other call centers in the same network but currently at a lower utilization level.

In batch manufacturing, capacity utilization is still matched to demand using Lean methods such as takt time and the careful scheduling and movement of work through their systems using visual or electronic queuing. In these systems, utilization varies with the ability of an organization to effectively match resources to demand. What is not preferred is the historically poor practice of loading a system to produce at high utilization rates and increasing inventory unless it is done for strategic purposes or because the system has design constraints. Lead time between subsequent production increases as inventory is built, thus reducing scheduling flexibility and increasing waiting time. Producing at high utilization rates may also push equipment and workers to a point where quality problems start to occur. Products may need to be scrapped or reworked and additional work added to schedules to meet customer requirements.

Table 6.6 has several other useful tools and methods. Process mapping helps us visualize the relationships between operations. Then we can apply a value-add lens to the process to eliminate nonessential operations. As discussed previously, the takt time ensures customer demand is satisfied even if a process is initially inefficient. Then standardizing work, mistake-proofing processes, continuing preventive maintenance, practicing quality improvement, utilizing specialized scheduling methods, reducing lead time (e.g., using SMED), cross-training employees, and reporting metrics are introduced to balance flow, meet external demand,

TABLE 6.6

Ten Lean Tools and Methods

Tool or Methods
1. Implement capacity planning (resources to meet demand).
2. Utilize process mapping and simplification (operational-spatial relationship).
3. Calculate takt time calculation (production per time).
4. Standardize work (used to balance flow).
5. Mistake-proof processes (used to stabilize takt time).
6. Continue preventative maintenance.
7. Maintain high quality in product and process design (do it right the first time).
8. Constantly reduce lead time through application of single-minute exchange of dies, transfer batching, mixed-model scheduling, and other methods (reduce lead time).
9. Continually cross-train employees and empower them within their local work groups.
10. Establish performance measurements and visual controls (constant improvement).

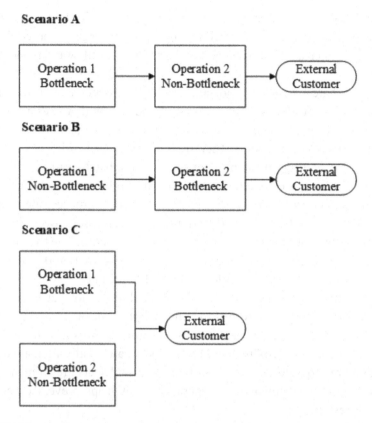

FIGURE 6.6
Bottleneck management.

and improve operational efficiency. We will discuss these later in this chapter.

Next, the system's bottleneck and capacity-constrained resources need to be managed. Figure 6.6 shows several bottleneck scenarios. In scenario A, a bottleneck is feeding a non-bottleneck resource. The throughput through the downstream resource needs to be balanced with the bottleneck throughput. To ensure operational efficiency, the downstream operation should be utilized at the same rate as the bottleneck (assuming equal production rates). In scenario B, the bottleneck is downstream of the non-bottleneck. The utilization rate of the non-bottleneck resource must match that of the bottleneck. The same utilization strategy is applied in scenario C, except that the two operations run in parallel. The throughput rate of the non-bottleneck must be balanced to the bottleneck resource. There is a final configuration, not shown in Figure 6.6, in which a bottleneck feeds several non-bottleneck resources. Ensuring that a bottleneck resource is fully utilized will increase the throughput of the process workflow and reduce lead time.

Transfer batches are an important strategy for reducing lead time. In a transfer batch production system, as opposed to one that uses a process batch, units (or material or information) are moved downstream to subsequent workstations as soon as they are built. In other words, they are not batched. Depending on the number of units in a batch, lead time reductions of 50% or more are attainable across all production operations. The example shown in Figure 6.7 shows that each unit requires one minute of work at each of the four workstations. If 100 units are moved through each of the workstations as a batch, the total throughout time through the four sequential operations using a process batch system, is 400 minutes or 100 minutes + 100 minutes +100 minutes +100 minutes. Using a transfer batch system, in which each unit is transferred to the downstream workstation as it is completed, results in a throughput time of just 103 minutes or 100 minutes + 1 minute + 1 minute + 1 minute. This is a throughput time reduction of approximately 74%. Transfer batches also increase quality compared to a process batch system because defects are immediately found by the next downstream operation. This helps prevent excessive scrap or rework.

A third major method used to reduce lead time is quick response manufacturing (QRM). QRM is used to reduce lead time in master production schedule (MPS) and materials requirements planning (MRP) systems. QRM dynamically matches demand, causing scheduling changes to available resources by providing lower-level operations (i.e., work cells) with updated demand information. QRM is an adjunct to (MRP) in which local control is enabled at a work-cell level. This contrasts with an MRP system that pushes out customer demand based on cumulative lead times and the MPS schedule. An MPS/MRP demand-push environment is based on higher-level, external product forecasts incorporated into the MPS and offset by the MRP using a product's bill of material (BOM) and component cumulative lead times. Operational problems occur if demand or capacity change within a product's cumulative lead-time or frozen time fence (i.e., a promise to produce at the cumulative lead time). This creates a situation where jobs are left incomplete due to materials shortages because the materials were not ordered. The cumulative effect

Process Batch

1. One minute per unit and 100 units process through each of the four operations, but in batches of 100 units, results in a total lead-time (cycle time) of 400 minutes.

Transfer Batch

1. One minute per unit and 100 units process through each of the four operations but results in a lead-time (cycle time) reduction of ~ 74% .

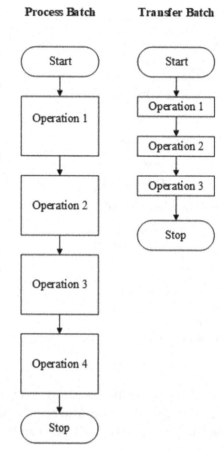

FIGURE 6.7
Transfer versus process batches.

is higher work-in-process (WIP) inventory levels and other scheduling issues.

Figure 6.8 shows a high-level view of a local work cell QRM application. In this example, local work cells communicate using a type of Kanban system that signals an upstream work cell to produce for the work center immediately downstream. This communication system is enabled by collapsing the BOM so that the MRP system is placing demand only at higher levels of the BOM and not at a work-cell level. This operational change enables local work cells to dynamically react to schedule changes. This creates a more stable production schedule and avoids process breakdowns because teams can make operational decisions based on the current

- Restructure to simple cellular product-oriented cells
- Rethink BOM
  - Design decisions
  - Materials
  - Make vs. buy
  - Collapse BOMs
- Use high-level MRP
- High-performance work teams (local decisions)

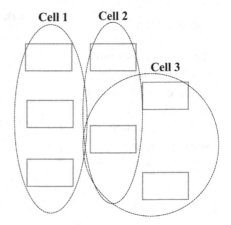

How Do Changes in System Status Inputs (MPS/ MRPII Changes) at Cells 2,3 & 4 Impact Capacity and Flow?

FIGURE 6.8
Quick response manufacturing (QRM). BOM = bill of materials.

process status, including available resources and capacity. Design-for-manufacturing methods can also help simplify and modularize designs to consolidate entire portions of a BOM and to outsource component manufacturing where possible.

A mixed-model scheduling system is another useful method to reduce lead time and increase throughput. Mixed-model scheduling is difficult to implement, however, because success depends on product and process design changes. Using this scheduling method, product differentiation is made at higher levels of assembly rather than at lower levels. If products or services have a high degree of design commonality, then their setup times will be reduced, allowing more setups and a more flexible system. This method dramatically reduces production lead times. Figure 6.9 shows a manufacturing sequence (i.e., schedule) of three products. Initially, each product is produced once every four weeks versus the mixed-model schedule of every two weeks, in which the lead time is reduced by 50%. The advantage is that if external demand changes, this system can flex to meet the revised schedule because the product is produced every two weeks

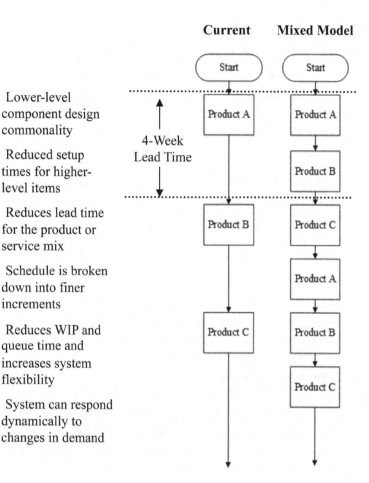

- Lower-level component design commonality

- Reduced setup times for higher-level items

- Reduces lead time for the product or service mix

- Schedule is broken down into finer increments

- Reduces WIP and queue time and increases system flexibility

- System can respond dynamically to changes in demand

FIGURE 6.9
Mixed-model scheduling.

rather than every four weeks. Inventory is reduced by 50% because it is proportional to the lead time.

Preventive and corrective maintenance systems are deployed to ensure equipment is available. Effective preventive and corrective maintenance programs rely on reliable equipment and developing optimum combinations of preventive and corrective maintenance of each piece of equipment. Takt time is more stable when equipment is up and running to support production. Table 6.7 describes planning for unscheduled (corrective) versus scheduled maintenance (preventive). Planning includes establishing equipment classifications, identifying failure probabilities,

202 • *Operational Excellence*

TABLE 6.7

Implementing a Maintenance Program

$$\text{Availability} = \text{Reliability} + \text{Maintainability}$$
$$\text{Maintainability} = (\text{Preventive} + \text{Corrective}) \text{ Maintenance}$$

Corrective Maintenance	Preventive Maintenance
1. Diagnose problem.	1. System has a failure rate which increases over time and is predictable (follows a known failures distribution).
2. Remove failed components.	
3. Order components for repair (if not in stock)	2. Cost of prevention is less than the cost of allowing the failure and correcting it at that point.
4. Repair or replace components which failed.	
5. Verify quality of the repairs.	

I.	Develop the goals and objectives for the maintenance program relative to unscheduled (corrective) versus scheduled maintenance (preventive) activities to ensure equipment availability.
II.	Determine equipment classifications, failure probabilities and other economics of maintenance by equipment classification.
III.	Assign responsibilities and budgets to each equipment classification.
IV.	Develop maintenance strategies based on equipment design.
V.	Develop systems to monitor and schedule maintenance activities with reporting relative to system performance and costs.
VI.	Train people in use of the system.
VII.	Periodically review the system performance and adjust as necessary to the system.

---

and managing information related to usage, schedule maintenance, and contingencies for handling breakdowns. Planning is used to assign maintenance responsibilities and budgets on the basis of equipment design, the systems to monitor and schedule maintenance, and metrics to track equipment performance and costs against budget. Training is also important for the people supporting the maintenance system.

SMED also contributes to takt time stabilization and lead time reduction by reducing and stabilizing job setups using a combination of tools and methods. Table 6.8 lists the ten steps of a successful implementation

TABLE 6.8

Ten Steps to Implement Single-Minute Exchange of Dies (SMED)

Step
1. Identify individual work tasks of setup using process maps, videos, and work and inspection instructions.
2. Separate internal work tasks from external work tasks associated with setup activities.
3. Move internal work tasks to external setup work tasks.
4. Simplify all work tasks associated with internal and external setups.
5. Design equipment to unload and load dies and align tools, as necessary.
6. Mistake-proof remaining setup work tasks to eliminate manual adjustments.
7. Standardize new setup procedures.
8. Apply 5-S methods to the setup areas to ensure efficient and accurate setups.
9. Train employees on the use of the new procedures.
10. Continually improve the setup process over time.

of a SMED program. The first step is to identify individual work tasks related to the setup using diagrams of the work area and identifying the sequence of work tasks needed to do the setup. Videos, current work procedures, and inspection instructions are useful for understanding the current setup process.

After an initial analysis of how setup work tasks are done and the time it takes to do each one, the SMED team separates internal or on-line setup work tasks from those that can be completed externally or off-line. In parallel, all work tasks, both internal and external, are simplified to the greatest extent possible. After the setup process has been simplified using SMED, equipment, fixtures, and other tools are designed to allow dies, fixtures, or other tools required to complete setups to be exchanged quickly. The improved setup process is standardized, and work and inspection procedures are updated to ensure the work is consistently done. The updated process is then mistake-proofed to eliminate manual adjustments.

Integral to SMED improvements is the application of 5-S methods to ensure standardization of the work and mistake-proofing. 5-S is a set of improvement actions applied to a work area. The first step is organizing the work area by sorting what is need from what is not needed for production. The second step is setting the work area up for efficient task completion by placing tools, equipment, people, and supporting materials in locations that are clearly marked. The third step is to assign cleaning or sweeping responsibilities in the work area. The fourth step is

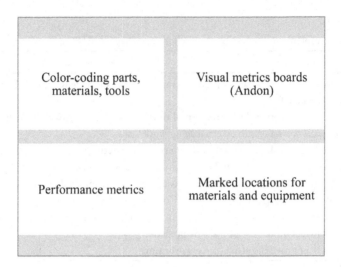

FIGURE 6.10
Implement a visual system to show equipment status, product locations, inventory, team, metrics status, etc.

standardizing the work for consistency using visual controls, checklists, training, and similar methods. The fifth step is sustaining the improvements though self-discipline and continuous improvement. Integrated with a Lean deployment are other initiatives such as total quality or Six Sigma. These initiatives improve process yields and are applied to a standardized process. Cross-training employees and empowering them to control the quality of work is an integral part of an effective Lean system. Performance measurements and visual controls show where to reduce waste to improve the process.

Figure 6.10 illustrates the deployment of visual controls as a sequential process requiring 5-S as its foundation. Visual displays in either electronic or physical form increase the ability of the local workflow team to actively control their process workflows. Studies indicate that people gain 60% of their information through visualization. In production systems, visuals are used to show equipment status, product status, inventory status, the team responsible for the work, and metric reporting performance to target, and so on.

Effectively deploying the Lean tools and methods listed in Table 6.6 creates a process that has lower cycle times and cost as well as higher quality and throughput rate. Inventory investment will also be lower. Let's return to our takt time example, now shown in Figure 6.11 as a modified

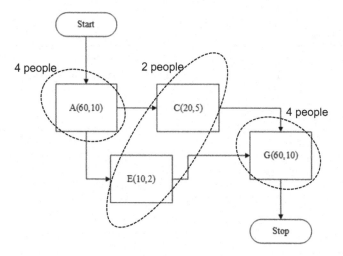

- Efficiency to new target % = 1– [(10–6)/6] x 100 = 100% – 67% = 33%
- Lead time on critical path A-C-G = 140 seconds
- Lead time reduction on critical path over baseline = [(140–290)/290] = 58%
- Reduction in initial number of workstations = [(10–14)/14] = 29%

FIGURE 6.11
Value-add operations remaining in the process.

and improved process. The optimum resources used by this process have been reduced from 12 workstations to 6 workstations over the initial baseline shown in Figure 6.3. This is because NVA work has been eliminated. Table 6.9 shows that now only 50% of the original people or workstations are required to maintain the takt time because the total time to produce on unit decreased from 290 to 140 seconds. Lead time on the critical path decreased by 58%. Note that the new efficiency is 33% because we now have a modified process design with only value-add operations. Additional efficiencies can be obtained by applying the Lean tools and methods summarized in Table 6.10.

SCHEDULING

Applying the discipline of Lean makes flexible scheduling possible by enabling materials and information to flow seamlessly through processes. The goal, if technically feasible, is to move toward unit-flow production

TABLE 6.9

Recalculating Workstations

Operation	Expected Time	Standard Deviation	Variance
A	60.0	10.0	100.0
C	20.0	5.0	25.0
E	10.0	2.0	4.0
G	60.0	10.0	100.0
Total	**150.0**		**229.0**

Demand per shift:	1,000.0
Allowed time (breaks):	3,600.0
Available time:	25,200.0
Takt time =	**25.2**
(seconds per unit)	

Theoretical minimum operations or stations:

Time to produce one unit:	150.0
Takt time	25.2
Number of people:	**6.0**

TABLE 6.10

Lean Concept Summary

Concept

1. Establish operational metrics to measure improvements relative to higher customer on-time delivery (schedule attainment), higher value-add time as a proportion of total time, higher throughput of materials or information, faster machine or job changeover (especially at bottleneck resources), higher machine uptime (available time), higher quality of work (reduced scrap/rework/warranty/returns), less floor space utilized, lower system inventory, higher supplier on-time delivery, and lower overall system cost.
2. Lean tools, methods, and concepts help simplify and standardize a process.
3. There are several critical components that should be sequentially implemented to deploy a Lean system.
4. Establishing a takt time is important to create a baseline from which waste can be systematically eliminated from a process.
5. There are five key tools that will greatly increase operational efficiency: process simplification, process standardization, bottleneck management, transfer batches, and mixed-model scheduling.

and away from batching work with large production runs, long lead times between product changeover, and high inventory.

There are different types of scheduling systems that vary by industry and the technical capability of associated organizations. At one extreme are processes in which lead time is long and calculated based on historical data. This approach creates inflexible systems. At the opposite extreme are production systems that are flexible and use a self-service scheduling strategy where capacity is matched exactly to demand. Scheduling methods evolve by creating new tools, methods, and concepts that enable jobs to be done more frequently because lead time is reduced. Production cost is lower and quality is higher if this is done properly. Schedule flexibility enables production schedules to quickly match demand variation. Some systems have already moved to self-service or service-on-demand scheduling strategies. Examples include online movies and entertainment, online ordering of almost anything, self-check-in at an airport, and scanning purchases at a grocery store. As technology becomes more sophisticated, systems that schedule the production of complex products and services will continue to evolve to enable customers to "pull" products or services themselves as needed.

Effective scheduling requires understanding how a system's available capacity and lead times change over time. Available capacity is calculated as the quantity of material or information that can be moved through a process during a given period. Throughput rate depends on total lead time across operation in the critical path of the process, capacity variation due to process status, and demand variation. The lead time of each operation is itself the sum of several smaller time components that include waiting for materials or information, job setup time, job processing time, the time to inspect the work, and time to transport it to the next operation. Work can be either material or information.

Scheduling flexibility depends on the design of a product or service. The greater the degree of design commonality between products or services, the greater the ability to bundle or aggregate products and services to schedule them together as one group. This strategy is the basis for the mixed-model scheduling system shown in Figure 6.9. The beneficial impacts of a mixed-model scheduling system are setup reductions. The ability to set up a job quickly results in reduced lead time and enables the product to be produced more frequently.

A system's service discipline, from a queuing perspective, is also useful for efficient scheduling. In Chapter 5, we discussed service disciplines based on queuing theory. These included first in, first out (FIFO), last in, first out (LIFO), service in random order (SIRO), prioritization of service (POS), and a general service discipline (GSD). Lead time varies with the service discipline used to schedule its production. A scheduling system also depends on the arrival pattern of customers or demand as well as its service distribution. Service discipline includes the design of a service system relative to the number of service channels or parallel servers in a system, as well as their phases or the number of sequential steps within a channel.

The goal of a production system should be to schedule its products or services only when they are needed by an external customer. This ensures available capacity is efficiently matched to actual customer demand to avoid situations in which too little or too much product is produced by a system. But this may be difficult if an organization produces thousands of products at different times and in geographically dispersed locations. It is difficult to match available resources to changes in customer demand at a set time if available capacity is allocated other products and locations. These inflexible systems rely on forecasting demand, which leads into the Master Production Schedule (MPS) and then into the Material Requirements Planning (MRP) system.

Operations scheduling requires allocation of enough capacity (rough-cut capacity planning) to meet an organization's strategic forecast. A strategic forecast estimates demand over three to five years by product group and location. This ensures there will be enough capacity in the form of fixed assets, equipment, labor, and materials to satisfy forecasted demand. Capacity can be increased by purchasing new facilities and equipment, hiring workers, or temporarily increasing inventory for planned downtime. In addition, labor can be hired, contracted, and trained as needed. In an intermediate forecast, which is typically between six and eighteen months, the MPS uses forecasted demand information and aggregates all expected demand streams for a product or service. Lean becomes effective at a short-range level where demand becomes more discrete and variable. It effectively optimizes available capacity using the tools and methods discussed in this chapter.

MPS and MRP systems are notorious for not being synchronized to changes production conditions or demand variation. This causes schedule changes and a need to expedite work by production activity control teams. If a system's resource status is known at an operational or work task level, then manual intervention is not required by production activity control teams. MRP "pushes" the work schedule through the supply chain using a cumulative lead-time offset determined by the production date of every product. The assumption, in these systems, is that allocated resources will be available to production and product demand will not change significantly during the cumulative lead time or frozen time fence. If changes do occur within the time fence, a process will eventually not be synchronized with the MPS and MRP systems.

"Push" scheduling systems use MPS and MRP systems to translate independent demand via a BOM into production schedules for dependent demand items based on net requirements for components and materials (after on-hand inventory has been subtracted from the scheduled quantities). The problem with push systems is that they tend to be inflexible if demand or resource availability change during a product's cumulative lead time or frozen time fence. Changes in demand or resource availability within a product's lead time have an effect of creating large amounts of partially completed products (i.e., work-in-process or WIP inventory). Production costs also increase when schedules are converted from one product to another.

Lean tools, methods, and concepts are applied to move a rigidly structured batch production system from "push" scheduling to one in which materials or information are "pulled" through the process. The latter system becomes self-scheduling using external demand and a calculated takt time. Our focus is on the application of Lean methods to scheduling work at a local level and with shorter time horizons. Table 6.11 maps attributes

TABLE 6.11

Scheduling at a Local Level

Characteristic	Current Paradigm	Goal
System Design	Make-To-Order or Stock	Mass Customization
System Demand	Variable	Level (Takt Time)
Lot Size	Batch	Transfer Batch
Capacity Strategy	Available Time	Balance to Takt Time
Production Control Strategy	Push (Old Paradigm)	Pull
Operations Layout	Operation Focus	Product Focus
Queue Time	High	Low

from current production methods to a make-to-stock where inventory is staged in distribution centers and batch-manufactured in a Lean system. The first paradigm shift is creating flexible production systems using common design; this will dramatically reduce lead times, enable the production of most of a product, and allow the product to be customized as late as possible based on actual customer demand. Customer demand is stabilized using a takt time to level the demand on the system. The takt time pulls and controls production though the system in contrast to pushing it using historical forecasts. The production focus on the takt time also enables production to move away from producing large batches to a transfer-batch system, which further reduces lead times. Integral to these paradigm changes is a focus on product versus process. In earlier chapters, it was mentioned that process design should follow product or service design, and not the other way around. The process layout also changes from a process focus to a product focus. Finally, waiting times decrease as lead times shrink.

Toyota developed the first pull system based on years of incremental improvements that stabilized takt time and squeezed out process waste. The result is an integrated supply chain system having less than 10% demand variation Toyota also uses design commonality and performs customization late in the assembly process. In contrast, in systems where demand variation is high, pull systems are difficult to deploy. Although pull systems were developed for the automotive industry, they have found applicability to varying degrees within other industries using a range of unique strategies to integrate Lean tools and methods into their systems. In each application, common product and process designs improve scheduling efficiency.

An ideal scheduling strategy for former batch manufacturing systems uses a pull system, visual controls, and Lean tools applied in combination with a Kanban scheduling system to achieve the takt time. Figure 6.12 reinforces the concept that pull systems are effective only after a significant amount of preliminary work has been implemented. We already discussed most of these topics. We discussed physical reconfiguration of a process in the queuing section of Chapter 5. In this section, we discuss process physical configurations from different perspectives.

Collocation of equipment, materials, and people are important to ensure a straight flow of materials and information through a process. This is especially important for batch or assembly operations where jobs are moved

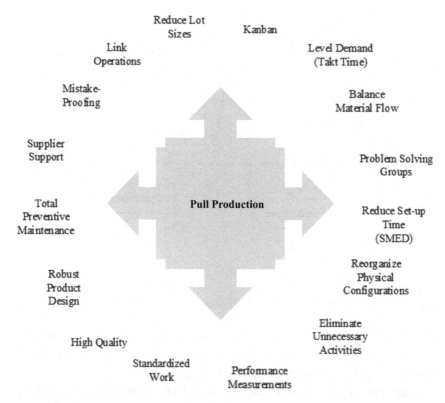

FIGURE 6.12
Necessary elements of a pull production system. SMED = single-minute exchange of dies.

between workstations. Figure 6.13 shows a convoluted and complicated process layout in which jobs move back and forth between the workstations. In contrast, Figure 6.14 shows four different process layouts that move jobs linearly based on available space. These include a straight-line layout, a U-shaped layout, an L-shaped layout, and an S-shaped layout. The best physical configuration for a given application requires a careful analysis based on the product or service design, the required work balance and operational cycle times to achieve the required takt time, and the potential for process waste reduction. Process waste includes scrap, rework, the unnecessary movement of materials, non-standard operational motions, and other waste. A U-shaped work cell layout is efficient because work entering a work cell is balanced with the work leaving it. Labor efficiency is improved in a U-shaped cell layout because workers can be added

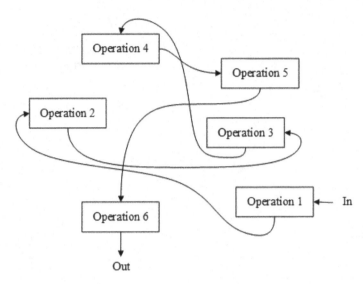

FIGURE 6.13
Collocation of equipment based on the build sequence – convoluted layout.

or removed as the takt time changes. This layout also promotes associate cross-training, which enables associates to move around the cell or to be reassigned as the workload increases or decreases.

Kanban scheduling systems can be deployed to balance the flow of work between work cells and suppliers after the Lean tools and methods listed in Figure 6.12 have been implemented. Kanbans are signals (if electronic) or physical cards (if manual) that authorize specific quantities of materials, services, or information at specific times. There are several types of Kanbans depending on the information being conveyed to downstream operations. Transport Kanban cards identify a part number, its quantity, where it was produced, and where it must be transported next. There are two types of Kanban cards: supplier and withdrawal. Supplier Kanban cards signal part orders to suppliers, so parts are delivered with an agreed-upon frequency to a requesting facility. These are called milk runs. They help maintain a stable lead time between the supplier and customer. Ideally, suppliers will be co-located with their customers. Withdrawal Kanban cards are used between internal workstations to signal that an operation immediately upstream needs to move a Kanban quantity of material to the downstream operation that is requesting material. Production Kanban cards are used to signal an upstream operation to produce a Kanban quantity to replace the one removed by the withdrawal Kanban card. A Kanban system is shown in Figure 6.15.

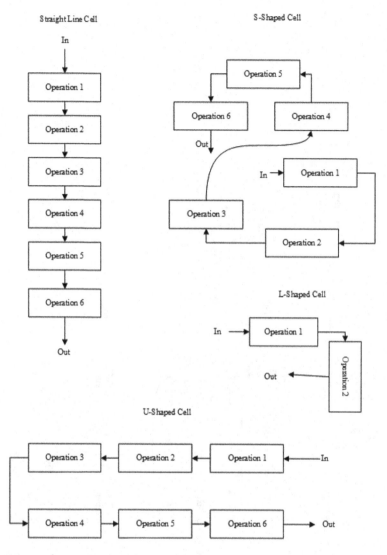

FIGURE 6.14
Process layouts to facilitate pull production – alternative designs.

Figure 6.16 shows how the number of Kanban cards is calculated using the expected demand during the lead time between operations, a safety-stock factor (usually set at 10% of the expected demand), lead time, and the container size for the material or part being placed into the Kanban. As example, if 100 parts are required per hour and the safety-stock level was set at 10%, the calculated quantity would be 110 parts. If a container

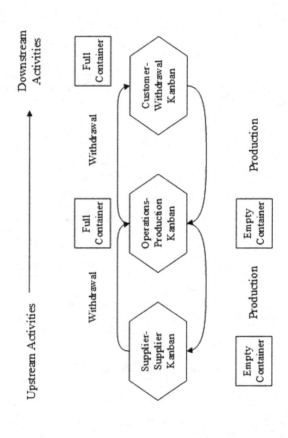

FIGURE 6.15
Kanban cards pull material from upstream operations.

$$\text{Kanbans} = \frac{\text{Expected Unit Demand During Lead Time} + \text{Safety Stock}}{\text{Container Size}}$$

Containers Include:	Items Pulled Include:
•Boxes	•Raw materials
•Totes	•Parts
•Pallets	•Assemblies
•Trucks	•Products
•Any standardized container volume and type	•Lots

FIGURE 6.16
Kanban facts.

holds 55 parts, then two containers and Kanban cards would be required to control the hourly flow of parts between operations.

Toyota developed its pull systems in an environment in which external customer demand was relatively smooth and detached from their MPS and MRP systems. The material flow was stable and linear, which meant that it could be managed manually by local work teams. Over time, it became apparent in other industries that pull scheduling systems could not be easily applied to low-volume production processes controlled by MPS and MRP systems using forecasted demand and batching of materials. As an example, one industry was consumer products that manufactured thousands of unique products. These products were placed in distribution centers as inventory. A modification of the pull system called quick response manufacturing (QRM) was developed to provide local work cell control of the material flow within higher level MPS and MRP environments. Figure 6.8 provided an example earlier in this chapter.

OTHER LEAN TOOLS

Once the value flow map is created, several analyses are overlaid to analyze the process. The first is distinguishing operations that add value from those that do not. This was discussed earlier in this chapter. This concept was useful to initially simplify a process. Then we discussed balancing to the takt time, transfer batching, and scheduling. To continually improve the value content of a process, we need to simplify, standardize, and mistake-proof it by using additional Lean methods. The next analytical method is applying the concept of process waste to our value flow map. There are seven classic process wastes, and safety was recently added to the list by some organizations. Process waste adds complexity and cost and increases the likelihood of product and service defects.

Transportation waste occurs if materials or information are moved unnecessarily. Examples include walking an invoice around for signatures or moving materials without processing. Inventory waste occurs when we build excess materials, information, people, or other resources. The risk of creating this excess capacity, unless it is planned, is that demand may change. The result is excess capacity that will not be used, thus causing higher cost; in addition, resources used to create this excess capacity will not be available for other work. Excess capacity must also be kept in storage, which carries a risk for damage and higher costs for the storage. Motion waste occurs if the number of work tasks performed within an operation are more than the defined work standard. As an example, if an operation should be completed in three motions based on engineering studies, but workers use more than three motions to complete the work task, then this motion waste results in a longer processing time. The workers may also make mistakes or injure themselves by these unnecessary repetitive motions. Waiting waste occurs if an operation cannot start because it needs materials, information, or other resources from an upstream operation that is not available when the operation is ready to start. Examples include a job that cannot be processed because a machine is being repaired or materials and people are not available, or an invoice that is waiting for a manager's approval. Overprocessing result from adding complexity to a process, such as adding features and functions with no value to customers. Examples include creating reports or other unneeded work objects. Defects are process waste because the work must be corrected or thrown out and redone. This wastes resources and time, thus increasing cost. The eighth waste is safety issues. These result in poor working conditions and operations that harm people, animals, property, or the environment. The advantage of understanding and seeing process waste is that these issues can be identified and projects can be created to resolve them. The concept of eight wastes is a powerful process-improvement method.

When we encounter a process issue, it useful to ask why it exists. It is vital to ask why several times to get as close as possible to root causes. This is known as 5-Why analysis, and it is a useful tool to identify root causes and other gaps that prevent process simplification and standardization. To ensure a root-cause analysis stays on track, it is useful for the team to have subject matter experts to unambiguously answer questions. A 5-Why example would be troubleshooting why a refrigerator does not work. The first question would be, "Why did the refrigerator stop working?" The team might verify through testing that the compressor motor stopped working. The next question would be, "Why did the compressor motor stop working?" The team might determine the compressor motor overheated. The third question would be, "Why did the compressor motor overheat?" The answer might be poor air circulation on a very hot day. The next question would be, "Why was there poor air circulation?" The answer might be the refrigerator was pushed against the wall and paper bags were stuffed around the refrigerator. Finally, the fifth question might be, "Why was the refrigerator pushed against the wall and paper bags stuffed around it?" The answer might be a poor process procedure. This is the root cause for the initial problem of the refrigerator failing. The solution would be to remove the paper bags to increase air circulation. In summary, a 5-Why analysis is a simple method to drill down deeper into a problem. It is best done with subject matter experts because each level of questioning needs to be verified before proceeding to the next question. The number of "whys" may be more than five if needed for resolution of the problem.

5-S is another useful method for process analysis and especially for process simplification and standardization. Most recently, some organizations have added safety and sustainability to the original 5-S method. This method is often successfully used for improving work areas. A before-and-after metric summary is created by the improvement team. These metrics are lead time through the process, yield, per-unit cost, percent value-add operations, floor space required for production, and required work-in-process (WIP) inventory. To start the 5-S project, a team is formed with the people doing the work and a Lean facilitator. In manufacturing, the 5-S project requires three to five days. After a leadership introduction, the facilitator trains the team in the 5-S basics. At the end of the project, the workspace will be transformed and there will be a second leadership presentation discussing the observations made prior to the project and the improvements made as a result of the project.

The first step is sorting or organizes the workplace (*seiri*). The team goes to the work area and identifies what is needed for production. This includes parts, inventory, equipment, tools, and materials. Anything else is red-tagged for potential removal from the work area. Red-tagging rules are specified in advance of sorting. Examples include placing a tag on inventory more than one week old, equipment not used in the last three months, or tools and equipment not needed for this work area. The tag has the name or number for the item, the location from which it is taken, the location where it will be either stored or disposed, the quantity, the reason for tagging, contact people for placing the tag or the owners of the item, the date the item was tagged, and other relevant information. Once items are red-tagged, they are evaluated with stakeholders to determine if they should be kept in the work area, stored for future use, discarded, sold, returned to the supplier, or transferred to another work area. It is important to understand that although items are not needed for the current work, they may be very valuable in the future. An example is large and expensive pieces of equipment used in process industries, such as paper manufacturing. The cast iron frames in a paper factory may be a hundred years old, but they are still useful for production because electromechanical innovations were added to them over the years. At the end of this step, the team makes the changes and removes unnecessary items from the work area.

Once the work area is cleaned up, what is left is set in order (*seiton*). The workflow may be changed, equipment may be placed in a new sequence to simplify the process, and production balanced to the takt time. The goal is to ensure little or no process waste. Considering the eight process wastes, when setting up a work sequence we want to minimize motion, unnecessary transportation, inventory, unsafe conditions, and the other process wastes. The team also standardizes the use of materials, methods, machines, tools, communication, training, etc. Visual controls are set up. All materials, tools, equipment, storage containers, templates, and fixtures are labeled and placed in the correct location. Marked lines, color coding, and other visual information are added to the work areas to communicate production status. In summary, the team puts each item in the right place in the sequence of work tasks.

The third step is shining or sweeping (*seiso*), i.e., cleaning the work area. Cleaning has two components. First, prior to placing the equipment in order, the workspace floor is usually painted. In some industries it is painted white to show oil leaks from equipment; alternatively, the equipment may be painted white to identify oil leaks to aid maintenance and troubleshooting. Assignments are made for team members to clean equipment, tools, walls, and work bench surfaces to eliminate dirt, oil, and loose materials, to upgrade lighting, and other similar activities. Inspection lists and cleanliness criteria are agreed upon, and schedules are created to keep the area clean. Audits will be performed based on the fifth step to ensure cleanliness continues.

In the fourth step, the work area is standardized (*seiketsu*). Going forward, every operation will be standardized based on the best way to do it. Supporting standardization will be color-coding, mistake-proofing, checklists, training, and visual controls. Any remaining process waste will be eliminated over time using continuous improvement methods. The fifth 5-S step is self-discipline or sustaining these habits (*shitsuke*). An auditing plan is created to support the improvements from the first four steps. This plan will ensure consistency over time.

Some organizations have added safety and sustainability to their 5-S projects. Reducing unnecessary clutter, organizing the work area, and improving lighting will directly improve safety. But additional actions may be needed, and a safety expert can be added to the 5-S team. As the team rearranges the work area, the safety expert will provide advice on best practices to improve the safety of the work area and procedures to prevent injury and death in ways that meet local regulations. These actions may include ensuring workers are trained in safety practices, have the right equipment, place protective guards on machines, and other actions.

Sustainability is now an important consideration to ensure an organization's practices save energy and resources and do not harm the environment over their useful life. Key areas of focus include recycling, repurposing, converting and properly disposing of materials, as well as minimizing the use of hazardous materials and using renewable energy sources. Metrics aligned to these focus areas include energy used per employee or unit of production, waste per employee, percent recycled materials, and the amount of carbon dioxide released into the environment per employee or for the total organization. Materials sourced in areas where people are exploited (i.e., conflict resources) are also a concern for organizations today.

Maintaining the balanced flow of work to achieve a takt time also requires that equipment and facilities be available to do work. TPM develops goals and measurements to manage unscheduled (i.e., corrective) versus scheduled maintenance (i.e., preventive) activities to ensure equipment availability. A TPM program consists of trained experts who determine equipment classifications, failure probabilities, and economics of equipment maintenance. TPM assigns responsibilities and budgets for equipment classifications, and it develops maintenance strategies based on equipment classification and design. Software applications are used to monitor equipment, schedule maintenance, and report status. A TPM system is periodically audited, and needed improvements are made. The guiding concepts in TPM are that availability depends on equipment reliability and maintainability, and maintainability in turn depends on preventive and corrective maintenance practices.

Maintenance activities are classified as preventive or corrective. Both are needed to control TPM costs and ensure equipment availability. Preventive maintenance uses equipment failure rates to schedule maintenance. In other words, maintenance interventions are predictable based on the component design, i.e., they are predictable and follow a known failure distribution. An example is scheduling maintenance for a personal vehicle based on recommended service intervals at critical mileage. These intervals are based on component designs from engineering tests by the manufacturer and its suppliers. The cost of preventive maintenance will usually be less than the cost related to simply waiting for a failure to occur.

Corrective maintenance is done when a component fails. Unexpected corrective maintenance for expensive equipment carries a high cost because the equipment is unavailable for use, as well as the cost of the repair. For low-cost components, such as light bulbs, several may be allowed to fail because the impact is minor (i.e., within safety parameters) and perhaps the entire population is replaced at once. In this situation, enough lighting is available and labor costs are kept low. In a corrective maintenance event, failed components are removed, analyzed for failure, and then repaired or replaced and tested.

Mistake-proofing has been mentioned in several chapters already. The concept is easily understood from the position that mistakes need to be prevented. But knowing how to prevent mistakes requires understanding key mistake-proofing concepts. Implementing effective mistake-proofing strategies requires an understanding of red-flag and error conditions that cause defects. Red-flag conditions include high complexity, an inability to measure performance, poorly written procedures, poorly maintained tools, little or no formal worker training, poor environmental conditions, stressful working conditions, and utilizing capacity beyond a stable level (i.e., the system's rated design throughput). If red-flag conditions exist, then the likelihood of an error condition occurring increases.

Error conditions may or may not lead to a defect, depending on whether the defect is prevented from occurring. Error conditions include processing omissions, processing errors, errors in setting up work, missing components, inclusion of incorrect components, completing the wrong job, operation errors, measurement errors, tool or equipment errors, and defects in job components. An example of an error condition using an invoicing example are no stamp on the envelope (processing omission), incorrect signature (processing error), incorrect spreadsheet formula (set-up error), left out the profitability analysis (assembly omission), incorrect postage (incorrect component), incorrect letter placed in the envelope (incorrect job), incorrect spelling (operations error), incorrect measurement of the envelope weight (measurement error), machine fails to stamp envelop (equipment error), and copy toner ran out (defective component). These error conditions are exacerbated by red-flag conditions.

Although error conditions may exist, this does not imply a defect occurs. The error may be identified as it is being created and then corrected. The important concept for mistake-proofing is to prevent red-flag and error conditions by simplifying and standardizing processes. If a defect does occur, correct it before it moves downstream to the customer, where corrective actions are more expensive and take longer to implement.

SUMMARY

There are numerous case studies about organizations that have successfully applied Lean tools and methods. These successes inspire others to deploy a Lean initiative in their organizations with varying levels of success. It is not that the Lean tools, methods, and concepts do not work, rather that they are often applied in an ad hoc manner and only sporadically. There is a sequence for creating an effective Lean deployment. It may take several years to stabilize a supply chain, although immediate cost savings, lead-time reductions, and higher quality levels are immediately seen, even with limited application of key Lean methods. But the full benefits, like pull scheduling and low inventory, require foundational work be implemented as shown in Figure 6.12.

Some key foundational work includes establishing metrics to measure operational improvements for on-time delivery (schedule attainment), increasing value-add time as a proportion of total time, increasing the throughput rate for a process (shortening the order-to-cash cycle), enabling faster machine or job changeovers (especially at bottleneck resource), increasing machine uptime (available time), improving the quality of work (reductions in scrap, rework, warranty, and returns), using less floor space through process simplification and changes to layouts, lowering inventory levels to expose operational problems, improving supplier on-time delivery, and lowering overall system cost. Other foundational work requires implementation of a takt time to create a baseline for a process from which waste can be systematically eliminated, and improvements in process simplification, standardization, mistake-proofing, bottleneck management, transfer batching, and mixed-model scheduling can be made. It is important that an organization determine the best scheduling rules and algorithms to manage their processes. These scheduling systems could be manual or automated based on the process. Scheduling will always be easier if the workflow has been optimally configured and Lean tools and methods are applied to simplify and standardize its operations. Finally, we discussed useful methods for reducing process waste: the eight wastes, 5-Why analysis, 5-S, Total Productive Maintenance (TPM), and mistake-proofing.

7

Measuring and Improving Productivity

OVERVIEW

This chapter covers how to link higher-level financial goals to operational projects to increase productivity. Highly competitive organizations focus on increasing productivity and shareholder economic value added (EVA). They align organizational resources to achieve their strategies in a highly competitive global environment. This helps them achieve strategic goals. These goals are also carefully selected to increase customer experience metrics, such as net promoter score, which correlates to repeat purchase intentions, and customer satisfaction. The strategy is balanced to ensure customers, employees, and other stakeholders are represented in the operational projects that enable the organizational strategy. Organizational behaviors are driven by metrics that help identify productivity and operational improvement opportunities to increase productivity. These are aligned to "voice of," financial, and operational metrics that provide a focus for resource alignment to ensure an organization works on things that will increase its competitive position over time.

There are thousands of metrics that organizations and industries use to measure, manage, and improve their products, services, and supporting processes. Some are financial, others operational, and, depending on the goal, they focus on customer satisfaction, sustainability, and interests of other stakeholders. They can be aggregated into higher classifications, such as time, money, quality, sustainability, safety, and other types, or condensed into basic lists organizations use to manage their business.

TABLE 7.1

Financial Metrics

Metric
1. Market Value Add (MVA)
2. Economic Value Add (EVA)
3. Return-on-Equity (ROE) using an average cost of debt and equity capital.
4. Productivity Measured Year-To-Year
5. Net Operating Profit After Taxes (NOPAT)

Table 7.1 lists some important financial metrics. These are business-level metrics and include shareholder EVA, which measures the profit in excess of return to shareholders (i.e., the net profit minus cost of capital), and return on equity (ROE) is the gain to shareholders over what they invested (i.e., the return on assets minus liabilities). Productivity is the ratio of sales revenue divided by operations costs to gain the revenue minus adjustments. Net operating profit after taxes (NOPAT) is revenue minus operating costs. These metrics will be used to identify projects to improve operational performance and are the basis for this chapter. The goal in this chapter is to show how higher-level financial metrics are calculated and disaggregated to identify and strategically align projects that will improve operational performance. This will ensure resources are allocated for operational effectiveness (i.e., doing the right things) and efficiency (i.e., doing them well).

Shareholder value and productivity are increased in organizations that have the right strategic direction and can execute strategies at a tactical level. Effectiveness and efficiency contribute to higher organizational productivity by effectively allocating and efficiently utilizing resources to produce products and services. Organizations do this by aligning financial measures to enable year-over-year productivity improvements as well as increase shareholder EVA and ROE. Productivity targets are incorporated into an organization's annual operational plan. This plan is based on strategic goals and is developed by the organization's leadership team to meet sales, cash flow, and operating income goals, among many others.

Examples include gaining market share and achieving safety, sustainability, and diversity goals. The strategy depends on achieving goals by deploying projects of various types. These projects are created to provide solutions for performance gaps and use different tools sets. Therefore, different initiatives are needed to improve organizational performance while implementing the strategy. It is a translation process that carefully aligns and maps higher-level goals to lower-level ones to achieve marketing, financial, and operational goals. To do this, projects must be identified, linked to strategic goals, and executed on schedule, and they must achieve the targeted benefits. They must also be realistic and provide practical solutions to close gaps.

Project linkage is where organizations sometimes lose momentum. The alignment process and execution require concerted effort and transparency. There must also be accountability for both good and poor performance. Some organizations have execution cultures. They move strategy down to a team and an individual contributor level. All employees know the impact of what they do on higher-level goals. Therefore, they work on the right things. In this context, communication is critical at all levels. The messaging must clearly link strategy at every organizational level and explain how those employees can execute the strategy. Execution cultures drive and reinforce the right behaviors through reward and recognition systems. They are laser-focused on what is important.

Some organizational cultures execute strategy well, and some do not. In the latter case, there is usually a lack of accountability, and the reward and recognition systems may be broken. There are several organizational attributes that help effectively execute strategy to increase productivity, EVA, ROE, and customer satisfaction. Organizations that have poor strategy execution and alignment to lower-level operational metrics will be hard-pressed to significantly increase productivity, even with excellent project execution. As an example, if marketing's strategic plans are inaccurate, the wrong products or services will be designed, produced, and sold. The processes may be efficient, but products and services will not be sellable at expected margins or perhaps not at all.

CALCULATING PRODUCTIVITY

Organizational productivity is calculated as an efficient utilization of labor, materials, and capital versus the revenue received by their conversion and sale. Productivity is calculated as a ratio of outputs to inputs based on inflation and economic adjustments as shown in Figure 7.1. It is calculated as a year-to-year index. Pricing adjustments and changes in international currency exchange rates are incorporated into a productivity index for the current year to ensure that, relative to internal operations, production efficiencies are accurately estimated net of the impact of external factors that are beyond an organization's immediate control. Figure 7.1 also shows that higher productivity results from simultaneously increasing sales, lowering costs, or a combination of both. Higher productivity makes an organization more adaptable because it has resources to invest well and a better ability to respond to disruptive changes. It also makes an organization more competitive. High competitiveness enables organizations to dominate their industries.

There are financial measurements that calculate the effectiveness for increasing sales, reducing costs, and managing assets. These are EVA, NOPAT, market value added (MVA), and ROE. These metrics measure the revenue versus the costs incurred to attain it. Revenue and costs are adjusted for macro-economic factors and estimated using a weighted cost of capital. They will not guarantee that future operational performance will be competitive, but they guide an organization toward improving its operational performance by ensuring resources are allocated to productive activities. The interrelationships between financial and operational performance measurements ensure alignment with available capital to increase revenue, reduce costs, or efficiently utilize assets.

NOPAT is another useful measure of organizational efficiency, unless the organization is highly leveraged financially. Higher net operating income drives higher cash flow and increases shareholder ROE. Higher operating income and cash flow enable organizations to invest in technologies such as digitization and automation to further reduce operating expense and increase cash flow. Alternatively, new products and services can be created to gain additional revenue. Evaluating NOPAT relative to the capital invested to create it enables calculation of EVA.

EVA is a measure of how well assets were managed to create the NOPAT metric. Like ROE, it can be distorted by how investments are financed and how assets are valued. Figure 7.2 shows that EVA measures the rate of return on total capital. It is calculated by dividing NOPAT by the total capital used to sustain operations. Capital is calculated as all of the cash

$$\text{Productivity} = \frac{\text{Current Year Index}}{\text{Previous Year Index}} - 1$$

$$\text{Previous Year's Index} = \frac{\text{Previous Year's Sales} - \text{Adjustments}}{\text{Previous Year's Operating Costs} - \text{Adjustments}}$$

$$\text{This Year's Index} = \frac{\text{Previous Year's Sales} - \text{Adjustments} - \text{Pricing} - \text{Exchange Rates}}{\text{Previous Year's Operating Costs} - \text{Adjustments} - \text{Exchange Rates}}$$

FIGURE 7.1
Calculating productivity.

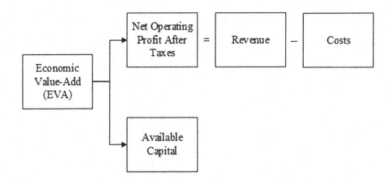

EVA = (Rate of Return − Cost of Capital) × Capital Invested

EVA = NOPAT − (Cost of Capital × Capital Invested)

FIGURE 7.2
Increasing economic value added (EVA).

invested in net assets over their useful life without adjusting for financing. The cumulative depreciation expense of assets is subtracted from their investment because their value decreases over their useful life. EVA can be increased by increasing profits with the same capital (e.g., inventory, accounts receivable, cash, facilities, and equipment), maintaining the same level of profit using fewer capital resources, or using a strategy that combines both approaches. EVA is also useful for measuring organizational performance because it focuses attention on growing sales, reducing costs, and managing assets better. These actions increase shareholder value by ensuring an investment's rate of return on invested capital is higher than the cost of that capital. This goal is to ensure capital is not assigned to projects or investments that provide a low return on invested capital. An analogy would be to invest a $100 in a bank that provides 10% interest rather than one that provides just 5%. The higher interest rate is more attractive to an investor. This is the basis for strategic alignment to tactical projects. Projects should be considered in the same way unless they must be undertaken because of laws, regulations, and other influences.

As a side note, G. Bennett Stewart III of Stern Stewart & Company describes a modification of the EVA concept in which an organization's value creation is based on its market value or MVA. The MVA is calculated by subtracting the costs of capital from an organization's market value. MVA information on 1,000 corporations is embodied in the Stern Stewart

Performance 1,000 report. However, the MVA method could be impacted by external economic factors such as stock speculation. This could bias an MVA analysis, although an argument could also be made that an organization's stock is fairly valued by the market based on an expected ROE to stockholders.

ROE shows the return shareholders received from an organization's operational effectiveness and efficiency. It is influenced by the ways in which assets are financed and valued as well as how expenses are accrued for acquisitions and how some overhead components such as research and development are recorded. In other words, the full cost of these assets may not be accurately accounted for, which would cause distortions of financial performance and, by implication, operational performance and productivity estimates. Higher ROE also favors use of debt rather than cash financing for the acquisition of capital. For this reason, it is often recommended that ROE be estimated using an average cost of debt and equity capital to provide better insight to measure shareholder equity. Productivity is directly correlated to ROE and EVA because they are aggregate measures for how well an organization manages resources and assets to support sales and revenue generation.

The ROE financial model shown in Figure 7.3 is also called a DuPont financial model based on where it was first used in practice. Average cost of debt and equity capital is used in our example. The example applies to the production of both products and services, including supporting operations such as manufacturing, purchasing, accounting, and other processes. The numbers shown in Figure 7.3 are simplified and are not related to the other examples in this chapter. The DuPont model is useful for identifying beneficial improvement projects across an organization. It helps with the evaluation of the right balance of projects to execute strategic goals while avoiding competition for scarce resources. There will need to be operational linkage to these projects when creating project charters. The model also shows how projects are linked to each other financially, as well as shareholder performance measurement (i.e., ROE). This analysis becomes a roadmap for increasing productivity.

The analysis of revenue, costs, and assets helps ensure a linkage between higher-level financial goals and the process improvements necessary to execute them. Project selection and the impact on ROE and productivity can be evaluated by varying the model's inputs, such as cost of goods sold (COGS), depreciation expense, selling expenses, and general and administrative expenses, or by increasing sales levels or pricing to evaluate the

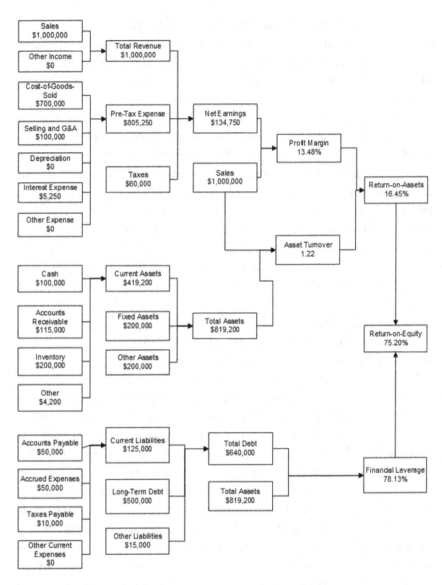

FIGURE 7.3
Return-on-equity (ROE) financial model.

impact of these changes on the model's higher-level financial and productivity ratios. Analysts can change the levels of these influential financial categories and metrics to evaluate the impact on ROE. The usefulness of this model is in guiding the focus of operational improvement efforts and

TABLE 7.2

Common Financial Ratios

Ratio	Variations of the Ratio
• Liquidity ratios measure how well an organization meets its current financial obligations.	• Current Ratio = Current Assets / Current Liabilities • Quick Ratio = (Current Assets – Inventory) / Current Liabilities
• Activity ratios measure the efficiency with which an organization uses its assets.	• Inventory Turnover = Cost of Goods Sold / Average Inventory • Days Sales Outstanding = Accounts Receivable / (Sales / 365) • Asset Turnover indicates how many dollars of sales are supported by one dollar of assets.
• Profitability ratios measure an organization's profitability.	
• Profit margin shows the percent of every sales dollar the organization converted into net income.	
• Return on Assets (ROA) relates net income to total assets.	
• Return on Equity (ROE) indicates the rate of return earned on the book value of owner's equity.	

in showing how they impact the higher-level financial metrics. This analysis also helps prioritize and align competing projects that may need the same resources. In summary, a financial model is also useful to improve MVA, EVA, NOPAT, ROE, and productivity year-to-year and to meet or exceed competitive productivity levels.

Table 7.2 lists common financial ratios used to measure operational efficiency. Improvement projects identified using these ratios will be directly tied to EVA, ROE, NOPAT, and productivity. High liquidity implies an organization is not highly leveraged with debt and can self-finance investments in areas such as digitization and automation as well as improvement projects to eliminate current process issues. It also reminds leadership that internal improvement projects need to generate returns higher than the cost of invested capital; that is, it will see higher improvements in its financial metrics (i.e., EVA, ROE, and productivity metrics). High liquidity makes an organization more competitive because it can quickly apply resources to areas experiencing competitive threats or to those where sales can either be increased or operating costs reduced. In other words, high liquidity increases an organization's adaptability.

Activity ratios show the efficiency with which assets are utilized. Competitive organizations have high activity ratios. As an example, inventory turnover measures how well inventory assets are managed to support sales as approximated by COGS. As an example, for constant COGS, the lower the required inventory invested in raw materials, work in process, and finished goods inventories, the higher the inventory turnover ratio. An inventory turnover ratio can also be calculated for a single product or all products in combination.

But activity ratios can also be misleading. A classic example is running a machine to achieve 100% efficiency, but without incoming demand. The results are high inventory build-up with all the associated issues and low relative throughput rates, which lengthen the lead time from order to cash. Recall the bottleneck example, where a resource should only be activated to match its throughput to a bottleneck. This implies if there is no demand then machines should be idle. This was a paradigm shift in the 1980s because many American manufacturers designed and employed large complicated machines with high throughput rates. These machines needed to be kept busy (i.e., 100% utilized) to generate positive payback. In contrast, Japanese manufacturers such as Toyota employed simple and low-cost machines in parallel that were idle until external demand required they be activated for production. Asset utilization needs to be carefully thought out to ensure no adverse impacts elsewhere in the organization.

Table 7.3 shows the general ledger of a hypothetical profit center for the years 2018 and 2019. This information will be used to demonstrate the usefulness of financial analysis by process improvement professionals to identify improvement projects to increase productivity and competitiveness. The ledger contains a large amount of information that can be used to identify projects. Just by looking at the changes to accounts between 2018 and 2019, there are some positive changes. These include lower inventory investment and a reduction of liabilities. But the negative changes are significant. Shareholder equity and revenue are down in 2019, and labor costs and accounts receivables increased. More detailed analysis will help focus on where operational and other improvements would be useful.

The next step is to create the income statement as shown in Table 7.4 for the year 2019 with income and expenses. This statement is a snapshot

TABLE 7.3

Profit Center General Ledger

#	Account Identification	2018 Baseline (000) Facility 1	Facility 2	Facility 3	Total	2019 Actual (000) Facility 1	Facility 2	Facility 3	Total	Difference
1	Cash	$ -	$ -	$ 85,000	$ 85,000	$ -	$ -	$ 168,000	$ 168,000	$ 83,000
2	Accounts Receivables	$ -	$ -	$ 2,500,000	$ 2,500,000	$ -	$ -	$ 3,100,000	$ 3,100,000	$ 600,000
3	Inventory	$ -	$ -	$ 3,250,000	$ 3,250,000	$ -	$ -	$ 2,500,000	$ 2,500,000	$ (750,000)
4	Inventory Reserve	$ -	$ -	$ (45,000)	$ (45,000)	$ -	$ -	$ (28,000)	$ (28,000)	$ 17,000
5	Plant, Property & Equipment	$ -	$ -	$ 8,000,000	$ 8,000,000	$ -	$ -	$ 9,500,000	$ 9,500,000	$ 1,500,000
6	Accumulated Depreciation	$ -	$ -	$ (6,000,000)	$ (6,000,000)	$ -	$ -	$ (7,500,000)	$ (7,500,000)	$ (1,500,000)
7	Additional Assets	$ -	$ -	$ 1,200,000	$ 1,200,000	$ -	$ -	$ 950,000	$ 950,000	$ (250,000)
8	Accounts Payables	$ -	$ -	$ (3,250,000)	$ (3,250,000)	$ -	$ -	$ (3,200,000)	$ (3,200,000)	$ 50,000
9	Additional Liabilities	$ -	$ -	$ 1,900,000	$ 1,900,000	$ -	$ -	$ (2,100,000)	$ (2,100,000)	$ (4,000,000)
10	Equity	$ -	$ -	$ 7,640,000	$ 7,640,000	$ -	$ -	$ 3,390,000	$ 3,390,000	$ (4,250,000)
11	Revenue	$ (675,000)	$ (450,000)	$ (600,000)	$ (1,725,000)	$ (700,000)	$ (500,000)	$ (650,000)	$ (1,850,000)	$ (125,000)
12	Equity Income	$ -	$ -	$ 1,200	$ 1,200	$ -	$ -	$ 1,200	$ 1,200	$ 1,200
13	Direct Labor &Fringe	$ 55,000	$ 20,000	$ -	$ 75,000	$ 61,000	$ 25,000	$ -	$ 86,000	$ 11,000
14	Indirect Labor & Fringe	$ -	$ -	$ 135,000	$ 135,000	$ -	$ -	$ 150,800	$ 175,000	$ 40,000
15	Overtime Premium	$ -	$ 8,000	$ -	$ 8,000	$ 8,700	$ -	$ -	$ 55,000	$ 47,000
16	Salary & Fringe	$ -	$ -	$ 280,000	$ 280,000	$ -	$ -	$ 302,016	$ 302,016	$ 22,016
17	Inventory Obsolescence	$ -	$ -	$ 250	$ 250	$ -	$ -	$ 1,500	$ 1,500	$ 1,250
18	MRO	$ 9,500	$ 8,500	$ -	$ 18,000	$ 9,100	$ 9,200	$ -	$ 18,300	$ 300
19	Depreciation	$ 19,000	$ 9,500	$ 4,100	$ 32,600	$ 29,000	$ 16,000	$ 4,300	$ 49,300	$ 16,700
20	Contracted Services	$ 5,800	$ -	$ 4,500	$ 10,300	$ 11,000	$ -	$ 5,000	$ 16,000	$ 5,700
21	Materials to CGS	$ 230,000	$ 65,000	$ -	$ 295,000	$ 196,000	$ 66,000	$ -	$ 310,000	$ 15,000
22	Scrap	$ 900	$ 900	$ -	$ 1,800	$ 800	$ 1,100	$ -	$ 1,900	$ 100
	Total Operating Cost	$ 320,200	$ 111,900	$ 423,850	$ 855,950	$ 315,600	$ 117,300	$ 462,416	$ 1,015,016	$ 159,066
	Volume	3,000	1,000	2,000		4,000	2,000	3000		

Note: Sales are positive and set negative for calculations on this table.

TABLE 7.4

2019 Profit Center Income Statement

Revenue		
Sales	$	1,850,000
Equity Income	$	1,200
Operating Expenses		
Direct Labor &Fringe	$	86,000
Indirect Labor & Fringe	$	175,000
Overtime Premium	$	55,000
Salary & Fringe	$	302,016
Inventory Obsolescence	$	1,500
MRO	$	18,300
Depreciation	$	49,300
Contracted Services	$	16,000
Materials to CGS	$	310,000
Scrap	$	1,900
Income	$	836,184
Taxes	$	-
Net Income	$	836,184

of a company's profitability over the specified period (i.e., 2019). It should be noted that an income statement can be impacted by the accounting method used to calculate expenses. As an example, most organizations use an accrual rather than a cash accounting system. In an accrual system, revenues from sales are recorded when they are earned, and expenses are recorded in anticipation of their incurrence. The accrual system contrasts with a cash system in which revenue and expenses are recorded as they occur without an accrual of future expenses. The choice of accounting method has an impact on income for the period under consideration.

Although this income statement can be used to identify projects by increasing revenue or reducing expenses, it needs to be compared to the prior year and percent changes must be calculated to determine negative or positive impacts. Ideally, several years would be used in this analysis. These should be carefully analyzed for their significance. As an example, an expense analysis would compare year-to-year expenses by type. If expenses increased more than the adjusted sales, projects can be used to investigate the root causes and reduce expenses. There could be several projects in any category, and several different projects could be focused across different categories. The advantage of a top-down approach for project identification is that the projects are financially linked to metrics that directly impact productivity. If they are also strategically aligned, then the organization will be more competitive with higher productivity. Alignment implies that projects promote the current strategic goals. These could be revenue increases in certain market segments, inventory reductions for products being obsolesced, direct labor reductions for products or services that have low profit margins, or other types of projects.

Next, we construct a balance sheet of an organization's profit using information shown in Table 7.5. Components of a balance sheet include assets, liabilities, and shareholder equity. Assets are resources owned by a business that are expected to benefit future operations by creating a revenue stream that exceeds the cost of the asset. The rate of return versus

TABLE 7.5

2019 Profit Center Balance Sheet

Assets		
Cash	$	168,000
Accounts Receivables	$	3,100,000
Inventory	$	2,500,000
Inventory Reserve	$	(28,000)
Plant, Property & Equipmen	$	9,500,000
Accumulated Depreciation	$	(7,500,000)
Additional Assets	$	950,000
Total Assets	**$**	**8,690,000**
Liabilities		
Accounts Payables	$	3,200,000
Additional Liabilities	$	2,100,000
Equity	$	3,390,000
Total Liabilities and Equity	$	8,690,000

the cost of capital invested in an asset is the basis of the EVA calculation shown in Figure 7.2. Asset acquisition, management, and disposal require ongoing evaluation.

Productivity improvement projects are created based on an evaluation for how assets are acquired, managed, and disposed of by an organization. Evaluations can be made to determine if assets should be purchased or leased. Financial models can show the advantages of each approach. Asset conversion, through the sale or leasing of assets to others, frees up cash for investments that could create higher rates of return on investment. This occurs if assets are used or consumed to increase sales or reduce operating costs. Examples include reducing inventory to such a low amount that a facility can be sold or used for other purposes. In addition to reducing asset investment, cost savings are realized by not having to maintain the asset or by paying interest expense to borrow capital. Remote working dramatically can reduce operating expenses associated with fixed assets such as an office building. Expenses such as energy, maintenance, and materials are also significantly reduced by remote work, and employees benefit from reduced commuting expenses. These are disruptive changes to how an organization works. They increase productivity and competitiveness.

Liabilities are debts or obligations to creditors. They reduce the asset value of a business. They include accounts payables, loans, and other debt. Projects can be deployed to reduce liabilities such as late fees or to pay off loans and debt. Examples include refinancing or selling an asset and leasing it from a third party. From a process perspective, these processes (e.g., the accounts payable and others that incur debt) can be simplified and standardized through process-focused projects. The third section of a balance sheet is shareholder equity. This is calculated as assets minus liabilities. It is a measure of a shareholder's net investment in the business. The relationship between the three balance sheet categories is assets = liabilities + shareholders equity.

Different types of financial analyses are made to examine financial and operational performance and their interrelationships. One type is shown in Table 7.6. It is an evaluation of changes to pricing for three production facilities for the years 2018 and 2019. We see pricing was negative for 2019 relative to 2018 for three production facilities. The negative pricing reflects the fact that there was price erosion of the aggregate products manufactured by all three facilities. The next step would be to evaluate the specific pricing of each product at the three facilities to identify the reasons for the price erosion. There

TABLE 7.6

Evaluating Price Changes

Sales =Volume*Price

2019	Facility 1	Facility 2	Facility 3
Sales	$ 700,000	$ 500,000	$ 650,000
Volume	$ 4,000	$ 2,000	$ 3,000
Price	$ 175	$ 250	$ 217

2018			
Sales	$ 675,000	$ 450,000	$ 600,000
Volume	$ 3,000	$ 1,000	$ 2,000
Price	$ 225	$ 450	$ 300
Price Change	-22%	-44%	-28%

All three facilities have a price erosion problem

could have been several causes, such as adjustments of warranty issues, price concessions to offset external competition, or other adjustments.

Pricing is important to maintain target profit margin, assuming the COGS is constant. Although competitiveness may be temporarily increased because of higher sales, productivity and longer-term competitiveness will decrease.

Issues associated with negative pricing help identify projects. As an example, warranty problems could have occurred due to design problems, poor user training, or poor production quality. Competitors may have lowered prices, forcing a temporary response. Or for situations characterized by poor product forecasting, forecasted quantities may have exceeded actual demand and created excess inventory or product obsolescence problems, and these products may need to be sold at a lower margin. In summary, there may be many different reasons for price erosion. A root-cause analysis of pricing issues and their elimination will have a positive impact on productivity and long-term competitiveness.

TABLE 7.7

Evaluating Year-over-Year operating Income and Margin

		2018		2019	Change	% Change
Revenue	$	1,725,000	$	1,850,000	$125,000	7%
Operating Expenses						
Direct Labor &Fringe	$	75,000	$	86,000	$ 11,000	15%
Indirect Labor & Fring	$	135,000	$	175,000	$ 40,000	30%
Overtime Premium	$	8,000	$	55,000	$ 47,000	588%
Salary & Fringe	$	280,000	$	302,016	$ 22,016	8%
Inventory Obsolescenc	$	250	$	1,500	$ 1,250	500%
MRO	$	18,000	$	18,300	$ 300	2%
Depreciation	$	32,600	$	49,300	$ 16,700	51%
Contracted Services	$	10,300	$	16,000	$ 5,700	55%
Materials to CGS	$	295,000	$	310,000	$ 15,000	5%
Scrap	$	1,800	$	1,900	$ 100	6%
Operating Income	$	869,050	$	834,984	$(34,066)	-4%
Operating Margin%		50%		45%	-10%	

Table 7.7 shows an analysis of operating income and margin. This financial statement is particularly useful for identifying operational improvements to increase productivity. Revenue variation stems from year-to-year changes in sales, inflation, and currency valuations as well as adjustments caused by returns, warranty, pricing changes, and other concessions. Changes to operating expenses are positively impacted by investment such as automation, process improvements, supplier discounts, or other factors that reduce expenses. Negative changes are caused by higher expenses. Many reasons for higher expenses require improvement projects be created to investigate them. Year-to-year changes in expenses are relevant if adjusted to revenue. Their magnitude is also an important criterion for further investigation.

Table 7.7 shows that sales revenue increased by 7% from 2018 to 2019, but operating income decreased by 4% and operating margin by 10% over the basis year 2018. The erosion of operating income and margin

TABLE 7.8

Measurement Net Income

	2018	**2019**
Operating Income	$869,050	$834,984
Equity Income	$ 1,200	$ 1,200
Taxes		
Measurement Net Income	$870,250	$836,184

Components: Operating Income/Royalties/Equity
Income/Other Income/Taxes

was caused by increases in all the expense categories listed in Table 7.7. The indirect labor and overtime categories had large increases, and the 2019 expenses were large relative to 2018. Projects can be deployed in these higher percentage categories. As an example, the causes for higher overtime and indirect labor cost could be investigated. Analysis and elimination of the root causes for high operating expenses will help improve operating income and margin as well as organizational productivity. An adjustment can also be made to operating income to evaluate it net of taxes and additional income sources. This is shown in Table 7.8. Higher income is important for internal investment, to pay down debt, or to pay dividends, or it can be retained to increase shareholder equity.

The lead time of an order-to-cash process is shown in Figure 7.4. The shorter the order-to-cash lead time, the higher the free cash flow available for supporting operations. In other words, money will be available sooner. Available cash can be used to finance additional production or for other purposes. In contrast, if free cash flow is low, then money needs to be borrowed to finance operations and investments such as equipment, facilities, and other assets, and borrowed money incurs interest expense. In some situations, organizations are highly leveraged because they build inventory, hire employees, or purchase assets. If this investment is not converted into cash, an organization's financial position deteriorates and productivity decreases. This situation occurred in the automotive industry when the wrong vehicles were made because of poor forecasting or demand did not

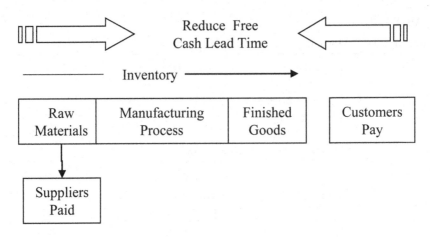

FIGURE 7.4
Compressing the cash flow lead time.

materialize. In some situations, inventory rapidly becomes obsolete and is never converted into cash. Instead it must be written off the balance sheet as a loss. This reduces competitiveness.

Analysis of its order-to-cash flow lead time enables an organization to understand how its cash is used and to develop strategies to manage it more effectively. This is the velocity flow of invested cash. For some highly efficient organizations, cash flow is optimized to where customers pay for products or services before the supplier pays for the labor, materials, and overhead that were used to create them. Organizations can utilize several strategies to compress their order-to-cash lead time, such as paying suppliers as late as possible or offering customers pricing discounts for early payment. Lead time can also be reduced by simplifying or leaning out supply chain processes.

Table 7.9 shows a cash flow analysis at a single point in time using the information from Table 7.3. The analysis shows cash increased by $1,186,184 in 2019 relative to the basis year 2018. This cash flow increase was based on reductions in inventory investment, the sale of other assets, and increases in depreciation expense that reduced income taxes. This extra cash can be used for capital investment to increase sales revenue or to decrease operating expenses. Improvement projects can also be applied to these processes.

TABLE 7.9

2019 Cash Flow Analysis

Cash Flow	2019
Measurement Net Income	$ 836,184
-Increase in Accounts Receivable	$ (600,000)
+Increase in Accounts Payable	$ (50,000)
+Net Change in Inventory	$ 750,000
+Change in Other Assets and Liabilities	$ 250,000
+Depreciation	$ 1,500,000
-Capital Expenditure Paid in Cash	$ (1,500,000)
Cash Creation	**$1,186,184**

Changes in working capital is bracketed alongside the rows "-Increase in Accounts Receivable" through "-Capital Expenditure Paid in Cash".

There are four methods commonly used to evaluate the investment cost versus benefits from projects: net present value (NPV), internal rate of return (IRR), payback period, and the average rate of return (ARR). These are shown in Table 7.10. When evaluating capital expenditures or other investment decisions, the time value of money is important, as is the interest earned if money were safely invested with a guaranteed rate of return. A dollar earned in the future will be worth less than one earned today for the simple reason that we could earn interest on today's dollar and external economic conditions such as inflation or currency exchange rates may impact the value of a future dollar. Earning guaranteed interest on money is a logical investment alternative. These concepts are used to evaluate whether cash should be invested in a project for productive purposes.

The NPV method compares the present value of a project's future cash flows to an initial investment cost. The comparison is made relative to its minimum rate of return compared to a safe investment. The rule is that an investment should be undertaken if its NPV is positive or its return is higher than what could be obtained from a safer investment. It is important to determine a project's expected cash inflows relative to project risks throughout the life of the project to ensure the NPV is accurate. As an example, in some projects, the cash inflows occur early while in other projects they occur toward the end of the project. Cash flows derived from

242 • *Operational Excellence*

TABLE 7.10

Evaluating Potential Investments

Cost and Benefit Method

1. Net present value (NPV) is a calculation of all cash inflows, positive and negative. Investments are negative cash outflows. Project savings are treated as positive cash inflows. When evaluating multiple alternatives select the project with the greatest NPV.

2. Internal-Rate-of-Return (IRR) is the rate of return that a project earns over the period of its evaluation.

Initial Investment	$20,000
Investment Useful Life	10 years
Annual Cash Inflow	$4,000
Cost of Capital	10%
Present Value of Annuity Factor	5
The Approximate IRR	16%

3. The "payback" method calculates the number of years that is required before a project recovers its initial investment. It does not discount future cash inflows.

Payback Period = Initial Investment/Annual Cash Inflow

4. The average-rate-of-return (ARR) method is the project's average cash inflows minus depreciation divided by the initial investment of the project.

ARR = [(Cash Inflows per Year)-(Depreciation)]/Initial Investment

the latter scenario will have more risk because external factors have more time to influence the project.

The IRR method evaluates the NPV of a project's cash inflows and out-flows. If the IRR is equal to or greater than the minimum required rate of return, then the project should be undertaken. The minimum required rate of return depends on project risk and the availability of other invest-ment alternatives. When an organization has more investment opportuni-ties than available cash, it may rank projects to invest in those with a target minimum IRR.

The payback method calculates a simple ratio of the initial investment divided by the project's annual cash inflow. It does not consider the time value of money, but it does provide a quick estimate of the project's costs versus benefits. The ARR calculation divides a project's cash inflows minus depreciation by the initial investment. The investment alterative having the highest ARR is selected. The time value of money is ignored in the ARR analysis, and income rather than cash flow data is used for its calculation. ARR also evaluates the full useful life of the investment. Organizations usually have finance policies that determine the preferred evaluation method. There may be others that are specific to an organization's industry.

The example shown in Figure 7.5 calculates productivity using the formulas from Figure 7.1 and the information in Table 7.3. The productivity improvement is shown to be 6.9% when comparing year 2019 to 2018. This implies the organization used less resources to achieve revenue gains by managing its operations effectively. This analysis can be applied to several organizational levels using cost center reports. The advantage is that it provides a direct view of how effectively and efficiently managed organizations use resources to gain incremental revenues. It also helps identify impactful improvement projects to further increase productivity. These would need to be aligned to strategy. Recall that the initial review of Table 7.3 showed some categories increased while others decreased. But by integrating all of the information into the analysis, we can evaluate progress made toward higher productivity and, by implication, competitiveness.

Several of the higher-level financial metrics in Table 7.3 have also improved from 2018 to 2019. This higher productivity is assumed to have occurred through process improvements that increased revenue, reduced cost, and utilized assets more efficiently. The productivity index was also impacted by pricing. As a final observation, productivity is a total supply chain concept. It needs to be calculated throughout a supply chain and optimized based on available labor, capital, technology, and knowledge. Recall that factor productivity was discussed in Chapter 1 from a macroeconomic perspective and is like the application of technology and knowledge to improve the use of productive resources (i.e., labor and capital). Productivity evaluations should be made across an organization's operations as well as the end-to-end supply chain participants. In other words, it makes little sense from a competitiveness perspective to only optimize productive operations but not other operations such as marketing, sales, design, and supporting back office processes.

$$\text{Productivity} = \frac{2.16}{2.02} - 1 = \boxed{6.9\%}$$

$$\text{Previous Year's Index} = \frac{1{,}725{,}000}{855{,}950} = 2.02$$

$$\text{This Year's Index} = \frac{1{,}850{,}000 + 185{,}000}{1{,}015{,}016 - 11{,}000 - 40{,}000 - 22{,}016} = 2.16$$

Pricing Impact = $1,850,000 × 10% = 185,000

Direct Labor Increase = $11,000

Indirect Labor Increase = $40,000

Salary Increase = $22,016

FIGURE 7.5
2019 Productivity analysis.

IDENTIFYING PROJECTS

Figure 7.6 shows how a production process should be managed to execute an organization's strategic goals and objectives. An organization's financial performance and productivity and competitiveness depend on how well it manages all resources relative to a competitive strategy. At an operational level, the goal will always be to select a combination of projects, tools, and methods to improve process yields, increase system availability and capacity, and reduce lead times to support the production of product and services. This is accomplished by effective application of enabling initiatives to create core competencies. As an example, to improve yield, Six Sigma tools and methods help identify the root causes of low yields and guide productive solutions. Lean tools and methods reduce lead times

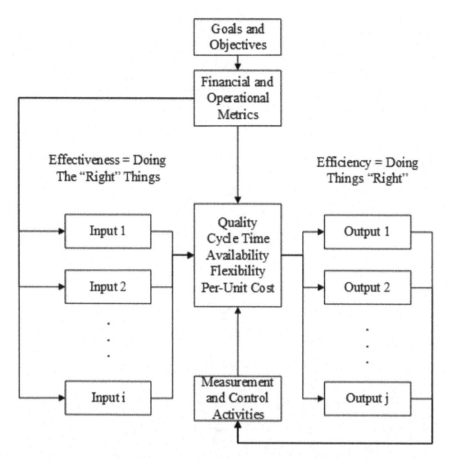

FIGURE 7.6
Evaluating productivity at an operational level.

through process simplification, standardization, and mistake-proofing using customer value and serves as a guide to eliminate process waste. This increases system availability and capacity to help meet demand, but with fewer resources.

Financial and operational data are used to identify productivity opportunities down to a process level. Figure 7.7 shows how this identification process is achieved using a flow-down model. It could start at any level of Figure 7.7, but, when completed, lower-level projects and their metrics should be aligned with higher-level metrics. As an example, we might

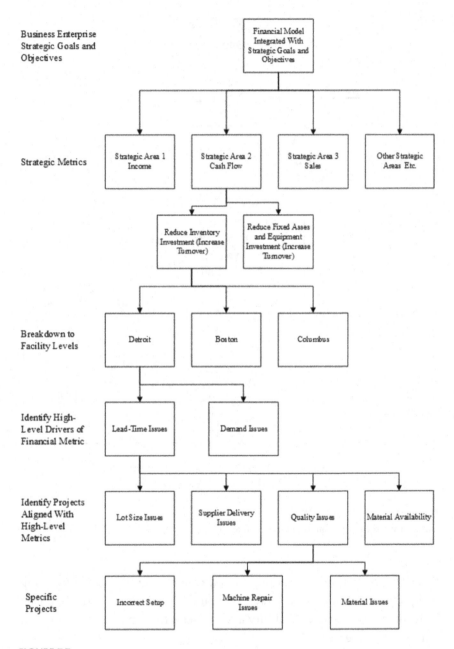

FIGURE 7.7
Aligning operational improvements with strategy.

begin the project identification at a business enterprise level and then successively move down to a project level. Alternatively, we could start the analysis from the bottom up, working upward from a major process issue. The top-down model is generally easier.

In the example shown in Figure 7.7, the high-level financial goal is cash flow improvement. Two areas impact cash flow and thus provide improvement opportunities. These are inventory reductions and fixed asset investment. The next step of the analysis might be to evaluate inventory investment (turnover ratio) for each of the facilities. Recall that the inventory turnover ratio is defined as the COGS divided by the average inventory investment necessary to support the COGS. The lower the inventory investment at a constant COGS level, the higher its turnover ratio. Taking the analysis down another level, the two major drivers of inventory are lead time (or demand over lead time) and demand variation. The longer the process lead time, the more work in process and finished goods inventory that will be needed until more inventory is received to replenish safety stocks. Also, the higher the variation of demand, the higher the safety-stock inventory required to meet demand at the targeted service level.

Continuing the analysis down through lead time shows several new categories that directly impact lead time. Any operational issues that increase the operation's cycle time also increases system lead time. Depending on lead time and inventory investment impacts, process issues are potential improvement projects. In this example, lot size, supplier delivery, quality, and material availability impact lead time and hence inventory investment. The larger a lot size, the more inventory being kept on-hand. Large lot sizes occur for several reasons. These include suppliers requiring minimum purchases, a lack of visibility of on-hand inventory, and inaccurate container calculations. Additional inventory needs to be kept on-hand to ensure internal operations are not disrupted in the event a supplier misses a delivery. Quality issues require work be redone, which interrupts production schedules and lengthens the lead time for receipt of goods from suppliers. If internal materials are not available, production must wait, and lead times are lengthened. Some reasons for lack of available materials include poor inventory records, damage when transporting materials, and poor quality that is detected only after taken from inventory storage. Lean or Six Sigma projects can be created to address these process issues.

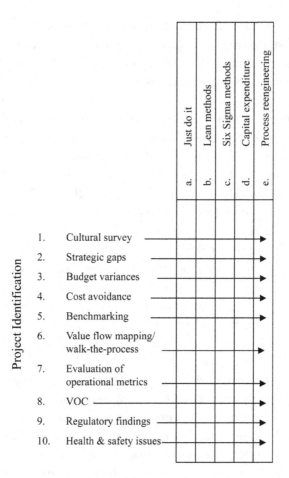

FIGURE 7.8
Project selection versus process improvement strategy.

Consultants gather information for each of the categories shown in Figure 7.8, looking for performance gaps when conducting operational assessments. These include cultural surveys, strategic gaps that need to be closed, financial analysis such as budget variances, identification of cost-avoidance opportunities, benchmarking other processes either internally or externally, value flow mapping (VFM), evaluation of other internal metrics including operational, the voice of the customer (VOC), regulatory findings and health incidents, as well as safety and environmental issues that impact the organization. These are analyzed and prioritized for action. The project charters are created and integrated into current organizational initiatives, and these are incorporated into the annual planning with periodic reporting of status.

Cultural surveys are one-on-one interviews or online surveys at different organizational levels. They help identify performance gaps using information provided by employees and other stakeholders. Online surveys are used to ask questions of selected employee groups, suppliers, or customers, depending on the survey's scope. There may also be follow-up questions. The goal of cultural surveys is to assess the organizations readiness for change. Questions should focus on previous initiatives and how they were deployed. Why were they successful? What were the benefits? What were the issues that should be avoided for future initiatives? Ideally, the questions will enable an analysis of the top issues, benefits, success characteristics, and similar themes. One good question format is, "What are your top three gaps or issues?," "What would be solutions to these issues?," and "Which types of improvement projects would create the greatest benefits for your organization?" Employee feedback gained from cultural surveys is useful for looking for areas that offer productivity opportunities.

Strategic performance gaps occur when strategic goals need to be executed but some have no solutions. Productivity opportunities (i.e., projects) have not been identified to close the gaps. The focus for identifying ways to close strategic gaps is to list the gaps and bring a team together to brainstorm actions or projects that would be good candidates for closing these gaps. The common approach is to analyze financial and operational reports that show the gaps and work the brainstorming exercise from that perspective. Then projects are created with charters and are integrated into current initiatives and their reporting.

This chapter discussed several approaches for identifying improvement projects using financial reports. Budget variances are used to identify abnormal changes in budgets. Cost avoidance projects are also good candidates for improvement projects if their basis is rigorously verified. An example would be a situation in which a material currently being used to build a product needs to be replaced in the future because of regulatory requirements. Failure to replace the material in a timely manner could result in future fines or prohibition of use, resulting in the product not being manufactured.

Internal and external benchmarking were discussed in Chapter 3. They were shown to be a useful for gathering process improvement information. Benchmarking can serve as a basis for identifying opportunity to increase productivity. In some instances, disruptive approaches for process improvement may dramatically improve performance. As an example, if an organization benchmarked an industry competitor to reduce facility costs, they may find that the benchmarked organization dramatically reduced facility costs by enabling remote work for a portion of their workforce. In addition to saving facility costs for things such as energy and maintenance, entire locations may have been sold or leases not renewed. An advantage of benchmarking is that, although an idea like remote working may have been discussed internally, seeing it work with testimonials is a powerful way to effect change. Another example would be finding a new solution to a chronic problem. Current policy may require sending invoices via mail to obtain signatures, whereas other organisms may use encrypted e-mail that controls access and provides sign-off approvals to dramatically reduce lead times and cost. In summary, benchmarking identifies differences between organizations' process performance that may illuminate opportunities for creating improvement projects.

Because some process issues are not captured in management reports (e.g., the hidden factory) it is always useful to walk a process to identify the process waste associated with non-value-add operations. VFM and other Lean tools and methods discussed in Chapter 6 are useful for these process walk-throughs. There are likely many opportunities to simplify, standardize, and mistake-proof processes. Normally a workshop is held to bring together a team representing the process and its inputs and outputs. The VFM is created or displayed on a wall, and the operations are evaluated for customer value. Process waste is added to the VFM, as are relevant metrics. These include cycle time, rework and scrap, inventory, uptime, throughputs, floor space, and other information for each operation to provide insights into issues and potential projects.

In Chapter 3 we discussed customer experience and how it can be used to identify gaps in that experience. These gaps span the activities customers engage in to research and decide to purchase through use of products and services as well as disposal. This customer journey focuses on customer satisfaction and customer intent to repurchase. Customer experience projects increase revenue while reducing adjustments to revenue. These types of projects directly increase the numerator in the productivity equation. The denominator is also decreased when concession expenses are reduced for poor quality and other issues. Listening to the VOC through marketing research, complaints, one-to-one interviews, surveys, and on-site visits also provides ideas for process improvement.

The final categories shown in Figure 7.8 are regulatory, health, safety, and environmental issues. These are also good projects for increasing productivity. In many situations they are required by law or regulation. Direct impact to the profit and loss statement is seen with fines, worker injuries, and other expenses. There are situations where complying with laws and regulations improves a competitive position. An example is deploying technology that has reduced environmental emissions. Some organizations invest in technologies that have this advantage, whereas those that do not cannot sell products in regulated markets.

Figure 7.8 also shows several solutions that are employed to execute a project. These are just-do-it projects, Lean methods, Six Sigma methods, capital expenditures, and process reengineering. Many projects have a known solution. For these projects, the root causes should be eliminated as soon as possible without extensive analysis. These are called just-do-it projects. In situations with a very complicated process, Lean methods are used to simplify and standardize the process as described in Chapter 6. Lean methods can also be applied to a specific set of issues. 5-S and mistake-proofing are examples, but there are many others. If root causes are process-focused and an analysis of the process is useful, then the application of well-known Lean tools and methods is recommended. In situations that require extensive data analysis, Six Sigma methods may be appropriate. These will be discussed in Chapter 9.

There are also situations where machines wear out and cannot hold a designed tolerance. The solution is known: new tooling or machines are needed to improve quality. In other situations, a new machine or process design is needed to produce upgraded or entirely new products and services. Enhancements may also be needed relative to digitization and automation. These require investment of capital expenditures.

Reengineering may also be required. This includes changes to policy, process, people (i.e., roles and responsibilities), outsourcing, or other major changes. These may or may not require investment. Projects may be required for these changes because a root-cause analysis is typically the reason for the recommendations for these changes.

The operational goal is to align the deployment of improvement projects and their tool sets and methods to improve financial performance and

TABLE 7.11

Linking Projects to Achieve Productivity Targets

Project Focus	Initiative/ Toolset	Key Productivity Enabler	Financial Statement Impact
Reduced Order to Cash Lead Time	Deploy Lean Projects	Increase Throughput	Labor and Increase Available Capacity
Increase Inventory Turns/ Reduce Investment	Lean Projects to Reduce Lead-Time	Reduce Average Inventory Levels to Increase Turns	Reduce Holding Costs and Material Handling Expenses
Increase Manufacturing Yield	Deploy Six Sigma Projects	Reduce Scrap and Rework	Reduce Material and Labor Expense
Reduce Unscheduled Maintenance	Total Productive Maintenance (TPM)	Increased Equipment Availability and Reduce Downtime Expense	Reduce Direct Labor Cost and Increased Capacity

productivity. Table 7.11 shows how to make this alignment. This discussion is an extension of Table 1.1, which describes enabler initiatives. The projects shown in Table 7.11 are aligned to the initiative and tool set most useful for its root-cause analysis and identification of solutions. The relevant operational and financial metrics are also shown. As an example, increasing throughput will reduce order-to-cash lead time when a process is simplified and standardized and the appropriate Lean methods are applied to maintain the takt time. Increasing manufacturing yields directly reduces the direct labor and material costs used by a production process. This is because scrap and rework are invested material and labor that need additional work. There are many other relevant examples throughout various industries and functions within a given industry. Table 7.11 shows that metric linkages should be set for all projects to ensure alignment between the customer, finance, and operations to optimally use scarce resources and increase productivity.

Administrative Information

•Project name
•Business unit
•Sponsor
•Schedule
•Date
•Stakeholders
•Project team
•Project lead
•Cost and benefits

Project Definition

•Business case
•Scope
•Metrics
•Problem statement
•Critical to customer outcomes (project deliverables)
•Cost
•Benefits

FIGURE 7.9
Common elements of a project charter.

Project improvement opportunities are incorporated into a project charter like the one shown in Figure 7.9. There are many different versions of project charters, but the list of common elements is used for most of them. A charter describes the problem and its extent (i.e., the scope), its impact on the organization, costs and benefits, its deliverables, its sponsorship, the leader of the team, the team, resource requirements, and the schedule. To fully document the costs and benefits, a project charter should have a separate section that shows the assumptions of the financial analyses of the project's cash inflows, outflows, required investment, applicable financial ratios such as payback and IRR, as well as their impact on customer satisfaction and productivity. Charters are also communication tools for stakeholders that help garner organizational support. Finally, project charters are useful when aggregating several projects into a program or initiative to align the work to strategic goals.

SUMMARY

Highly competitive organizations focus on increasing productivity and shareholder EVA. They align organizational resources to achieve their strategies in a highly competitive global environment. This moves them closer to competitive goals. These are carefully selected to also increase customer experience metrics such as a net promoter score, which correlates to repeat-purchase intentions and customer satisfaction. Project linkage is where some organizations lose momentum. The alignment process and execution require concerted effort and transparency. There must also be accountability for both good and poor performance. Some organizations have execution cultures. These organizations move strategy down to a team and an individual contributor level. Employees understand the impact of what they do on higher-level goals. Therefore, they work on the right things. In this context, communication is critical at all levels.

Organizational productivity is calculated as an efficient utilization of labor, materials, and capital versus the revenue received by their conversion and sale. It is calculated by taking a ratio of outputs to inputs based on inflation and economically adjustments as shown in Figure 7.1. It is calculated as a year-to-year index. There are several approaches for identifying improvement projects using financial reports to increase productivity. Project charters help describe productivity projects. A charter describes the problem and its extent (i.e., the scope), its impact on the organization, costs and benefits, its deliverables that are tied to strategic goals, its sponsorship, the leader of the team, the team, resource requirements, and the schedule. To fully document the costs and benefits, a project charter should have a separate section that shows the assumptions of the financial analyses of the project's cash inflows, outflows, required investment, applicable financial ratios such as payback and IRR, as well as their impact on customer satisfaction and productivity.

8

Information Technology Ecosystems

OVERVIEW

Twenty years ago, data accuracy focused on metadata across one or a few systems, and the analysis was usually local. Information technology ecosystems were few in number and accessible only through a few subject matter experts. In large corporations today, hundreds of systems are stitched together end-to-end with the metadata needed to execute the quote-to-cash and related workflows. In large organizations, there may be several hundred workflows and thousands of process steps, each containing work instructions and other information needed to transform data into usable information. Figure 8.1 describes a generic quote-to-cash ecosystem. Other workstream examples include new product introduction, manufacturing planning, procurement and sourcing, marketing, master data management, sales enablement, reporting of various types, accounting and tax compliance, customer service issues and reverse logistics management, human resources and talent life cycle management, as well as information technology (IT). Additional complexity exists when different tools are used for similar functions (e.g., quoting or ordering in different regions and languages). As an example, if an organization has been acquiring other organizations, legacy IT platforms and applications proliferate. The flow of metadata through the combined IT ecosystem becomes more complicated, and specialized software is required to map and extract it for analysis.

Metadata is information about data fields. Sales and invoicing examples include account name; company name; first name, last name; e-mail

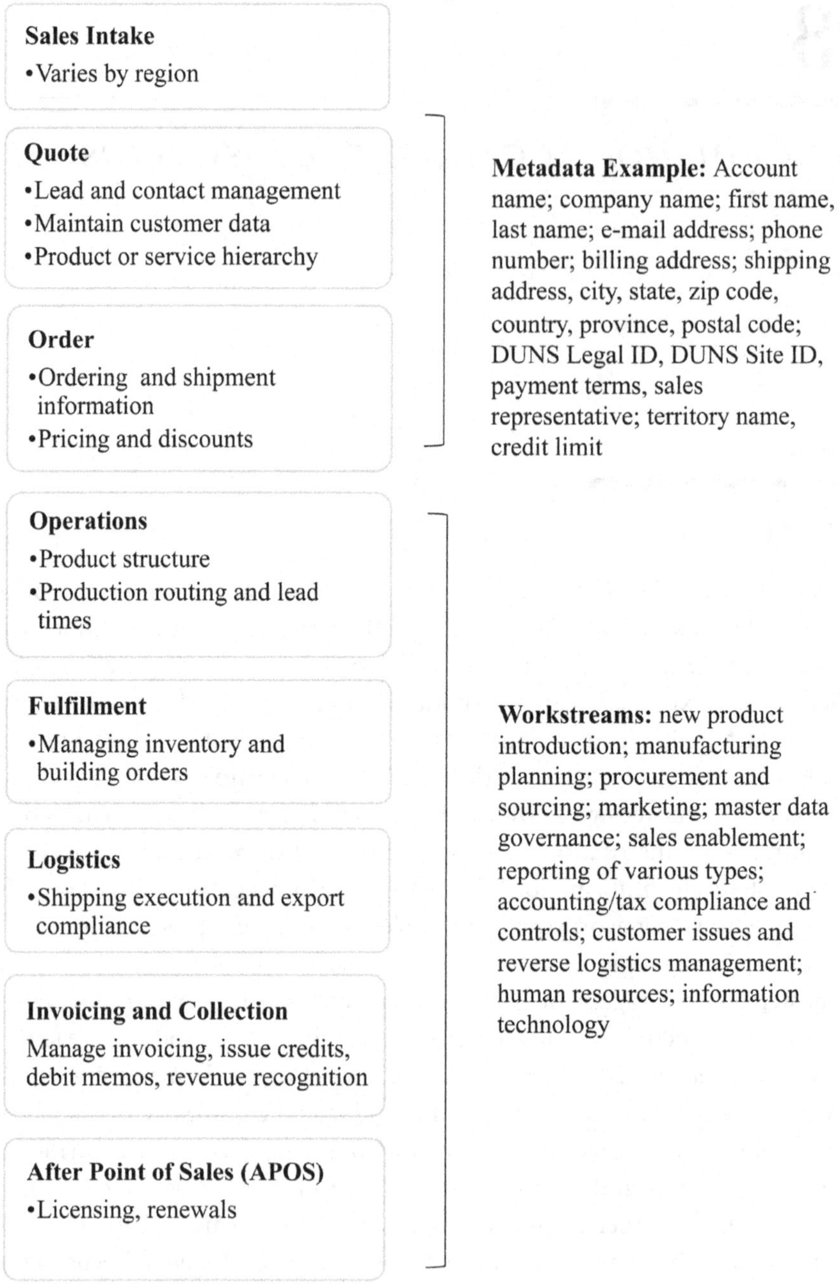

Sales Intake
• Varies by region

Quote
• Lead and contact management
• Maintain customer data
• Product or service hierarchy

Order
• Ordering and shipment
  information
• Pricing and discounts

Operations
• Product structure
• Production routing and lead
  times

Fulfillment
• Managing inventory and
  building orders

Logistics
• Shipping execution and export
  compliance

Invoicing and Collection
Manage invoicing, issue credits,
debit memos, revenue recognition

After Point of Sales (APOS)
• Licensing, renewals

Metadata Example: Account
name; company name; first name,
last name; e-mail address; phone
number; billing address; shipping
address, city, state, zip code,
country, province, postal code;
DUNS Legal ID, DUNS Site ID,
payment terms, sales
representative; territory name,
credit limit

Workstreams: new product
introduction; manufacturing
planning; procurement and
sourcing; marketing; master data
governance; sales enablement;
reporting of various types;
accounting/tax compliance and
controls; customer issues and
reverse logistics management;
human resources; information
technology

FIGURE 8.1
Quote-to-cash ecosystem.

address; phone number; billing address; shipping address; city, state, zip code, country, province, postal code, Dun & Bradstreet Universal Numbering System (DUNS) Legal ID, DUNS Site ID, payment terms, sales representative; territory name or code, credit limit, and many more. There are literally thousands of metadata fields across the systems in large organizations. Actual data are created, reviewed, updated, and deleted (shortened to CRUD in IT lingo) in metadata fields.

Let us review the quote-to-cash example in Figure 8.1. It is gathered using multiple sources (intakes) within a large IT ecosystem. Salesforce. com (SFDC) is a common intake platform that can be configured to intake quotes and other customer data to create orders that are passed on to other systems. It is a customer relationship management application that provides a single view of a customer across an organization. It also can provide personalized marketing, enable e-commerce, assist customer support, automate routine sales work tasks, run analytics, and more. The data flowing through this application and others complicates our ability to analyze process issues. First, SFDC is a complicated application requiring help from subject matter experts to capture and analyze its stored metadata and data. Second, there may be different instances (i.e., different configurations) of SFDC in an organization. Third, organizations may have other intake applications to capture customer information, which can range from controlled systems to informal ones. In addition, different market segments may have dedicated Internet portals that capture customer or partner information.

The intake tools obtain metadata from other systems such as a customer master data management application. There can only be one master data management system; however, if an organization acquires others or evolves, master data management may exist in several systems and will need to be reconciled. Customer master data include metadata related to DUNS information for sites and legal entity, as well as account name, billing and shipping addresses, contact preferences, and sales-relevant metadata such as sales territory identification, sales representative, and other information. Customer and sales intake information is merged with pricing, credit, service, and entitlement information. Then it is passed to the order management system.

In large organizations, there may be several ordering management systems across different regions. The order will be checked by the order management and revenue teams and scheduled for production in the manufacturing IT systems. Each of these teams works through an IT ecosystem that controls ordering, manufacturing, fulfillment, logistics, returns, and other work. The result is thousands of different metadata fields employed to process the quote-to-cash process. The data complexity increases as additional workstreams are engaged.

How does the IT ecosystem impact process improvement efforts? Let's use order accuracy as an example. Starting at the highest level, assume we were provided first with a historical baseline of order accuracy (i.e., the percent of orders received by customers without complaint because the order was delivered in the right quantity, quality, and on time). And then we were given a second piece of information, namely that the percentage of order accuracy is decreasing over time. We would begin analyzing (i.e., stratifying) the historical data to identify the major contributors of lower accuracy over time. This type of analysis has become more complicated as the number of systems and subject matter experts needed to complete it increases. Complicating any supply chain analysis is the enormous size of current databases (i.e., Big Data). We will discuss Big Data and its analytics in Chapter 10. Although IT ecosystems have become complicated, process improvement methods are evolving to manage this complexity to gain meaningful insights into the root causes for process issues.

The capability to create and improve processes is enabled, in part, because of the explosive growth of sophisticated diagnostic software designed to acquire data across an IT ecosystem and then analyze it using specialized algorithms. Global collaboration tools also allow the exchange of information between teams on projects that span all global supply chain functions. Technological sophistication has evolved through the major IT functions as shown in Table 8.1. These include the business process management suite (BPMS), business process management (BPM), business process modeling and analysis, business intelligence (BI), business activity monitoring (BAM), enterprise application integration (EAI), and workflow management, as well as Internet transactions, e-mail, and standardized enterprise resource planning (ERP) systems. In this chapter, our goal is to discuss these systems, including their tools, methods, and concepts as they apply to the design and management of global supply chains.

The benefits of successfully implementing IT technology include work task automation and elimination of manual work. In addition to automation, the emphasis has shifted to adding intelligence for monitoring, management, and control of processes. This has been the focus for the

TABLE 8.1

IT Applications

System	Description
• Business Process Management Suite (BPMS)	• An application that integrates several other IT applications to improve system coordination
• Business Process Management (BPM)	• An application that manages a process to coordinate it operations.
• Business Process Modeling and Analysis (BMA)	• Tools that use rules to model workflows and report change sin metrics relative to time, cost and quality to determine an optimum configuration.
• Business Intelligence (BI)	• Using tool to gather data across an IT ecosystem to identify underlying patterns for insight.
• Business Activity Monitoring (BAM)	• Decision rule applied to a model to monitor and control a process or system.
• Enterprise Application Integration (EAI)	• A system that integrates several supply chain functions and their user interfaces (UI) into one UI.

deployment of BAM, BI, business process modeling and analysis, and BPM. Intelligent IT applications promote the sharing and leveraging of information across an organization's supply chain. IT system modularization also enables greater system configurability and flexibility and promotes global integration and coordination, increasing organizational productivity.

A BPMS integrates and coordinates the diverse applications in an ERP system. Prior to BPMS, applications were scattered across an IT ecosystem. The BPMS enables users to exchange data at several levels within the system to coordinate functions of supply chain management, such as ordering, receipt, fulfillment and shipment of products, inventory transactions, customer transactions, service interactions, accounting and payroll functions, materials planning and purchasing activities, sales and marketing forecasts, and bill of material control. There are other ERP functions that vary by industry. Systems configured in BPMS format can be reconfigured to match modifications to the design of a process as material or information changes. Figure 8.2 shows an example of a BPMS application where operations have been removed and others sequenced differently. A BPMS system links to internal and customer and supplier supporting processes (i.e., interfaces), and these external interfaces remain unchanged when internal processes are modified by business analysts.

Figure 8.3 shows how a BPMS application is integrated into a BPM system with rules, process models, software systems, and manual interfaces. Some BPMS software is highly specific for industries such as financial services or call centers. In these applications, the software will usually be configured based on an organization's customer-segmentation strategy. Organizational resources may be allocated differentially by these BPMS systems. The rules assigned to each customer segment will usually differ. As an example, in financial service industries, customers may be segmented based on their net worth. One rule may state that highly affluent customers wait no more than ten seconds for their call to be answered versus other customer segments having a small net worth. Also, the type of services provided may vary, perhaps with highly affluent customers being routed to highly trained agents.

A BPMS system can be configured to monitor and control the volume of traffic in a call center. An additional capability may include product and service cross-selling or providing useful information to customers. In some applications, BPMS software must be initially configured by IT, but, once deployed, it can be modified easily by business analysts with minimal IT support. The rules driving BPMS software can be ranged from a few to several hundred, depending on the complexity of the process being monitored and controlled.

BPMS applications use three implementation components. First are manual modifications by its business users. In these situations, work lists can be modified by users to specify different process sequences based on process modifications. A second implementation element could include invoked software applications such as a system forecast. Finally, a third implementation element could be one of several ERP applications. The coordination and execution of BPMS software can be internally managed or web hosted by third-party providers. An important difference between BPMS versus ERP software is that ERP software must be compiled and is somewhat inflexible because its rules cannot be changed without direct IT support.

BPM is an IT management discipline enabling processes to be easily modified, monitored, and controlled. It provides a process-centric approach to workflow management. The business impact of BPM implementation is

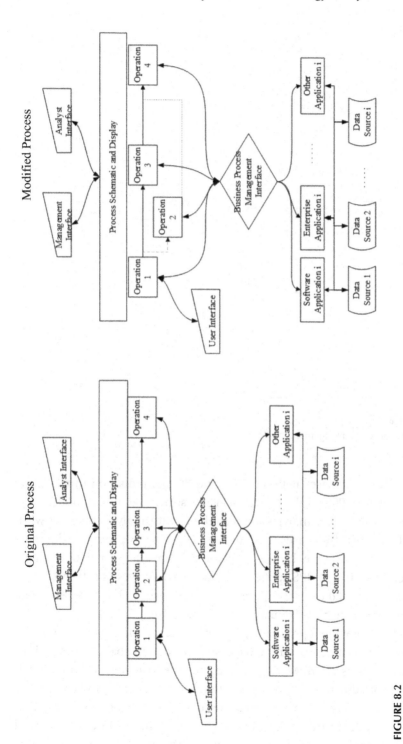

FIGURE 8.2

Business process management suite (BPMS). BPMS is a rule engine that manages the business processes.

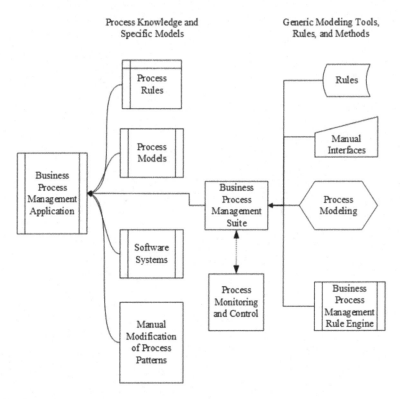

Process Knowledge and
Specific Models

Generic Modeling Tools,
Rules, and Methods

FIGURE 8.3
Business process management application.

productivity increases between 50% and 80%, a reduction in transition errors between 90% and 95%,. Also, IT investment savings is another benefit because business analysts can reconfigure and analyze processes without IT support. BPM uses loose process coupling. It promotes the reuse of lower-level software. In fact, software functionality is not 100% implemented in an initial BPS application, but rather evolves as software applications are refined by user experience. This reduces software development and maintenance costs from an Agile perspective.

A BPM deployment process begins with determining business modeling specifications and the required user-specified design goals and objectives. The initial focus of a BPM team is to capture the basic required functionality and work down into lower application levels until rules and procedures are set for the process being modeled. Supporting higher-level functionality are middleware applications such as system hardware, peripheral hardware components, software components, and telecommunications equipment and related hardware. These components are integrated through language mapping. Software is used to enable dynamic scheduling and real-time modeling of a process. Supporting this capability are modeling and metadata specifications and data. Other related functionality includes structuring mechanisms for transaction data collection and time management, as well as object location and security management. Additional features include object management group domain specifications, which vary by industry, as well as embedded intelligence and security specifications. A BPM system provides higher-level system capabilities and flexibility through these normalized and standardized processes.

BPM, including simulation, queuing, and liner programming models, have been in use for decades. More recently, however, they gained popularity because of increasing computing power, a greater need for process productivity, and the increasing complexity of the systems being modeled. The first step is to create an electronic version of the process. This is like constructing detailed process maps of material and information flows. Once a process has been mapped, workflow rules are associated to model's operations with rules for how to transform material and information into mathematical representations of the transformation processes for each operation. These representations are statistical distributions that describe the parameter distributions, including their initial and final states. Once a process is quantified, an analysis is made to estimate costs, lead times, quality levels, capacity, and other system characteristics, such as yield and uptime. The transition state probabilities for the operations, including frequencies and rates, may also be required to construct the model.

Once the model is populated with the necessary information and its rules are established, analysts evaluate alternative processing scenarios to determine the optimal levels for each resource relative to bottlenecks and capacity-constrained resources. Throughput rates and operational costs are also calculated. Simulations can be run to evaluate process changes, from eliminating non-value-add operations to making modifications to the remaining value-add operations. Final modeling activities include the evaluation of alternative solutions.

BI uses data mining methods to search and aggregate information from diverse and disparate databases for analysis. The resultant information could be a simple list of relevant information associated with the questions that prompted the analysis or incorporated into decision-support algorithms to provide information that can be used to answer other questions. BI methods rely on metadata such as part numbers, customer numbers, and key search words and phrases. These correlate one piece of information to another across disparate databases using a common key or metadata field. Increasingly, algorithms mine text in disparate databases without relying on metadata fields or tags for collecting and aggregation data. An example would be typing in phrases that enable Internet searches of specific topics. BI methods improve the efficiency of clustering, classification, and taxonomy-related analytical methods by identifying data patterns that are associated with event outcomes of interest. As an example, if we find a subset of call center agents with higher productivity and customer satisfaction ratings than other agents, we could use BI data-extraction methods to analyze digital recordings of customer calls and extract key phases associated with customer interactions to provide clues as to which behavioral patterns drive higher productivity and quality. BI methods combined with decision support and process-modeling capabilities can greatly enhance the ability to optimally configure and manage processes.

BAM is used for several important business applications, such as monitoring the status of processes in real time for better control and decision making, or understand relationships between process output metrics and the variables that influence them. This enables an organization to drill down to identify the root causes of process variation or poor performance. In these systems, an alarm event usually signals a potential process issue. This is like mistake-proofing efforts in which error conditions are eliminated from a process to prevent defects. If prevention is not possible, then alarms are placed within a process to predict the likelihood of defect based on transformation models that predict output metric or variable performance based on inputs. BAM is enabled through an integrated messaging system. Alternatively, BAM can be used to proactively improve a process.

A prerequisite for BAM implementation is development of a stable process. Once the process is stable, its key metrics are identified and used to identify the status of process operations. Decision rules and support systems are layered on top of the basic process model to show status and abnormal events. The algorithm analyzes process metrics for patterns and trends as well as violations of business rules and constraints. Notifications are sent to predetermined users with recommendations for action. BAM also enables offline analysis of event occurrences using what-if scenario analyses. Examples include changes in capacity and other process modifications to understand costs, lead times, and other performance criteria.

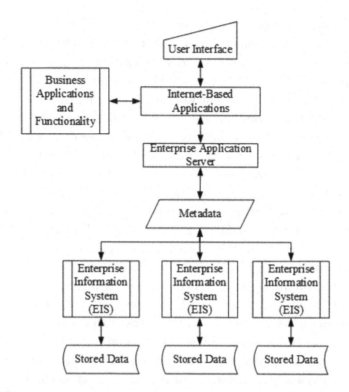

FIGURE 8.4
Enterprise application integration (EAI).

EAI systems integrate several global supply chain functions. Examples include transactions related to purchasing, accounts payables, accounts receivables, production activity control, fulfillment, order management, inventory transactions and material flow, invoicing, financing, and other functions. Figure 8.4 shows that EAI systems coordinate several IT systems using one interface versus previous configurations that employed numerous system-to-system connections. These previous configurations were not able to integrate IT applications and share information across a global supply chain. The high level of integration in modern supply chains is supported by hardware and software standardization and Internet technologies. The flexible configurability of the IT ecosystem is streamlined using EAI integration. Other benefits are intelligent information routing including instructions, middleware that supports messaging to monitor and control system applications, and an ability to manage several processes virtually.

Previous issues that inhibited the implementation of EAI included lower-level incompatibilities between application programming interfaces (API) and conflicting programming models and client APIs among some EAI platforms. Legacy systems to be integrated also made integration difficult because of security clearances or an inability to create new user accounts or support new APIs. To the extent EAI can be deployed within a global supply chain, its benefits include workload balancing, asynchronous messaging, distributed communications, and business process application sharing as well as access to and sharing of disparate databases. EAI systems support BPMS as well as BMA, BI, BMA, and workflow management.

Table 8.2 summarizes the most common global supply chain IT platforms with a description for each one. These systems include enterprise resource planning (ERP), material requirements planning II (MRPII), material requirements planning (MRP), distribution requirements planning, master production scheduling, forecasting systems, capacity requirements planning, manufacturing automation protocol systems, and warehouse management systems, including auxiliary software systems and the advanced shipping notification system that is used to control material flow between suppliers and their customers.

An ERP system is a more sophisticated version of an MRPII system that includes accounting-related information and the resources needed to plan, manufacture, and ship customer orders. ERP systems also have graphical user interfaces. MRPII was an earlier version of ERP in that it had higher functionality than the original MRP. MRPII functionality includes operational and financial data conversion that enables business planning, and it integrates sales and operations planning, master production planning functions, material requirements planning, and capacity planning. The original MRP systems used bill of material, inventory, and master production schedule information to calculate their net requirements for materials and components that were required for manufacturing and supplier orders. These net requirements were offset by material and component lead times. Distribution requirements planning is a system that replenishes inventory at branch locations throughout a distribution network. It uses time-phased order points or similar logic to translate planned orders to suppliers for every item and its location throughout the distribution system. The master requirements planning schedule is a system that uses sale's forecasts and order book or firm demand, estimated gross capacity, on-hand inventory levels, and other manufacturing planning information to develop a netted manufacturing schedule. The forecasting system uses historical demand and time-series algorithms to predict future demand by forecasting time intervals over a forecasting time horizon.

TABLE 8.2

Global Supply Chain IT Evolution

IT Platform	Description
• Enterprise Resource Planning	A more sophisticated version of the original MRPII system that includes accounting-related information as well as the resources needed to plan, manufacture, and ship customer orders. These systems also are characterized by graphical user interfaces.
• Material Requirements Planning II (MRPII)	A system with higher functionality than material requirements planning. It includes operational and financial data conversion and allows business planning. It integrates functions related to sales and operations planning, master production planning, material requirements planning, and capacity planning.
• Material Requirements Planning	A system that uses bill of material, inventory, and master production schedule information to calculate net requirements for materials and components for manufacturing and suppliers. The requirements are offset by material and component lead times.
• Distribution Requirements Planning	A system that replenishes inventory at branch locations throughout a distribution network using a time-phased order point or other logic for every item and location to translate planned orders via MRPII to suppliers.
• Master Production Schedule	A system that uses the sales forecast and order book demand, gross capacity, and on-hand inventory manufacturing planning to develop a "netted" manufacturing schedule.
• Forecasting System	A system that uses historical demand and time-series algorithms to predict future demand by forecasting time intervals over the forecasting time horizon.
• Capacity Requirements Planning	A system that uses MRPII information related to open and current manufacturing orders as well as routings and time standards to estimate required labor and machine time across facilities.
• Manufacturing Automation Protocol	A system based on the International Standards Organization, which allows communication between systems from different organizations and depends on the International Standards Organization's open systems interconnections standards.
• Warehouse Management System	A system that dynamically manages received materials and components and assigns an inventory storage location. More advanced versions of these systems enable efficient order fulfillment and cycle-counting activities.
• Advanced Shipping Notification	An integrated system that allows customers and suppliers to know all the items making up an order by their pallet and vehicle using barcode scanning. A prerequisite is a supplier certification program and deployment of information technology.

A capacity requirement planning system uses MRPII information related to open and current manufacturing orders as well as product routings and time standards to estimate the required labor and equipment across a supply chain and at a local process level. The manufacturing automation protocol system is based on the International Standards Organization's open systems interconnections standards that enable communication between systems of different organizations.

Warehouse management systems enable distribution centers to dynamically manage materials and component receipts and assign inventory storage locations. Advanced versions of these systems enable efficient order fulfillment and cycle counting. Finally, advanced shipment notification systems provide customers and suppliers with visibility relative to the items making up their orders by pallet and vehicle and using barcode-scanning systems. A prerequisite to deployment of an advanced shipment notification system is a supplier certification program and an IT deployment to ship and receive orders.

Workflow management focuses on the design and management of processes. Software is used to create virtual representations of processes. Virtual process maps are easy to modify and, once quantified, enable analyses, simulations, and other models. More recently, advanced adaptive systems can optimally reconfigure a system dynamically. Business process management (BPM) systems are used to integrate processes. Agile project management is used to coordinate and manage these projects. In summary, the design, management, and control of processes have evolved from highly manual models to virtual models. Virtual process models enable easy reconfiguration as well as the addition, deletion, and modification of operational and governing business rules. These concepts are listed in Table 8.3.

ROBOTIC PROCESS AUTOMATION

As the transaction volumes in IT ecosystems increase, automation is being applied to reduce manual work tasks that have high cost, long lead times, and lower quality. RPA automatically accesses applications to create, read, update, and delete (CRUD) metadata and data. Sometimes an automation initiative is large in scale and creates entirely new applications or features

TABLE 8.3

Workflow Management

Capability	Method	Comment
Manual processes and systems	Simple functions (e.g., calculating and checking text)	Ad hoc design based on local content
Virtual versions of manual operations and systems	Process monitoring and reporting	Standardized process structure and definition allowing systematic improvements to the process over time
Virtual versions of the process with modeling and analytical capability	Process optimization based on current or predicted data	Rapid ability to analyze a process to create alternative designs and optimize the best design
Adaptive processes enabling simple responses to changes in inputs	Process reconfiguration due to changes in system status caused by variation of input levels and external influences.	The system changes the process design based on rules and logic programmed by its users to optimize certain critical outputs
Advanced adaptive systems that reconfigure a system dynamically to optimize several outputs	Optimization algorithms to ensure goal alignment and convergence	Characterized by an ability to reconfigure, add, delete, and modify processes dynamically

and functions having higher performance. In other situations, islands of automation are applied to a sequence of process steps based on business rules and a macro algorithm that improves process efficiency and quality. These focused applications are called RPA projects. RPA applies software tools to complete tasks formerly performed by humans. RPA differs from an enterprise application in that the focus is on lower-level manual work activities that interface with larger IT applications. A common application is the use of macros to replicate work activities step by step.

These processes must be rule-based in that software code can be built with defined inputs and outputs. These are modeled using if-then statements, e.g., if conditions A and B exist, then update this status. This requires the inputs to be structured so they can be read by the system. The format is structured as numbers, optical character recognition, or text searches using rules (e.g., frequency counting). Processes that rely on unstructured data that cannot be reliably read are not good candidates for

RPA. A manual process should also be repetitive, and its work activities should follow a sequential pattern that repeats. The process must also be mature and stable with large volumes or batch sizes. Finally, the manual activities should have a high cost or quality levels should be low so the return on investment for RPA is high. Examples include filling metadata fields with customer data based on a DUNS customer number. Once the RPA robot (bot) reads the DUNS Ultimate Customer ID (UCID), additional metadata from other systems can be collected by the bot to build a customer profile. Other examples include inserting delivery addresses in an e-mail or creating an e-mail targeted to specific persona and use cases based on business rules.

Table 8.4 shows three steps. These are creating the RPA foundation, transforming the process for higher productivity, and sustaining performance improvement. The team begins by confirming feasibility (i.e., the process is mature, stable, rule-based, and will exist for the foreseeable future). A formal project charter is created that defines project scope, deliverables, and their schedule. The next step is to walk the process by capturing screen shots and recording the sequence of operations needed to complete the work task. The current-state process is documented to identify automation opportunities based on known RPA success criteria. The team also captures the business rules that govern the creation of the work product of the process. There may be variations of the types of work done by the process based on user persona and their use cases. Other relevant actions at this RPA step include confirming baseline metrics. The focus is on the confirmation of operational and work task rules. The automation is tested under controlled conditions and, once approved and shown to be effective, it is turned over to the process owner. At the end of the project, process documentation is updated and roles and responsibilities are modified to reflect the higher automation.

AGILE PROJECT MANAGEMENT

Agile project management (APM) has gained widespread acceptance as an important set of tools and methods shown to be useful for managing software design projects. It is characterized by high quality work, adaptability to changing customer requirements and solutions, transparency of work,

TABLE 8.4

Robotic Process Engineering

Phase	Business	Process Engineering	RPA Questions	RPA Engineering
	• Process request RPA Engineering support • Confirm project charter and plan and help establish project deliverables	• Build project charter, team, plan including schedule	• Is the scope correct? • What are the metric baselines? • What are the performance targets? • When is the work to be competed and by whom?	• Support Process Engineering team
	• Support the team relative to feasibility analysis	• Create process documentation including screen shots and step by step work instructions		• Recommend documentation needed for automation feasibility
Create the RPA Foundation			• Are these steps rule based? • Are the process steps standardize i.e. repeatable? • Is the process high volume (or large batch)?	
	• Confirm feasibility recommendations	• Identify which steps can be automated	• Are inputs/outputs readable by applicable systems • Are the transformation rules and metadata lineage understood? • Is the data structured versus unstructured? • Is this process scheduled for obsolescence in the future?	• Confirm feasibility for automation
Transform the Process and Performance	• Confirm cost/benefit analysis • Conform business impact of proposed changes	• Business requirements documentation with cost/benefit analysis • Proposed process changes (before/after screen shots, work instructions and process flows, changes to roles & responsibilities and policy changes as required) • Update combined Process Engineering and RPA Engineering plan	• Pilot the RPA plan and monitor performance • Scale the RPA plan	
Sustain Performance	• Process owner confirm deliverables have been met including performance targets.	• Update process documentation with business owner and team and verify process performance		• Develop the macros and BOTS to automate the process steps

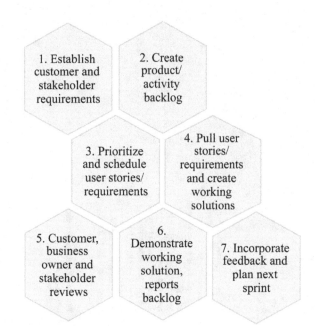

FIGURE 8.5
Agile project management (APM).

a high degree of customer collaboration, effective solutions delivered rapidly, and empowered teams. APM tools and methods have been adapted from analogous Lean tools and methods. Figure 8.5 shows basic elements of APM. These include gathering customer and stakeholder requirements and prioritizing them using a visual product backlog on a white board to promote collaboration. Visual displays of work tasks, activities, and milestones help manage and effectively communicate the project's status. The Agile team brainstorms user stories around features, functions, and requirements as well as the work tasks that need to be performed to complete user stories. User stories are in the form of "as a (role), I want to do (this task), so that (this result will occur)." As an example, a user story might be, "As a sales maker, I want to be able to update currency type so my expense report will be accurate for any country I visit."

The product or activity backlog facilitates an open exchange of backlog status and what needs to be done. This rapid feedback system, which includes incremental software development cycles (i.e., sprints) ensures the design functions properly in the customer's environment. Sprints are created as team members pull items from the sprint backlog, and then a focused effort is made to complete the selected backlog items. At the end of the sprint, one or more user stories are solved, and a review is made with the customer and stakeholders to validate the working solution. Based on customer and stakeholder feedback, additional work tasks may be added to the activity backlog and the next sprint. The APM philosophy is to communicate often to avoid working on non-value-add user stories that create unnecessary features and functions.

APM starts with support from Agile leadership. Leaders promote agility, align Agile work to strategic goals, and provide resources and assistance. This helps ensure adoption throughout an organization's software development cycle. The concepts can also be applied to any design process where features and functions are created and periodically reviewed by customers and stakeholders. APM should be integrated into an organization's strategic initiatives to promote efficient software development. It is also useful with modifications for managing other types of work because of its clear roles and responsibilities, the visual execution of work, and the periodic feedback cycles. In this context, it is similar to Lean project management methodology because the focus is on simplifying work through cross-functional collaboration and support for removing technical, resource, and other barriers.

A product owner is a critical business role in APM. There is only one product owner for a scrum team. A scrum team works to deliver increments of features and functions of a product design. The owner is responsible for the product, which is a compilation of user stories with workable features and functions. The product owner works with the customer, business owner, and other stakeholders to develop clear requirements that form the basis for the product or activity backlog. The backlog is the list of user stories or requirements that need to be resolved to successfully finish the Agile project. The product owner updates the backlog as the scrum team completes sprints and determines when the backlog has been successfully completed.

The scrum master is the team's coach. The person in this role understands the principles of APM, trains team members, and works with the product owner to remove barriers that inhibit the team's work. Scrum masters accelerate the execution of the backlog by ensuring the status of work is visible to everyone. The Agile team is multidisciplinary and self-managing. It is dedicated to this Agile project for the period needed to complete the product and sprint backlogs. The scrum team is small, consisting of four to ten dedicated members, including the product owner and scrum master. Ideally, the team will be collocated to enable collaboration.

The Agile team is empowered to make design trade-off decisions to complete the user stories.

The backlog is a white board that is visible to the team and key stakeholders. It is a list of prioritized user stories, requirements, or ideas that need to be completed in the sprints. The backlog may need periodic refinements during the project. Updates to the user stories will clarify and refine the backlog. The product owner and scrum team rank the priority of the major pieces of work needed to deliver workable solutions to the user stories during each sprint, and the product owner is responsible for decisions regarding the final ordering of the backlog list.

The visual backlog board is like the visual display boards used in Lean deployments. Recall that these are of various types, including metrics boards placed in a work area and value flow maps used to describe a process flow with metrics, gaps, and potential projects. Visualization is always useful for communicating the status of complicated activities as opposed to storing information on a computer and sharing it only occasionally with a team. In addition to having a user story, the backlog should also estimate the business value for each user story or requirement as well as a test or evaluation method to measure successful completion. Backlog actions may be periodically reprioritized based on the team's work status and product owner prioritizations.

Sprints are created using the product backlog, but backlog activities are not incorporated into a sprint until they have a user story, quantified benefits, and defined methods to measure success criteria. Sprints are organized to deliver workable solutions to user stories (i.e., features and functions) for review and feedback from the product owner, customer, and stakeholders. At the start of a sprint, the scrum team agrees on its goals and the amount of work that can be reasonably completed during the sprint. The work is sized to deliver discrete features and functions that satisfy the user stories. The sprint plan includes which team member will work on which activities and when they need to be completed.

During the sprint, the scrum team continuously prioritizes its work. Only the scrum team can reprioritize work within its sprint. Some requirements and their work tasks may be found to be unnecessary and will be deleted from the sprint backlog, or others may be modified based on new information. A sprint will last between one and several weeks depending on the amount of work to be completed.

During each sprint, the team also holds a daily fifteen-minute stand-up meeting to discuss the previous day's progress to determine what work was completed and if there is any carryover work to do. The day's work is discussed, and previous day's uncompleted work tasks are added to the schedule. Resources are confirmed. This enables an Agile team to discuss what is working well and refocus resources. The scrum master helps remove barriers that inhibit the work and collaborates with the product owner, the business owner, the customer, and other stakeholders. During the sprint, the team continues to refine its prioritized work, adding ideas for solutions and collaborating to develop working solutions to the user stories and requirements.

At the end of a sprint, a working solution should be ready to review with the customer, business owner, and stakeholders. This review includes a demonstration of the working solution that satisfies one or more user stories. The backlog status is also reviewed, as well as plans for the next sprint. Finally, feedback from the business owner, customer, and stakeholders is used to make updates to the Agile project backlog and schedule. This information will be incorporated and prioritized into the next sprint. A retrospective is also conducted by the scrum team to identify ways to make the next sprint more efficient. A working solution is the best measurement of sprint success. This solution will demonstrate working features or functions that satisfy user stories.

METRICS

IT ecosystems and their project teams rely on performance metrics and dashboards for ongoing process control and improvement. Several metrics related to cost, time, and quality were discussed in previous chapters, such as actual versus budgeted cost, actual versus planned schedule, project completion time, and others. Software projects have specific metrics that help evaluate the creation of code and features and functions. These are associated with the general categories of project management, problem resolution, unplanned design iterations, and the types of quality problems found and resolved by the team. Metrics are created and evaluated from different perspectives. Because questions differ across stakeholder groups, metrics dashboards exhibit a variety of formats.

Metrics are designed to answer questions from customers and internal stakeholders. Customers are interested in product and service availability, cost, quality, performance, and time to delivery. Other evaluation criteria are ease of use, availability, maintainability, upgrades, reuse, and disposability and sustainability. Marketing and sales need to know how products and services help grow market share, that is, their unique features and functions that excite customers and increase profitability. Finance needs to know revenue and profitability as well as compatibility with current products and services. From an operational perspective, questions are focused on global producibility, ease of use, and ease of maintenance, as well as disposability and sustainability. Other stakeholders will pose different questions. Metrics and dashboards are created to answer these types of questions.

Work activities measure the creation and deployment of hardware and software systems. Some of these include ongoing maintenance and upgrades, as well as refresh and disposal of equipment. Others are stratified by software modules, features, functions, lines of software code, and similar product attributes. Software is periodically released as versions that build on previous versions. Two types of metrics associated with releases include resource measurement (e.g., total labor hours and lead time per release) and numbers of errors and customer complaints from early test releases. Software and configuration metrics relative to features and functions delivered by a team include the cost per configuration, the time to resolve issues, and the percentage of design changes. From a customer perspective, measures include the cost per service issue, the time to resolve a service issue, actual versus planned service level by feature and function, the percent of service-related issues, and the accuracy of the measured service-related information.

In addition to these metrics, others are used to evaluate the software itself. These include the efficiency, ease of use, reliability, maintainability, and reusability. Efficiency measures the software's performance relative to the time to accurately execute lines of code and calculations. Ease of use measures how easy it is for users to use the software through user interfaces. The software should be intuitive to use and should guide users through it with tips, drop-down menus, and other aids that provide clear instructions. Reliability measures the failure incident rates of hardware and software components. The overall system reliability depends on these failure rates as well as how they are organized (i.e., their architecture and especially the design of parallel and serial paths). Reliability with proactive and preventive maintenance contributes to a system's availability for use. Maintainability measures the ease of repairing a system's hardware or software. Reusability measures the degree to which hardware or software can be repurposed for new solutions.

Metrics are also classified as lagging, coincident, or leading. Lagging metrics measure historical performance. Examples that affect customers include lost revenue, percent complaints, returned goods and warranty expenses, and others. Examples that affect projects include actual versus budgeted cost, actual versus planned schedule attainment, and the average time to resolve a problem. Process improvement teams use historical information to create projects to eliminate chronic problems so that, over time, the customer experience improves. Coincident metrics measure current performance. Examples that affect customers include recent late deliveries, quality issues by type, and similar events. These events occur within the current reporting cycle and can be acted upon immediately to correct them. Examples that affect projects include total completed work activities, person days required to complete scrum sprints, forecast versus actual expenses, the cycle time per software release, the cost per service issue, and planned versus actual service levels by software feature and function. Leading metrics predict future performance and enable preventive actions that save time, reduce costs, and prevent deterioration of the customer experience. Project examples include accurate estimates of a project's remaining work activities as well as the time to complete them, the person days required to complete remaining scrum sprints, and the amount of budget remaining.

SUMMARY

Organizations need to have a strategic approach to IT ecosystems. Ecosystems contain hundreds or thousands of applications with multiple types of metadata. Those focused on data domains (e.g., marketing, sales, finance, and production) would comprise a subset of the larger ecosystem and contain focused applications. Ecosystems may not be formally organized. Some may also be closed except to participants who have defined points of access. Open ecosystems are usually associated with e-commerce platforms. Supporting back-end operational systems in those applications need to adapt to open ecosystems if they exist, as well as the closed systems within their organization. Strategies should be developed to coordinate the use of a platform and its applications to ensure operational efficiencies are maintained for participant satisfaction. This approach often leads to unique ecosystem designs in which subgroups of participants

work together to share information, work products (e.g., analytics), algorithms, and reports with the hosting organization that provides platform
governance.

Hosted ecosystems are also supported by a variety of third-party applications that provide information or a vehicle to create work products.
Key roles include the hosting organization, suppliers, consumers, and
experts of various applications. Data are easily shared by all participants
based on data and business rules through cloud platforms and portals.
Normalization of data is straightforward using metadata governance and
rules. The second level of the ecosystems is the production of discrete
workloads for data domains. This enables participants to contribute information to the work product. The highest level of the ecosystem are the user
interfaces or portals that control access to the metadata, rules, and work
products. These are organized by participant groups. Also supporting the
ecosystem are engineers and analysts who conceive new applications and
coordinate the use of current applications through analytics, algorithms,
and functions and features. These roles include discipline experts associated with coding, data domain experts, and application developers who
improve the value of current applications or create new ones. This leads
to the question of which organization owns the customer experience?
Strategy is important. Customer satisfaction and the efficiency of internal
operations, both IT as well as supporting systems, need to be governed
across the supply chains to ensure excellent customer experience and
productivity.

Having the ability to create an IT ecosystem that supports adaptable
and flexible processes enables organizations to compete effectively on a
global basis in diverse markets. IT ecosystems are very complex, having
hundreds or even thousands of software applications supported by IT
platforms with thousands of metadata fields. These need to be formally
governed though a council. Clear roles and responsibilities are necessary,
as well as an understanding of the metadata flowing from various sources
to consuming systems. These systems and their metadata must have owners and supporting governance processes. IT ecosystems may also have
redundant systems if an organization acquired other organizations that
had their own IT ecosystems.

Over the past few decades, advanced software applications have been
designed to automatically navigate these ecosystems to collect and organize enormous amounts of data to make it useful for reporting, providing insights, and making decisions. Operations has also benefited through

direct IT automation across the ecosystem as well as focused process automation (i.e., RPA). RPA is applied to mature and stable processes having high volumes or large batch sizes where the business rules for doing work are logical. An RPA algorithm or macro mimics a highly manual process used to produce work, but at a lower cost and higher quality. This can include automated access to metadata in other applications to copy, delete, or modify it to build reports, models, invoices, and other work products.

Agile project management (APM) is an effective methodology for coordinating and managing IT projects. APM promotes the gathering of customer user stories and requirements by displaying them visually. This helps the scrum team associate work tasks with discrete features and functions tied to user stories. These can be executed in a scrum sprint. At the end of a sprint, a working solution is reviewed by the business owner, customers, and stakeholders. Software development productivity will be higher and lead times will be reduced when APM is used effectively.

9

Six Sigma

OVERVIEW

High quality is a core competency every organization should develop to maintain customer satisfaction, retain customers, and increase productivity. This ensures that customer requirements and internal specifications are met by an organization in its day-to-day activities. Competitive quality management systems continuously improve the capability of their processes to reduce failure expenses, such as warranty claims, returned goods, scrap, and rework. Table 9.1 lists several of these attributes. In this chapter, we discuss the roles of quality management from two perspectives. First, we discuss quality management relative to its classic functions. This discussion will include a brief history of some of the important quality initiatives deployed over the last several decades. Then we will discuss important quality tools and methods, from the basic to more advanced methods, with an emphasis on Six Sigma methodology.

Table 9.2 lists ten quality activities ranging from identification of the voice of the customer (VOC) to new product or service designs to enabling customer reviews of requirements such as drawings and specifications through the concurrent engineering (CE) team. Others include process auditing and creation of control procedures for new products and services, inspections of work, the evaluation and approval of testing and measurement equipment, fixtures, inspection procedures, and training. Quality assurance also performs capability analyses and product or service performance analyses as required by a CE team and has a role in developing quality control plans for new products and processes. This role includes

TABLE 9.1

Competitive Quality Metrics

Metrics
1. Customer satisfaction and customer retention ratings
2. Percent productivity due to quality improvements
3. Process capability
4. Percent of quality expenses spent on proactive versus reactive issues
5. Warranty claims, returned goods, scrap, and rework expenses as a percentage of sales

ensuring that failure mode and effects analyses (FMEA), specifications, audit schedules, product performance testing, and related supporting activities and documentation are created on schedule. Quality assurance supports the CE team by verifying that the new products and processes meet customer requirements during pre-production trials. This information is incorporated into an organization's customer quality control plan. Quality assurance also engages in the day-to-day auditing, inspection, and management of production and other processes to ensure work is done right the first time.

The Six Sigma quality initiative helped coalesce various quality tools, methods, concepts, and theories of quality into a phased problem-solving

TABLE 9.2

Ten Quality System Activities

Activity
1. Review customer requirements as specified in contracts, drawings, and specifications.
2. Assist the product planning process with the CE team.
3. Assist in the development of the design and process procedures with CE team.
4. Assist in the development of the sign-off documentation with the CE team.
5. Assist in the design and development of inspection, testing, and measurement equipment, fixtures, procedures, and training with CE team.
6. Assist with capability analysis and similar performance analysis as required by the CE team.
7. Develop quality control plans based on design and process information including failure mode and effects analyses.
8. Develop auditing procedures.
9. Assist in product and process verification with the CE team as specified by customer requirements.
10. Provide feedback to the CE team and the production team on product and process capability as determined by the quality control plan.

CE = concurrent engineering.

methodology applied to current processes. The tools can be used individually or in groups to solve specific quality issues. As an example, prior to the increased popularity of Six Sigma in the mid-1990s, there were specific workshops that focused on individual tools such as control charting, quality function deployment, experimental design, FMEA, quality control plans, and others. A problem with this approach is that the tools were not integrated into a coherent methodology to solve business problems. The tools and methods also did not appeal to higher levels of management or to associates who were not trained in their practical use. Because of these highly technical and acronym-filled workshops, organizations relegated the use of upcoming quality tools and methods to subject matter experts.

However, in recent years, diverse approaches to quality assurance and control have coordinated approaches and tool use for success. As an example, in some organizations, Six Sigma and Lean are used together as Lean Six Sigma. The International Standards Organization (ISO), which originally developed a set of auditing activities, developed updated ISO systems that recommended proactive approaches for process quality. Another example is the Malcom Baldridge Award, which acknowledges organizations that adhere to a series of standards, policies, procedures, and philosophies designed to improve quality. The Malcom Baldrige criteria were modified to make them more holistic and proactive from a process-improvement perspective.

Table 9.3 describes several common quality initiatives and cross-references their attributes. Properly integrating these initiatives has helped improve quality in many organizations. Several of these initiatives formed the basis of Six Sigma. We will discuss Six Sigma tools, methods, and concepts with the assumption that several of these initiatives, such as ISO, Automotive Industry Action Group (AIAG), Malcom Baldrige, Lean, and total quality management (TQM), are also operative in an organization.

DEPLOYING SIX SIGMA

The Six Sigma improvement model is designed to dramatically improve performance in existing processes. It was originally conceived at Motorola using a Juran breakthrough improvement model, and it is considered one of the most successful process improvement models ever developed because it enables a systematic analysis of current process performance

TABLE 9.3

Current Quality Programs and Methods

Quality Method	Description
Deming/Shewart	Dr. W. Edward Deming advocated that the system was the problem, not the people. Deming and Walter Shewart proposed a process improvement model called the Deming Wheel, which consists of four phases: Plan, Do, Study, Act.
Juran	Key concepts of Dr. Joseph Juran were quality improvement could be achieved using continuous improvement or breakthrough methods; quality experts need to speak the language of senior management and ensure quality is customer- and business-focused, and organizations should invest in preventive measures to reduce failure costs associated with quality, such as scrap, rework, and warranty expenses.
Total Quality Management (TQM)	A continuous-improvement program that is designed to involve everyone in an organization to improve their processes using simple quality-oriented tools. Although the concept is good, deployments are usually targeted isolated processes, so customer and business benefits are sporadic.
Continuous Improvement	A variation of the total quality management concept, it has been recently revitalized by the tool sets contained in Lean and Six Sigma.
Kaizen Events	Similar to continuous improvement, except the process analysis and improvements are focused on a small portion of a process or workstream over a short time period, resulting in immediate benefit to an organization. Simple Lean and Six Sigma tools are used in Kaizen Events.
Lean	A process improvement program that focuses on simplification, standardization, elimination of process waste, and mistake-proofing of processes to improve quality.
Six Sigma	A phased methodology to improve quality characterized by five phases: define, measure, analyze, improve, and control. It was initially developed at Motorola using Juran's breakthrough method.

(continued)

TABLE 9.3 (*Continued*)

Current Quality Programs and Methods

Quality Method	Description
Malcom Baldrige Award	A system for measuring organizational performance relative to measurement and control of processes; it is based on how well procedures are followed, and it utilizes a point system. Quality is improved through an auditing process that identifies process breakdowns.
International Standards Organization (ISO)	A group of standards that organization must follow. These standards set forth a minimum level of quality that organizations must maintain to sell their products around the world.
Automotive Industry Action Group (AIAG)	The AIAG system consists of five sets of deliverables designed to design and produce a product to service: (1) quality product planning and VOC; (2) product design and design for manufacturing; (3) process design and development; (4) product and process validation; and (5) control plan methodology.

and provides a detailed roadmap to identify root causes and eliminate them to improve process capability. It aligns to the VOC and the voice of the business (VOB) to increase quality and productivity and to sustain higher performance. An effective quality improvement strategy drives operational excellence across an organization, from the business-unit level to the local process level. Figure 9.1 describes a general quality improvement model. This deployment process is generally faster than that of TQM, but it depends on well-defined and well-executed projects. Figure 9.2 shows the major differences between TQM and Six Sigma. TQM focuses on the elimination of a problem's root causes using simple quality tools and methods. TQM activities have migrated into the Six Sigma Green Belt role in some organizations. Six Sigma offers several advantages that were initially absent from TQM deployments.

Six Sigma is a top-down alignment versus the bottom-up approach that is a characteristic of TQM. A second advantage is that Six Sigma provides significant business benefits for organizations, and these benefits can be realized relatively quickly once projects are deployed. As a result, TQM was augmented by Six Sigma in the mid-1990s. Different organizations approach quality improvement from either a TQM focus with Six Sigma augmentation or vice versa. Six Sigma has often been deployed as

1. Analyze current performance

2. Predict the quality of products/processes

3. Benchmark products, services, and processes

4. Identify Best in Class and areas of focus

5. Plan and design processes for robustness

Strategy
Improve Voice of the Customer
and Voice of the Business

Strategic Options
Project Selection
Initiative Selection

Workstream Improvement Focus

FIGURE 9.1
Quality improvement model. Quality improvement projects are selected to improve operational competencies, drive improvements in profit & loss statements and the balance sheet, and improve customer value.

a project-based initiative that must be integrated into an organization's quality assurance systems. A reliance on Six Sigma alone to improve and sustain process improvements is risky because, in the absence of formal quality systems and TQM, in which most employees are trained, Six Sigma process improvements will deteriorate over time. The program was always

Rapid Change

Six Sigma Breakthrough

- Modified Process Requirements
- Modified Process Model and System
- Modified Learning Systems
- Modified Technology

Slow Change

Total Quality Management

- Time Reduction
- Activity Reduction
- Variance Reduction

FIGURE 9.2
Rate of process improvement.

Six Sigma Goals	Six Sigma Vision
•Understand customer requirements	•Integration into culture
•Reduce process variation	•Maturity to Six Sigma performance
•Center process on target	•Six Sigma skills enable learning organization
•Focus on cause not symptom	
•Ensure improvements are sustained	•Six Sigma used in developmental training

FIGURE 9.3
Key characteristics of Six Sigma. Six Sigma helps organizations make the transition from tactical problem solving to business process development and customer excellence.

designed to include a fraction of employees to achieve breakthrough improvement while most employees engage in continuous improvement.

The concept of "breakthrough" improvements in quality and aligning projects with goals that are important to leadership helps secure resources for projects. Figure 9.3 shows important characteristics of an effective Six Sigma program. The deliverables are achieved using the five Six Sigma phases: define, measure, analyze, improve, and control (DMAIC). The DMAIC phases are further expanded into ten to twelve steps (depending on the organization), with each step having key deliverables. Over an extended period, an organization will mature into a Six Sigma performing culture if it has quality assurance and management infrastructure that supports continual improvement.

The DMAIC methodology is applied to improve the performance of customer critical-to characteristics (CTs). Figure 9.4 shows the breakthrough concept applied to a single CT characteristic, namely a critical-to-quality (CTQ) variable or key process output variable (KPOV). This could be processing defect percentage, lead time, or another quantified variable. Notice that this KPOV exhibits variation around its average (or mean) level. There may also be periodic disruptions occurring within a process, or spikes in the CTQ, causing non-random patterns. These are called assignable causes of process variation. In the absence of assignable causes of variation, a process exhibits common case variation or random variation of the CTQ around its mean value.

The concept of assignable versus common cause variation will be discussed later in this chapter in the control charts discussion. A process that exhibits common cause variation remains at its mean, which may good or bad from a customer's perspective. If the mean is not at an optimum level or exhibits high variance (or both), then the root causes of the common

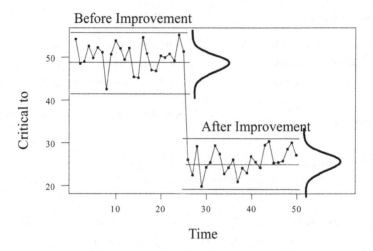

2 Sigma ...... Low customer satisfaction

3 Sigma .... Average customer satisfaction

4 Sigma .... Above average customer satisfaction

5 Sigma + ... Customer excellence

FIGURE 9.4
What is Six Sigma? Six Sigma is a methodology to proactively enable the transformation of an organization from a functionally oriented, reactionary operation to a cross-functional, process-focused, continuously improving, learning organization.

cause variation should be investigated through data collection and analysis to eventually eliminate it from the process. If this is a chronic problem and the process variable is stable, it can be a difficult task to eliminate root causes without a project having focused resources. The goal of the DMAIC methodology to achieve breakthrough performance levels. This concept is shown in Figure 6.4 as before-and-after curves. Figure 9.4 also lists some common "Sigma" levels correlating to customer satisfaction. These "Sigma" levels will be discussed later in this chapter.

The DMAIC phases are broken down as shown in Table 9.4, with deliverables and the tools and methods used to achieve the deliverables within each phase. There may be additional tools depending on the application. Some of these tools and methods may be used in more than one DMAIC phase. This methodology helps define a process problem relative to its extent, occurrence, and impact on customers. A Six Sigma team first estimates accurate CT baselines using measurement system analyses,

TABLE 9.4

DMAIC Problem-Solving Methodology

Phase	Deliverables	Tools and Methods
Define	Define the problem including its extent, occurrence frequency, customer and business impact.	• Problem statement • High-level process mapping • Metrics analysis • Cost of Quality Analysis (COQ)
Measure	Verify the CT can be measured accurately and precisely, determine baseline capability of the CT and develop a data collection plan on the inputs and the CT.	• Problem statement • High-level process mapping • Metrics analysis • Cause and effects • Failure mode and effects (FMEA) • Measurement system analysis (MSA) • Basic statistics/process capability • Cost of Quality Analysis (COQ)
Analyze	Eliminate the trivial inputs and develop a short list of KPIVs impacting the CT or KPOVs.	• Basic statistics • Graphical analysis tools • Hypothesis testing/contingency tables • One-way ANOVA • Multi-Vari analysis • Correlation/regression • Detailed process map
Improve	Experiment with the KPIVs and KPOVs to determine their interrelationships and select the best combination of KPIV levels to optimize the KPOVs.	• General full factorials • 2^k full factorials • Fractional factorials • Response surface designs
Control	Ensure the improved process will be sustainable and remain in control.	• Statistical process control/mistake-proofing • Measurement control • Maintenance/training • Validate capability • Control plans • Final Cost of Quality Analysis (COQ) review

CT = critical-to characteristic; KPIV = key process input variables; KPOV = key process output variables; ANOVA = analysis of variance.

capability analyses, and data collection and analysis. The analysis is completed in sequence in the define, measure, and analyze phases. In the improve and control phases, the process is modified based on the root-cause analysis, and solutions are implemented to eliminate the root causes to a move the CT to a new performance level. We will now discuss the tools and methods of each DMAIC phase.

DEFINE PHASE

There are many tools and methods available to clearly define the VOC and the VOB. These range from financial, operational, and value stream mapping to the application of marketing research methods. Some of these methods were discussed in earlier chapters. Our assumption is that a project has been created and it can be solved using an application of the DMAIC methodology. In other words, the hypothetical project is going to address a chronic process problem that has no known solution. In Table 9.5, three tools help a team define the project more clearly from VOC and VOB perspectives: a high-level process map called a Supplier-Input-Process-Output-Customer (SIPOC) chart, a project charter, and a quality improvement team. A SIPOC is used to clearly define the project scope (i.e., where it starts and ends). A project charter describes a project from several perspectives including the problem it must eliminate, the impact to customers and the business, estimated business benefits, and the resources required to move it forward. This enables the selection of a team consisting of suppliers to the process, customers receiving its output,

TABLE 9.5

Basic Tools in the Design Phase

Tool	Description
SIPOC	A high-level process map showing the inputs and outputs between suppliers, the process, and customers, as well as the metrics at the input and output boundaries (i.e., Supplier-Input-Process-Output-Customer).
Project charter	A formal document, either electronic or in paper format, that describes the project's objective, its anticipated customer and business impacts, the project timeline, the required resources, and the project's team members.
Quality improvement team	Two or more individuals assigned to a project and having roles and responsibilities necessary to complete the project or associated work.

TABLE 9.6

Six Sigma Project Deliverables

Deliverable
1. Project title
2. Black Belt name
3. Team picture
4. Problem statement
5. Project objective
6. Process baseline
7. High-level process map
8. Cause and effect analysis
9. Failure mode and effects analysis
10. Initial measurement systems analysis
11. Capability analysis
12. Initial business benefit estimate
13. Elimination of many trivial input variables
14. Selection of the few vital variables using a root-cause analysis and statistical tools solution to eliminate the root causes
16. Integrated control plan
17. Mistake-proofing strategy
18. Final measurement systems analysis
19. Instructions and training plan
20. Verified final business benefits
21. Next steps
22. Project translation opportunities
23. Lessons learned
24. Proof of process control

and others that work in the process. A project's team members are selected based on where the project is focused (i.e., its scope) and specific knowledge of the process.

Once formed, the team led by a Black Belt works to complete the project's key deliverables by DMAIC phase as listed in Tables 9.6. A Black Belt is the Six Sigma expert and project lead for the team. This person has been trained in the tools and methods of the initiative. Project definition requires identifying customer requirements, business benefits, and their strategic alignment. As data are collected, a project's objective should become focused to ensure it remains within the defined scope and can be executed according to the project's schedule. The project's definition also requires a baseline of CT or KPOV metrics. Figure 9.5 lists operational

1. Customer satisfaction
2. Business benefits and strategy alignment
3. Narrowly focused
4. Historical baseline
5. Measurable
6. Resources available
7. Team members available

- Customer billing adjustments
- Sales policy errors
- Product destroyed in field
- Returned product
- Warranty expense
- Shipping errors
- Premium freight
- Margin improvement
- Sales success rate
- Inventory holding costs
- Inventory obsolescence
- Emergency maintenance
- Overtime expense
- Product transfer
- Rework expense
- Scrap expense
- Past-due receivables
- Cycle time

FIGURE 9.5
Project definition: How to select projects.

areas where projects have been successively deployed within organizations. There are in fact thousands of project applications across different industries. If an existing process is not achieving its designed performance levels, there may be an opportunity to create a DMAIC improvement project.

A SIPOC describes a process at a high level. It may also help identify new projects. An example is shown in Figure 9.6. This version is quantified and helps identify new projects. It helps refine the scope of a project to a part of the process and on a single or several metrics. There are four business metrics in Figure 9.6 for each of the four operations. Depending on priorities, sixteen integrated projects can be deployed within this process. They could reduce cycle times, defect rates, or costs, or they could improve yields. Using this concept, a team can be assigned to improve any of these metrics. If a SIPOC does not currently exist, then a team can use the questions listed in Figure 9.6 to begin constructing a SIPOC and quantify it in a similar manner.

Inputs				Outputs
Category	Operation 1	Operation 2	Operation 3	Operation 4
Expense %	10%	50%	30%	20%
Defect %	15%	10%	2%	1%
People	100	500	800	200
Cycle Time	1 day	20 days	5 days	100 days

- Why does this process exist?
- What is the purpose of this process?
- What are the process outputs (Ys)?
- Where does the process begin and end?
- Who are the customers of this process?
- What are the inputs and outputs for every high-level process step in the SIPOC?

FIGURE 9.6
How to build a SIPOC.

A project charter is a formal document that communicates the problem a team is investigating. The charter has several important components that were discussed in Chapter 7 and are shown in Figure 7.9. A charter describes the process where a project is deployed, its starting and ending dates, as well as its project leader, champion, and process owner. These terms were discussed in Chapter 2. In this chapter, we want to focus on metric definitions. Metrics need to be carefully defined and have the characteristics shown in Figure 9.7. At a project level, there are two categories of metrics: primary and secondary. The team is focused on improving primary metrics but does not want to inadvertently induce a deterioration of the secondary metrics. The secondary metrics balance the primary metrics. An example would be maintaining customer service levels if inventory investment is reduced. The primary metric may initially be at a higher level and represented as a business metric. A business metric is linear and can be aggregated across an organization. An example is the inventory turnover statistic that can be calculated for any product, aggregated by product family and across facilities. Recall that an inventory turnover ratio is calculated as the cost of goods sold divided by the average inventory investment needed to support it. The higher the ratio, the lower the required inventory investment that is needed. If the initial primary metric is inventory turnover, then eventually lower-level metrics will be added to

Actionable …Tough to Beat … Drive the Right
Behavior… Aligned With Strategic Goals …Easy to
Measure…Link Across an Organization

Primary Metric: A yardstick used to
measure project success. Consistent with
the problem statement and its objective.
Includes two time series: baseline
performance (average over past 12
months) and actual performance versus
the project's objective.

- Business Metric
- Project Metric
- Financial Metric

Secondary Metric: Used to drive the
right team behavior. Tracks potential
negative consequences of the project
improvements. More than one secondary
metric may be required.

FIGURE 9.7
Project definition: Business metrics.

the project if a root-cause analysis shows they impact the inventory turnover ratio. A financial metric is in monetary units. In the inventory turnover example, inventory investment would be a financial metric used to
measure a project's success as its level is reduced.

As a team works through a root-cause analysis, the reasons or root causes
for low inventory turnover or high inventory investment will be identified
and eventually eliminated. Root causes could be of different types. These
are the operational factors such as lead time, large lot sizes, delivery issues,
poor forecasting and inventory models, or other issues. At this point in a
project, the business and financial metrics may be augmented with project
specific metrics such as reducing lead time or improving forecasting accuracy, etc. In fact, a root-cause analysis could lead to several other projects,
each having a different operational metric or "project metric" tied to a
project's business, financial, secondary, and operational metrics from the
root-cause analysis.

As a project charter is updated its problem statement, goal, or other
information are refined. Table 9.7 shows attributes of good versus poor
problem statements. A good problem statement communicates a complete
description of a problem and strategically links it to leadership's goals and
objectives. It does not contain solutions that are not based on a root-cause

TABLE 9.7

Project Definition: Good Problem Statements

Good Problem Statements	Poor Problem Statements
1. Complete description of a problem.	1. Customer requirements are not known.
2. Shows current baseline performance metrics.	2. No linkage to business objectives.
3. Describes customer requirements.	3. Quantification is not reliable.
4. Links to business objectives.	4. Measurement sources are not defined.
5. Contains no solutions.	5. Little linkage to customer metrics.
6. Is quantified.	6. Its solutions or causes are stated in advance.
7. Defines its measurement sources.	

analysis. Figure 9.8 shows that a poor problem statement can be improved. Once it is refined, several smaller projects may be identified that narrow the scope of the initial project. The reasons for a high inventory investment might be due to several different root causes as described above, with each cause requiring a separate project.

Team members have different roles and responsibilities as shown in Table 9.8. Some are directly related to project execution, and others are

Problem Statement

- Focus the team on a process deficiency.
- Communicate the significance to others.
- Does not contain solutions or causes.
- Is as quantified as possible.

Poor Problem Statement

Product returns are too high and will be reduced by analyzing first- and second-level Pareto charts.

Better Problem Statement

Product returns are 5% of sales, resulting in a loss of $5 million and reduced market share of 10%.

Project Objective

- Part of the problem statement.
- Address problem statement.
- Quantify performance improvement.
- Identify timing.

Poor Project Objective

Reduce product returns by implementing individual performance measures and objectives

Better Project Objective

Reduce returns of product line XYZ from 5% to 2.5% of sales by year end to reduce overall business unit returns by 1% and save $1 million.

FIGURE 9.8

Project definition: Writing a problem statement and objective.

TABLE 9.8

Roles and Responsibilities

Role	Description
Project champion	Breaks down barriers inhibiting the project.
Process owner	Manages day-to-day process activities and controls local resources.
Project manager	Leads the team and works with the champion and process owner.
Team members	Support brainstorming, data collection, data analysis, and process improvement work.
Financial representative	Validates project definition, alignment, and financial benefits.
Other functional experts	Provide information, advice, or specific resources such as data extraction for the team.

indirectly related. They may also have other names depending on the context of the discussion. In some organizations, a project manager is also called a Black Belt. A project manager or Black Belt leads their team through the DMAIC methodology. The Black Belt has been highly trained to apply tools and methods to work through a project definition, root-cause analysis and solution. These tools and methods the focus of this chapter. A project champion secures the resources and stakeholder support to help accelerate project completion. The champion will coordinate the work of several Black Belts and liaison with the process owners and leadership. The role of the process owner is to work with a DMAIC team to ensure that it remains on track, to provide resources, and to implement solutions. The process owner will own the solution and has a special interest in ensuring the solutions are effective and sustainable. The improvement team may also have ad hoc members from finance, information technology, and other functional teams.

MEASURE PHASE

The tools and methods of the measurement phase ensure the critical-to (CT) characteristics or KPOV baseline are identified and accurately measured against the target level. During this phase, the team brainstorms potential input variables (or Xs) for data collection activities that impact CT performance. Table 9.9 lists the common tools and methods used in the measure phase. These include measurement systems analysis (MSA),

TABLE 9.9

Measurement: Basic Tools

Tool/ Method	Description
Measurement systems analysis (MSA)	Determining the components of measurement system including its resolution, accuracy, stability, linearity, repeatability, and reproducibility.
Capability analysis	Determining how well a process output (i.e., a Y or CT characteristic) meets customer requirements relative to its central location and variation.
C&E diagrams	A brainstorming tool that qualitatively relates causes to their effects. It is used to identify potential Xs for data collection.
C&E matrix	A matrix that allows ranking of potential Xs to several Ys or CT characteristics using information obtained from several C&E diagrams.
Data collection	The process of collecting data on the potential process inputs (i.e., Xs) thought to impact the process outputs (i.e., Ys).
Statistical sampling	A series of efficient data collection methods that select some members of a population for data collection and analysis, but not all members of the population. This information is used to estimate the magnitude of the population's statistical parameters with a stated level of statistical confidence.

C&E = cause and effect; CT = critical-to characteristic.

capability analysis, cause and effect (C&E) diagrams, the C&E matrix, data collection planning, and statistical sampling.

The MSA is used to verify that a CT can be measured accurately and with sufficient precision to detect changes in its level as a DMAIC team implements solutions in the improve phase. Although an MSA is applied to the evaluation of a CT characteristic or a KPOV (or Y), it may also be used to evaluate KPIVs (or Xs). Table 9.10 shows six components of an MSA: resolution, accuracy, reproducibility, repeatability, stability, and linearity. Four of the MSA components are relatively easy to evaluate. Resolution requires that a measurement system should be in units smaller than the CT characteristic it is measuring. As an example, if we historically measured lead time in days but need to make process improvements in the range of hours, then the resolution should be hours or minutes. The second component, accuracy, can be estimated and corrected. If measurements consistently read low or high on average, we can adjust the system to eliminate this bias and bring it on target. Stability can also be managed.

TABLE 9.10

Measurement System Analysis (MSA)

Analysis

---

1. **Resolution:** The ability of the measurement system to discriminate changes in the characteristic being measured (1/10 rule). This rule ensues that the measurement system is in smaller increments than what is being measured. As an example, if a project metric is in hours, we would want a resolution of minutes or perhaps seconds.
2. **Accuracy (Bias):** The ability to measure a characteristic and be correct on average over many samples.
3. **Reproducibility:** The ability of two or more people (or machines) to measure a characteristic with low variation between each person (or machine).
4. **Repeatability:** The ability to measure a characteristic with small variation when a sample is measured several times under constant conditions.
5. **Stability:** The ability to measure a characteristic with the same person (or machine) and obtain the same measurement value over time.
6. **Linearity:** The ability to measure the characteristic over its entire range with equal variation (error).

For example, if we are using visual color standards to evaluate product quality, then inspection procedures and training can be created to periodically replace the color standards if they fade over time. The fourth of these MSA components is linearity. Our measurement tools should be used within the range it was designed (i.e., where variation remains constant). We should avoid situations in which the MSA tools are highly variable.

Reproducibility and repeatability involve people and tools. Reproducibility measures the consistency of two or more people to agree on average when measuring the same part with the same measuring tool. Repeatability is the consistency of one person measuring the same part several times using the same tool. These components are evaluated with a Gage Reproducibility and Repeatability study. Reproducibility and repeatability differ based on the distribution of the CT characteristic. If a CT characteristic is distributed as a continuous variable, then a "Variable Gage R&R" is used to evaluate reproducibility and repeatability. If the CT characteristic is discrete (e.g., pass or fail), an Attribute Agreement Gage R&R is used to evaluate reproducibility and repeatability. Not all six measurement components may be applicable for evaluating some systems. As an example, if the measurement system is automated within a single system that does not require manual intervention, then its reproducibility component does not need to be estimated.

Capability analysis is a set of tools and methods designed to compare the process performance of a CTQ characteristic to customer requirements. A capability analysis compares the VOC, in the form of specifications,

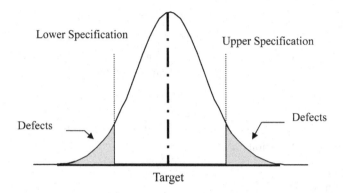

$$\text{Capability} = \frac{\text{Specification Range}}{\text{Process Variation}}$$

Specification Range = Upper Specification – Lower Specification

Process Variation   = Number of Process Standard Deviations

FIGURE 9.9
Capability analysis.

to the VOB, in the form of a simple ratio in a manner shown in Figure 9.9. It is important that an improvement team be able to measure a CT characteristic with sufficient accuracy and precision to determine its capability level. An ideal situation is one in which the distribution of a CT characteristic is centered on a target and with small variation. If six standard deviations of a CT distribution can be fit on each side of a specification's lower and upper limits, then the CT characteristic is at Six Sigma. There are different versions of capability metrics, each of which can be converted into the other metrics using transformation equations. As an example, Motorola adopted the Six Sigma capability metrics "Z" and "Sigma," while many other organizations adopted the AIAG terminology of C_p, C_{pk}, P_p, and P_{pk}. The capability metrics shown in Figure 9.10 have a simple transformation equation of Z_{st} = Sigma = $3 \times C_p$. They show that Cp = 2 at the Six Sigma performance level. This is because C_p = 1 is defined as a process capability of ±3 standard deviations within the upper and lower specification limits with the process centered on target, but a Six Sigma process has ±6 standard deviations, or C_p = 2.

The yield metrics shown in Table 9.11 are also commonly used in quality programs such as Six Sigma. These include defect per unit, parts per

	On-Target	Off-Target
Short-Term Variation	C_p $Z_{st} =$ Sigma $= 3 \times C_p$	C_{pk}
Long-Term Variation	P_p	P_{pk}

FIGURE 9.10
Capability metrics.

million (PPM), and rolled throughput yield (RTY). RTY measures of the number of units that pass through all the process operations defect-free. Defect-free means that no units were scrapped or reworked as they were transformed by the process. The more complicated a process, the lower the RTY, all other things equal. In the Six Sigma program, the concept of

TABLE 9.11

Process Yield Metrics

Metric Definition
1. Defects-Per-Unit (DPU) = Total Defects Found in Sample / Total Units In Sample
2. Parts-Per-Million (PPM) = DPU X 1,000,000
3. Rolled Throughput Yield (RTY) = Π / I [(Defect Free Units at Each Step$_1$) / (Total Units At Each Step $_1$) x100]
4. . RTY = Yield 1) x (Yield 2) x (Yield 3)
Over a very large number of workflow operations the RTY approximation is:
5. RTY = $e^{-DPU}{}_{Total}$
Opportunities = Number of workflow operations which are right or wrong:
6. Defects-Per-Million-Opportunities (DPMO) = PPM/Opportunities/Unit
7. Sigma = Z value from a normal table corresponding to DPMO *(Must be converted to short-term Z)*

opportunity counting was also introduced to measure process yield and complexity simultaneously. PPM is calculated for each CT characteristic of a product or service. Dividing the PPM number by the opportunity count (i.e. the number of value-add operations) of the process enables calculation of the defects per million opportunity statistic. This is the metric from which the Z_{st} or Sigma of the overall process is calculated.

Although organizations use variations of these quality metrics, several of them are equivalent, as shown in Figure 9.10. There are four groups, and placement depends on whether a CTQ characteristic is on-target or off-target and on how its standard deviation is estimated. A target is the mid-point between bilateral specifications' lower and upper specification limits. A standard deviation is calculated using short-term or long-term historical baseline data. A short-term historical baseline is calculated using the standard deviation of samples collected as rational sub-groups. A rational sub-group is defined as a set of observations taken from a process that represents the smallest practical variation the process will produce. As an example, if the hour-to-hour variation of a process needs to be evaluated, then a rational sub-group would be an hour. This implies that there will be higher observed variation between hourly sub-groups than within them. In Figure 9.10, the improvement strategy is to improve process capability by moving the mean of a CT characteristic to the target, and then reducing its variation.

A complication was added to capability estimation in the original Six Sigma deployment at Motorola when a constant of "1.5" was arbitrarily added to a calculated Z or sigma value. This is seen in Table 9.12, where the classic probability calculations are shown in the long-term section of the table, and the Six Sigma calculations are shown with a 1.5 constant or sigma shift added in the other section. Statisticians do not accept an assumption of a 1.5-sigma shift in every process. Our recommendation is to use long-term capability calculations and to directly calculate short-term or sub-group statistics specific for the process being analyzed. As an example, the area under a normal distribution curve at 0.5 (or, in our analysis, a defect percentage of 50%) correlates to a Z value of 0. This is the mean of a standard normal distribution. In contrast, the Six Sigma scale shifts the 0 by +1.5 standard deviations. The resultant defect percentage decreases from 50% to 6.68%. This practice may significantly overestimate process capability. The practical way to calculate short- and long-term capability is to use actual process data without this 1.5-Sigma shift.

Once the CT characteristic baseline and its capability for meeting the specification are calculated, the team begins to brainstorm the potential

TABLE 9.12

Tabulated Probabilities

Short-Term		Long-Term (Actual Percent)			
Sigma	Cₚ	PPM	Percent	Zlt	CPk
1.50	0.50	500,000	50.00%	0.00	0.00
2.00	0.67	308,549	30.85%	0.50	0.17
3.00	1.00	66,809	6.68%	1.50	0.50
4.00	1.33	6,210	0.62%	2.50	0.83
5.00	1.66	233	0.023%	3.50	1.16
6.00	2.00	3.4	0.000%	4.50	1.50
2 parts per billion		3.4 parts per million			

Note: Statisticians do not assume a 1.5 sigma shift in every process. The recommendation is to use "long-term" calculations; and directly calculate shorter term or subgroup statistics to calculate an actual shift for your process.

causes for poor performance. This will form the basis for the data collection plan. A C&E diagram and similar methods are used to identify potential causes that may impact the CT characteristic or KPOV. The C&E helps the DMAIC team brainstorm all causes of poor capability for subsequent prioritization. In Figure 9.11, a C&E diagram is applied to an inventory investment example. The causes are grouped by the standard categories of measurements, methods, procedures, and people. In other applications, categories might include machine, measurements, methods, materials, people, or environment. A team can use other categories that fit their situation. If the C&E diagram is used effectively, then the root-cause analysis will show that one of more of the causes on the C&E diagram have a significant impact on the CT characteristic. These inputs (or Xs) are now called KPIVs. In the improve phase, we will experiment by changing the levels of these Xs to understand their impact on the KPOV (or, Y), which is the CT characteristic.

The C&E matrix shown in Figure 9.12 is used to rank Xs for data collection relative to several CT characteristics or Ys. The C&E matrix is useful if the team has two or more C&E diagrams each containing several common Xs. The team uses the matrix to assign a weighting to each X relative

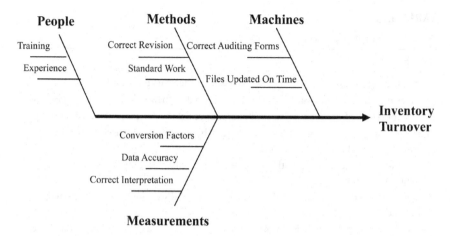

FIGURE 9.11
Cause and effect diagram.

Rating of Importance to Customer	10	8	7	6	8	
	1	2	3	4	5	
Process Inputs	Yield%	Cost	Strength	Color	Cycle Time	Total
1 Temperature	5	1	3	8	10	207
2 Pressure						
3 Catalyst Level						
4 Material A						
5 Material B						
6 Line Speed						
Total						

FIGURE 9.12
Cause and effect matrix.

TABLE 9.13

Data Collection Activities

Action

---

1. Ask the right questions to ensure the assessment meets its goals and objectives.
2. Determine the type of information and data required to answer the assessment questions.
3. Bias the data collection efforts toward quantitative data to increase analytical sensitivity.
4. Develop a data collection plan that specifies where the data will be collected, by whom, and under what conditions.
5. Review the collection plan with your team and the people who will be part of the data collection activities.
6. Develop data collection forms that are easy to use and will not be misinterpreted; include all instructions as well as examples.
7. Remember to collect data in a way that makes for easy data entry into Minitab, Excel, or other software packages.
8. Ensure the team is trained in the correct procedures, tools, and methods, including measurement of the data.
9. Periodically analyze the assessment data to ensure it provides the necessary information.
10. Allow resources and time in the schedule for follow-up data collection efforts as necessary.

---

to its correlation to each Y and the overall ranking of the Ys to each other. In the example shown in Figure 9.12, a single calculation is made for the independent variable temperature relative to each of the Ys. The weighted total for temperature, across all of the Ys, is 207. After the ratings of the other Xs are calculated, they are prioritized in descending order based on the weighted totals. Data collection efforts are focused on the Xs having the highest weighted total scores. This method is useful when there are many variables.

The data collection activities listed in Table 9.13 are used to measure the Xs identified in the C&E matrix and their corresponding Ys. Each combination of Xs and the associated Ys will be analyzed in the third DMAIC phase (i.e., the analyze phase). The team starts the data collection planning by listing all of the questions that will need to be answered in the analyze phase. These questions should correspond to the root-cause analysis. Additional questions may arise during the data collection because the process is iterative, but good planning will already have listed most questions. Table 9.13 lists several useful ideas to help improve data collection. Finally, a periodic review of the data collection strategy and its related activities is important for project success.

Statistical sampling becomes important once the specific activities of the data collection plan (i.e., where data will be collected, by whom, under

Universe: A set of characteristics that define the complete set (i.e. the complete population).

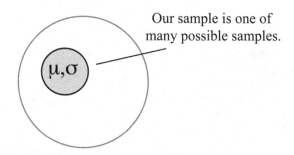

Sample: A subset of members possessing the same characteristics as the universe or entire population.

FIGURE 9.13
What is sampling?

what conditions, how it will be measured, its frequency of measurement, and the sample size) are established. Figure 9.13 shows two attributes of statistical sampling (i.e., sampling is conducted when an entire population cannot be counted, and samples should be representative of the population with respect to the parameters being estimated and large enough to make inferences about the population's parameters using the sample). The sample size depends on the statistical methods to be used, the risk we assume when stating statistical conclusions, and the distribution of the CT characteristic or Y (the metric) that is being analyzed. Ensuring a sample is representative implies we have collected data from each variable combination. As an example, if our CT characteristic is the cycle time of four machines across three shifts, we need to collect data from each machine on each shift to answer questions concerning overall performance across the four machines and three shifts, which is our population. In contrast, if a project focus is only one machine and shift, then data would be collected for the one machine and shift, which is the population. In summary, a sample drawn from a population should reflect the questions that need to be answered in the root-cause analysis.

Sampling can be complex, but there are simple guidelines that are useful for most applications. Figure 9.14 shows four common sampling methods. Simple random sampling is used if a population is not stratified relative to its Xs or independent variables. In simple random sampling, a sample

1. **Simple Random Sampling:** Drawing a sample from a population at random.

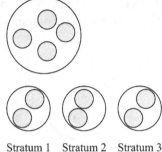

2. **Stratified Sampling:** Using a stratification variable to divide a population into groups (strata) then drawing a random sample from each group.

Stratum 1   Stratum 2   Stratum 3

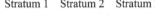

Sequence or Time

3. **Systematic Sampling:** Drawing a random sample at equal intervals by sequence.

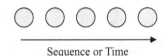

4. **Cluster Sampling:** Drawing a random sample from naturally occurring groups.

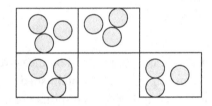

FIGURE 9.14
Common sampling methods.

of size *n* is randomly drawn from the population and sample statistics are calculated to estimate the population's central location and dispersion. If there are several variables at several levels, a sample can be stratified by the number of independent variables and their discrete levels. Random samples are then drawn from each stratum. In the previous example, samples of cycle time were to be collected over the four machines and three shifts. A third sampling method is applied if a process changes over time. This is systematic or rational sub-group sampling, in which samples are periodically collected from a process. The subsequent analysis provides information of the Y or dependent variable as a time series. Finally, if a population can be represented using several naturally occurring groups or clusters then cluster sampling would be used to collect data.

Although sampling can be complex, some simple guidelines are provided in Figure 9.15. These guidelines should be verified using an exact sample size formula prior to their usage. A final consideration in sampling

Continuous data measured along a scale such as temperature:

•One sample test ~ 20 to 30 observations.

•Two sample test ~ 10 to 15 observations per subgroup.

•One Way ANOVA ~ 5 to 10 observations per subgroup.

•Two-level factorial designs use 2 to 6 replicates per experimental combination.

Discrete data either pass/fail or a set of discrete counts:

•One sample proportion test >100

•Two sample proportion test > 100 per group

•Contingency tables ~ sample until there are at least 5 observations per cell

FIGURE 9.15
Sampling guidelines.

is when a dependent variable or Y is highly skewed. The required sample size must be larger for a skewed distribution than for a normal distribution because variance will be greater. If the sample data are not normally distributed but this is the test assumption, then several actions can be taken that may help normalize the sample data. First there may be errors in the data that skew it, and these errors can be removed. There could also be outliers that are far from the sample mean. This condition would also skew the data. Outliers should be investigated, and if they are not representative of the whole sample, they can be removed from the sample. If they cannot be explained and removed, however, then the distribution may be skewed. The measurement system could also be biased or could contribute to sample variation. A measurement analysis should be done to verify its accuracy, precision, and other components. If portions of the sample were collected at different times, there may be more than one distribution present. If this is true, the samples should be analyzed separately. If the sample is very small or is not representative, then a larger sample could be collected. Finally, if the sample remains skewed, then a distribution test should be made, and the data fit to the correct distribution.

ANALYZE PHASE

Once sampling for the independent variables or Ys and dependent variables or Xs has been collected, analytical tools can be used to understand relationships between independent and dependent variables. Each method is designed to answer a very specific question and requires that the data be in a specific format. These tools and methods include process maps, histograms, Pareto charts, box plots, scatter plots, time series graphs, and many others that will answer the questions the data collection was created to answer.

There are several types of process maps. Each one provides insight into how a process works, but from different perspectives. We have already discussed SIPOC charts and value flow maps. The discussion will focus on functional process maps. These maps show how material and information flow operation by operation over time through a process. The operations are organized within workstreams or swim lanes that are usually functional in nature. An advantage of this approach is that rework loops and multiple hand-offs are easily seen as work moves between functions. The operational work tasks, inspection tasks, movement of materials and information, and other activities taking place within a process are shown.

There are three common versions of this type of process map. The first is the current state or as-is version of the process. This version, which may be how the process is expected to work, is often inaccurate. The team must verify the accuracy of the current-state process map by walking the process operation by operation with the people who do the actual work. The second version of a functional process map is the future state, or what the process should be. The future state map is an optimized process. All non-value-add operations and rework loops will be eliminated in the future-state process. This methodology is like that used in value flow mapping, except there is a focus on swim lanes by function. Portions of value flow maps are often broken into functional process maps to study them in detail. Table 9.14 provides useful ideas for building a functional map. Process maps, in different formats, are also used throughout the DMAIC process, depending on the required analytical questions. Figure 9.16 shows how different types of process maps are used in the DMAIC phases.

Histograms are graphical summarizations of continuously distributed data. The histogram shown in Figure 9.17 shows the central location and dispersion of the number of returns by month. Notice the distribution

TABLE 9.14

Building Effective Process Maps

Action
1. The project's problem statement should be well defined.
2. Include all required functions on the mapping team.
3. Brainstorm for solutions to how the team should analyze the process.
4. Interview people who are part of the process workflow.
5. Include people who perform work tasks within the process on the team.
6. Define "as-is" (current) and "should-be" (future) process maps.
7. Understand the process by walking it.
8. Be willing to identify process workflow shortcomings.
9. Team members should provide constructive solutions to problems.
10. Use open-ended questions when investigating the process.
11. Collect all available process information.
12. Map the process workflows.
13. Include the process boundaries using a SIPOC chart.
14. Analyze all metric linkages.
15. Ensure the correct level of detail in the process map.
16. Analyze the current process metrics.
17. Analyze the current process interfaces.
18. Create the "as-is" and "should-be" process maps.
19. Compare the maps.
20. Migrate the process to the "should-be" process map.

is highly skewed right. Subsequent statistical analysis of the population's central location or median will require the use of non-parametric tools and methods because the data are not symmetrical around the mean (i.e., the data are not normally distributed). Non-parametric methods will test

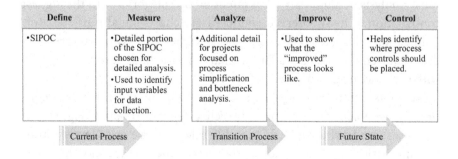

FIGURE 9.16

Where are process maps used? SIPOC = supplier-input-process-output-customer.

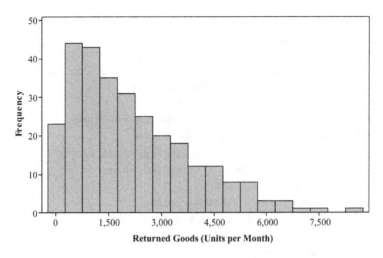

FIGURE 9.17
Histogram of returned goods.

a continuous distribution's median rather than its mean. The median is a better estimate of central location for a skewed distribution. The returns histogram shown in Figure 9.17 could be used to describe the project's baseline prior to the starting an improvement project to reduce returns. After a project is completed, it is useful to compare the before and after returns distributions to see of the median returns or its variation was reduced over the baseline scenario.

Pareto charts are useful for ranking discrete categories of a variable by relative count or frequency. In Figure 9.18, a second-level Pareto chart classifies inventory classes by four machines. Notice the inventory classes having the highest observed counts by machine are placed first on the chart and the others in descending order. Pareto charts are useful for root-cause analysis because they focus attention on categories with the highest contribution to total observed count. Pareto charts are also useful communication vehicles to stakeholders because they are easy to interpret. The data required to construct a Pareto chart must include several categories with each having an observed count.

Box plots graphically depict the central location and range of a continuous variable for one or more discrete categories or levels. Figure 9.19 shows a three-level box plot of monthly sales at three price levels within two industries and two regions. Notice that the average monthly sales changes for price level, industry, and region. The variation also changes for each discrete level of the three variables. The advantage of using a box

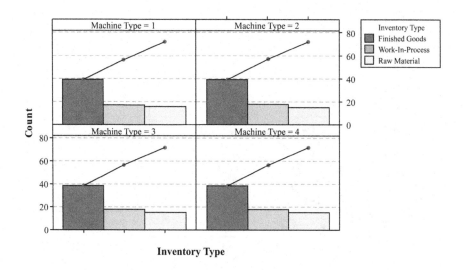

FIGURE 9.18
Pareto chart of inventory type by machine type.

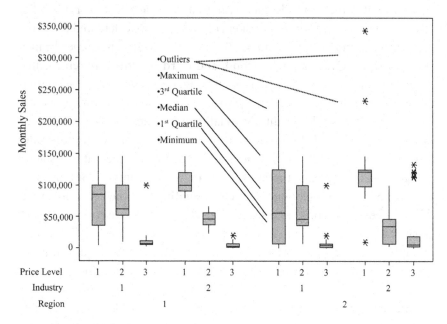

FIGURE 9.19
Box plot of sales vs region, industry, price level.

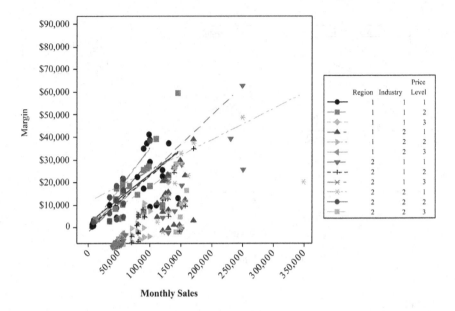

FIGURE 9.20
Scatter plot of margin vs sales.

plot is that it depicts sample data without assuming a specific probability distribution. The ends of the whiskers of each box are calculated using the following formulas: lower limit = Q1 – 1.5 (Q3 – Q1), and upper limit = Q3 + 1.5 (Q3 – Q1). The first, second, and third quartiles are represented by horizontal bars as shown in Figure 9.19. Box plots are useful for qualitatively comparing several variations and at several levels for each variable.

Scatter plots describe qualitative relationships between two continuous variables. In Figure 9.20, gross margin is plotted against monthly sales and stratified by price level, region, and industry. In the pattern shown in Figure 9.20, it appears that margin increases as monthly sales increase. Scatter plots are useful for qualitatively evaluating how the dependent variable changes in response to a second variable. They are useful for preliminary analysis and prior to developing more quantitative models. As an example, if a scatter plot shows a curvilinear pattern, a subsequent higher-level mathematical model may show its quantitative relationship as $Y = a + b_1 \times X_1^2$.

Time series plots show changes in a continuous variable over time. They are like scatter plots except that the independent variable or X is ordered by time. The continuous variable is on the Y axis and the time index is

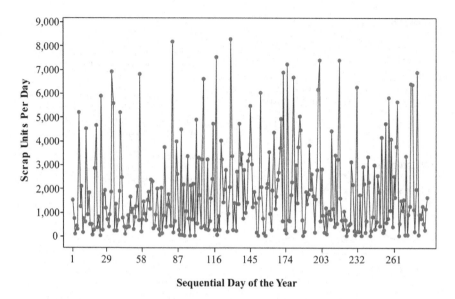

FIGURE 9.21

Time series plot of scrapped units for all machines.

the X axis. Figure 9.21 shows a time series graph of scrapped units per day for several machines and the day of the year independent variable is sequential. The average scrap rate appears constant over the time period, but scrap variation appears high. Examples of useful time series include forecasting models and control charts.

ADVANCED METHODS

Root-cause analysis requires the use of the simple analytical tools and methods just discussed. More advanced methods are also useful for root-cause analysis and are essential for some analyses. These include distribution fitting because statistical tests assume a specific probability distribution, tests of means and medians for continuously distributed data, test of proportions, when the data are pass or fail, and other advanced tools and methods.

Hypothesis testing formulates a statistical statement dependent on a practical question. The statement is also associated with a specific statistical test method that has specific assumptions. Figure 9.22 shows nine

Two -Sided Test

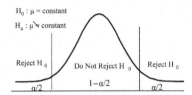

$H_0 : \mu = \text{constant}$
$H_a : \mu \neq \text{constant}$

Reject H_0 | Do Not Reject H_0 | Reject H_0
$\alpha/2$ | $1-\alpha/2$ | $\alpha/2$

1. A one-sided test is more sensitive than a two-sided test (i.e., the critical value is less).

2. Correctly reject the null hypothesis with 1-α confidence (i.e., when the calculated "p" value corresponding to the test statistic s less than 0.05, then reject H_0).

3. Minitab correctly calculates "p" based on either the one-sample or two-sample or two- sample situation.

One -Sided Test

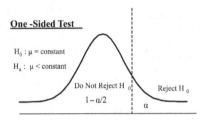

$H_0 : \mu = \text{constant}$
$H_a : \mu < \text{constant}$

Do Not Reject H_0 | Reject H_0
$1-\alpha/2$ | α

1. Set up the hypothesis and its alternative.
2. Set the significance level of the test α and β.
3. Choose a test statistic to test H_0.
4. Determine the sampling distribution of the test statistic.
5. Set up the critical region where H_0 is rejected.
6. Set the sample size.
7. Choose a random sample and collect data.
8. Compute test statistic and look at "p" statistic.
9. Make decision on H_0.

FIGURE 9.22
Hypothesis testing overview.

sequential steps to set up a statistical hypothesis. In all hypothesis tests, the null hypothesis (H_0) is a statement of equality, and the alternative hypothesis (H_a) is a statement of not equal, less than, or greater than. There is also a test method with the practical question, and it has a test statistic. The magnitude of the test statistic is evaluated relative to its statistical significance. The larger the magnitude of the test statistic, the smaller the area to right side (for this discussion) of the critical value. The area is also called a probability value p. This area is also the probability of incorrectly stating that the null hypothesis is false, i.e., it is incorrectly rejected in favor of an alternative hypothesis.

TABLE 9.15

Statistical Risk

		Your Decision	
		Reject H_0	Don't Reject H_0
Reality	H_0 True	Type I Error $P\ (Type\ I\ error) = \alpha$	Correct
	H_0 False	Correct	Type II Error $P\ (Type\ II\ error) = 1{-}\alpha = \beta$

Table 9.15 describes statistical risk. Alpha risk is related to a decision of correctly rejecting a false null hypothesis, whereas beta risk is failing to reject a false null hypothesis. As an example, if a null hypothesis is true but we do not reject it, then we have made a Type I decision error. Alternatively, if a null hypothesis is false but we do not reject it, then we have made a Type II error. Statistical risk occurs because samples are used to estimate population parameters such as a mean or variance.

Each statistical test is based on an underlying probability distribution and assumptions of its test statistic. We confirm distribution assumptions using a goodness-of-fit analysis to confirm a sample follows a specific probability distribution. This is also a hypothesis test with a null assumption that the sample data follows the presumed distribution. A common assumption of most analyses is that the sample is drawn from a normal distribution. The assumption needs to be proven using a goodness-of-fit test. The null hypothesis can be correctly rejected with $1{-}p$ confidence of not making a Type I error, or stating that the sample data is not from a normally distributed population when in fact it is.

In Figure 9.23, sample data representing monthly demand show an Anderson-Darling goodness-of-fit normality test. The p value indicates we can reject the null hypothesis correctly with $1{-}0.123 = 87.7\%$ confidence of not making a Type I error. It should be noted that by convention we usually set a critical probability of $p = 0.05$ (or $1{-}p = 95\%$ confidence) of not making a Type I error. In the current example, because the p value of 0.123 is greater than 0.05, we do not reject the null hypothesis and assume the sample was drawn from a normal distribution. We can now use statistical tests that require normality.

Tests on means and medians are used when data are continuous and the questions are relative to central location. Tests of means include one-sample t-tests, two-sample t-tests, and one-way analysis of variance (ANOVA) tests. The one-sample t-test answers a simple question: "Is a sample mean

Summary for Monthly Demand (Units)

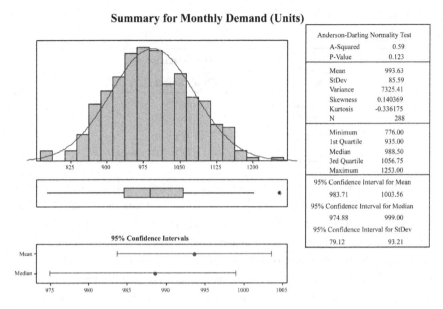

Anderson-Darling Normality Test	
A-Squared	0.59
P-Value	0.123
Mean	993.63
StDev	85.59
Variance	7325.41
Skewness	0.140369
Kurtosis	-0.336175
N	288
Minimum	776.00
1st Quartile	935.00
Median	988.50
3rd Quartile	1056.75
Maximum	1253.00
95% Confidence Interval for Mean	
983.71	1003.56
95% Confidence Interval for Median	
974.88	999.00
95% Confidence Interval for StDev	
79.12	93.21

FIGURE 9.23
Distribution fitting.

equal to a constant?" A two-sample *t*-test answers the question, "Are two means equal?" Figure 9.24 shows an example of the two-sample *t*-test for the question, "Is the mean monthly demand equal to the mean monthly units shipped?" The calculated test statistic is shown to be 17.65, and the *p* value is close to 0. This implies we should reject the assumption of equal means and conclude that the samples differ at a statistically significant level (i.e., 1–*p* confidence of not making a Type I error).

A one-way ANOVA test answers the question, "Are these *k* sample means equal?" In all three statistical tests, an assumption is that the sub-groups are drawn from a normal distribution. The one-way ANOVA also assumes that the variances of the *k* sub-groups are equal. If the sample distributions are continuous but highly skewed, non-parametric tests of medians are used to compare central location of sub-groups. The one-sample Wilcoxon test compares a sample median to a test median, whereas Mood's median test or a Mann-Whitney test compares two sample medians to each other, and a Kruskal-Wallis test compares several sample medians. In all comparative tests, when a *p* value associated with the calculated test statistic is less than 0.05 (or 5%), we can reject the null hypothesis of assumed equality with 1–*p* = 95% confidence of not making a Type I error and state that there is a difference in central location.

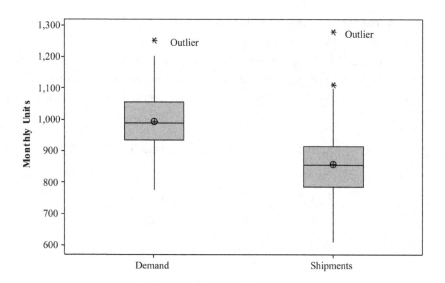

Two-Sample T-Test and CI: Demand, Shipments

Two-sample T for Demand vs. Shipments

	N	Mean	StDev	SE Mean
Demand	288	993.6	85.6	5.0
Shipments	288	857.5	99.1	5.8

Difference = mu (Demand) − mu (Shipments)

Estimate for difference: 136.146

95% CI for difference: (120.992, 151.299)

T-Test of difference = 0 (vs not =): T-Value = 17.65

P-Value = 0.000 DF = 562

Statistically significant

FIGURE 9.24
Box plot of monthly demand and shipments.

Tests of proportions answer practical questions related to differences between proportions. As an example, a one-sample proportion test answers the question, "Is the sample proportion equal to a known test proportion?" A two-sample proportion test answers the question, "Are these two sample proportions equal?" The underlying assumption in proportion tests is that the test statistic follows a binomial distribution because it is a success or a failure (i.e., discrete).

A contingency table answers a practical question, "Are two variables related to each other based on an observed count or frequency?" In Figure 9.25, the null hypothesis states the observed counts of defective

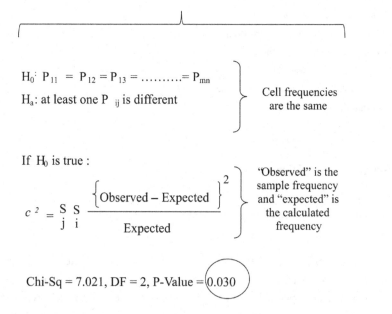

	Shift 1	Shift 2	Shift 3	Total
Form A	5	8	20	33
	7.64	11.51	13.75	
	.912	1.123	2.841	
Form B	20	30	25	75
	17.36	26.39	31.25	
	.401	.494	1.250	
Total	25	38	45	108

$0.694 \times 38 = 26.4$ $0.306 \times 45 = 13.8$

H_0: $P_{11} = P_{12} = P_{13} = \ldots\ldots = P_{mn}$

H_a: at least one P_{ij} is different

Cell frequencies are the same

If H_0 is true :

$$c^2 = \underset{j}{S}\,\underset{i}{S}\ \frac{\{Observed - Expected\}^2}{Expected}$$

"Observed" is the sample frequency and "expected" is the calculated frequency

Chi-Sq = 7.021, DF = 2, P-Value = 0.030

FIGURE 9.25
Contingency tables.

invoices are the same regardless of the type of form used or the shift using a form. The observed counts are shown in Figure 9.25 to be 5, 8, and 20 for Form A and shifts 1, 2, and 3, respectively. The observed counts for Form B were 20, 30, and 25 for shifts 1, 2, and 3, respectively. The calculated or expected counts (rounded) are shown to be 7.6, 11.5, and 13.8 for Form A and shifts 1, 2, and 3, respectively. The expected counts for Form B are 17.4, 26.4, and 31.3 for shifts 1, 2, and 3, respectively. Contingency tables help answer the question, "Are the observed counts close enough to the expected counts to be considered a random pattern?" If the p value of the calculated test statistic is less than 0.05 (or 5%), the null hypothesis with its assumption of equality is rejected and we conclude the counts differ by the type of form or shift with $1-p$ confidence of not making a Type I error.

Equal variance tests answer the practical question, "Are the variances of two or more sub-groups equal?" The null hypothesis is that sub-group variances are equal. If the sub-groups are normally distributed, then the more sensitive Bartlett test can be used for the analysis. However, if one or more sub-groups are not normally distributed, then the Levene test (non-parametric assumption) should be used for the analysis. In Figure 9.26, we see that the p value associated with the Bartlett test is 0.166, which exceeds 0.05. Based on this high p value, we conclude the sub-group variances are equal. Equal variance tests are also used to determine if an assumption

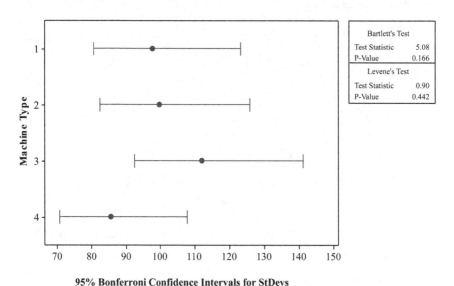

95% Bonferroni Confidence Intervals for StDevs

FIGURE 9.26
Test for equal variances for monthly shipments (units).

of equal sub-group variance is satisfied prior to using tests such as two-sample *t*-tests and one-way ANOVA that require this assumption.

One-way ANOVA tests answer a practical question: "Are the means of the sub-groups equal?" The null hypothesis is that the sample means are equal. The assumptions necessary to use this test are that the sub-groups are normally distributed and have equal variance. In the example shown in Figure 9.27, the mean monthly shipments of four machines are compared to each other. The null hypothesis is that the machines have the same mean number of shipments. The high *p* value of 0.591 indicates that we reject the null hypothesis and conclude that the mean numbers of shipments of the

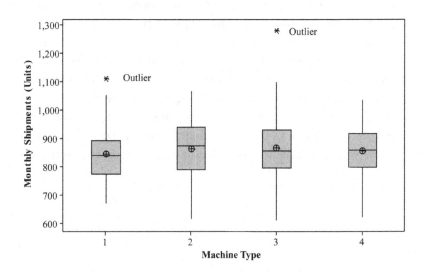

Source	DF	SS	MS	F	P
Machine Type	3	18,846	6282	0.64	0.591
Error	284	2,798,358	9853		
Total	287	2,817,204			Not statistically significant

S = 99.26   R-Sq = 0.67%   R-Sq(adj) = 0.00%

FIGURE 9.27
Box plot of monthly shipments by machine type.

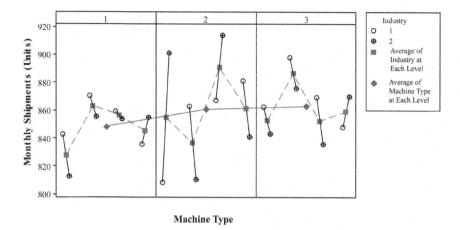

FIGURE 9.28
Multi-Vari chart for monthly shipments by industry, machine type, and price level.

machines are equal. If the assumptions for the one-way ANOVA are not met, then a non-parametric test such as the Kruskal-Wallis test can be used to test the null hypothesis that the sample medians are equal.

A Multi-Vari chart is a sophisticated graphical tool comparing several independent variables or factors to a continuous dependent variable or Y. An example is shown in Figure 9.28, where the dependent variable is monthly shipments. The chart shows how the level of a dependent variable changes when the levels of several independent variables change. The independent variables shown in Figure 9.28 include machine type, price level, and industry. The highest variation in shipments is associated with industry.

Whereas a scatter plot compares relationships between two continuous variables without calculating a model, a correlation analysis assesses the linear relationship between two independent and continuous variables from samples and provides a model to explain a linear relationship. In a correlation analysis, the r or simple correlation coefficient varies between -1 and $+1$. A value of $r = -1$ indicates a perfect negative correlation where one variable increases, the second deceases. A value or $r = +1$ indicates a perfect positive correlation where as one variable increases, the second variable increases. In Figure 9.29, several continuous variables are compared pairwise, and simple linear correlation coefficients are estimated for each pair-wise comparison. A p value is also calculated for the null hypothesis: "There is no linear correlation between the variables."

In the example, the correlation between warranty and rework is 0.629, or weakly positively correlated, but the associated p value is 0, which is lower

	Margin%	Percent Error	Warranty	Returned Goods
Percent Error	0.005			
	0.934			
Warranty	0.099	0.032		
	0.094	0.591	Not Statistically Significant	
Returned Goods	0.099	0.032	1.000	
	0.094	0.591		
Scrap	0.031	0.060	0.629	0.629
	0.600	0.311	0.000	0.000	Statistically Significant
Rework	0.031	0.060	0.629	0.629
	0.600	0.311	0.000	0.000

FIGURE 9.29
Correlation.

than our critical value of 0.05 (or 5%). As a result, we reject the null hypothesis of no correlation and conclude that the variables are linearly correlated to each other with at least 95% confidence of not making a Type I decision error. The algorithm made the p calculation based in part on the sample size. In contrast, warranty and margin% have a correlation coefficient of 0.99 and a p value of 0.094, indicating no statistically significant linear correlation at a 95% confidence level.

These tools and methods help build a regression model by identifying potentially important variables that explain the level and variation in the KPOV (or Y). As we work through the analyze phase, we ask questions such as, Does prior information suggest a tentative model? How are data being collected? What are the independent variables? Then when we create the regression model, check its assumptions, look for influential observations (i.e., outliers), and validate it using confirmatory experiments. Recall that we have used various terms for the dependent variable, including CT characteristic, Y, and KPOV. For the independent variables, we have used terms like X or KPIV. Regression explains relationships between the dependent variable and one or more independent variables. The coefficients of the model are linear in that the terms can be added together if

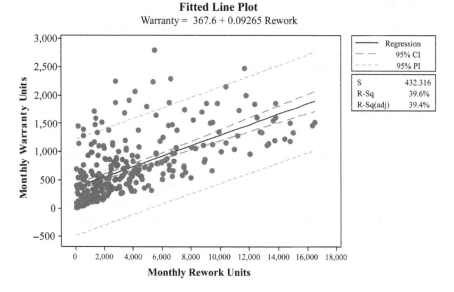

FIGURE 9.30
Simple linear regression.

independent to predict the dependent variable. But the X terms may have a first or second order effect on Y. In other words, they may have a format of X or X^2. In more advanced models, the independent or dependent variables may be either continuous or discrete. In all the models, a one-unit change in X increases Y by the coefficient of X, and these terms are added to the constant of the equation, assuming the Xs are independent of each other.

We begin the regression discussion by discussing simple linear regression as an analytical tool used in the analyze phase of the DMAIC methodology. Figure 9.30 shows a simple example of monthly warranty units versus the number of monthly rework units. The assumption is that as the number of reworked units increases, there will be leakage to customers. Based on the analysis shown in Figure 9.30, there appears to be a positive correlation between the numbers of reworked units and warranty units. But there is noise in the analysis because the $R^2_{adjusted}$ value is just 39.9%. This means it explains only 39.9% of the variation in Y, whereas we require an $R^2_{adjusted}$ value of 90% or higher.

The analysis also calculates a regression equation: Warranty = 367.6 + 0.09265 Rework. This means that, on average, a one-unit increase in rework increases warranty units by 376.6 + 0.09265 = 367.7 units. The line through the sample data is the equation. The data vary within the confidence intervals (CI) 95% of the time, and individual values vary within the

TABLE 9.16

Model Assumptions: A Residual Is a Difference between the Predicted Y from the Regression Equation and the Actual Y

Predicted Y	Actual Y	Residual
10	8	2
8	10	−2
10	10	0

Assumption	How to Verify
Independence of the residuals	Checked by plotting the residuals versus the time sequence of observation to verify randomness and using the appropriate test (e.g., Durbin-Watson)
Normality of the residuals	Checked by running a normal plot of the residuals
Constant variance of the residuals	Checked by running a normal plot of the residuals

prediction intervals (PI) 95% of the time. Recall that, if there are outliers, these should be investigated and eliminated if possible to create a better model. In addition to the outlier investigation, the results of the model should be analyzed. A residual is a difference between the predicted Y from the regression equation and the actual Y. The larger the differences, the poorer the regression model and the farther the sample data are from the regression line. If the residuals are close to the regression line, the higher the R^2 statistic. R^2 is a ratio of the variation explained by our model to the total variation of the dataset. Table 9.16 describes how residuals are calculated and the rules that ensure a good model.

Figure 9.31 shows the equations for the R^2 and $R^2_{adjusted}$ statistics. The total variation is calculated as the difference from each data point from the mean of all the data. The sum of squares of error (SSE) is the difference at each level where the model does not predict the actual values. The simple linear regression model is sum of squares of total variation (SST) = sum of squares of variation explained by the model (SSM) + SSE. SST, SSM, and SSE are calculated using other equations. When we move from simple linear regression having one independent variable to multiple linear regression with several independent variables, R^2 is adjusted because the addition of any independent variable to the regression model, however irrelevant, will cause a decrease in the SSE term and create a marginal increase in R^2. This correction term balances the effect of the addition of irrelevant independent variables to the model against the required increases in sample size and reduction in the SSE.

- The addition of any independent variable to the regression model, however irrelevant, will cause a decrease in the SSE term, producing a marginal increase in R^2

- The correction term balances the effect of the addition of irrelevant independent variables to the model against the required increases in sample size and reduction in the error sum of squares.

$$R^2 = 1 - \frac{SSE}{SST} \qquad\qquad R^2_{adj} = 1 - \frac{SSE/(n-k-1)}{SST/(n-1)}$$

- Where k = number of independent variables in the regression model.

FIGURE 9.31
What is R^2? SSE = sum of squares for error; SST = sum of squares for total.

Figure 9.32 shows some common regression-based models. In this chapter, we will discuss multiple linear regression models (MLR) using several independent variables. MLR models explain variation of a dependent variable by using a least squares algorithm. The algorithm fits an equation or line through a dataset in a way in which the sum-of-squared deviations from every data point to the fitted line is minimal relative to any other line that could be fit through the same dataset. We will also discuss several other statistical tests that how good the fitted line is for explaining the variation of the dependent variable.

MLR requires parameters of a model be linear so they can be estimated with a least squares algorithm. Referring to Figure 9.32, we see additional assumptions that must be met. These are residuals should be normally and independently distributed around zero with constant variance. Recall that a residual is the difference between the models' fitted value (Y_{fitted}) minus its observed value ($Y_{observed}$) for each experiment or observation of a dataset. An experimental observation consists of a Y or dependent variable (e.g., monthly sales) and the levels or values of each independent variable (i.e., Xs) are used to build a predictive MLR equation represented as $Y = f(X) = \beta_0 + \beta_1 X_1 + \beta_2 X_2 + \ldots + \beta_k X_k$. As an example, if the MLR model is fitted to the monthly sales of \$100,000, but the actual observed value of monthly sales was \$90,000, then the residual would be \$10,000. The larger the residual, the poorer the fit of an MLR equation.

In addition to the MLR model, there are several specialized regression models used for specific situations. Several of these are shown in Figure 9.32. In the MLR model, the parameters or coefficients are linearly

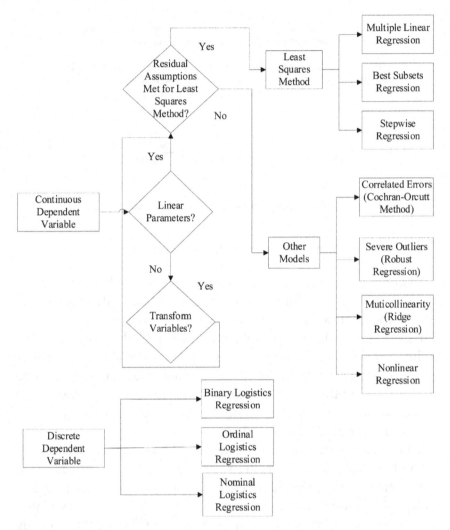

FIGURE 9.32
Regression models.

related to a dependent variable Y, although the form of the independent variables can be quadratic (e.g., x^2) or may contain other higher-order terms. There are other types of regression models shown in Figure 9.32 that are used to explain the variation of a dependent variable Y when the assumptions required for using an MLR model cannot be met. As an example, non-linear regression is used if the estimated parameters of the equation are not a linear function of the dependent variable. An example would be if the parameters were in the form of an exponential function such as $Y = \beta_0 + \beta_1 e^{X_1}$ In this application, a transformation of the non-linear equation might be useful for building the linear relationship of $Y = f(X)$, but this may not always be possible. The Cochran-Orcutt method is another regression model wherein the MLR assumptions are not satisfied. In this application, residuals are correlated by time and are not independent. An MLR analysis requires the serial correlation information contained in its residual pattern be incorporated back into the MLR model as a term to explain the variation of the dependent variable more adequately. The Cochran-Orcutt method can be directly used to explain the variation of the dependent variable. If independent variables are correlated to each other (as determined using a variance inflation factor), ridge regression can be used to build a regression model. A robust regression method is used if MLR assumptions are not met due to severe outliers in a dataset. Finally, if a dependent variable is discrete, logistical regression can be used to build a model. There are three major types of logistic regression models: binary (pass/fail), ordinal (1, 2, 3, 4, etc.), and nominal (red, white, blue, etc.), depending on how the data of the dependent variable are structured.

Several statistics are associated with MLR models. Figure 9.31 showed an R^2 statistic and its adjusted version, $R^2_{adjusted}$. These statistics measure the percentage of variation of the dependent variable explained by an MLR equation. As an example, an R^2 statistic of 0.9 implies 90% of the variation of Y is explained by an MLR equation. It is apparent that high R^2 statistics imply a good model fit to a dataset. $R^2_{adjusted}$ adjusts R^2 downward to account for the number of independent variables incorporated into the MLR model relative to the sample size used to build it. This is because R^2 can be increased by simply adding variables to the MLR model, even if they do not explain changes in Y.

A second important test is the Durbin-Watson (DW) statistic, which measures serial correlation of the model's residuals (assuming data are ordered by time) as shown in Figure 9.33. One assumption of an MLR model is that its residuals are not serially correlated over time. Figure 9.33 shows it is possible to have positive or negative serial correlation in a fitted model. In actual practice, the calculated Durbin-Watson test statistic is compared to critical values in a statistical table. These critical values are determined considering sample size, the number of independent variables in the model, and the Type I error required by the test. As a rule, an ideal range of the Durbin-Watson test statistic is between 1.5 and 2.5. Serial correlation requires that serially correlated data points or experimental

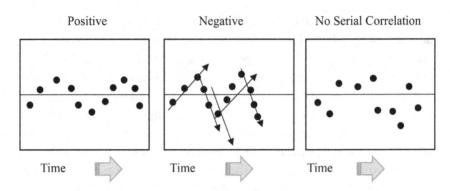

FIGURE 9.33

Durbin-Watson test for serial correlation. A formal statistical test for serial correlation of the residuals is based on the Durbin-Watson test. For no serial correlation, the test statistic $d \sim 2.0$; for positive serial correlation, $d < 2.0$; and for negative serial correlation, $d > 2.0$. If d is in the range of 1.5 to 2.5, do not suspect statistically significant serial correlation. Note: the d statistic varies by sample size.

observations be removed from the MLR model, or that additional terms be incorporated into the MLR model to incorporate the effect of serial correlation of the residuals. Alternatively, the Cochran-Orcutt method can also be used to build the MLR model.

Figure 9.34 summarizes the analytical strategies for building models with serial correlation. These are in fact quite common in situations where time is relevant (e.g., forecasting). A useful approach is to add a lagging dependent variable to the model. A failure to account for residual serial correlation will create either an inefficient model (without lagging dependent variable terms in the model) or an inconsistent model (with lagging dependent variable terms in the model). Inefficient implies the estimated coefficients of the model are accurate on average, but they have a large variance (i.e., a larger sample will be required to precisely estimate them). Inconsistent means the estimated parameters are incorrect and will change from sample to sample.

A third useful statistic is the variance inflation factor, which measures the degree of correlation between two independent variables. Highly correlated independent variables, if left in the final model, will result in inefficient estimates of the independent variable coefficients. This will require a larger than necessary sample to precisely estimate them. Changes in one independent variable would be confused with changes to other independent variables with which it may be correlated.

Regression Model	No Correlated Residuals (Errors)	Correlated Residuals (Errors)
Simple Linear Regression	Use Least Squares Method	Least squares parameters estimates are inefficient; use Cochran-Orcutt method.

◄──── *Use Durbin-Watson test to detect serial correlation* ────►

Models Having Lagged Dependent Variables	Use Least Squares Method	Least squares parameter estimates are inconsistent; use nonlinear regression.

◄──── *Use Durbin-h test to detect serial correlation* ────►

FIGURE 9.34

Correlated residuals. Inefficient = produces a larger variance of the parameter estimate, and a larger sample size is required to reject the null hypothesis: parameter = 0. Inconsistent = the estimated values of the parameter will not correspond to the true value.

Table 9.17 shows how to interpret the suitability of a regression model using the $R^2_{adjusted}$ statistic and residual patterns to adjust it to better estimate the dependent variable (or Y). The $R^2_{adjusted}$ statistic and non-random residual patterns may be caused by poor data collection, including incorrect independent variables, the wrong model format (i.e., perhaps it is not a straight line but a curve, which is better explained using X^2 terms). Or perhaps additional independent variables should be added to the model or provide a better fit to the data. It is a useful tool to evaluate how well an MLR model fits a dataset using its R^2 value and residual pattern. R^2 is a simple ratio of the variation explained by an MLR model (i.e., SSM divided by the total variation of the dataset as measured by deviations from the average of all the data points SST).

Table 9.17 also shows a slightly modified version of an R^2 statistic in terms of the SSE: 1–(SSE/SST). SSE is the variation of the dependent variable not explained by an MLR model. The total variation in a dataset equals the variation explained by the MLR model and the variation not explained by it (i.e., SST = SSM + SSE). The higher the SSE term, the poorer the MLR model fit, and vice versa. If a model fits the dataset poorly, its residual pattern should be first analyzed to look for clues as to how best to modify it to more exactly fit the dataset (i.e., to explain more of the variation of the dependent variable). As an example, in Table 9.17,

TABLE 9.17

Interpreting Model Residuals

$$SS_{Total} = SS_{Model} + SS_{Error} \qquad \text{Larger the residuals the higher } SS_{Error}$$

	Random Low Variation of Residuals	Random High Variation of Residuals	Non-Random Pattern of Residuals
R^2 Low	• N/A	• Poor Model • Incorrect KPIVs • Measurement Accuracy	• Poor Model • Add terms to model • Transform KPIVs, KPOVs or Both
R^2 High	• Good Model • Correct KPIVs	• N/A	• Good Model • Add terms? • Transform?

What Is R^2 Adjusted?

The addition of any independent variable to the regression model, however irrelevant, will cause a decrease in the SSE term ...producing a marginal increase in R^2 ... the correction term balances the effect of the addition of independent variables to the model against the required increases in sample size.

$$R^2 = 1 - \frac{SSE}{SST}$$

$$R^2_{adj} = 1 - \frac{SSE/(n-k-1)}{SST/(n-1)}$$

Where k = number of independent variables in the regression model.

where R^2 is low (i.e., < 0.90), the residuals are large. One or more of the potential causes discussed above might be operative (i.e., there could be measurement errors with the data collection). If there is a non-random residual pattern, it may be possible to transform the dependent or independent variables to obtain a more exact model fit. Another option might be to add an additional term to the MLR model. As an example, if a quadratic pattern is observed in the residual pattern, it might make sense to add a X_i^2 term. This assumes serial correlation is eliminated and the independent variables are not collinear (i.e., their variance inflation factors are equal to or close to 1).

IMPROVE PHASE

Six Sigma was initially deployed in manufacturing. Experimental designs were revolutionary for understanding how to optimize machines depend on several variables. These methods are still important when experiments should be done. But the Six Sigma program has migrated to different industries over the past thirty years, including those focused on services. The application of formal experimental designs outside manufacturing is limited, but at times it can be useful. The process of planning experiments is useful in any application because it presents a logical sequence for data collection and analysis. In this section, the intent is to briefly describe these methods.

Why use experimental design instead of regression analysis to build a model? Regression analysis relies on historical data to build a model. These data may be inconsistent and inaccurate. Running a carefully controlled experiment ensures data collection will be consistent and its data accurate. Historical data often are not collected at the full ranges of the independent variables. As a result, regression models can only interpolate within the limited data range. If an independent variable's range is only partially sampled, some information will be missing. Planned experiments provide a full range over which a variable is studied. The solution space will be larger. Also, data collected haphazardly may contain correlated errors if there is an underlying periodicity. This will cause some variables to appear important when they are not or vice versa. Experiments randomize data collection, factoring out the effect of time. Finally, some independent variables may be correlated to each other, causing spurious modeling relationships. There are statistical tests to identify multilinearity, but experimental design avoids this situation because the independent variables are not correlated to each other. Independence also maximizes the solution space and enables the evaluation of combinations of independent variables through their interacting effect on Y.

The improve phase of the DMAIC methodology uses the information gained from the analysis phase. This includes information describing those KPIVs that impact the KPOV. These independent KPIVs are important for changing the level of the KPOV, dependent variable, or Y. Once a list of KPIVs has been determined, the DMAIC team experiments by changing their levels in an organized way and evaluating their combined impact on the KPOV. This evaluation is done using experimental designs that measure the impact of each KPIV by itself and in combination on

TABLE 9.18

Experimental Designs

Experimental Design	Description
Full factorial designs	An experimental design in which the independent variables are studied at two or more levels. Normally used when the independent variables are discrete.
2^k designs	An experimental design in which the independent variables are studied at two levels relative to their linear relationship with the dependent variable. Normally used when the independent variables are continuous.
Fractional factorial designs	A 2^k experimental design in which not all factor combinations are evaluated. In fact, higher-order interactions are traded away to reduce the size of the experiment.
Screening designs	Special types of 2^k experimental designs in which the fractionation is at a very high level. A special class of screening designs called Plackett-Burman designs allow intermediate numbers of experiments versus the 2^k situation to further reduce the number of required experiments.
Response surface designs	Experimental design that allows quadratic modeling between several continuous independent variables and a continuous dependent variable.

the KPOV. Full factorial designs study independent variables at two or more levels and assume a linear relationship between the Xs and the Y. Fractional designs are efficient ways to use full factorials by running fewer experiments and trading off unnecessary information on variable combinations or interactions. There are several versions of this concept where relationships between the Xs and Y may not be linear or the variables may be discrete rather than continuous. Other models are used to explain how changes in Xs impact the Y. A few examples are shown in Table 9.18.

Table 9.19 shows the five steps to create an experimental design: planning, selecting a design, conducting an experiment, analysis, and building the model. Planning an experiment is the most important step. It is important that a team agree on the types of information an experiment will need to provide to run an experiment and determine the KPIVs, including an initial evaluation of how they may interact with each other to affect the KPOV. Other considerations include the distribution of the KPOV (i.e., continuous versus discrete), risk mitigation if the experiments do not

TABLE 9.19

Planning Experiments

Step	Actions
1. Planning	• What functions must the product or process perform? • Set the experimental design objective(s). • Define the time frame of the study. • Select responses (i.e., outputs or Ys). • Select factors (i.e., independent variables or Xs) whose levels will be varied in the experiment; sources of Xs are the cause and effect matrix, FMEA, SIPOC, etc.). • Determine resource requirements.
2. Select design	• Select the best design type. • Consider relationships between independent variables (i.e., interactions). • Establish the degree of confounding (i.e., alias structure). • Randomize runs and factors. • Allocate factors to the array. • Document non-linearity of effects
3. Conduct experiment	• Make sure everyone knows about the experimental plan. • Know how to measurement of inputs and outputs. • Record experimental conditions.
4. Analyze data	• Develop the relationship between the dependent and independent variables (i.e., $Y = f(x)$). • Analyze each variable independent of others (i.e., main effects). • Analyze variables acting together on the output (i.e., interactions). • Understand the optimum levels to set each of the Xs to put Y on target (i.e., best factor settings). • As the Xs vary within specification, how does Y vary (i.e., prediction interval)?
5. Build model: $Y = f(x)$	Confirm the regression model's terms (i.e., Ys and Xs).

FMEA = failure modes and effects analysis; SIPOC = supplier-input-process-output-customer chart.

go as planned, and resource requirements. A continuously distributed KPOV requires significantly fewer experiments to detect its change relative to changes of the KPIV levels. Another important consideration in planning an experimental design is the selection of the KPIVs that are included in the experiment and the range over which they will be evaluated. Important questions include, "Is a KPIV continuous or discrete?" or "Over which range should we evaluate the KPIVs?" Once KPIVs and the KPOV have been selected for experimentation, the design can be selected.

The second step is to carefully plan and conduct the experiment. This includes ensuring all team members know their role during the experiment, how the data will be collected, and the tools and methods to be used, and developing a risk mitigation plan. The analysis of experimental data will be straightforward if experiments are well executed according to the plan. After the experiment and the model is determined, the DMAIC team confirms the model through confirmatory experiments.

Full Factorial Designs

Full factorial experiments are used if the KPIVs have two or more discrete levels. These designs use linear transformation equations, which means that, although a low level and a high level of a KPIV are run in the model (this is a type of regression model), we cannot interpolate between the discrete factor levels. Figure 9.35 provides an example of a full factorial experimental design that optimizes monthly sales. Price level is the most significant variable for predicting monthly sales. This is confirmed by its probability value of ~0.00 in the ANOVA table. Recall that a variable is statistically significant if its probability value (of not making a Type I error) is less than 0.05 (or 5%). The other variables all have probability values greater than 0.05 and are not statistically significant. The factor plots show large discrete changes in monthly sales as the price level changes. In contrast, the other factors show no change as price level increases.

2^k Experimental Designs

A 2^k factorial design is shown in Figure 9.36. In these designs, all factors have just a low and a high level for k factors. Some KPIVs may be discrete at two levels, whereas other KPIVs may be continuous and, though run at a low and a high level, formulas are used to interpolate linearly between the two values. An assumption of linearity requires only two levels for evaluating the effect of each KPIV on the KPOV. The analysis shows that price is a significant predictor of monthly sales. Its associated probability value is 0.008. Notice that the $R^2_{adjusted}$ statistic of the current model that includes all KPIVs and interactions is 63% (i.e., it explains 63% of the variation of monthly sales). Referring to Table 9.17, we may be able to improve the predictability of the equation. But first the model needs to be simplified reduced by eliminating statistically non-significant KPIVs with high p values. Regardless of the final model and its $R^2_{adjusted}$ statistic,

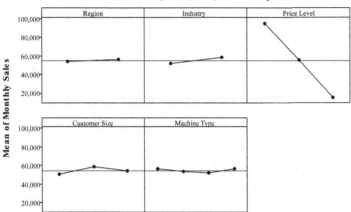

General Linear Model: Sales versus Region, Industry, and Price Level

Factor   Type Levels Values

Region   fixed   2 1, 2
Industry   fixed   2 1, 2
Price Level   fixed   3 1, 2, 3
Customer Size   fixed   3 1, 2, 3
Machine Type   fixed   4 1, 2, 3, 4

Analysis of Variance for Sales, using Adjusted SS for Tests

Source	DF	Seq SS	Adj SS	Adj MS	F	P	
Region	1	540262278	540262278	540262278	0.30	0.582	
Industry	1	2648573371	2648573371	2648573371	1.49	0.223	
Price Level	2	3.07080E+11	3.07080E+11	1.53540E+11	86.52	0.000	Statistically Significant
Customer Size	2	2736877373	2736877373	1368438687	0.77	0.463	
Machine Type	3	897503568	897503568	299167856	0.17	0.918	
Error	278	4.93360E+11	4.93360E+11	1774675039			
Total	287	8.07263E+11					

FIGURE 9.35
Full factorial designs.

price level will remain an important predictor of monthly sales. This design shows the impact of each KPIV on the KPOV independently as well as in combination with other KPIVs (these are interactions between the independent variables). Interactions exist if combinations of KPIV levels cause unusual changes to the level of a KPOV. In fact, in some models, the KPIVs by themselves may not be significant, but combinations of the KPIVS may be statistically significant. In this example, the

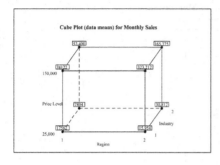
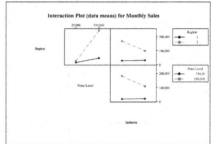

Factorial Fit: Sales versus Region, Price Level, Industry

Estimated Effects and Coefficients for Sales (coded units)

Term	Effect	Coef	SE Coef	T	P	
Constant	81530	18015	4.53	0.002		
Region	104,616	52,308	18,015	2.90	0.020	
Price Level	126,994	63,497	18,015	3.52	0.008	Statistically Significant
Industry	-34,365	-17,182	18,015	-0.95	0.368	
Region × Price Level	93,916	46,958	18,015	2.61	0.031	
Region × Industry	-37,125	-18,562	18,015	-1.03	0.333	
Price Level × Industry	-36,915	-18,457	18,015	-1.02	0.336	
Region × Price Level × Industry	-49,433	-24,716	18,015	-1.37	0.207	

$S = 72061.4$ R-Sq = 80.27%   R-Sq(adj) = 63.01%

FIGURE 9.36

2^k Design.

interaction between Industry and Price Level is statistically significant with a probability value of 0.031.

Fractional Factorial Designs

Fractional factorial designs are a special type of 2^k experimental designs in which not all combinations of the KPIVs or factors are evaluated in an experiment. Fractionation can be very useful in situations with many KPIVs because some of their higher-order interaction information is usually not practically useful. This is shown in Figure 9.37, in which a 2^3 experimental design containing three KPIVs was fractionated into two parts, or a one-half fraction, for experimentation. Fractionation saves experimental resources, and it reduces the information obtained from an experiment. As an example, in Figure 9.37 we saw that, prior to fractionation, each of

Run	A	B	AB	C	AC	BC	ABC	
(1)	-	-	+	-	+	+	-	
a	+	-	-	-	-	+	+	block 2
b	-	+	-	-	+	-	+	
ab	+	+	+	-	-	-	-	
c	-	-	+	+	-	-	+	block 2
ac	+	-	-	+	+	-	-	
bc	-	+	-	+	-	+	-	
abc	+	+	+	+	+	+	+	block 2

Factors	2^k	Main Effect	1st	2nd	3rd	4th	5th	6th
5	32	5	10	10	5	1		
6	64	6	15	20	15	6	1	
7	128	7	21	35	35	21	7	1

1. Resolution III: Retrieves all main effects in a 2^k fractional factorial, but each will be aliased with some two-way interactions.

2. Resolution IV: Retrieves all main effect clear of two-way interactions, but some two-way interactions are aliased with each other.

3. Resolution V: Only three-way or higher order interactions are aliased.

FIGURE 9.37
Fractional designs.

the KPIVs (i.e., A, B, and C) and their interactions AB, AC, BC, and ABC had different patterns of +1 and –1 levels. After fractionation, factors A and BC, factors B and AC, and factors C and AB had similar patterns. In other words, we cannot know if the change in the KPOV will be caused by level changes in either factor in these factor pairs. This fractionalization is also called aliasing because some variables are indistinguishable relative to their effect on the KPOV. It is also called confounding because there is confusion related to which factors are affecting the KPOV (i.e., the main factor or its interaction). The interpretation of fractional factorial designs is like full factorial interpretation, except not all KPIV and interaction terms are required. Screening designs are created when the fractionalization is continued to a point that all KPIVs are aliased with lower level interaction information. In these highly fractioned experimental designs statistically insignificant variables and their aliases can be eliminated from the analysis to save experimental resources. Then the statistically significant variables and their aliases can be studied as full factorial designs. The number of overall experiments is reduced with the reduction in KPIVs studied.

Response Surface Designs

The previously discussed experimental designs were linear relative to relationships between the KPIVs and the KPOV. In contrast, response surface models explain curvilinear relationships between one or more of the KPIVs and the KPOV. Figure 9.38 shows a relationship between adhesion, which is the KPOV, and the KPIVs of temperature and pressure. The KPIV terms are of the form X^2 and X. There are also several versions of these models, with the central composite and Box-Behnken designs being the two most popular. Figure 9.38 shows that a central composite design can be built from a 2^k level design using axial points if a curvilinear relationship is found by running an intermediate center point in the 2^k level design.

CONTROL PHASE

As we enter the control phase, we have identified the major root causes of poor KPOV performance. We know how to maintain optimum performance levels to the original targets by modifying the KPIVs, either because we have a regression model from analysis of historical data or experimentation or we have a non-mathematical solution derived using Lean tools and methods. Controls need to be placed on these KPIVs to ensure the solutions are sustainable. The controls will be incorporated into a control plan and the project will be transitioned to the process owner. Important questions will need to be answered at this time: Which variables need to be controlled? What is the control strategy (e.g., control charts, FMEA, audits, checklists, others)? How will controls be implemented? Who is accountable for monitoring and taking corrective actions? When will a control activity start and finish? How will we know if the process is not under control?

The important actions to ensure effective process control include listing the process steps in the updated future state map and identifying KPIVs from the analyze and improve phases on the map. If the project was focused on a product, the KPIVs will be features, functions, and

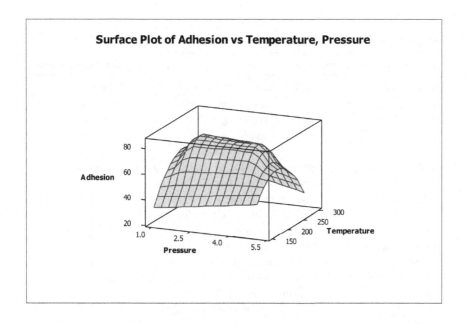

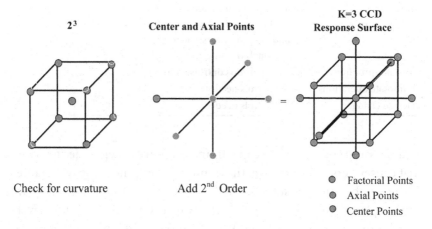

FIGURE 9.38
Response surface methods.

attributes. Table 9.20 describes common solutions to eliminate root causes and controls that help sustain the solutions. In the third column, a note is made relative to how easy it will be to sustain the solution. Eliminating root causes for a problem may require using a combination of solutions. As an example, perhaps updated procedures, training, and audits are all needed to sustain a solution. We want to avoid situations where only the less sustainable solutions and controls are used, instead using robust

TABLE 9.20

Controls on Process Improvements

Solution/Improvement	Controls	Ability to Sustain
Verbal instructions	Audit, checklist, written procedure, testing	Difficult
Written instructions	Audit, visual, web-link to ensure compliance, testing	
Training	Audit of frequency, content, web-link to ensure compliance, testing	
Audits	Set schedule, skills, templates, feedback, and corrective action	Requires frequent audits
7-S methods	Visual control, roles and responsibilities, audit, feedback, and corrective actions	
Statistical process control	Visual control, operator involvement, reaction plans (other control charts)	
New roles and responsibilities	Monitor effectiveness through audits and measurements, incorporate thorough training and procedures	Easier
Total productive maintenance	Set schedule, skills, templates, feedback, and corrective action	
Policy changes	Monitor effectiveness through audits and measurements, incorporate thorough training and procedures	
Mistake-proofing	Limited or no controls (FMEA)	
Eliminate operations	No controls needed	
Design change	No controls needed	

solutions and controls. If we can eliminate a process step or design feature that causes poor performance, the improvement is more easily sustained.

The combination of solutions is incorporated into the formal quality control plan shown in Figure 9.39. The two versions differ in their level of detail. Important questions are, Which outputs and inputs are important from the root-cause analysis and need controls on their solutions? How should the inputs be controlled and to what level? How should we measure each input and output to ensure it remains at its target level? What is the frequency of measurement, including inspection and testing? Who is responsible for control of the outputs and inputs, including training and work instructions? Everything needs to be documented in the control plan and integrated into the organization's quality management systems. The control plan integrates all control actions and ensures process outputs and key inputs are under control. The control plan is a formal document

Less Detailed

What	Why	Who	How	Reaction Plan
1. The project metrics	To ensure performance to target is met over time	The process owner and work team	Control chart unless root causes were eliminated	Procedures and recommendations should be part of management control systems and describe what to do if the process goes out of control
2. Controls on improvements that could fail (e.g., 7S, training, procedures, manual operations etc.)	To ensure performance to target is met over time	The process owner, work team and 3rd parties *(internal or external)*	Periodic audits using checklists, management reviews using agenda, periodic training with compliance testing etc.	Procedures and recommendations should be part of management control systems and describe what to do if the process goes out of control

More Detailed

Title:											
Process Name:		Prepared by:						Page: 1 of 1			
Location:		Revised by:						Document #:			
								Revision: 1.0 Date:			
Process Step	Description	Output (Y) or Input (X)	Specification LSL	Target	USL	Measurement Method	Size	Frequency	Who	Where Recorded	Action

FIGURE 9.39
Control plans.

with supporting information that shows the KPIVs and how to control them so the KPOV stays on target with minimum variation. In addition, reaction plans are created and incorporated within the control plan to bring a process back under control if KPIV levels change dramatically. It is used throughout product or process life cycle and is a living document to ensure quality control and continuous improvement.

FMEA is used in the control phase of a DMAIC project to reduce the probability that KPIVs will move from their optimized levels. An example of an FMEA is shown Figure 9.40. At this point in the project, the FMEA is used as a risk management tool as opposed to helping identify causes for poor performance as in the earlier DMAIC phases. The risk assessment is used to evaluate the effectiveness of the current controls, the likelihood of their failure, and reaction plans to eliminate the failure. There will usually

Process or Product Name: Responsible:								Prepared by: Date (Orig) ___ (Rev) ___		
Process Step/Part Number	Potential Failure Mode	Potential Failure Effects	S E V	Potential Causes	O C C	Current Controls	D E T	R P N

- Failure Mode : Description of a non-conformance at a process step.
- Failure Effect : Effect of a failure mode on key process output variables.
- Severity: Assessment of the seriousness of the failure effect on the customer using a scale of 1 to 10.
- Failure Cause : Describes "how the failure mode could have occurred."
- Occurrence: An assessment of the frequency with which the failure cause occurs using a scale of 1 to 10.
- Controls: Prevention, design or process activities to prevent, reduce or detect failure modes or causes.
- Detection: An assessment of the likelihood (or probability) that your current controls will detect the failure mode using a scale of 1 to 10.
- RPN : *Risk Priority Number (RPN)* = (Severity) × (Occurrence) × (Detection). It is used to prioritize recommended actions. Special consideration should be given to high *Severity* ratings even if *Occurrence* and *Detection* are low.

FIGURE 9.40
Why is an FMEA useful?

be extensive supporting documentation added to the FMEA, such as process, testing, and maintenance instructions, as well as roles and responsibilities and other information, to quickly bring performance back on target. The FMEA is integrated into the quality control plan. There may be versions for both design and support processes. These enable tracking and prioritization of control risks and mistake-proofing the process based on risk.

Control charts are time series graphs that have been modified using control limits to aid in evaluation of the non-random patterns. Control limits are commonly set as ±3 standard deviations from the mean of the variable being charted. A normal (symmetrical) probability distribution will encompass 99.73% of the variation within ±3 standard deviations from the mean. Table 9.21 summarizes the most common charts in terms

TABLE 9.21

Common Control Chart Summary

Attributes	Individual Moving Range Charts	X-Bar and Range Charts	P-Chart/NP-Chart	C-Chart/U-Chart
Data format	Continuous	Continuous	Percentage or proportion	Counts
Use these charts for stated data format	We are measuring cycle time, hours, incident rates, temperature, weight, costs, or other continuous numbers.	We are measuring cycle time, hours, incident rates, temperature, weight, costs, or other continuous numbers that are sub-groups (e.g., if we measure delivery time each working day, the sub-group is "week," which has 5 days).	We take a sample of things and classify them as pass or fail based on a standard or evaluation criterion (e.g., if we take 100 pumps per day and classify them as clean or dirty, the percentage of clean pumps is plotted every day; if we take 200 invoices and classify them as accurate or not, we plot the percentage of accurate invoices per day).	We count the number of defects per sampling unit (i.e., the number of inaccurate data fields per invoice, the number of accidents per month). We could also classify an invoice as accurate or not if any data field has an error; this gives us a percentage.
Sample size	25–125 observations in the total sample with sub-group size = 1	4–6 observations per sub-group and 20–25 sub-groups in the initial baseline sample	50 or more observations per sub-group; p-charts are constructed using sub-groups of equal or unequal size, whereas np-charts are used in situations where sub-group sizes do not vary.	Convenient sampling unit (1,000 square feet, every 1,100 people, incidents per month, etc.) that is constant from one sample to another; U-charts are used in situations where the size of the sub-group varies.
Assumed distribution	Normal/moving range chart in control	Normal/moving range chart in control	Binomial	Poisson

of the data format, sample size, and assumed distribution. There are many other specialized control charts based on other assumptions such as short production runs or other distributions. Control charts are applied to the analysis of process variation and are used to monitor a process over time. If the process is stable, its behavior can be predicted and statistical conclusions can be drawn from the analysis. These charts differentiate process variation due to common versus special causes (i.e., trends, cycles, shifts, changes in variation, outliers, etc.). This allows identification and removal of special causes (e.g., outliers and non-random patterns) and prevents excessive tweaking of a process so that the process operates with less overall variation.

This is possible because a representative sample from the process is used as the reference distribution to set up the control chart's statistical limits. The theory is that subsequent samples taken from the same process should match the reference distribution if the process has not changed over time. Data points exhibiting common-cause variation remain within a control chart's upper and lower control limits without exhibiting non-random patterns, whereas special cause variation data exhibit non-random patterns such as outliers, trends, cycles, or other patterns. Control charts are constructed by taking sequential samples of size n from a process. Over time, additional samples are taken from the same process workflow of size n and compared to the reference distribution. If the process has not changed relative to its mean or variation, then the two patterns should be similar.

The control charts shown in Table 9.21 have as their basis different underlying assumption and practical uses. The most common difference is relative to the distribution of the variable being charted. As an example, if a variable is continuously distributed and sub-groups are taken from a process, then the resultant distribution of sub-groups will most likely be normally distributed (central limit theorem). This is the basis of the X-bar and R control charts. If a variable is measured as pass or fail, however, then the resultant probability distribution will be binomially distributed and discrete control charts such as p or np charts will be constructed. The fourth common control chart is based on counting the number of defects. In this application, the C control chart will be based on the Poisson distribution.

A p-Chart example is shown in Figure 9.41. It is constructed using sample proportions based on data collected in groups over time and classified as pass or fail. An application would be gathering 50 parts every hour from a process and classifying them as pass or fail based on evaluation

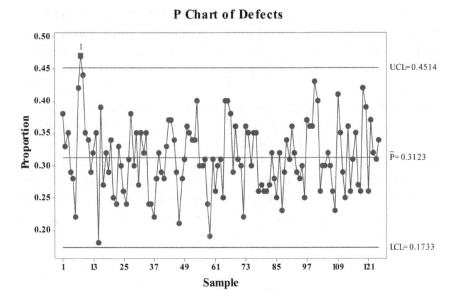

P Chart of Defects

UCL= 0.4514

P̄= 0.3123

LCL= 0.1733

FIGURE 9.41
Control chart example.

criteria. In Figure 9.41, we see that the process is stable within the control limits, except for one outlier that is above the upper control limit. This data point should be investigated. It may have occurred by chance or it might be an assignable cause of variation whose root cause must be eliminated from the process.

Table 9.22 shows control and capability are different but both important. A process will need to be under control and stable before we can

TABLE 9.22

Control versus Capability

		In Statistical Control?	
		No	**Yes**
Capable?	No	Bring process into statistical control and determine entitlement; then make improvements	Create an improvement project **(DMAIC Projects)**
	Yes	Bring process back into statistical control	OK

rely on sampling statistics such as capability indices, which are calculated using samples from the process. When we begin the DMAIC project, the first actions are to construct the baseline of the KPOV metrics using the appropriate control chart and to ensure it is stable before estimating performance to target. If the process is stable but not capable, we start the DMAIC project because this indicates a chronic process issue.

At the end of the control phase, we should be able to demonstrate that the process is both stable at the target performance level and under control as shown in Figure 9.42. Each project is different relative to its root cause analysis and solutions. Some are highly quantitative whereas others focus on Lean tools and methods. In each of these examples, the KPOV metric was significantly improved. In the process map, the percent of

Target = Reduce NVA operations by 50%

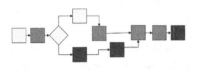

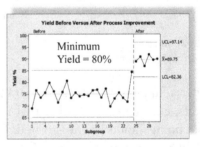

Process mapping to identify process wastes. Eliminate red (wasteful) operations to simplify the process.

Create time series plot of the yield to show before and after performance.

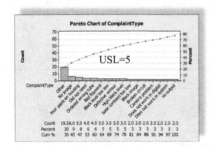

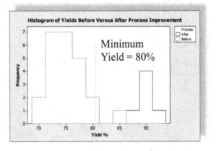

Create a Pareto chart of defects to show before/ after performance e.g. reduced counts.

Create a histogram of and show before/ after performance e.g. yield improvement.

FIGURE 9.42

Project metric baselines — are we capable? NVA = non-value-add; UCL = upper confidence limit; LCL = lower confidence limit.

non-value-add operation was reduced by 50%. Yields were improved and complaints were reduced in the other three examples.

SUMMARY

In this chapter, we discussed the most common tools and methods used in the Six Sigma program from a management perspective. The Six Sigma initiative became popular in the mid-1990s as hundreds of organizations embraced its breakthrough methodology. The initiative revolutionized the way that quality improvement was applied not just to manufacturing but also to services and supply chains. It showed that quality management and improvement are critical for improving an organization's competitiveness across diverse industries. In this chapter we continued the decision that it is important to align quality assurance and control activities with the concurrent engineering team to ensure products and services are designed to have high capability to meet customer requirements under a variety of actual use conditions. High quality products and services create competive advantages by simplification, standardization and doing things right the first time. In addition to breakthrough projects, an organization must also embrace continuous improvement and other quality initiatives. A quality program should be integrated to include continuous improvement. Six Sigma breakthrough and other initiatives that enhance customer experience. Associate training in basic quality tools, methods, and concepts to continuously improve their process helps change a culture and make it more customer centric, productive and competitive.

10

Big Data

OVERVIEW

What is Big Data? It is a collection of data in very large and complex databases that defy previous management and processing methods. Big Data has large volume, large velocity, and large variety in data formats. The growth of databases has increased exponentially in recent years, and the differing data formats (e.g., numbers, text, pictures, videos, voice, etc.) require enormous amounts of computer storage, server speed, and specialized analytical software to access, process, and interpret the data. The size of these databases is enormous. The world moved from discussing databases in terms of kilobytes in the 1990s, which represents approximately half of a page of text, to terms of terabytes a decade later, which is equivalent to about 75 million text pages. Today's information technology (IT) systems create multiple terabytes in a matter of hours. Table 10.1 lists database sizes and provides examples. Large databases require data conditioning, transformations, and new statistical methods because most standard methods to organize and analyze it are inadequate. There are challenges in storage, searching, transferring, and visualizing these large and diverse databases.

Big data is driving global transformation of the ways we learn, work, and produce goods and services. First, there is the IoT, composed of interconnected devices and sensors that provide information on status, predict performance, and control these connected devices. Currently there are more than twenty billion of these connections. They control global

TABLE 10.1

Database Size Comparison

Name	Binary Usage	Value	Typical Year	Example
Kilobyte	2^{10}	10^3	1980	half of a page text
Megabyte	2^{20}	10^6	1990	
Gigabyte	2^{30}	10^9	1995	
Terabyte	2^{40}	10^{12}	2000	
Petabyte	2^{50}	10^{15}	2005	
Exabyte	2^{60}	10^{18}	2009	150 exabytes represents several times the size of all books written

production and services across supply chains. They also offer opportunities to improve efficiency while meeting customer expectations. Second, there is virtualization in the design of almost anything today. This enables physical objects to be created using models and algorithms, and the model can be tested in virtual environments to identify design flaws that can be corrected prior to production. Service system models can also be simulated to analyze their response to changes in incoming demand and capacity if systems fail. Data virtualization promotes the use of Big Data because it can be organized and presented in easily consumable formats that provide insights of relationships and status for decision making. It also provides a single source of trusted truth.

Analytics are enhanced through access to cloud platforms that enables sharing of disparate, very large databases using new methods to organize them. Artificial intelligence and machine learning are also applied to provide new insights into data relationships. User-friendly interfaces allow easy querying of the large databases. Big Data methods combined with cloud access also help identify and repurpose dark data, or data that is accumulated but not used. The reasons that dark data is not used are its size, its unstructured format, or other reasons that make it unavailable. Although some obstacles still remain, most barriers for making efficient use of dark data have been overcome. This enables organizations to put the data to use and oftentimes to monetize it. The key for using previously dark data is sorting out useful data. The balance of the data may need to be archived because of laws or regulatory status but does not provide insights for operational management. Storing old and unusable data is called cold storage, and such data are not placed in the cloud but rather are stored on physical media.

BIG DATA

At an analytical level, there are three types of data. The first is structured (e.g., organized), and defined formatting with Excel worksheets is a good example. The second type is semi-structured data from which patterns and models can be created with analytical effort (e.g., parsing numbers and text using Excel to provide structure). The third type is unstructured data with differing formats (e.g., text, pictures, voice, video, etc.) and little structure that can be read by a machine. New analytical methods are being created and applied to the unstructured data type. Unstructured data are seen as modeling large systems, video imaging, microphones capturing audio, security cameras creating images, thousands of sensors on complicated equipment (e.g., aircraft have thousands of sensors), and wireless networks transferring large amounts of data across global networks from mobile and other connected devices. But how big is big? In the past forty years, business analytics evolved from business activity monitoring (e.g., simple applications focused on dashboards and reports or simple automation that is dependent on a few inputs) to systems dependent on thousands of inputs. These larger and more complicated analytical applications require mega-byte (10^6), gigabyte (10^9), and even larger databases. As applications moved through business intelligence (i.e., data mining of structured data across several databases) through modeling (i.e., what-if scenarios) to predictive analytics (i.e., using structured, unstructured, and other data formats), the largest database sizes exceeded terabyte (10^{12}) to petabyte (10^{15}) and larger. The impact on process design, analysis, and improvement has been challenging. From a hardware consideration, Big Data requires large systems with numerous servers, high capacity, and hardware and software architecture that enables fast data creation, reading, updates, and deletion (CRUD).

How data are designed, controlled, structured, interconnected, and conditioned is relevant for process improvement professionals. Process improvement projects need to use newer tools and methods to collect data and apply analytical methods for root-cause analysis. This field in IT is called information (or data) governance. Data stewards organize data access and ensure it is available and has integrity across the ecosystem's many applications. Specialized governance software is used to ensure metadata ownership, standard definitions, and the ability to trace the flow of metadata through the many applications comprising the ecosystem. This is data mapping to establish metadata lineage.

The process for ensuring measurement accuracy and precision applied to a project's data now requires evaluations of accuracy (attribute correctness); consistency (relative integrality when compared to similar data in other parts of a database); completeness (no missing data); timeliness of data (data is collected relative to other data elements in the same timeframe); conformity (relative to required formatting); uniqueness (there is a single instance of the data element within a metadata field), and synchronization (data elements in a database are consistent from one record to another and across the data elements). Table 10.2 summarizes the dimensions for data quality. Reporting dashboards are used to baseline and improve data quality. An example will be discussed later in this chapter. This is in addition to the classic measurement system attributes commonly evaluated in measurement systems analysis.

A Big Data analytics ecosystem consists of users, hardware devices, specialized software, storage arrays, private or public clouds, the data sources, as well as required conditioning and analytical software that enable access to large databases. These are shown in Figure 10.1. Users include disparate institutions and organizations including government, education, industry, entertainment, defense, or others, depending on the application. The myriad devices and hardware that provide the data (i.e., its inputs) may include computers, sensors across different applications, mobile phones, video platforms, complex equipment such as airplanes and automobiles, and numerous other data input sources. Hardware storage of incoming data streams is provided by different suppliers. A Big Data system has supporting software that efficiently manages data input, processing, and output transactions. Note that cloud storage is resident on hardware organized by

TABLE 10.2

Metadata Dimensions

Dimension	Description
Accuracy	Attribute is correct.
Consistency	There is relational integrity of a data element compared to the same data element elsewhere in similar data fields.
Timeliness	The data element is within required timeframe.
Completeness	There are no missing (null) values in the data fields.
Conformity	The data element has the required format.
Uniqueness	There is only one instance of the data element in the field.
Synchronization	Data elements are consistent from one database to another.

Users
Financial, healthcare, defense, government, entertainment, research, communications, education, etc.

Devices/ Hardware
Cell phones; video, medical scanner, ATM, computers, tablet, GPS, cable, satellite, etc.

Storage
Cloud providers (EMC, Oracle, Dell, IBM, Microsoft, Amazon, etc.) store and organize data for usage by others for cross-selling, other analyses.

Sources of Data
Government, retail, financial, healthcare, Internet, communications, cable providers, and anyone collecting data on users or other systems, etc.

Data Conditioning/Analytics
Infor Chimps, Mechanical Turk, GalaxyZoo, SaS

Open Source Tools
Cloudera, Hadoop

FIGURE 10.1
Big Data ecosystem.

specialized software and resident in redundant data centers that are geographically dispersed to improve data availability. The data conditioning and analytical tools are software driven. They may be proprietary or open source code. Finally, there are open source tools such as Hadoop that help organizations efficiently manage very large databases to enable their efficient read and write access as opposed to traditional databases.

How does this impact process improvement efforts in service systems, especially large-scale systems? One example is an automotive parts supplier that needs to increase product sales velocity across a major retailer's store shelves to maximize profit per cubic foot. Millions of point-of-sale (POS) transactions are created per year with extensive customer demographic information. Models need to be built based on key demographic variables and local vehicle types by zip code so the right products will be at the right location at the right time. Another example is building models to understand and predict the spread of a new disease moving across South America into the Caribbean and the southern United States. Which people based on demographic variables are most correlated to susceptibility? How many people are likely to become infected, and when and where? A credit card issuer's website processes millions of transactions per day. It also allows customers to review statements, transfer money, and pay invoices. How can the company identify customers to cross-sell and up-sell to? What are the important demographic variables that indicate a higher likelihood for additional sales? Finally, a new aircraft engine has several thousand sensors generating enormous amounts of performance data per flight. How can this data be analyzed to predict engine failure or optimize fuel efficiency?

In Chapter 9 we discussed several analytical methods that required collecting sample data for analysis. Big Data applications rely on automated data collection and analytics because of the large number of transactional records. In most practical, non-Big Data applications, sample sizes are calculated without analytical issues. However, when analyzing large data sets, sample sizes can become a problem. Insignificant variables may become significant because the error mean square can be artificially reduced because its denominator (i.e., the degrees of freedom) is increased, and the F statistics of the independent variables are calculated using the mean square error in their denominator. This inflates the F statistics and decreases their probability values, resulting in a high significance of variables just because of the sample size. In other words, all variables in a model would appear to be statistically significant. As another example, goodness of fit tests will reject the null hypothesis of the assumed distribution because the p value will be low due to the degree of freedom inflation. We would conclude a statistically significant relationship even if one does not exist. As a third example, control chart limits are calculated using sample size in the standard error formula. Very large sample sizes will reduce the term and artificially reduce the widths of the control limits. Therefore, special analytical methods are needed to analyze large databases. The normal issues for building models are also exacerbated. These include incorrect historical records, outliers that bias regression equations, underlying non-random patterns, multi-collinearity of independent variables, and other issues.

METADATA

Metadata are the data fields where data are created, reviewed, updated, and deleted. We will use a customer profile as an example. Figure 8.1 listed the various metadata fields used to describe a customer profile. These included account name; company name; first name, last name; e-mail address; phone number; billing address; shipping address, city, state, zip code country, province, postal code; the Dun & Bradstreet Universal Numbering System (DUNS) DUNS Legal ID, DUNS Site ID, payment terms, sales representative; territory ID, credit limit. Information from various customers within these fields is in the same format but varies because different customers will have differ universal customer identification (UCID) numbers and information.

Customer account metadata is organized as a hierarchy that enables an organization to structure data relationships for process control and reporting. Figure 10.2 is an example for accounts and uses DUNS metadata. The hierarchy of a customer account is important for reporting and understanding customer account relationships such as invoicing, services, shipments, and other functions. In a large, multinational organization with several international subsidiaries, reporting will be aggregated to the legal UCID, and lower levels of an organization will have unique numbers. These include a global ultimate UCID, a domestic ultimate UCID, a subsidiary ultimate UCID, and a site UCID for locations within a subsidiary. An example would be different manufacturing facilities in a corporate division within a specific country. This metadata field is useful if purchasing or leasing equipment with warranties or other entitlements associated with a specific machine. This ensures service technicians and remote support teams provide services and parts to the correct machine at a location. If an organization deviates from this hierarchy (e.g., because of poor database design), it will have difficulty merging and sharing metadata with other organizations because the hierarchal relationships will be different. From a process engineering perspective, the consequences of poor hierarchal design will be costly data collection and poor reporting and process control across the IT ecosystem.

Business data stewards measure the quality dimensions of metadata to ensure accurate billing, delivery, invoicing, and other workstreams. Table 10.3 describes these dimensions and common data quality rules. Most people

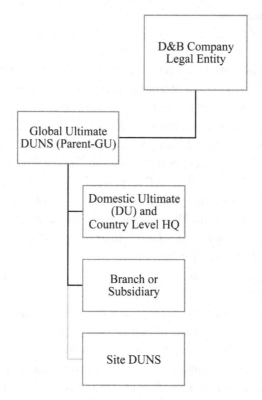

FIGURE 10.2

Customer data taxonomy. DUNS = Dun & Bradstreet Universal Numbering System.

TABLE 10.3

Data Business Rules

Metadata Field	Business Rules
Company Name	UCID legal name corresponds to a physical address.
	Name not abbreviated.
	Name must not be blank.
	Name cannot be all numbers or special characters.
Address	UCID site must be a physical address or post office box.
	Address must not be blank.
	Address cannot be all numbers or special characters.
E-mail	E-mail has an @ symbol.
	No blank spaces.
	E-mail has a valid domain extension such as .com, .net, etc.

are familiar with a few of them (e.g., accuracy, completeness, etc.), but from the perspectives of data governance and process efficiency, all of them are important. To better measure these dimensions, data quality rules are applied to enable automatic verification of each dimension to its rule. As an example, the UCID legal name must exist, it cannot be abbreviated or be blank, and it cannot be all numbers or special characters. The other data quality dimensions would also be applied to this metadata field. Data quality is reported using a format shown in Table 10.4. Reporting is stratified to understand data quality for location, account, source system, and other relevant factors.

A business process from a data perspective is an aggregation of metadata from several sources that build work products such as a customer order profile. How an organization's systems use metadata is important for information governance. Data mapping or data lineage traces the sources of metadata and how it flows through various IT applications to create work products, such as an order or invoice. Data lineage shows whether metadata came from a trusted source. It is also important if there are quality issues or if the business rules need to be modified. Software tools are used to crawl though IT applications and trace the end-to-end flow of metadata. Visualization of metadata lineage is important to see high-volume transaction flows to focus process improvement efforts, including the evaluation of metadata performance against business rules. In summary, because of the number of applications and platforms used by organizations, process improvement professionals need to understand metadata quality, lineage, and governance to work effectively with business data stewards, business stakeholders, and others to improve process quality and efficiency.

INFORMATION QUALITY GOVERNANCE

Information governance is a relatively new discipline. Its purpose is to standardize the use of core and extended metadata across data domains. The need for metadata standardization is important because of the proliferation of IT systems and metadata as well as the evolution of Big Data. Industries such as medical devices and pharmaceuticals need strict controls over data definitions and usage to adhere to governmental regulations and to reduce risk. These industries have been leaders in information governance. In the past decade, other industries have been working to

TABLE 10.4

Data Reporting

Workstream	Metadata	Accuracy	Consistency	Timeliness	Completeness	Conformity	Uniqueness	Synchronization
Quote to Cash	**Account Name**							
	Company Name	99% ○	98% ○	95% ☺	90% ☺	98% ○	90% ☺	85% ●
	First Name							
	Last Name							
	Email address	95% ☺	98% ○	93% ☺	90% ☺	98% ○	90% ☺	85% ●
	Phone Number							
	Billing Address	98% ○	99% ○	96% ○	88% ●	98% ○	90% ☺	85% ●
	Shipping Address	99% ○	98% ○	94% ☺	90% ☺	98% ○	90% ☺	85% ●
	City							
	State							
	Zip Code							
	Country							
	Provence							
	Postal Code							
	DUNS Legal ID							
	DUNS Site ID							
	Payment Terms							
	Sales Representative							
	Territory ID							
	Credit Limit							

○ = Meets Target (>95%)   ☺ = Marginal (90%-95%)   ● = Requires Improvement (<90%)

improve the efficiency and quality of data use because of the proliferation of applications using data and the advent of Big Data. Data quality has always been a cornerstone for process improvement, but in IT ecosystems, with Big Data and automation, process improvement efforts depend on newer analytical tools and methods. In the absence of effective governance, severe issues arise that impact the ability of an organization to manage information across data domains and business processes. Examples include inconsistent data capture from multiple intake sources; inconsistent data quality rules for accuracy, consistency, and other quality dimension gaps; and unclear roles and responsibilities for data ownership, allowing unauthorized metadata changes.

The application of governance is important to ensure consistent definitions and use of shared metadata. Organizations have thousands of data elements (i.e., metadata). Some are more important than others because they are used across several IT applications and processes. As an example, customer profiles are used for quoting, order, delivery, and invoicing. Metadata is associated with business processes. This association is called a data domain, and there are different data domains with unique data owners (e.g., customer, procurement, manufacturing, finance, and others), with metadata used to control their work. An assumption is that metadata fields have business and IT owners by functional group. As an example, marketing controls customer and contact metadata; manufacturing controls production metadata; and supply chains control metadata related to suppliers, logistics, and inventories.

Governance is facilitated by classifying metadata into core and the extended data elements used by functional groups to govern their data domains. Core data elements are used by several IT applications and require strict control by their owners and conformance to quality dimensions like accuracy, consistency within a database over many transactions and across various databases (i.e., synchronicity), timeliness (i.e., availability), completeness, adherence with a required format, uniqueness (i.e., one instance). The data lineage must also be known from source to consuming systems, and clear roles and responsibilities must be controlled through policies and standards. These are coordinated by a leadership governance council that approves how core data elements are defined and used across the organization.

The process for building information governance begins with a proof of concept using impactful business use cases. Maturity increases as the number of new use cases expands to include more core metadata that is managed though a governance framework. Table 10.5 describes a

TABLE 10.5

Data Governance Maturity

Organizational Environment	Maturity Phase	Key Actions to Increase Maturity
Reactive	Assessment	• Create core stakeholder council • Identify major business problems impacted by data quality • Create persona/use cases • Define and gather key metrics
Foundational	Governance framework	• Solve persona/use cases • Expand stakeholder council • Define and assign roles and responsibilities • Create governing policy for data definitions and rules, course systems, and roles and responsibilities • Integrate all information into a data quality platform to coordinate collaboration
Proactive	Reporting infrastructure	• Profile core data and assess against data dimensions • Create formal dashboards and reporting with exception management and disposition through the stakeholder council • Formalize core data governance
Strategic differentiation	Improve performance	• Improve dashboard quality dimension ratings • Document end-to-end data lineage • Expand end-to-end persona/use cases • Continue to solution and build project portfolio
	Sustain	• Scale data governance to the functional team level • Transition reporting to how the business is run

simplified version of five maturity stages: assessment, governance framework, reporting structure, improving performance, and sustaining the improvements. In the assessment phase, a core stakeholder council is created, and a few data domains are chosen to prove the governance concept using a few major business problems impacted by poor data quality. Relevant persona and use cases are created to align to the business benefits associated with higher metadata quality. Examples include reducing customer returns caused by inaccurate customer address, or reducing high field-service costs incurred when technicians are sent to service equipment at a wrong location. Preliminary scorecards are also created to start measuring metadata quality dimensions.

Building the governance framework requires solutioning the persona and use cases, expanding the leadership governance and working councils based on data domains, defining and assigning roles and responsibilities, and creating policies, standards, definitions, and business rules. This information is formally incorporated into a collaborative IT platform that controls metadata ownership, policies, standards, reporting, definitions, and related information as well as CRUD. Roles and responsibilities are used to control access to the collaborative platform. This begins with a leadership council that approves policies and investments aligned with data quality that provide impactful business benefits. The next level is the working council.

The working council is composed of data domains. As an example, in the manufacturing data domain, there would be owners of the bill of materials, testing, routing, and production metadata. The working council includes data stewards who are aligned by data domain. Data stewards approve data policies, standards, and definitions. They also coordinate data clean-up, create data models, and develop the policies, standards, and other supporting collateral for council approval. Collectively, the working council determines which roles create, review, update, and delete metadata. Based on its governance actions, the working council also recommends investments to the leadership council to solve poor data quality issues that impact business owners. Additional members of the working council may include various IT roles associated with maintaining the ecosystem or managing its information as well as team members who maintain and ensure data are available. Team members execute policies, standards, and procedures with the business teams. Working councils help improve data quality to reduce service errors, delivery errors, and other business process errors by measuring and reporting the dimensional quality of metadata and engaging process improvement professionals.

In the reporting phase, metadata quality dimensions are profiled and correlated to metrics of the impactful use cases using a scorecard like the one shown in Table 10.4. Exception reporting identifies outliers or nonrandom patterns that require investigation. Then projects are created to improve one or more data quality dimensions. Information governance then becomes a closed loop with reporting made to the councils and projects approved to improve data quality. This momentum leads into the improve performance phase. The scorecard ratings become progressively higher as projects are completed. As part of this phase, end-to-end metadata lineage across the IT ecosystem is mapped using automated algorithms to understand metadata flows from source to consuming systems (i.e., who is using the metadata and how they are using it). The number of use cases continues to expand across the data domains. Business benefits accrue and serve as a basis for further investment to improve data quality.

In the sustain phase, data governance is transitioned into the organization and data quality information is integrated into the collaborative platform that coordinates data access and CRUD actions by role. The data domains and all of the councils formally coordinate all data governance through the collaborative platform. This limits the ability of one group to make unilateral changes to metadata rules and other attributes that may adversely impact other domains and business owners. Governance is now formal and is the basis for approved policies, reporting, and control of definitions, ownership, key performance indicators, and remediation plans for root-cause analysis.

A lack of ownership and standardization causes metadata to be interpreted differently in IT applications and their functional groups, and this leads to an inconsistent taxonomy. Inconsistent taxonomy results in inconsistent metadata usage (e.g., building inconsistent customer and sales account profiles or creating different profiles for the same customer in different IT applications). This results in proliferation of duplicate and inaccurate transaction records, which can cause operational issues (e.g., referencing information for CRUD, or identifying the root causes for process issues). As an example, when there are different customer profiles with different shipping addresses for the one customer, the likelihood of shipping products to the wrong location increases, as does the time to look up information. Localized interpretation of metadata also creates different metadata definitions and models.

DATA QUALITY IMPROVEMENT

An effective framework for improving data quality is shown in Table 10.6. It helps identify impactful persona and use cases, projects, and the root

TABLE 10.6

Data Governance Roles

Executive Steering Committee
•Governance prioritization and resource allocation •Policy Changes Organization Changes Roles & Responsibility Changes Funding approval
Working Governance Council
•Investment recommendations to improve data quality •Approve core data standards, policies and business rules •Coordinate data quality improvement projects •Sets roles and responsibilities for who can create and change core metadata
Business Data Stewards
•Review core data standards, policies and business rules •Understand data models and lineage mapping across systems •Recommends data clean-up and remediation
Subject Matter Experts (Analytics)
• Advanced analytics, methods and tools • Maintenance to ensure data and conforms to data quality rules across is dimensions

causes for poor data quality, and it helps prioritize projects for solution. Business data stewards use a sequential methodology. In data governance, the improvement methodology is modified to the following steps: Develop, Onboard, Profile, Implement, and Control (DOPIC). We will discuss the DOPIC methodology and how it is used to improve data quality as opposed to the Define-Measure-Analyze-Improve-Control (DMAIC) improvement strategy.

In the develop phase, an opportunity assessment is made from the business owner and stakeholder perspectives to define impactful personas and use cases, key metrics, core metadata, and its quality dimensions relative to the business metrics that need to be improved (e.g., on-time delivery, reduced returns, low sales, missed schedules, and other use cases). These are prioritized by business owners, stakeholders, data quality stewards, and the information governance team. Prioritized projects are added to governance roadmaps to secure resources and funding. It is essential to show the return on investment for the larger initiative. The time frame for this work is between three and six months.

If these are initial projects, a data governance foundation is built as described by the maturity model. Business owners, stakeholders, and subject matter experts are brought onboard to the initiative using the initial projects or to the larger governance initiative if it is mature. A team is built around the project's use case on the basis of the metadata as well as its data source and consuming systems. This initial analysis identifies business and IT owners needed to support the project. Once onboarded, these roles help define and align the metadata to the project's relevant business metrics and benefits. The project team documents data lineage from the source to consuming systems, definitions, data quality rules and other information in the collaborative platform. If this work is foundational based on initial projects, the time required to complete it is between three and six months; if maturity exists, the project time is often between one and two months.

In the profile phase, user stories are created from an Agile Project Management perspective. These are used to start data quality profiling. Profiling is useful for answering relevant questions. Baselines are established for the metadata and business metrics and tracked to targets using a reporting dashboard. This helps show data quality and business metric performance. Models are also built to include leading, lagging, and coincident indicators as well as independent variables that impact the quality of metadata and the associated business and process metrics. Stakeholders are engaged to provide feedback according to the Agile methods to integrate the analysis with respect to systems, metadata, metrics, and process. The time to complete the project work is between one and two months if maturity exists, or between three and six months otherwise.

In the implementation phase, data policies and standards are either formalized if these are initial projects or updated through the working and leadership councils. Metadata lineage is documented with the help of supporting applications that map data lineage from source and consuming systems. Solutions for data quality gaps are piloted to improve business performance. The reporting dashboards are updated. Remediation activities (e.g., data clean-up) is also initiated using the updated definitions, standards, and algorithms. Ideally these solutions will be performed at an enterprise level and will be permanent to avoid the recurrence of the data issues. This phase typically requires between one and three months for projects that are part of a mature governance framework, or several months dependent on funding for data clean-up or capital investment.

In the control phase, governance is optimized for source and consuming systems. Policies and standards are used to identify impactful projects and use cases to improve data quality. New use cases bring more data domains, systems, and business owners into the governance community. Working councils are established for these domains. Advanced analytics form the basis for improvements to standards, policies, and business rules, building data models, and understanding data lineage across source and consuming systems. The organization moves from remediation planning and data clean-up activities to proactive infrastructure improvements that prevent data quality issues from occurring. The governance leadership council provides ongoing funding approval, prioritization, and resource allocation to improve business performance. Improvement projects are aligned to this strategy and its capital investment roadmap. Data governance roles and responsibilities are incorporated into policies.

DATA SECURITY

Data security is always a concern for organizations. A major problem is that not all organizations govern data effectively for a variety of reasons. One reason is that security may be controlled by different groups across an organization without formal governance because most organizations are not subject to strict regulatory requirements such as that for medical industries and other highly regulated industries. Highly regulated industries have formal policies, procedures, and processes designed to secure data creation, review, updating, and deletion (CRUD) through defined roles and responsibilities and infrastructure controls on access.

Governance implies metadata is known and each field one has a single owner. Owners control the metadata policy, definitions, and rules that impact how it is used. Metadata cannot be modified except by its owner, and only after other stakeholders are informed of planned changes. This is especially true for core metadata that impacts several business processes. Governance also implies metadata lineage is known from source to consuming systems, including all intermediary systems. Finally, metadata should be stored and accessed through a secure collaborative application that controls read, write, and deletion privileges based on data domain roles and responsibilities.

Data security is an important goal, but it is especially important relative to how an organization collects and uses personal data. Internally created metadata that is not personal is fully under an organization's control and can normally be used for internal consumption without regulatory constraints. Data supplied from external sources, including consumers, must be carefully controlled and used. Recently, new regulations were created to control the historical abuse of private information by some organizations. Examples include selling personal information without permission for profit to telemarketers or not controlling its access properly, allowing security breaches that result in loss of personal reputation or property.

The General Data Protection Regulation (GDPR) was created by the European Union (EU) and became effective in May 2018. It controls use of personal data of EU citizens stored within IT systems located in the EU as well as any such personal data stored or used in systems outside the EU. Potential penalties for non-compliance are up to 4% of an organization's annual revenue. Personal data are defined as information associated with an identified individual who is called a data subject in the GDPR. Examples include names, phone numbers, home address, e-mail address, credit history, health information, and similar data. Scrutiny and regulation of social media companies and other organizations that collect and use personal information is accelerating because Big Data enables them to piece together accurate consumer profiles from personal details.

An organizational framework is needed to start a GDPR initiative because additional governance is required to control personal metadata that can identify individuals. A GDPR initiative is initially created as a separate initiative, but it is often integrated into the information governance leadership council once priority systems have been made compliant to GDPR requirements. GDPR representatives include the legal compliance and human resource teams. Recall from Chapter 8 that a large

TABLE 10.7

General Data Protection Regulation Workstreams

Requirement	Definition
Notice and consent	Online notice and consent notices at source systems where consumers can opt in or out of sharing personal information.
Data subject rights	Consumer rights to access their personal information or to act on a request to revise or delete personal information.
Incident response	There is a 72-hour GDPR requirement to notify the GDPR regulators of a serious data breach.
Third-party processes	All documentation and processes with third-party vendors, such as contracts and supplier agreements, must be GDPR compliant.
Data minimization	Internal policies and procedures should be revised to only request information needed to do work.
Recordkeeping	Record keeping must be secure and available on request by GDPR regulators.
International data transfers	All documentation and processes related to the transfer of personal information between EU countries or to non-EU countries with EU information must be GDPR compliant.
Data protection impact assessment	Organizations must develop a governance framework to manage GDPR audits and non-compliance risk.
Communications strategy and training	Organization must create communications systems to notify their team members and suppliers of GDPR compliance actions.

organization's IT ecosystem will have hundreds or thousands of software applications. Many of these are source systems that capture personal information. Examples include quoting and ordering applications used by sales staff or customers and are accessible via the Internet, marketing and quality surveys, and other sources. Controls need to be placed on the source systems and on systems that consume personal data for reporting or other transactions.

Table 10.7 describes the GDPR requirements. Notice and consent require consumers to be alerted that personal information will be collected to complete their transaction. The notice should explain how personal information will be used, including the data subject rights. This notification must be available to consumers for all source systems that collect personal information. Prior to proceeding with a transaction, the consumer must be given an option to explicitly opt into the terms of use rather than only be notified they exist. Data subject rights include an option to request deletion of personal information unless there is a legitimate business reason for keeping the data (e.g., service or warranty contracts that require the information for a time). There are other data subject rights as well, such as a right of access to personal information to confirm its accuracy and completeness. Consumers can also request inaccurate information be corrected. Other rights include portability of data from one organization to another, as well as the ability to review automated processing decisions such as a credit decline created by an algorithm.

If an organization's system is compromised and personal data are stolen, then another requirement is to notify GRPR regulators within 72 hours. This requirement also includes third-party processers handling personal information that should have signed a GDPR compliance agreement with their customer. The overall goal is data minimization, which is another GDPR requirement. Minimization implies that only essential personal information is collected for transactions, and that the number of people accessing personal data should be minimized. Recordkeeping needs to be secure and available on request by GDPR regulators. A secure collaborative governance platform will help an organization meet its GDPR requirements. It will also help auditing compliance and communication amongst the domain communities.

The GDPR governing council is organized by GDPR requirements as shown in Table 10.7. Each requirement workstream has a lead and a small team to define the scope and execute the work. These workstreams are supported by IT, communications and training, information quality governance, human resources, the legal department, and other groups. The focus is on identifying all systems subject to GDPR oversight, including their owners, and prioritizing them to control the collection and use of personal data. This process can take several months to years, depending on the number of systems that need to be made GDPR compliant. Because of the required work and investment, the GDPR core team should create a formal roadmap and execution plan for the initiative for communicating to implementation status and future compliance plans to GDPR auditors.

The trend for more data privacy regulations is growing. This impacts internal audits and other compliance requirements. Data breaches are forcing the U.S. Securities and Exchange Commission (SEC) and other accounting agencies to regulate cybersecurity. Organizations should refresh their cybersecurity policies and ensure supply chain participants sign on and adhere to them. The GDPR data privacy rights are a good place to begin making a list. But more is needed relative to platform and application security. The IoT is proliferating sources of data collected by organizations, and these data are vulnerable to security breaches. In response, organizations are building out their cybersecurity teams and compliance controls.

SUMMARY

Big Data is a collection of very large and complex databases that defy previous management and processing methods. Big Data has large volumes, large velocities, and a large variety of data formats. Big Data has grown exponentially, and differing data formats (e.g., numbers, text, pictures, videos, voice, etc.) require enormous amounts of computer storage, server speed, and specialized analytical software to access, process, and interpret them. As a result, Big Data analytics ecosystems have evolved to include users, hardware devices, specialized software, storage arrays, private or public clouds, a variety of data sources, and conditioning and analytical software to enable access to the large databases. Big Data also impacts classic process improvement tools and methods, such as those used by Six Sigma practitioners, because these methods rely on statistical sampling and small samples. In contrast, Big Data analytics usually counts 100% of a database's records and uses modified methods to analyze patterns and relationships between the variables. New process improvement tools and methods have been created to work in these ecosystems.

Metadata are data fields where data is created, reviewed, updated, and deleted (CRUD). Organizations have thousands of metadata fields. Some metadata is more important than others because it is used by several IT applications and processes. As an example, customer profiles are used for quoting, order, delivery, and invoicing. Metadata is associated with various data domains, each having unique processes and owners. Because of the need to share core metadata, the application of information governance is important to ensure consistent definitions and use.

Data security is also a concern. Most organizations have policies, procedures, and processes designed to ensure secure data creation, review, updating, and deletion (CRUD) depending on roles and responsibilities. Some are more effective than others, as seen by periodic breaches of personal data. The GDPR was created by the EU to regulate the security of personal data. Personal data are defined as information associated with an identified individual, who is called a data subject under GDPR. GDPR applies to personal data stored in IT systems located either within the EU or personal data of EU members stored and used in non-EU systems. Potential penalties for non-compliance are up to 4% of an organization's annual revenue. Improvement projects can be created to prevent these enormous fines or take corrective action when fined.

11

Operational Assessments

OVERVIEW

Organizations should step back periodically to assign a team or bring in consultants to review how work is done and how it could be redesigned to focus more on customers, or how it could be digitized or automated. Operational assessments are a proven strategy for increasing productivity. They are also used to evaluate changes to policies, processes, roles, and responsibilities that impede productivity. This chapter discusses the planning and execution of such assessments as well as the methods for analyzing the information that is gathered. Although it requires an up-front commitment of time and resources, a well-done assessment creates a diverse project portfolio. The portfolio identifies opportunities for increasing business benefits and how to align them to strategy. Whereas available reporting shows known performance gaps, assessments identify gaps that have not yet been identified. These are incremental additions to current operational planning. The resultant impactful projects can be deployed either across an organization to start a new initiative or can be focused on a single function, such as manufacturing or distribution, and then expanded over time.

Assessment preparation begins with forming a core planning team, conducting initial employee surveys, obtaining feedback from key stakeholders, and gathering operational and financial performance information. Stakeholder and contact lists are also created with an assessment plan. Integral to the assessment planning will be identifying where to create value stream maps to analyze the end to end supply chain or value flow maps of key processes. Data gathering helps focus an assessment on areas that have greater potential to create projects with high productivity opportunities.

They also identify which processes would benefit from a value flow map workshop. These are used to fill in reporting gaps. The advantage of creating value flow maps of major processes is that information is gained by walking a process. This is also called a Gemba Walk to reinforce that the concept that it is important to see how work is done in person rather than relying on formal reports. Building a value flow map with the people who do the process work provides accurate information beyond that available from higher-level management reports. Normally the assessment team will find some non-value-add work being done. Examples include workarounds, rework loops, and other causes that together are called the "hidden factory." A hidden factory is a term used to describe all the undocumented and non-value-add process activities that take place within an organization. An organization is unaware of these activities because they are not captured on current reports, hence the term hidden factory.

A useful tool when doing an assessment is the operational SWOT format shown in Figure 11.1. It uses feedback (opinions) from the employee surveys and interviews to identify, based on opinion, operational strengths, weakness, opportunities, and threats (hence, SWOT). Other information can be also be used to supplement the analysis. The analysis considers an

	Promote Productivity	Inhibit Productivity
Internal	Strengths in operations over competitors or new markets	Operational weaknesses relative to competitors
External	Opportunities to increase operational efficiency	Competitive, macro-economic, or other threats
	Future trends, macroeconomic factors, culture, legislation, demographics, global competition.	People, physical resources, financial position, market share , competitive advantages.

FIGURE 11.1
SWOT analysis for productivity.

organization's current and future operational environment, strategic goal alignment, and current and anticipated operational performance, including how well an organization executes its goals and objectives in its current business environment. Employees are also surveyed to gather opinions regarding the organization's operational strengths relative to competitors in current and new markets. Operational weaknesses are also included in the SWOT analysis. These identify gaps to help the assessment team focus its work. Subject matter experts such as marketing, sales, design engineering, and others are also surveyed, with additional questions to provide feedback on external conditions.

Employee surveys are also a useful start to an assessment. They provide feedback for subsequent data collection that can be used for process mapping and financial and operational analysis. Surveys help identify unknown interdepartmental issues that cause organizational friction. Chapter 3 described ways to plan, execute, analyze, and report survey information. Surveys are sent to employees, managers, and executives online (e.g., via e-mail or a website) or in person for key managers. These surveys explore the key themes of the organization's culture relative to stated values versus expectations, its customer focus, vision, and mission statements, as well as the clarity and alignment of its operational strategy. The survey, or cultural assessment, is the voice of the organization relative to what needs to be improved, when, and sometimes how. The operational assessment will validate whether these employee opinions were correct.

Gathering financial and operational reports and performance data is another critical deliverable from the assessment. These are augmented with interviews with leaders, process owners, key employees, and others to help interpret the report and identify additional non-value-add expenses, barriers for customer satisfaction, and lower-level causes of poor performance. The assessment information will eventually be translated into projects that identify and eliminate the root causes of poor process performance. Financial and operational analysis is also used to benchmark processes internally to differentiate poorer from better performing processes to adopt best practices. During the assessment or shortly after its conclusion, project charters are defined, financially justified and approved by process owners. This creates a project portfolio in areas where the assessment was deployed.

In previous chapters, we demonstrated that several different types operational strategies are needed to execute projects. These depend on the anticipated root causes and solutions. Examples are Lean, Six Sigma,

Total Productive Maintenance, capital expenditures, process reengineering, capital expenditures for new equipment, and savings from purchasing price negotiations, among many others. If an organization does not have an internal capability to do this work, then either external consultants should be hired or employee training is needed to understand and use the required tools and methods. A well-executed assessment will usually identify a portfolio of projects with a potential productivity impact of between 0.5% and 4% of the budget for the area in which the assessment was done. The range depends on the organization's size and its industry.

In Chapter 7, we discussed ways to translate productivity and other metrics such as economic value added (EVA), return on equity, return on investment, and other financial measures into an organization. The translation process started with the next level of metrics (i.e., sales, cash flow, and operating expenses) and worked deeper into the organization to identify operational initiatives and projects. Assessments use the methods from previous chapters and especially from Chapter 7 to ensure that the project portfolio is logically built and that business benefits are systematically identified to align with operational strategy.

The translation process was shown in Figures 1.1, 1.2, and 7.7. Chapter 7 described ways to analyze financial statements to identify impactful projects that were aligned to higher-level business metrics. Table 7.11 also described how projects should be linked to both enabler initiatives and their tools as well as resultant financial benefits. This is the purpose of an assessment: to ensure the portfolio projects are linked to real productivity opportunities and potential benefits are estimated well.

PREPARING FOR AN ASSESSMENT

An assessment impacts several organizational functions. It may also impact some customers and suppliers, depending on its end-to-end scope. As a result, the assessment needs to be well organized for efficiency. It also needs to provide sufficient information to create actionable project charters. To initiate assessment activities, there will be a meeting with the organization's leadership to understand strategic initiatives and operational goals so that they can be integrated into the assessment's objectives. This ensures the assessment is aligned with the organization's strategy and goals. There may also be some training to familiarize leadership with the assessment methods. The goal is to present a plan, obtain feedback to finalize the assessment planning and create a communication package to begin planning with the locations that will be part of the assessment.

Using information from the leadership team helps focus the up-front analysis of current financial and operational reports to identify performance issues that need solutions. The types of reports vary based on the assessment's scope, including the locations where the assessment will be conducted. The various financial reports discussed in Chapter 7 are evaluated to identify where the assessment team should initially focus the work. Operational reports are also used to focus the work. The plan is updated to include the gathering of process information to verify the reporting accuracy and to determine the best approaches for creating project charters and their scope. Once at the location to be assessed, a second meeting is held with the local leadership team. During this meeting, the assessment team will describe the assessment plan, methodology, and initial areas of focus for the assessment and obtain feedback relevant for that location's assessment. Once at a location, interviews will be held to obtain additional insight from employees in the proposed focus areas. The interviews will start discussions for where to focus value flow mapping workshops.

The assessment for the locations is added to the plan once focus areas are known for each site. Teams will be deployed based on the expected work and benefits for each site. Site planning includes up-front gathering of local contacts, organizational charts, operational and financial reports, and other relevant information. The first assessment deliverable will be to interview the local management teams and successively interview members of the process work teams based on opportunity. At the process-owner level, local teams will be formed to begin value flow mapping and data collection. These teams consist of people who do the process work and assessment facilitators. The deliverables from this work are project charters supported by financial, operational, and other supporting information for that work area.

Communication will also be initiated with the site leaders and their management teams. There may be training for the site management teams as well as for process owners. This will help them understand the assessment's methods prior to deploying the assessment teams. Useful feedback for customizing the planned activities may be obtained from these initial discussions. Once on-site, the assessment team continues the discussions face to face, but with a focus on the site assessment plan.

The management meeting discusses how the site assessment will be conducted, what help may be needed, and the expected benefits and next steps for executing the projects. Specific tools and methods will also be discussed depending on the initiative. An important topic is the financial and operational performance gaps to be investigated. The critical-to strategic flow down also acts to ensure that the project charters are aligned and the assessment meets its goals. The strategic flow down concept introduced in Figure 7.7 is important to ensure that projects are incremental to leadership's current plans or will help execute currently planned projects. It is important the assessment does not duplicate currently identified opportunities under active review and whose solution paths are already known. It is also important not to deploy the assessment teams to processes that may be divested or redesigned soon. This is particularly important for projects that will require capital expenditures and investment. Process owners may also need to be trained in the use of technical assessment tools and methods, or they may need just-in-time training to assist the assessment team. This is also called "project champion" training in Six Sigma initiatives or "Lean Leadership" training in Lean deployments. Once this plan is reviewed and updated, and any necessary training is completed with the site management team and process owners, the work to collect operational data begins.

CONDUCTING THE ASSESSMENT

After the assessment team arrives, the management and process owner meetings have been held, and the assessment's objectives, activities, and deliverables are approved, interviews are started at the site. In these interviews, the critical-to flow downs that were constructed during the leadership and site management training or orientation sessions are updated with relevant information. Using this information as a starting point, the assessment team and now site teams begin to verify the original project ideas and to identify new opportunities though local interviews. It is important to confirm the process issues that were originally on the assessment list. These activities help identify the process teams needed to help with data collection, process mapping, and other assessment activities.

The operational assessment gathers information using one or more of the methods that were introduced in Figure 7.8 and discussed in Chapter 7.

These may include, depending on the assessment's scope, the evaluation of strategic gaps, budget variances, cost avoidances, internal benchmarking, value flow mapping, evaluation of operational metrics, voice of the customer, and regulatory, health, and safety issues. Information from the employee survey can also be incorporated into the analysis.

Performance gaps exist if operational performance differs from strategic goals. Budget variances are indicative of abnormal expenses that may be observed as unexpected shifts, trends, or outliers. An assumption is that the original budgets were realistic. Cost-avoidance gaps are also a good source for projects if there is risk from not doing them. Internal benchmarking is a good source of projects if the processes that are compared to each other are similar. As an example, when looking for process improvement ideas, it would make little sense to compare inventory investment at one distribution center against that in another distribution center if the first distribution center had a policy of inventory centralization with distribution as needed to other locations while the second had a decentralized inventory policy. These processes cannot be compared unless the project was to decide whether to convert one policy to the other. These project-identification methods rely on information available from reports.

Using Figure 7.7 as a guide, higher-level goals are successfully broken down to lower-level goals to identify projects that have operational relevance so an owner and team can be assigned and start the definition work. Ideally, the project portfolio will contain very concisely defined projects such as incorrect setups, machine repairs, and issues with missing materials. Table 1.2 also provides a list of common metrics associated with operational projects. In fact, using a list like Table 1.2 as reminder of potential projects is a useful adjunct for operational assessments. Specific organizations will have other metrics that can be investigated. These are the types of projects an assessment should identify for evaluation. In summary, a critical-to flow down should be used for project identification. This requires analytics be used for data analysis. The goal is to align assessment in a way that projects do not compete for resources.

In Table 7.7 we discussed the profit and loss (P/L) statement. The P/L statement is useful for identifying projects directly linked to productivity. Increases in revenue or decreases in operating expenses increase productivity. Budget variance and trends may indicate a breakdown of internal processes. The year-over-year P/L is also useful for showing operating expenses in several budget categories and at different times. This enables several different projects to be added to the assessment portfolio and avoids situations where one process has too many recommended projects. The P/L categories also align directly with the teams that will be needed to investigate root causes and help identify and implement solutions.

There are several ways a P/L can be analyzed to identify projects. First, any line item that shows a monetary variance greater than budgeted may be a good project. But an investigation is required to confirm whether it is actionable (i.e., whether the amounts can be reduced). There is a possibility that the original budget was not properly set or that the process changed (e.g., the incoming volume increased over the previous years). The percent changes in expenses for a category year over year is another good place to start an investigation, but the same caution must be noted. As an example, in Table 7.7, the overtime and inventory obsolescence percentages are high. Revenue and its adjustments can also be analyzed. If revenue has not grown at the forecasted rate, assessment projects can be identified to investigate and address the causes. If sales adjustments such as returned goods and allowances exceed those stated by sales policies, projects can be created to mitigate or reduce their impact. Chapter 7 and other chapters provide many ideas for ensuring a successful operational assessment.

An assessment also benefits from using Lean, Six Sigma, and other analytical tools and methods disused in previous chapters. One useful method for identifying projects is comparing similar processes in different locations to identify better versus poorer performance. This is known as internal benchmarking, and it is a common assessment approach. Analogous applications are evaluations of several similar internal processes, teams, products, and other categories. Figure 11.2 shows scrap percentages for three internal facilities. In this example, Detroit has a higher scrap percentage than Boston or Columbus for this time series. Detroit's scrap percentage appears to be increasing in contrast to the stable patterns shown by Boston and Columbus. The performance gap between Detroit when compared to the other facilities indicates a project should be created to investigate the percentages and to quantify the potential project benefits. The improvement strategy will be to identify the good practices being utilized by the Boston and Columbus processes and apply these in Detroit to reduce that facility's scrap percentage.

Figure 11.3 analyzes the scrap percentages from a different perspective. In this analysis, which uses a box plot, we find the Detroit scrap percent is 4.8% versus the scrap percent of approximately 2% in both Boston and Columbus. The differences of scrap percentages without overlap of the

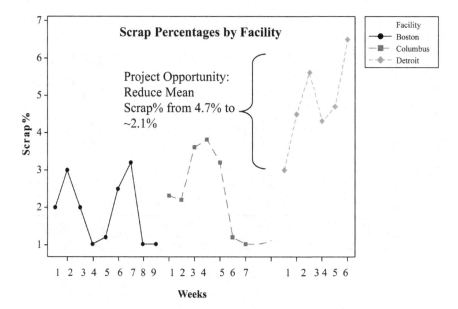

FIGURE 11.2
Internal benchmarking.

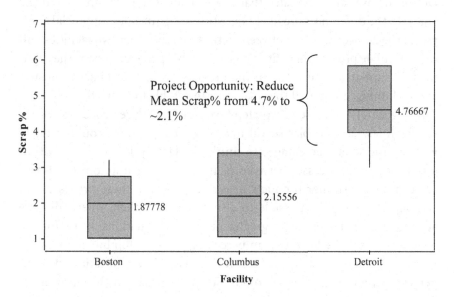

FIGURE 11.3
Internal benchmarking of facility scrap percentages.

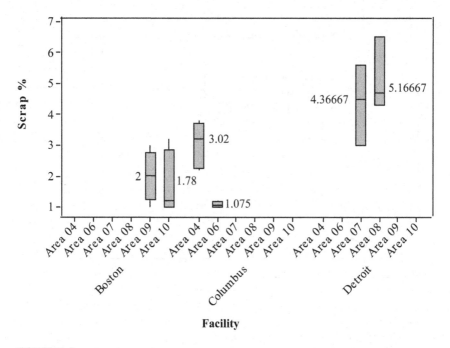

FIGURE 11.4
Internal benchmarking by process within facilities.

Detroit dataset also indicates that if a statistical test was applied to the analysis, the differences are likely statistically significant. A financial analysis of the 2.8% difference between Detroit and the other two facilities will help calculate project's benefit from closing this percentage gap. The argument is similar to that made in the previous example: What are Boston and Columbus doing well that may be transferable to Detroit?

In Figure 11.4, we use a two-step box plot to analyze processes within the facilities. This enables serval investigations. First, we could evaluate whether the scrap percentage are similar by facility, by processes within a facility, or by processes between facilities. The assumption is the processes produce similar products or services. Two of these processes are comparable; it will be possible to also benchmark them internally. The advantage is that there are a greater number of situations to use for the benchmarking. The lowest scrap percentage is in Columbus for area 06, which has a scrap percent of ~1%. It also has a lower variation in scrap percentage, meaning the Columbus site is consistent in their processes. The question now becomes: Why can't all the processes in all facilities be like this one? Figure 11.5 shows the same concept but using a different

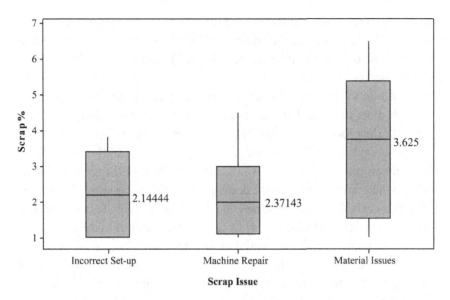

FIGURE 11.5
Internal benchmarking by cause.

example (i.e., incorrect setups, machine repairs, and material issues for three facilities). Material issues appear to be the major contributor to the scrap problem across all the facilities. Figure 11.6 uses a Pareto analysis to count the number of incidents by facility as well as the processes within each facility. This would be a useful approach for reducing the numbers of

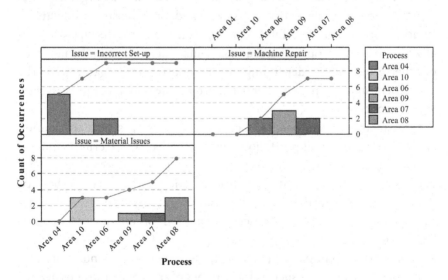

FIGURE 11.6
Internal benchmarking by scrap cause and process.

incorrect setups, material issues, and machine repairs. In addition to the many other tools and methods discussed in this book, an assessment team could use analyses like these to identify and financially justify improvement projects.

In addition to operational and financial analyses and all of the analytical methods that can be used to identify project opportunities, it is important to also walk the processes using audits, process mapping, gathering data right where the work is done, and involving the people who do the work rather than rely on intermediaries. It is important to see how things are done as well as where and when they are done in a representative way. That is, it is critical to evaluate several process conditions and ideally the best-case and worst-case scenarios to look for root causes and solutions. Chapters 5 and 6 provided many useful tools and methods to aid in this process analysis. Figure 6.2 shows an example in which the three non-value-add operations are highlighted for elimination. After their elimination, the remaining inefficient process steps that have components of value-add and non-value-add work tasks and that negatively impact process yield, cost, lead time, or throughput can be eliminated, improved, or automated. When process inefficiencies are identified using a value flow map created by the process teams, projects that can be added to the assessment portfolio will be identified. As discussed in previous chapters, these projects will not appear in operational reports because they can only be identified using a hands-on process analysis rather than with analytics alone.

The assessment team should work between and within organizational functions to ensure the entire site is evaluated for increasing productivity. In addition to Table 1.2, Table 11.1 lists common projects that are usually identified from operational assessments. There are literally hundreds of other project ideas, depending on the industry and organization. The assessment should have a master list of project ideas to integrate with their assessment goals.

Assessment projects need to be prioritized using several evaluation criteria before the final portfolio is recommended. These criteria include business benefit, effort, and timing of benefit realization. The criteria need to be carefully defined before prioritization so there is no ambiguity. Benefits are normally defined as time savings and cost savings, and sometimes as more focused benefits such as reductions of complexity (i.e., number of handoffs reduced) and similar types. Effort will usually be defined as people hours to implement a project, investment costs, and sometimes more focused categories such as the number of stakeholder groups needed

TABLE 11.1

Project Ideas

Finance	Marketing
Reduce finance charges	Increase market share
Reduce operational cycle times	Increase market penetration
Reduce auditing errors	Reduce marketing expenses
Reduce accounts receivable billing errors	Increase customer loyalty
Reduce accounts payable errors	Reduce the cycle time for market research studies
Sales	**Human Resources**
Improve quote success rate	Increase employee retention rate
Increase sales revenue	Increase employee satisfaction
Increase sales per person	Reduce employee hiring cycle time
Reduce rework expense	Reduce hiring expenses
Increase sales quote accuracy	Reduce termination expense
Administration	**Production**
Reduce facility maintenance expense	Reduce operational scrap and rework
Reduce facility energy usage per employee	Reduce operational lead time
Optimize materials and operating supplies cost per employee	Improve schedule adherence
	Reduce standard cost
	Reduce emergency maintenance

for approval of a solution. The effort/impact prioritization matrix shown in Figure 11.7 helps organize projects based on these criteria. This matrix helps the assessment team identify the ideas with high benefits and requiring little effort; these are the highest priority projects); in the opposite corner of this matrix are ideas that provide little benefit and require high effort (i.e., the lowest priority projects). These latter projects are not prioritized highly in the project portfolio. Projects with low benefits and low effort are also recommended to be done. The last category high benefits and high effort usually require investment, but the benefits can be substantial.

The usefulness of this visualization is that other criteria can be overlaid on the matrix to provide addition insight into the prioritization. As an example, projects can be color-coded to show the anticipated implementation lead times. The preference would be for projects that can be executed more quickly than others. Similar projects can be grouped by circling them. The similarity may be related to root causes having common solutions (e.g., training issues, policy issues, design issues, and others). This approach

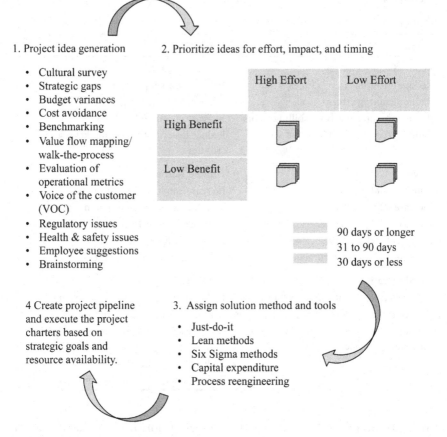

1. Project idea generation

- Cultural survey
- Strategic gaps
- Budget variances
- Cost avoidance
- Benchmarking
- Value flow mapping/ walk-the-process
- Evaluation of operational metrics
- Voice of the customer (VOC)
- Regulatory issues
- Health & safety issues
- Employee suggestions
- Brainstorming

2. Prioritize ideas for effort, impact, and timing

	High Effort	Low Effort
High Benefit		
Low Benefit		

90 days or longer
31 to 90 days
30 days or less

4 Create project pipeline and execute the project charters based on strategic goals and resource availability.

3. Assign solution method and tools

- Just-do-it
- Lean methods
- Six Sigma methods
- Capital expenditure
- Process reengineering

FIGURE 11.7
Project prioritization.

is useful for assigning similar projects to a single team. The assessment team's portfolio recommendations should include different projects to balance benefits (e.g., operational productivity versus customer satisfaction), include diverse parts of the organization, and avoid competition for resources.

CLOSING THE ASSESSMENT

Once the team reaches a consensus for the types of projects needed to improve productivity and customer satisfaction, the report is finalized to provide local site leadership with the assessment findings, recommendations, and the final plan. These include the project charters and specific processes where productivity improvements can be achieved reasonably given resource constraints. These findings and recommendations are summarized for a review with site management.

The report provides the plan for increasing the site's productivity over the current plan. Findings include the recommended project charters with initial sponsors, team lead and team members, time-phased benefits, required resources, and other relevant information. It is important that recommended project charters are not ideas or abstractions but are well-defined and financially justified project charters with required resources and anticipated barriers to implementation. The SWOT analysis is used to aggregate key interview themes to show local leadership the key issues employees believe are impacting performance and how the recommendations will focus on these as well as other identified gaps. Quantitative analyses of financial and operational metrics and value flow analyses of major processes are also integral components of the report.

Once the report is agreed to by the team and verified with the process leads, an exit meeting is scheduled with the site leadership team to close the engagement. The findings include projected productivity levels, return on investment, and other relevant information necessary to deploy an initiative at the site level. The agenda include an executive summary, the purpose and deliverables of the assessment, key interview themes around financial and operational goals, the updated SWOT analysis, the project portfolio, and the deployment plan. Also discussed will be the analyses of the major processes from the value flow mapping with analyses. The site leadership team's recommendations are used to update the final site assessment report that will be integrated with other site locations.

SUMMARY

Assessment preparation begins with forming a core planning team, conducting initial employee surveys or obtaining feedback from key stakeholders, and gathering operational and financial performance information. In addition, stakeholder and contact lists are created along with an assessment plan. Integral to the assessment planning will be identifying where to create value stream maps to analyze end-to-end processes or value flow maps of key processes. Data gathering helps focus an assessment on areas that have greater potential to create projects with high productivity opportunities. The assessment information will eventually be translated into projects that identify and eliminate the root causes of poor process performance. Financial and operational analysis is also used to internally benchmark processes to differentiate poorly performing processes from better performing processes to identify and adopt best practices. During the assessment or shortly after its conclusion, project charters are defined, financially justified, and approved by process owners. This creates a project portfolio in areas where the assessment was deployed.

After the assessment team arrives, the management and process owner meetings have been held, and the assessment's objectives, activities, and deliverables are approved, interviews are started at the site. In these interviews, the critical-to flow downs that were constructed during the leadership and site management training or orientation sessions are updated with relevant information. Using this information as a starting point, the assessment team and the site teams begin to verify the original project ideas and to identify new opportunities through local site interviews. It is important to confirm the process issues that were originally on the assessment list. These activities help identify the process team that will need to help with data collection, process mapping, and other assessment activities. Once the team reaches a consensus for the types of projects needed to improve productivity and customer satisfaction, the report is finalized to provide local site leadership with the assessment findings, recommendations, and the final plan. These include the project charters and specific processes where productivity improvements can be made practically, given resource constraints. These findings and recommendations are summarized for a review with site management.

12

Virtual Teams

OVERVIEW

Project management is being influenced by the same macro trends discussed earlier in this book. One of the most impactful is virtualization of project teams, which is the topic of this chapter. Virtualization has several benefits, including lower cost, diversity of teams, and global access to skills and experience. Digitalization is influencing how teams work and the work they do. It includes automation of many types, artificial intelligence, Big Data, and other topics previously discussed in earlier chapters. There are also trends specific to project management.

Project management is increasingly focused on initiatives containing many integrated projects that together to deliver measurable improvements in customer experience and productivity. Increasingly the project management strategy is to focus on project portfolios as opposed to isolated projects. Operational ecosystems are now highly complex, and a portfolio approach is often more effective than isolated projects because solutions require a combination of aligned projects. Portfolios are needed when there are dependencies between several projects. If there is a single project there are different approaches available, including classic project management with milestones, agile project management (APM) with scrum sprints, the Six Sigma phased method, Lean, and others. Teams can use any one of these methods or they can use a hybrid approach. But if a solution requires multiple projects to implement a solution then they must be managed as a portfolio. Digitalization and analytics also influence project management methods as well as data gathering, analysis, and solutions because of the size and number of the accessed databases. Whereas previous project teams could see and touch work products, digitalized work moves around the world and across many systems, with different formats and complexity. In addition to classical project management methods, artificial intelligence provides information and insights for team decisions. Artificial intelligence is already applied to the mundane project management tasks of scheduling work, resource allocation, and project balancing on the critical path, budgeting, and other activities.

Today, products and services, as well as their supporting processes, are decentralized across integrated technology platforms. These platforms employ hundreds or even thousands of software applications that sit on integrated technology platforms. The software applications, the information that is updated, and the associated work is distributed across virtual clouds. Clouds are physical collections of hardware and software located in controlled environments and accessed via the Internet. Clouds aggregate information from many sources to increase hardware and software utilization to lower cost. They also increase software application and information availability and reliability because cloud facilities are duplicated across large distances to reduce downtime.

VIRTUAL TEAMS

Recent studies show significant productivity increases from remote working. And there is a growing ability and opportunities to work remotely and still relate to others. Some jobs, however, cannot be made remote. These include on-site manufacturing, distribution, and most server jobs that have face-to-face customer contact. Also, not all people enjoy working remotely, and some lack the skills or the technology to be effective. To the extent that remote working can be implemented, there are several benefits to individuals and organizations. Expenses are reduced by not commuting to work and not traveling for business meetings. These savings are significant. For individuals, the savings may total several thousand dollars after tax from the reduced use of vehicles or other transportation and associated costs. Also, living in less expensive areas can reduce living expenses for individuals. Organizations can save even more. Reduced office space, rents, and lower utility and insurance expenses are just a few examples. There is also less risk to employees by not traveling for business. This is especially true for international travel. Another significant advantage is the dramatic reduction of an organization's carbon footprint to support corporate sustainability initiatives. Some teams are 100% remote and others are mixed, with both in-office employees and remote workers. The strategies for working remotely are the same except and depends on universal access to the same information and resources for all participants.

Organizations can also take advantage of global talent both from a skill variety perspective as well as through lower labor costs. In some situations, an organization may be able to pay more for certain talent because other employment costs (e.g., rent, travel, and related expenses) are lower. Workforce flexibility is increased because a remote workforce can be easily scaled. Employee retention in some situations may be higher if a remote workforce has lower work-related expenses and more personal time. Employees can work for organizations located in countries or locations where they would not normally be able to live. Global teams can be organized to service customers around the clock. This reduces the lead times or service levels for handling customer inquiries and to do other work. Productivity will be higher, in part, because travel time is reduced. There are also fewer non-productive meetings, and side conversations are reduced significantly.

There are also disadvantages associated with remote working. First, there is the potential for disconnection from other employees. This is especially applicable for people that have a work style requiring high social interaction. Second, distractions may reduce productivity if a home office is not set up to minimize interruptions. Third, the technology may not be suitable relative to hardware and software performance, or telecommunications may not be efficient. Finally, it may be difficult to separate work time from personal time. These situations contribute to employee burnout.

Prior to forming a virtual project team, there are several important considerations: building trust, maintaining connections between team members, managing work, and eliminating barriers for doing remote work. It is important to build trust between remote workers and central teams through policies, procedures, and work standardization. Policies and procedures must be documented for the teams to work together. Remote and central teams need to understand their roles and responsibilities as well as the team's goals. Consistency is very important for any team, and especially so for remote teams. Consistency is enhanced by meeting regularly, complete with agendas and other team facilitation tools and methods. It requires that each team member follow the team's agreed-upon rules for working. In fact, many remote teams have an informal agreement on how to work together.

An agreement describes how the team will communicate and keep promises to finish work that is in scope and agreed upon in advance. This approach will also be useful when new team members onboard. The team leader should maintain transparency between the members to ensure equal contributions by all. This means work should be evenly divided based on skills and the team agreements. Information should also be shared equally within the team, except when it is personal and private. This does not imply that team members would not be recognized when they go above and beyond their expected contributions, rather that the recognition criteria should always be equally applied to everyone in similar circumstances. Team members may also have expertise or certain skills that enable them to lead team projects. More experienced team members should be encouraged to coach new team members.

Remote teams should be supported with technology to interact with the global IT ecosystem. Remote client computers and Internet speeds are important considerations. Internet speeds need to match the software applications being remotely accessed. There needs to be enough bandwidth in the broadband connection, and phone, video conferencing software, printers, and other peripherals are necessary to enable efficient work. Remote technology deployment strategies vary. An organization could supply the hardware, software, and peripherals at an employee's home office or enable an employee to use low-cost equipment, or the employee may purchase their own equipment and be reimbursed later. The same would be true for contractors. Policies, procedures, and processes must be in place to govern remote work to ensure devices are properly serviced and secured as well as available for work.

Remote or virtual teams usually have members in different countries and time zones. Team effectiveness is increased if the team is culturally aware. One method to increase awareness is to learn about each team member's culture. Different cultures have differing perspectives of communication, work, and other factors important for team effectiveness. It is recommended to study cultural etiquette in advance of the first team meeting to modify behavioral styles. An example is speech (e.g., using slang or speaking versus being silent). These behaviors matter in most cultures. It is also important to listen to the team. Who is speaking more versus members who are silent? Relative to logistics, remote and especially global teams should schedule meetings considering the different time zones, country-specific holidays, and team members' personal commitments. It may be useful to schedule meetings at different times to allow members to share the inconvenience of meeting either late or early in the day.

Technology has enabled easy video conferencing and information transfer around the world, and international organizations routinely use such technology to do work. In the past, entire products or services were offshored and either served local, in-country markets or shipped complete solutions outside a country. To an extent, technology leveled the cultural differences within teams relative to how they do work for the organization. Effective project management has never been more important because team members may never meet in person. And although they do meet virtually, they will move to other projects and may not work together for months or years. The team maturation model that was discussed in Chapter 2 has been modified through corporate initiatives, communications, and policies that promote rapid team formation and efficient work to achieve goals. The project management basics, however, remain the same, albeit with modifications for virtualization.

Project management is an integrated set of activities that require effective planning and execution of interrelated actions. These activities ensure projects achieve their goals on schedule. Project management activities include leading a team and ensuring its project remains on schedule, within budget, and meets goals and their deliverables. An improvement team is formed around a project charter supported with financial and operational justifications and focused (or scoped) around a defined process having a starting point and an ending point. The business case ensures the project is strategically aligned. The charter will have identified the initial team members, at least by organizational function, based on the project's scope. The supplier-input-process-output-customer (SIPOC) map, such as was shown in Figures 3.11 and 9.6, is particularly useful for helping identify a project's team members. Team members should be selected across the process including those doing the work and people receiving materials or information. Team members should also have the requisite skills and knowledge to help the team drive toward the root causes of a process and develop solutions. The team leader will expand on this list with stakeholders to finalize the project team and obtain time commitments based on their expected roles and responsibilities.

Team management is important for successful project execution. Table 12.1 lists metrics that are effective for evaluating team performance.

TABLE 12.1

Metrics for Managing Projects

Metric

1. Working days used versus days allocated
2. Work tasks to be completed within 24 hours
3. Work tasks starting in the next 10 days
4. Work tasks in progress
5. Work tasks completed
6. Work task resources consumed
7. Work tasks started late
8. Work tasks over budget
9. Project expenses to budget
10. Work tasks "crashed" to reduce project time

The project leader balances time and resources, including expenses, to achieve goals and their deliverables. Deliverables are features or functions associated with a product, service, or supporting process. They consist of work tasks, which are logically grouped based on sequence and similarity into milestones. When the work tasks are complete, then the deliverables are complete. When all the deliverables of a milestone are complete, then the milestone is completed. Stakeholder reviews are conducted at project milestones. When the milestones are complete, the project goals are complete. Each deliverable has one to several work tasks that need to be completed on schedule using predetermined resources. The metrics in Table 12.1 are focused on measuring work according to schedule and resource usage. Work tasks are often interrelated. Some cannot be started before others, and sequence relationships are important to measure relative to when tasks begin and end. The metrics in Table 12.1 measure work task adherence to schedule. The list is redundant, and some teams will use some but not all the metrics. There are also others specific to different industries. The last metric in Table 12.1, "Work tasks that can be crashed to reduce expected completion time," refers to adding resources to critical tasks to do them more quickly to reach project completion. This topic will be discussed later in this chapter.

Prior to forming a team, an organization needs to ask the question, "Is a team really needed to investigate and execute this project?" Not every project requires a project team. If a project is small in scope or its solution is obvious, a formal team is not necessary. In contrast, a formal team is needed to execute a complex project that requires different stakeholders,

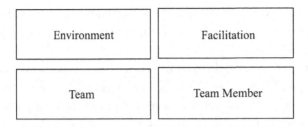

Form a team if ...

- There is a strong problem statement
- Leadership is aligned
- Resources are available
- Different perspectives are needed
- Solution is not known

FIGURE 12.1
Developing virtual teams.

resources, and skills. A project team should also not be formed, nor should a project be formally chartered, if there is no clear management directive to initiate the project, such as a lack of alignment with organizational strategy, a weak problem statement, ambiguous objectives, or a lack of resources and other required support. Figure 12.1 summarizes this discussion.

Once a project team is formed, issues may arise that need to be resolved. Every team may face such problems to one degree or another. A project manager should be aware of these potential issues and develop plans to mitigate their impact on the project's schedule and cost. Figure 12.1 shows the four categories of external environment, facilitation tools, and team evolution, and team member perceptions. The external environment impacts project prioritization and available resources. A project charter is the best way to internally prioritize and obtain resources from stakeholders. Resources include people who work in the process, access to information, and a budget. The external environment may pose several project risks, including competitive threats, technological and regulatory barriers, and adverse economic conditions. Competitive threats include the loss or gain of major customers, products, or services. Technological threats occur if a project relies on new or major improvement in technology. Regulatory and economic risks occur if an organization is not well positioned relative to competitors to meet new or updated regulations or to survive adverse economic conditions of various types, including international economic factors. External threats to a project vary by industry and organization.

Facilitation is also critical to team performance, especially if the team is highly diverse. Diversity is an important success factor for teams because it provides different perspectives for root-cause analysis and solutions. But diversity may result in disagreements as to how to proceed with project work. These disagreements must be facilitated to ensure project goals and schedule are met. Facilitation does not need to be complicated, and it is always helpful. As an example, using a meeting agenda, ensuring team members are heard and feel free to contribute their ideas, outlining clear roles and responsibilities on the team, and sending out meeting minutes and action items will ensure meetings are efficient. In contrast, if team members are homogeneous and agree on actions without discussion, it is more likely that wrong actions will be pursued. This is groupthink, and it contributes to dysfunctional behaviors because alternative and optimum solutions are often missed.

The opposite of groupthink is diversity in thought and is the preferred methods of working problems and solutions. There are several systems that measure personal perceptions of work. These show different people solve problems from different perspectives. One evaluation technique is the Meyers-Briggs method, which ranks people along four dimensions. The first is introversion versus extroversion. The second is sensing versus intuitive. The third is thinking versus feeling. The fourth is judgmental versus perceptive. These are organized into sixteen discrete categories. A person may be highly introverted or highly extroverted, or somewhere between these extremes. Without proper facilitation, the extroverts in a team will dominate conversations. This reduces contributions from introverted team members. A facilitation method to avoid this issue is to ask each person if they would like to contribute an idea to the team's conversation. This ensures everyone has a chance to contribute to meetings. Another Meyers-Briggs dimension is sensing versus intuitive. Individuals who naturally evaluate a problem sequentially are sensing types, whereas intuitive personalities will seek a solution without necessarily following a sequential process. To an intuitive personality, the sensing personality may seem to move too slowly when collecting the necessary facts and information to objectively investigate a problem. In contrast, to the sensing personality, the intuitive type may attempt to move through a root-cause analysis without factual justification. In these situations, the facilitation would involve following a problem-solving methodology that requires a sequential approach. The team would agree on the data collection plan and, once analyzed, decisions will be made based on the analytical results. Later in a project, the strength of the intuitive personalities will come into play by envisioning different solutions and alternatives, whereas sensing types may continue to focus on data collection and analysis. Team members may disagree on how best to proceed with work because of different perceptions; without facilitation, this will cause conflict.

The last category in Figure 12.1 is team evolution. Project teams move through four stages as they mature into a high-performance team. This model was discussed in Chapter 2. Recall that the maturation stages were forming, storming, norming, and performing. In the forming stage, team members develop initial impressions. Not much serious discussion of project objectives occurs during this stage. As the team starts to discuss the project's goals and deliverables and how to achieve them, disagreements may occur without facilitation. If the team is facilitated effectively, it can quickly pass through the storming stage to develop a consensus of how to work through the project's deliverables. Over time, as the team performs its roles and responsibilities and completes milestones on schedule, mutual trust increases and the team enters the performing stage.

There are positive and negative sources for team conflict. Conflict by itself is a necessary precursor to the investigation of a project's problem because it is based on diversity of thought. It is based on differences in the group's cultural values and psychological perceptions, differences in goals and expectations based on cultural perceptions and lack of understanding of cross-cultural norms. Positive effects from conflict are increased solution alternatives once understanding is achieved through group facilitation, communication is increased through awareness of cultural and psychological differences and increased motivation within the team occurs because of group goal alignment. Facilitation will eliminate or reduce stress due to misconceptions caused by different cultural expectations. This will improve solution alternatives and enhance agreement on problem statements and data interpretation. The result will be more effective communication, and higher morale. Facilitation will help a team achieve project milestones on schedule. Cultural differences also necessitate modifications to how teams are formed and managed in different regions of the world. First, the teams are virtual, and its members are scattered around the world. They must quickly move through the maturation stages to be effective, and only facilitation can do this.

A checklist is useful for ensuring facilitation of virtual teams. The list reflects some of the information from the team's chapter and includes clear roles and responsibilities including the team leader, the facilitator, team members, ad hoc technical experts, a timekeeper, and a note taker, the project goals and deliverables and other relevant information. A SIPOC should also be created to confirm the team's scope or work. The SIPOC's input and output boundaries should be aligned with the project's problem statement, goals and their deliverables or milestones. The team should include members having diverse viewpoints, perspectives, and skills. These people should be part of the process in scope. Outside assistance and resources should be requested when needed. The team should collect and analyze data to answer project questions in a fact-based manner and to drive solutions based on fact rather than only on team consensus. Several of the project management models discussed in earlier chapters provide a structured framework.

PROJECT MANAGEMENT

Once a problem statement is finalized, it is broken into deliverables that are further broken down to work tasks. Work tasks are grouped into higher level project milestones. Milestones are control points for the project. An objective of a project team is to time phase the milestones and work tasks using the work breakdown structure method. This method creates a list of sequential and well-defined work tasks that are aggregated hierarchically into milestones for project management and reporting. Each work task or activity has a starting point and an ending point, a measurable output, and a defined resource requirement and time duration.

A Gantt chart and Project Evaluation and Review Technique (PERT) model of a project's work tasks can be represented as a network that describes activity sequence and relationships. Figure 12.2 shows an example. This network has six activities spatially arranged into two parallel paths. For simplicity, we will not go deeper into the work task level of detail, but instead demonstrate how to build a network model using the work breakdown structure and the Gantt chart, calculating the critical path, and estimating the probability of completing this project example on schedule.

The analysis starts by estimating the time to complete each activity within the network. In the absence of historical or current lead time data

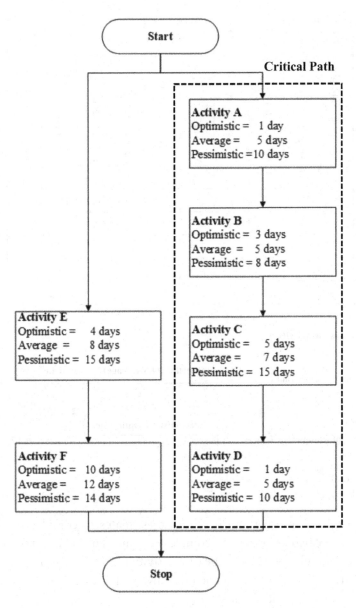

FIGURE 12.2
Developing a work breakdown structure.

for each activity, the team estimates the "most optimistic," "expected," and "most pessimistic" times to complete each activity based on the team's collective knowledge. Depending on the required analytical detail, activities can be disaggregated into work tasks. Each activity in Figure 12.2

Activity	Optimistic Completion Time	Average Completion Time	Pessimistic Completion Time	Expected Completion Time	Variance	Earliest Start (ES)	Latest Start (LS)	Earliest Finish (EF)	Latest Finish (LF)	Slack	Critical Path
A	1	5	10	5.17	2.25	0	0	5.17	5.17	0	YES
B	3	5	8	5.17	0.69	5.17	5.17	10.33	10.33	0	YES
C	5	7	15	8	2.78	10.33	10.33	18.33	18.33	0	YES
D	1	5	10	5.17	2.25	18.33	18.33	23.5	23.5	0	YES
E	4	8	15	8.5	3.36	0	3	8.5	11.5	3	NO
F	10	12	14	12	0.44	8.5	11.5	20.5	23.5	3	NO

Calculations for Activity A:

Expected Completion Time (t) =
$$\frac{\text{Optimistic} + (4 \times \text{Average}) + \text{Pessimistic}}{6} = 5.17 \text{ days}$$

Variance of Completion Time =
$$\left[\frac{\text{Pessimistic} - \text{Optimistic}}{6} \right]^2 = 2.25 \text{ days}$$

FIGURE 12.3
Gantt chart.

has optimistic, average and pessimistic estimates to complete it. These are used to calculate expected completion times and their variance. The expected completion time of the first activity is 5.17 days and its variance is 2.25 days. Calculations for the other five activities are summarized in Figure 12.3 with related statistics.

The work breakdown structure is shown in the Gantt chart in Figure 12.4, where the parallel paths of the network are clearly shown. The network's critical path is through operations A,B,C, and D, and the calculated expected project completion time for these four operations is 23.5 days. The total time required to complete all six operations is 44.0 (rounded) days. This implies that operations 5 and 6 have slack or extra time available on their parallel path.

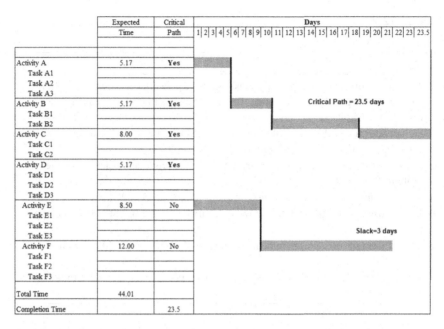

FIGURE 12.4
PERT and critical path summary statistics by activity.

Table 12.2 calculates the critical path by estimating the earliest starting time (ES), earliest finishing time (EF), latest starting time (LS), and latest finishing time (LF) of an activity. In complicated networks, these statistics are usually calculated using software. First, take the expected completion time of each activity and make a forward pass through the network to estimate the ES and EF statistics for each activity. This is shown in Step 2 of Table 12.2. Once the earliest finish time (EF) has been calculated for the last operation or activity of a project network (in this example, 23.5 days), a backward pass is made through the network. This backward pass is used to help calculate the LS and LF statistics as described in Step 3 of Table 12.2. The slack time of each activity is calculated as described in Step 4 of Table 12.2. An activity with zero slack must be started and finished on time and is on the critical path. The statistics described in Table 12.2 are summarized in Figure 12.4, where they are used to find the probability of completing the project in 20 days or less. Other completion (or lead) time targets can also be calculated. In Table 12.3, a completion probability of 34% is calculated using a hypothetical lead time of 20 days or less and assuming the distribution of completion times is normal. An interval can also be calculated assuming the expected time is 23.5 days

TABLE 12.2

Calculating a Critical Path

Step

1. A "path" is a linked sequence of work tasks within a network beginning with a "start" node and ending with an "stop" node. The critical path is the longest sequence of network work tasks.
2. Earliest Start time (ES) and Earliest Finish time (EF) for a work task is defined by "EF = ES + t," where "t" is the duration of the work task.
3. Latest Start time (LS) and Earliest Start time (ES) for a work task is defined by the relation "LS = LF–t."
4. Slack time for a work task is designed by the relation "LS–ES = LF–EF."
5. Make a forward pass through the network calculating the EF and LF times for every work task.
6. Make a backward pass through the network using the total calculated completion time as the LF time.
7. The critical path is defined as the sequence of work tasks having zero slack time as defined in Step 4 above.

TABLE 12.3

Statistics for Critical Path Operations

Step

1. Expected completion time (t) = 5.17 + 5.17 + 8.00 + 5.17 = 23.5 days
2. Variance of completion time = 2.25 + 0.69 + 2.78 + 2.25 = 7.97 days
3. Probability of completing project in 20 days = probability $Z \leq (20-3.5) / 7.97) = -0.41 = $ 34%

with a 7.97 day variance. The 95% interval based on a Normal distribution assumption is $23.5 \pm (1.96) (2.83 \text{ days}) = 23.5 \pm 5.5 \text{ days} = 18$ to 29 days.

SUMMARY

Teams are formed for different purposes. They differ in goals, duration, and form. Organizations are organized around work teams. Everyone is part of a work team. This is a formal construct with a leader and a reporting hierarchy. Roles and responsibilities are clearly documented, and performance is evaluated accordingly. The team leader will often make decisions and allocate work to team members although some work teams are self-managing to varying degrees. They can be collocated, virtual, or a combination of both. At times, organizations bring together teams to complete focused goals on a high-priority basis. These teams require formal project charters to identity scope, goals, deliverables, team members, sponsorship, resources, a schedule, and other relevant information. The charter is needed to avoid ambiguity of effort. These teams can be highly cross-functional depending on the project scope.

Recent studies show significant productivity increases with remote working, and there is a growing ability and increasing opportunities to work remotely and still relate to co-workers. Prior to forming a virtual project team, there are several important considerations. These are building trust, maintaining connections between team members, managing work, and eliminating barriers for doing remote work. It is important to build trust between remote workers and central teams; to this end, policies and procedures for the teams to work together must be well documented.

Not all teams are immediately successful. First, they move through a maturation process discussed earlier in this chapter. But there are potential barriers to high performance. Teams need rules of engagement and norms that govern how they will work. A project charter is a good start, and meetings must be facilitated to enable good decision making based on a full consideration of topics and then to move on to fact-based action. Full consideration implies that all member participate in meeting discussions and that the team is diverse with respect to ideas to avoid groupthink. Facilitation also minimizes team conflicts and promotes mutual trust. Transparency is crucial for effective teams.

Projects have associated risks that must be identified, eliminated, mitigated, or managed depending on their likelihood of occurrence and impact. Effective project management organizes people and resources to ensure activities remain on schedule, within budget, and with minimal project risk. Using a Gantt chart to organize activities and their work tasks is important to show the sequence of activities and their work tasks that must be completed on the critical path to minimize the time for project completion. In addition to estimating work task duration, the milestone schedule is estimated to enable periodic stakeholder reviews. Project status is communicated to the right audience, in the right format, and with the right frequency.

Project management requires an attention to detail to enable a project manager to keep a project on schedule and within budget. Understanding details and using the methods discussed in this chapter help manage projects when conditions change. These methods are also incorporated into project management software. Software enables a team to create simulations of a project network's activities and work tasks to analyze the impact of adding resources on the critical path. Alternatively, if a project's activities are delayed, resources can be reallocated to the delayed activities to maintain the schedule. This is useful if a project can be completed ahead of schedule and incremental revenue is obtained that offsets the incremental resource cost. In summary, project management is a complicated series of activities requiring specialized tools and methods. Effective project management requires an attention to detail at a work task level, but also an ability to keep the overall project schedule in view to achieve the schedule, the target cost, and other benefits required by the project's charter.

13

Supply Chain Excellence

OVERVIEW

Supply chains continue to undergo rapid evolution. Operational capabilities are increasing in ways that were not possible only a few years ago. Some organizations now deliver products or services on the same day as they are ordered based on digitization and advanced inventory models. Energy efficiency and sustainability are now a focus in the context of ethical supply chains. These trends have already been operative in manufacturing and other operations for several years. Global supply chains now have unique IT platforms and applications that integrate with supply chain participants through cloud infrastructure. Previously discussed trends such as customer experience, Big Data, and the other initiatives directly impact global supply chains. RPA and the IoT applications are everywhere. Machine learning and artificial intelligence are being applied across supply chains just as they are in manufacturing and services. Cybersecurity has never been more important because of remote access to sensitive data. Operational changes are being pushed by digital transformations. Nevertheless, the basis for supply chain operations and improvement remain the same: meeting service-level agreements with enough capacity, and reducing lead times and operational cost. Supply chains are becoming more complicated with different transportation modes, changes in laws and regulations, and competition from different directions. The focus is also on enabling the workforce and the importance of effective project management and team virtualization as competitive differentiators. A deep understanding of where value is created and reconfiguration of supply chain design will be the key differentiators in an era of global supply chain digitization and competition.

Current digitization trends include blockchain, drones and artificial intelligence deliveries, same-day or last-mile deliveries, layered third-party logistics, as well as those discussed in previous chapters (e.g., artificial intelligence, RPA, and Big Data). Blockchain technology enables secure transactions between all supply chain participants. Drones and remote self-driving machines are increasingly being used to transport materials. Airborne drones provide an advantage in that deliveries can be made efficiently over otherwise difficult terrain. Last-mile deliveries include partnerships with third-party logistics suppliers as well as retail organizations and other participants to coordinate inventory availability in ways that allow fast access as well as lower cost. Layered third-party logistics incorporates third-party providers with enabling technologies that link e-business providers into the supply chain.

Global supply chains continue to evolve because of increasingly competitive environments, technology, changing consumer preferences, and increased access to local markets around the world. This evolutionary process has been supported through enabling technologies and newly developed tools, methods, and concepts that increase supply chain responsiveness and flexibility to match supply and demand. In parallel, customers have been demanding higher quality and lower costs for products and services. To satisfy evolving customer requirements, delivery strategies and systems have evolved to transport these highly differentiated global products and services. New types of businesses have been created, and older ones have reinvented themselves. Many of these newer organizations were formed around completely new products and services that did not exist several years ago. Global supply chains continue to evolve at a rapid pace.

Productivity and shareholder economic value added are goals of supply chain strategy. Transaction costs continue to be dramatically reduced because the cost for moving information is low and materials can be located optimally anywhere in the world through enabling technologies. In addition to infrastructure advancements, people have learned to work more effectively using team building and project management methods. Manufacturers have also benefited from globalization with lower production costs and new market opportunities. In addition to making internal operations more effective and efficient, the insourcing of value-add work or the outsourcing of non-value-add work that is not associated with core competencies dramatically increases supply chain capacity and productivity. Dominant supply chains are profitable, dominate their markets, manage assets efficiently, and continually improve operations relative to supply, demand, logistics, and supporting activities. But organizations that use globalization only to lower cost rather than to focus on the critical strategy of enhancing the value of products and services from a customer perspective will likely see lower productivity over the long term.

Customers often prefer differentiated offerings and will not necessarily trade desired features and functions for lower cost alone As a result, it is important to build adaptable and flexible operations to produce products and services that customers need and want (i.e., that customers value). In this context, operational strategies, including supply chain strategies, should align to marketing strategies. Sometimes an industry is too heavily invested in outdated products, services, and supporting processes to effectively align to changing operations. Measurements become important to align an organization with its strategic vision and enhanced operational capabilities. Some good measurements for global supply strategic alignment are profit, gross margin, market share, customer satisfaction, asset utilization, service levels, lead-time reduction, and value-add work percentage stratified by demographic factors of interest (e.g., product, service, location, etc.).

Global supply chains also need to align tactical competencies to strategy to mitigate global competitive threats; various forms of local governmental regulations, incentives, and sanctions; and myriad other factors that could impact operational efficiency. The operational focus remains on improving the many supply chain processes including forward logistics, including demand planning, sourcing, operations, supplier relationships, and reverse logistics associated with customer dissatisfaction for various reasons.

Figure 13.1 describes global supply chain activities from a value perspective that emphasizes process integration backward from the voice of the customer. This approach pulls value through a global supply chain and balances customer needs and value expectations against operations. In fact, order fulfillment processes become more sophisticated through IT applications that enhance operational flexibility. Lean methods have also increased supply chain flexibility through process simplification, standardization, and mistake-proofing strategies that significantly reduce lead times. On the demand management side, the acquisition of point-of-sale

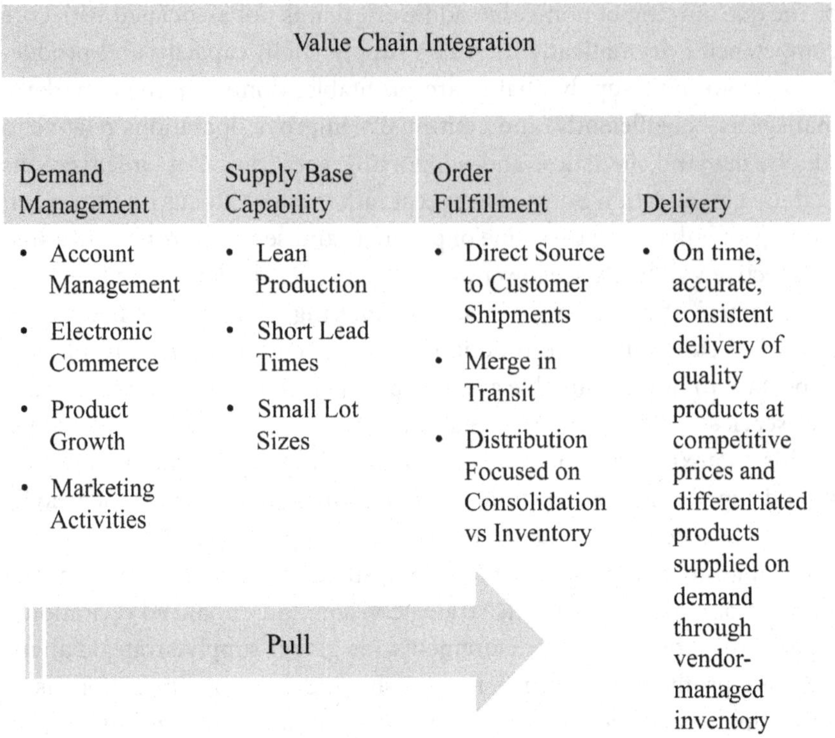

Value Chain Integration			
Demand Management	**Supply Base Capability**	**Order Fulfillment**	**Delivery**
• Account Management • Electronic Commerce • Product Growth • Marketing Activities	• Lean Production • Short Lead Times • Small Lot Sizes	• Direct Source to Customer Shipments • Merge in Transit • Distribution Focused on Consolidation vs Inventory	• On time, accurate, consistent delivery of quality products at competitive prices and differentiated products supplied on demand through vendor-managed inventory

Pull →

FIGURE 13.1
Global supply chains integrate value.

(POS) data and similar real-time collection of information can minimize the use of forecasting models having notoriously poor accuracy. In parallel, electronic commerce (i.e., e-commerce) increasingly enables the capture of localized customer preferences

Important characteristics of successful global supply chains include high collaboration between all participants, a high multi-cultural presence, adherence to global operational standards, high product availability, low costs, low order-to-delivery lead times, high transaction accuracy, and high asset availability and flexibility. High collaboration is enabled by virtual meetings, e-mail, and other communications systems. Collaboration helps identify where assets should be positioned across the supply chain to increase return on assets. Supporting this asset positioning are virtual and local project teams. There is also adherence to global design and operational standards relative to packing, fulfillment, and logistics. This ensures products and services consistently meet customer requirements across diverse regions. Standards also help simplify product and service designs and enable them to be used in different countries. Cost is also lowered.

High product availability is another important characteristic of a successful global supply chain. Availability implies supply is efficiently matched to demand. It is important to use demand-management strategies that ensure accuracy by moving away from a reliance on mathematical forecasting models toward firm demand commitments such as customer contracts (i.e., order book), POS information, and other systems that accurately capture demand. Integral to improving supply chain productivity is the elimination of intermediaries through simplification of products, services, and supporting processes. The application of operational initiatives such as Lean, Six Sigma, total productive maintenance, product and network design, and others can improve availability, flexibility, and productivity. Finally, standardization, mistake-proofing, and similar Lean tools, methods, and concepts can help improve supply chain productivity and reduce cycle time. The overall business benefits of a global supply chain using these combined initiatives are higher asset utilization and efficiency.

Table 13.1 lists strategic objectives of global supply chains. These include the development of strategic partnerships and other business relationships with incremental value, high margins across supply chain participants, differentiated products and services to increase competitiveness in local markets, ongoing rationalization of asset utilization and efficiency across the supply chain, and technology deployment. Chapter 8 discussed technology deployment relative to the business process management suite, business process management, business modeling and analysis, business intelligence, business activity monitoring, enterprise application integration, workflow management, and enterprise resource planning systems. Additional strategic objectives include ongoing rationalization of the distribution and logistics networks, rationalization of insourcing and outsourcing, optimizing global capacity planning, and increasing the percent of high-value operations while ensuring localized operational differentiation. Effectively integrating the flow of materials and information through a supply chain is an ongoing evaluative process that uses a hierarchy of IT platforms, tools, and methods to create useful information to manage a supply chain's processes.

Strategic partnerships help expand a supply chain's available capacity as well as new marketing opportunities. If properly designed, such partnerships will also increase operating margins for all participants. This is done

TABLE 13.1

Ten Strategic Objectives of Global Supply Chains

Objective	Description
1. Global strategic partnerships	Strategic partnerships expand a global supply chain's resources to satisfy demand. All participants need to extract value relative to alternative strategies.
2. High margins across the supply chain	Margins should be at their entitlement level. Entitlement infers every part of the supply chain extracts a margin reflective of its capital investment, risk, and value contribution.
3. Highly differentiated products to increase competitiveness in local markets	Products and services must be designed to reflect local culture and consumer needs, but designed in a way that allows mass customization principles to be employed when possible.
4. Ongoing rationalization of asset utilization and efficiency across the supply chain	Questions surrounding what assets are required, where should they be located, and who should own them is an ongoing series of analyses designed to ensure all parts of the supply chain have high asset-utilization efficiencies.
5. Technology deployment	Integration of the flow of materials and information through a supply chain is an ongoing integrative process that uses a hierarchy of information technology platforms, tools, and methods to create useful information to manage workflows.
6. Ongoing rationalization of transportation modes	The development of optimal routing sequences analyzes networks using operations research tools and methods designed to reduce network length along a critical path and cost by evaluating constraints related to demand, supply, and other relevant information.
7. Insourcing and outsourcing rationalization	The analysis and decision regarding where work should be performed within a supply chain is an ongoing activity based on where the most value can be added to reduce overall supply chain lead time and cost to increase asset utilization.
8. Match supply and demand	The ability to determine item demand by location and time enables the efficient matching of supply to demand. Demand estimation is enabled using real-time data obtained from the customer regarding actual demand for products or services.

TABLE 13.1 *(Continued)*

Ten Strategic Objectives of Global Supply Chains

Objective	Description
9. Process driven operations having high value content	Processes should be designed around similar output requirements related to time, cost, and quality as well as similar product or service design.
10. High operational standardization	High standardization is required to ensure operations are completed in a minimum amount of time without error. However, a system should be easily reconfigurable, with the resultant standards reflecting the newly configured system.

through optimally managing assets and determining where they should be located and which participants should own them. This becomes an evolving series of analyses that ensures all participants have high asset utilization and productivity. Optimal routing is also important. This requires a continual evaluation of a supply chain's demand and supply constraints using operations research tools and methods. Decisions regarding where and how work is done is an ongoing set of planning activities that evaluate where the highest value can be added to optimize asset utilization and reduce overall order-to-cash lead time and cost. Finally, global supply chains need to be easily reconfigurable. Ideally, operations including standards, reports, communications, network routing, and other operations are automatically enabled through digitization to create newly reconfigured systems.

Supply chains contain thousands of different work tasks that are aggregated into the functions shown in Figure 13.2 using a high-level Supplier-Input Boundary-Process-Output Boundary-Customer (SIPOC) chart. On the supplier side of the SIPOC, suppliers ship products or provide services to customers or distribution centers. Important integrative systems include distribution requirements, material resource planning, and enterprise resource planning systems. Material resource systems procure materials, components, and other items needed for immediate production requirements or for placement into inventory for later usage. Distribution requirements systems manage inventory across the global distribution network. Supporting activities include the management of purchase orders, accounts payables, and coordination of suppliers or others in the supply chain. Logistics also coordinates freight rates, shipping modes, and how a product is transported within a supply chain. Other activities include

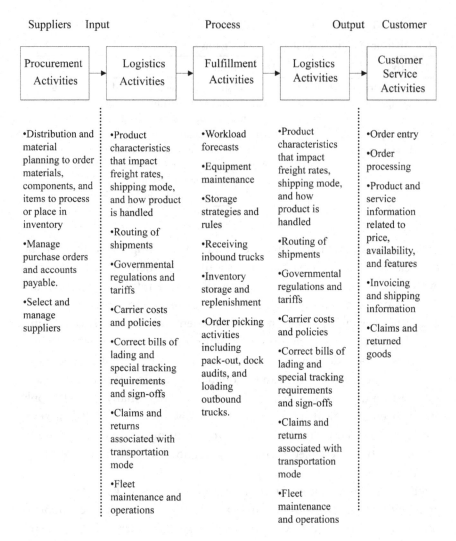

Suppliers   Input   Process   Output   Customer

Procurement Activities	Logistics Activities	Fulfillment Activities	Logistics Activities	Customer Service Activities
•Distribution and material planning to order materials, components, and items to process or place in inventory •Manage purchase orders and accounts payable. •Select and manage suppliers	•Product characteristics that impact freight rates, shipping mode, and how product is handled •Routing of shipments •Governmental regulations and tariffs •Carrier costs and policies •Correct bills of lading and special tracking requirements and sign-offs •Claims and returns associated with transportation mode •Fleet maintenance and operations	•Workload forecasts •Equipment maintenance •Storage strategies and rules •Receiving inbound trucks •Inventory storage and replenishment •Order picking activities including pack-out, dock audits, and loading outbound trucks.	•Product characteristics that impact freight rates, shipping mode, and how product is handled •Routing of shipments •Governmental regulations and tariffs •Carrier costs and policies •Correct bills of lading and special tracking requirements and sign-offs •Claims and returns associated with transportation mode •Fleet maintenance and operations	•Order entry •Order processing •Product and service information related to price, availability, and features •Invoicing and shipping information •Claims and returned goods

FIGURE 13.2
Global supply participants.

shipment routing, regulations and tariffs, carrier costs and policies, accuracy of bills of lading, special tracking requirements, and required signoffs.

In parallel, customer claims, returns, and fleet maintenance are controlled at a distribution center. Distribution centers also receive and warehouse materials for shipment to customers. There may also be packaging and light assembly operations within a distribution center. Supporting activities may include developing workload forecasts, maintaining equipment, receiving inbound trucks, managing inventory storage and replenishment activities, and picking orders, including pack-out, dock audits, and loading outbound trucks. Each of these operations requires systems to control their material and information flows. These processes may be complicated and may require unique operational tools and methods. If order entry and processing functions reside within a distribution center, then information related to products and services, including pricing, availability, and performance features, must be made be available to the people handling order entry to provide customers with the information necessary to place their orders.

Table 13.2 views supply chain operations at a more detailed level. Imports and exports from one country to another require specialized processes to ensure orders are put together quickly using the most efficient means of transportation for shipment to customers. Supply chains also rely on different types of software systems that enable information systems in disparate locations to communicate. The optimal routings and transportation modes must also be determined for products in a supply chain. At an operational level, products are loaded onto trucks or containers in sequence and according to weight and volume requirements to ensure arrival at their destination without damage. It is also important that the correct numbers and types of equipment are available on demand. In summary, adequate tools and methods must be available to ensure enough labor and material capacity exists, and they must be efficiently utilized to move materials and information through the supply chain.

Table 13.3 summarizes financial metrics and ratios that are useful for measuring the effectiveness and efficiency of a global supply chain. Chapter 7 described several important metrics from an operational perspective. Recall that the profit and loss statement summarizes revenues and expenses for a specific time. The value of assets, such as inventory, buildings, and equipment, are recorded on the balance sheet. Inventory investment can be evaluated as an expense or as a turnover ratio. Excess inventory is associated with poor inventory management. It can be calculated in several ways, but from an operational perspective multiples of lead time or days of supply are useful metrics. If days of supply exceeds the demand quantity expected over the order cycle or the required lot size, there may be excess inventory. Net operating profit after taxes (NOPAT) is calculated by dividing income after taxes by total revenue. Higher NOPAT levels are better than lower ones; NOPAT tracks industry averages, however, so it is difficult to compare performance across different supply chains. Asset efficiency or turnover is calculated by dividing

TABLE 13.2

Fifteen Important Global Supply Chain Functions

Function	Description
1. Import/export	Imports and export from one country to another require specialized processes and training.
2. Electronic data interchange	Software systems that enable information technology platforms and applications in disparate locations to communicate with each other.
3. Transportation analysis	The tools and methods used to determine the best routing and mode of transportation in a network or supply chain.
4. Carrier management	The tools and methods used to select, negotiate, and monitor organizations that transport products or information across a supply chain.
5. Load optimization	The tools and methods used to ensure products are loaded correctly relative to weight, volume, and quality to ensure they arrive without damage and at the intended time.
6. Fleet management/ maintenance	The tools and methods used to ensure that a supply chain has the correct number and types of equipment and that they are available on demand.
7. Traffic routing	The tools and methods used to direct the flow of products or information through different transportation modes and networks to achieve the lowest lead time and cost.
8. Claims management	The tools and methods used to identify, manage, and reduce customer claims relative to errors, high cost, or longer than expected lead times.
9. Distribution requirements planning	A system of tools and methods that matches supply with demand across a supply chain and inventory investment levels by item and location.
10. Network analysis	A model used to describe a supply chain including its operations and their spatial relationships with constraints on demand and supply.
11. Materials handling	The tools and methods used to move materials within fulfillment or distribution centers.
12. Packaging	Operations within a fulfillment or distribution center that remove items from stock and insert them into protective packaging for either direct shipment to customers or for storage as inventory.
13. Inventory management	The tools and methods used by organizations ensure inventory is available to satisfy customer demand by maintaining inventory at an optimum level as determined by lead time, expected demand, and target service levels.
14. Light assembly	Operations within a fulfillment or distribution center that require work other than packaging.
15. Workload management	The tools and methods used to ensure sufficient labor, material, and other capacity exist to meet work schedules.

TABLE 13.3

Global Supply Chain Financial Metrics

Metric	Description
Profit/loss	A profit and loss statement summarizes an organization's revenues and expenses for a specific time period. Expenses on this statement are costs incurred during business operations.
Inventory investment	Inventory investment is the amount of money invested in inventory. Inventory investment is evaluated in with an inventory turnover ratio.
Excess and inventory	Excess inventory is calculated based on multiples of lead time. A correlating metric is days of supply. If days of supply either exceeds the demand quantity expected over the order cycle (or lead time in some situations) or the required lot size, there may be excess inventory in the system.
Net operating profit after taxes (NOPAT)	NOPAT is calculated by dividing income after taxes by total revenue. Higher NOPAT levels are better than lower ones, but NOPAT tracks industry averages, so it is difficult to compare performance across different supply chains. As a result, NOPAT should be evaluated against direct competitors and an organization's competitive strategy.
Asset efficiency	Asset efficiency (or turnover) is calculated by dividing total sales revenue by the total asset investment necessary to obtain the sales for the time under analysis. Asset efficiency is an important metric to measure the degree of supply chain "leanness." Lean supply chains have high asset efficiencies relative to competitors.
Fixed asset efficiency	Fixed Asset Efficiency (Turnover) = Sales/(Average Property + Plant + Equipment)
Receivables efficiency	Receivables Efficiency (Turnover) = Net Credit Sales/Average Accounts Receivables
Profit margin	Profit Margin = Gross Profit/Sales
Return on assets	Return on Assets = Net Profit Margin × Asset Efficiency
Gross margin return on investment (GMROI)	GMROI = Gross Margin/Average Inventory Investment at Cost

total sales revenue by the total asset investment necessary to obtain these sales for the time under analysis. Asset efficiency (especially inventory) is an important metric that measures how lean a supply chain is relative to utilization. Lean supply chains have higher asset efficiencies relative to competitors. The other financial metrics shown in Table 13.3 represent additional key efficiency ratios.

Important supply chain operational metrics are described in Table 13.4. Service level targets are expressed as unit, line, or order fulfillment. Service level targets can also be defined as on-time delivery or delivery-to-promise, as well as manufacturing schedule attainment. The second metric, supplier on-time delivery performance, is calculated based on an agreed-upon versus actual delivery date. There could also be several variations of an on-time delivery metric, depending on the organization and industry. It is important all supply chain participants agree on the on-time delivery definition and its measurement. Overdue order backlogs occur for several reasons. In most situations, available capacity does not exist, but there could be different reasons based on the industry and organization.

The fourth metric, inventory efficiency (turnover), has been described as a ratio of annualized cost of goods sold (COGS) divided by monthly average inventory investment, and it can be determined at a product level or aggregated. There are many reasons for an unplanned order, such as poor forecasting, internal process breakdowns, or a failure to adhere to lead time promises or capacity requirements. Schedule changes are different from unplanned orders in the sense they are caused by unforeseen circumstances that result in products not being produced as originally planned. Unplanned orders are one cause for schedule changes. Data accuracy has a significant impact on decisions regarding how much and when to manufacture products or to provide services and their location. It is important to understand the extent, types, and locations of measurement errors across a supply chain. These include manual and automated data collection, analysis, and reporting. Lack of materials, other resources, or information that is required for production requires capacity be held in reserve to meet service levels. In manufacturing, raw materials and work-in-process (WIP) inventories remain unutilized because of scheduling issues.

Poor forecasting accuracy causes many production issues and wastes capacity, including inventory. The tenth operational metric, lead time, is impacted by several issues that increase the time from order to cash. Lead time can be defined several ways. In one context, it is the time required to perform a single operation; this is also called the operational cycle time to produce one unit. In another context, it could be the end-to-end time to move through a process. Individual components of lead time include preparation time, queue or waiting time, processing time, movement or transportation time, and inspection time.

TABLE 13.4

Global Supply Operational Chain Metrics

Metric	Description
Customer service target	Service level targets are expressed as unit fill, line fill, order fill, and financial terms. Service level targets can be defined as on-time delivery or delivery-to-promise, as well as manufacturing schedule attainment and other processes that touch the customer.
On-time supplier delivery	Supplier on-time delivery performance is calculated using agreed-upon versus actual delivery time. There could be several variations of the metric.
Overdue order backlogs	Overdue order backlogs occur for several reasons. Available capacity may not exist (for a variety of reasons), or the backlog represents the industry practice of make-to-stock, or the problem based on technology constraints (i.e., make-to-order systems).
Inventory efficiency (turnover)	The number of times that an inventory turns over during a year is calculated as the ratio of annualized cost of goods sold divided by monthly average inventory investment.
Unplanned orders	There are several reasons for unplanned orders, including poor demand forecasts, internal process breakdowns, or failure to adhere to standard operating procedures regarding lead time and capacity requirements.
Schedule changes	Schedule changes are different from unplanned orders in the sense they are caused by process changes or unforeseen circumstances.
Data accuracy	Data inaccuracies existing in a supply chain impact decisions regarding how much product to make, what services to offer, which subcomponents to order, and other decisions. It is important to understand the degree of measurement error in supply chain information systems.
Material availability	Lack of material, other resources, or information drives up inventory investment because raw material and work-in-process inventories remain unutilized and impact production schedules. The same concept holds true in any system where other resources wait.
Forecast accuracy	Poor forecasting accuracy causes demand and supply mismatch. There are many reasons for poor forecast accuracy.
Lead time	Cycle time is the time required to perform a single operation, and lead time is the time to complete two or more operations in a network. Individual components of cycle time or lead time include order preparation time, queue or waiting time, processing time, transporting time and, time to inspect the work.

Some industries measure capacity by the number of production facilities, pieces of equipment, or the number of available people. These organizations are large and well capitalized and dominate national and international markets; market entry is difficult, and barriers to competition are significant. However, entire new industries have been created recently in which capacity is dynamic and markets are highly differentiated and globally dispersed. Capacity management has evolved to incorporate virtualization as well as decentralization. This has dramatically changed the competitive landscape as well as the strategies and tactics used to compete.

CAPACITY

Insourcing, outsourcing, offshoring, automation, and other strategies are used to create, expand, and manage global productive capacity. Organizations now create capacity to satisfy expected demand anywhere, anytime, and based on service agreements at the lowest possible investment cost and risk. Information, technology, virtual teams, and new process structures are critical components of capacity around the world in recent years. In these new systems, capacity has some physical presence, but it also has an increasingly greater virtual content. An example is subject matter expertise accessible anywhere in the world at any time, as opposed to creating a local team that is off schedule part of the day.

Capacity is the ability of a transformation system to produce goods or services according to a schedule at an agreed-upon time, location, and quantity. It is a measure of a system's ability to efficiently transform inputs, represented by materials, labor, machines, information, energy, etc., into outputs, represented by products, services, or information. Capacity is also measured on a fixed time basis under predefined conditions related to system availability and service-level agreements. Based on predefined demand, delivery promises can be met if the predefined conditions exist. For a given system, its capacity can be modified to satisfy demand and delivery promises dependent on its design limitations. Capacity can also be thought of as a combination of labor, materials, and capital brought together to do work. Capacity will be reduced if the effectiveness and efficiency of resource utilization are below standard. It can be considered from different perspectives such as available, temporarily stored, or made available at a future date by planning. Processes can be designed to have each of these three forms of capacity in various parts. As an example, in some systems, 100% of the capacity is on-site and available. In other systems, it can be made available as needed through supplier agreements, leasing equipment, temporary labor, self-service systems, and related strategies that create capacity based on demand.

A system's capacity is dynamic. It changes based on the types of products or services flowing through a given process at a given point in time. Variations in the efficient use of labor and capital or the impact from external factors are additional causes for dynamic fluctuations in a system's available capacity. Capacity can also be defined as design capacity, available capacity, and actual capacity. Design capacity is the throughput of a process or system if all labor and capital are working at optimal levels. Available capacity is the system's design capacity minus expected or planned loses in operational efficiency because of technology or process constraints. These are caused by known time lost due to inefficient job setups, inspection of work, processing of work (e.g., moving materials or information), and waiting. The third type is actual capacity and is defined as the available capacity minus time lost due to unexpected events that negatively impact the throughput. Examples include scrap, rework, schedule variations, lack of resources, and other unexpected causes.

Recall that a system's throughput is the measure of available capacity at its bottleneck resource and, depending on operational variation within the system, its capacity-constrained resources, which may periodically become system bottlenecks. This requires increasing bottleneck capacity. Operational capacity at non-bottlenecks is also increased by simplifying, standardizing, and mistake-proofing processes and using other Lean tools and methods. Examples discussed in Chapter 6 included establishing a takt time to utilize capacity only if needed to satisfy external customer demand, operational balancing of work, the use of transfer batches, the application of mixed-model scheduling, waste elimination to reduce rework and scrap, and deployment of pull systems. Quality improvement tools and methods, such as Six Sigma or Design for Six Sigma, can also be used to reduce process variation to improve yields.

Economies of scale also increase capacity. If a system is operating below its available capacity, indirect costs must be allocated across a smaller throughput quantity. This increases unit costs. As a system's throughput increases, unit costs decrease because of operational efficiencies. A model is shown in Figure 13.3. As an example, there are fewer required job setups and changeovers from one product to another. This enables greater

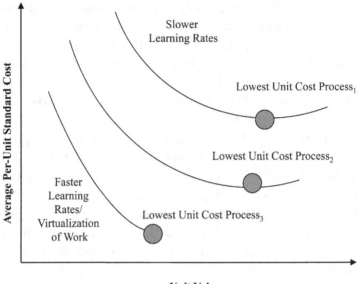

FIGURE 13.3
Economy of scale.

standardization of production methods. The result is an increase in the system's utilization and indirect costs can be allocated over larger production quantities, which reduces per-unit cost. The goal is to achieve economies of scale but also to be adaptable in meeting changes in demand though design standardization and process improvements such as mixed model scheduling.

At this point, we should distinguish between resource utilization versus activation. This is best understood in the context of the bottleneck resource. When upstream operations feed a downstream bottleneck, they should be activated only when the bottleneck needs material or, in service industries, information for production. Recall that a non-bottleneck resource should be balanced to the system bottleneck to avoid excess inventory and other issues. In other words, the utilization of non-bottleneck resources should match the bottleneck's activation and likely should not be utilized 100% of the time. A complicating factor in this scenario is that other products may be starved for materials and components if a production schedule changes if non-bottleneck resources are utilized unnecessarily. If additional system capacity is needed, then it should be added at the bottleneck. Examples include adding low-cost redundant machines, allocating multiskilled workers, or improving yield and reducing operational cycle times at the bottleneck.

As workers learn better ways to do work and engineers optimize the process technology, the lowest cost curve shifts downward, reflecting decreasing per-unit costs even at lower system throughput volumes. How is this possible? Learning curve theory assumes that an improved understanding of a process is gained though experience and contributes to higher operational efficiencies. These in turn contribute to higher available system capacity. Historically, less than optimal and more expensive product and service process designs drive supporting process and infrastructure design and cost to create go-to-market capacity. If markets become differentiated and move toward niches based on customer preferences, it becomes increasingly difficult to gain economies of scale to lower costs without design and process changes.

Adapting strategies for good design, organizational structure, automation, virtualization, and other methods must be used to lower costs. Technology deployment enables an increasingly higher percentage of virtualization to allow information to be transmitted quickly to do work. This eliminates the need for building physical infrastructure. It also creates supply chains where capacity can be inexpensively increased to match demand. In industries requiring production infrastructure such as oil, gas, utilities, and manufacturing, product design and supporting process design drive cost and system flexibility. Economies of scale are still applicable in these industries, as are the many tools and methods discussed in previous chapters.

Entire industries have moved away from a heavy reliance on physical infrastructure, although infrastructure is still integral to operations, just to a lesser degree. The telecommunications industry is an example where technology shifted the economy-of-scale model to lower costs as system throughputs dramatically increased. As an example, new cell phone technologies were set up using satellite technology without laying down expensive cabling in many regions of the world. There is still infrastructure, but not at the previous level.

FORECASTING

The goal of an organization should be to build closer customer relationships to better understand demand patterns rather than rely only on forecasting models. Closer customer relationships reduce the need for developing models. In the last part of this chapter, non-mathematical tools and methods will be discussed relative to demand management. But if forecasting needs to be done, then the accuracy of the forecast should be measured and improved by investigating the root causes for poor demand management practices.

To predict future demand, organizations use a combination of methods, both qualitative and quantitative. Qualitative methods include gathering opinions by bringing together people who are knowledgeable of customer demand (i.e., a jury of executive opinion) and asking the sales teams using interviews or surveys (i.e., build a sales force composite forecast by market segment or vertical and other stratification factors). Quantitative methods include time series analysis, regression-based models, and specialty models. In time series analysis, a forecasting model is built with lagging values of the dependent variable to predict its future demand. An example would be predicting sales next month based on sales from previous months. In contrast, regression models forecast future sales using lagging, leading, and coincident values of a dependent variable, as well as one or more independent variables. Leading variables enable a model to predict future demand based on variables known to predict future demand. An example would be real disposable income in this month as a leading indicator for retail sales next month.

Forecasts are used by different teams across an organization to plan their work. As an example, marketing uses forecasts to plan advertising and other promotional activities for direct and indirect sales. These forecasts are made at a product group level monthly and into a future time horizon. Sales teams use forecasts to measure performance to sales targets. Sales forecasts are made by product group and other demographic factors, such as region, on a monthly basis and into a future time. Logistics needs forecasts to know where, when, and how much capacity is needed (e.g., inventory) to satisfy demand, and to plan capital expenditures to efficiently move materials and information across its global supply chain. Forecasts are required for items at stocking locations at the appropriate time and into the future. The common time interval for forecasting was monthly, but now the lead time to meet demand is measured in weeks, days, and even hours. Manufacturing requires forecasts for purchased materials and components or dependent demand items aligned to its manufacturing schedules and offset by component lead times. Finance needs accurate forecasts to set sales, cost, profit, and cash flow projections and targets at business, divisional, and product line levels.

Selection of a forecasting time horizon is an important requirement for all types of forecasting methods. The forecasting time horizon is the period over which a forecast is estimated and used. It is also called a time fence, within which schedules should not be changed. A forecast also has a time interval. This is the actual length of time for building the forecasting model (e.g., hour, day, week, month, or another convenient interval). When a product's production schedule arrives at its cumulative lead time or time fence, it becomes firm (or "frozen") and orders are placed for its dependent demand items (i.e., the components based on cumulative lead time and the bill-of-material dependencies). Orders become firm and scheduled once they are within their time fence or cumulative lead time. A demand forecast not in the frozen window and beyond the cumulative lead time is not fixed and can be modified as shown in Figure 13.4.

Forecasting models also require differing levels sophistication. The simpler time series models such as moving average or exponential smoothing require little skill. In fact, they can be automated. If seasonality is modeled, then 36 to 60 months of data is required to accurately estimate the seasonal indices month-over-month. However, if seasonality estimates are not required, then only 12 to 24 months of data is required to build a nonseasonal model. More complex econometric models, based on multiple linear regression, require advanced analytical skills. The data required to build these types of models is usually a minimum of 10 observations

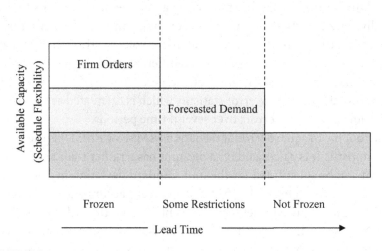

FIGURE 13.4
Time fence.

or time periods per estimated parameter. If a model has three independent variables, then approximately 36 months of demand is required. Digitization over the past decades has enabled the immediate acquisition of sales information by supply chain participants. Highly flexible organizations are moving away from a heavy reliance on forecasting models based on statistics.

A heavy reliance on statistics-based forecasting models with high error rates is detrimental to operations. Forecasting error rates only increase the further out a forecast is made. Forecasts made at a lead time of 30 days or less will be more accurate than those made on a quarterly or an annual basis, all other things equal. Forecasts are also more accurate when aggregated to a product group than at lower levels such as a specific item at a specific location. Studies have shown that, at an organizational level, statistical forecasting can be successfully applied to forecast product revenue with error rates between 1% and 5%. In contrast, at an item and location level, error rates can easily exceed 25% from month to month. Because forecasting error is difficult to reduce, organizations should develop strategies that do not rely exclusively on statistics-based forecasting.

Figure 13.5 shows how error statistics are calculated for forecasting models with an example. Forecasting errors are calculated after actual demand is realized and then compared to the original forecasted quantity by time interval. Although there are several forecasting error statistics, two are commonly used by most organizations. The first is percentage error, which is calculated by subtracting actual demand from its forecast and dividing by actual demand. The advantage in this calculation is the error statistic is a percentage and adjusted for volume. This makes it useful for comparing error percentages across different products having differed demand patterns. A modification of the percentage error statistic is the mean absolute percentage error statistic, which is calculated as the average of absolute percentage errors over several time periods.

The root mean square error or deviation (RMSE or RMSD) is the second error statistic. It is calculated on a per-unit basis rather than a percentage basis. It can be substituted for the unit standard deviation in safety-stock calculations. As an example, if a forecast is very accurate as measured by its RMSD, its required safety-stock inventory quantity will be less if the RMSD is used rather than its standard deviation. The concept is this: if I can forecast perfectly, I do not need safety stock. This situation is very unlikely because the levels of safety stock are calculated based on average

	January	February	March	April
Original Forecast	200	180	210	190
Actual Demand	190	200	220	200
Error	10	−20	−10	−10

$$\text{Mean Absolute Percentage Error (MAPE)} = \frac{\sum_{t=1}^{n} \left| \frac{Forecast_t - Actual_t}{Actual_t} \times 100 \right|}{n}$$

$$\text{Root Mean Squared Error (RMSE)} = \sqrt{\frac{\sum_{t=1}^{n}(Forecast_t - vActual_t)^2}{n}}$$

FIGURE 13.5
Calculating forecasting error.

demand over lead time, service level, as well as the standard deviation of demand.

Forecasting error statistics are an important basis for continuous improvement and can be used to identify beneficial projects. Table 13.5 lists several common process issues caused by low forecasting accuracy. Major impacts include customer service, manufacturing, operations, finance, transportation, marketing and sales, inventory management, logistics, and others. Each issue is a major project focus area and creates a portfolio of several projects to implement a solution. Business benefits are easy to calculate for these types of projects because the root-cause problems increase cost and lead time and lower customer satisfaction.

Forecasting models rely on underlying non-random patterns such as trends, periodicity, seasonality, or cycles. These should also be relatively stable and repeatable over several time intervals. Several years of historical data are required to build a seasonal model using a period of one month

TABLE 13.5

Poor Forecasting Impact

Manufacturing	Service
Production	**Operations**
• Schedule changes	• Schedule changes
• Overtime expense	• Overtime expense
Finance	**Finance**
• Increased inventory carrying expense	• Increased labor expense
• Lower cash flow	• Lower cash flow
Transportation	**Transportation**
• Unnecessary product transfer	• Unnecessary information transfer
• Higher premium freight expense	• Higher premium freight expense
Marketing	**Marketing**
• Excess and obsolete inventory	• Excess and obsolete promotional materials
Inventory Management	**Inventory Management**
• Lower inventory turns	• Lower transaction expense
• Higher inventory obsolescence	• Employee skill obsolescence
Logistics	**Facility**
• Excess warehousing space and expense	• Excess warehousing space and expense
• Damaged product expense	
Customer Service	**Customer Service**
• Poor line item availability	• Customer complaints
• Backorders	
• Customer complaints	

to estimate the monthly seasonal indices. Regression models require incorporating forward-looking information such as leading economic indicators as well as extensive historical records when long cycles exist at a macroeconomic level. There are circumstances where standard forecasting methods cannot be used to build a model. These include unusual events including a loss of market share, recessions, and other major events. Forecasting models are also ineffective for one-off events without underlying patterns. Examples include disruptive technology that threatens an industry.

The sources of independent demand for end items (as opposed to dependent demand items that comprise the end item) are aggregated by the demand management module within a forecasting system to build the models. The two common types of forecasting models are time series, which use exponential smoothing algorithms, and multiple linear regression models. Exponential smoothing models are built using historical demand, with smoothing parameters to fit the model to the historical pattern, a time interval, and for a specific length of time. A forecasting system also creates management reports of various types that break forecasts down by time period, geographical location, organizational level, product group, and other variables. The forecasts are calculated using a unit basis but are converted into monetary units using standard cost data. Forecasting accuracy metrics are also created by these systems to aid in continuous improvement efforts.

An effective forecasting system must have certain attributes to create efficient and accurate forecasts. First, it is important that a product's actual historical demand be used to develop models. Some organizations use shipment history to forecast demand. The problem is that shipments are influenced by inventory availability. If inventory is not available for shipment, then demand may appear lower than actual. Forecasts based on shipment histories create chronic backorders because inventory will always be set lower than actual demand. Basing forecasts on actual customer demand is the proper method to build a forecasting model. If items are not available for shipment, the forecast will still be based on original customer demand and the product's target inventory level will be constant except as the shortage is made up. It is very useful to simultaneously record shipment history, actual demand, and forecasted demand. Differences between any of these histories enables an analysis to eliminate ordering discrepancies due to forecasting errors.

Time series with periodic patterns such as seasonality require at least three to five years of month-over-month observations to ensure the monthly seasonal indices are estimated accurately in the model. The time horizon should set at least as far out as the annual operating plan and even further to plan future capacity. It is also important that forecasting accuracy be very high based on the time fence concept that was shown in Figure 13.4. This ensures manufacturing schedules are accurately estimated.

Non-random patterns caused by product promotions or other atypical demand patterns must also be analyzed and incorporated into a product's forecast. In some industries, quarterly or seasonal adjustments are made. In effect, there would be four similar forecasting models. Forecasting analysts should also specify the periodicity of a forecasting model and truncate the time series' historical basis if there are recent changes to its underlying pattern. This might occur if a product is at the end of its life cycle and demand exhibits irregular patterns. Analysts would use the most recent demand history to ensure the model is current. Depending on the application, additional information may be needed, such as underlying macroeconomic trends (e.g., recessions or expansionary cycles).

Effective forecasting systems should automatically create and track product forecasts. This is useful to organizations that sell thousands of products. Automatic tracking of a model enables analysts to focus attention on products with unusual demand patterns or are critical to the organization's operation. Aggregation and desegregation of product forecasts are also made, from an item's location up to the product group level. A forecasting system should also enable continuous improvement by providing accuracy metrics for each model.

The strategy of an effective demand management system is to make an increasingly larger proportion of its product demand firm while simultaneously decreasing the percentage of forecasted products. Expanding customer relationships and leveraging digital technology facilitates less reliance on product forecasting by capturing demand at its source. Demand estimation accuracy is especially important for industries that sell expensive products, such as capital equipment. Alternatively, the application of advanced technology can be used to measure customer demand at its POS in some industries. If POS information is available, manufacturing schedules will be accurately updated.

An effective demand management strategy optimizes resource effectiveness and utilization. This enables analysts to focus on creating the right forecast models for different demand patterns. Table 13.6 shows how products are stratified by unit volume and variation. It may be possible to place low-volume products with low demand variation on a minimum/maximum (min/max) system and managed using a simple rule. This rule states that when inventory reaches a certain level, more of the product is scheduled for production. The set level is the product's or component's reorder point. This stratification strategy enables forecasting analysts to focus on higher-volume or critical products. On the other hand, high-volume products

TABLE 13.6

Strategic Forecasting

	Low Demand Variation	High Demand Variation
Low Volume	Standard forecasting models	Special teams to investigate
High Volume	Min/max systems	Special models used to predict unusual demand patterns

having low demand variation can be automatically forecast using time series models. For products with low volume but high demand variation, special forecasting methods are needed to estimate their future demand.

Reconciliation of forecasted demand across an organization helps ensure operational plans and schedules are aligned to a "one number" consensus forecast. The strategic forecast is reconciled by a sales and operations planning process based on a cross-functional consensus. This reconciliation is developed as marketing and sales plans are broken down to a product group level and demand forecasts are verified by each team. The allocation is applied linearly from the one number down through product groups and locations to an item location level. Discrepancies related to capital, labor, and available capacity to meet production schedules are reconciled through the sales and operations planning process. Updated forecasted quantities, once verified by stakeholder groups, are aggregated upward in reverse. The updated consensus forecasts are represented in several forms, including unit quantities and revenue calculated using quantity and standard cost. The strategy for managing demand by progressive organizations is that it needs to be managed rather than pushing unintelligent forecasting models to drive scheduling. Forecasting models are needed and used by almost every major corporation to estimate demand, but these should only be used when more accurate methods cannot be cost effectively utilized.

The common time series forecasting models are listed in Table 13.7. These have several components that describe the time series average level, a trend if present, seasonal variation if present, and longer-term cyclical patterns. These components are modeled by using the appropriate model listed in Table 13.7. Models forecast demand into the future at time periods $t+1$, where t is the current period. They use actual demand from the current period and previous time periods (i.e., t, $t-1$, $t-2$, $t-3$, etc.). These previous time periods are the lagging dependent variables. As an example, the sales forecast in units next month is estimated using sales from this month and from previous months. For this example, sales last month lag the forecasted sales of the dependent variable of "sales next month." Time series models also use smoothing parameters to weight the impact of various lagging dependent variables. By modifying the parameters, lagging dependent variables can be weighted to make more recent history more impactful or not.

Figure 13.6 shows monthly sales data collected over eleven years. The graph shows a periodic pattern in the sales data and an upward trend.

TABLE 13.7

Time Series Models

Model	Description
Trend plot	Plots time series data versus time without creating a mathematical model.
Time series decomposition	Breaks a time series into its level, trend, seasonal, and irregular components. It models both trend and seasonal patterns using constants calculated from the decomposition.
Moving average models	A time series model created by taking the average of observations from the time series to smooth out seasonal or other data patterns.
Simple exponential smoothing	Models a level (stationary) time series (i.e., no trend or seasonality) using one smoothing parameter.
Double exponential smoothing (Holt's method)	Models a level (stationary) time series with a trend but no seasonality using two smoothing parameters.
Triple exponential smoothing (Winter's method)	Models a level (stationary) time series with a trend and seasonality using three smoothing parameters.
Autoregressive integrated moving average models (ARIMA)	Statistically based time series models that model level, trend, and seasonal components of a time series.

It will be obvious from Table 13.7 that some time series models fit this historical pattern better than others. Best model fit can be verified using the mean absolute percentage error statistic. The accuracy of a time series model requires fitting a model to historical data and measuring the deviations of forecasted to actual values at each forecasted period. As a side note, when statisticians compare a new forecasting method against previous ones, they use a standardized database that is available to all researchers. It consists of several hundred time series having differing patterns. In these evaluations, forecasting models are compared by fitting them to earlier parts of each reference time series (historical basis) and forecasting demand for the most recent part of the time series called the holdout period. The error statistic is calculated by comparing the forecast to the data in the holdout period. Either Winter's method or a time series decomposition model will be suitable for modeling the level, trend, and seasonal components.

The decomposition method breaks this time series' pattern into components. Table 13.8 shows the logic for doing a decomposition. The first step

Time Series Decomposition Plot for Sales
Multiplicative Model

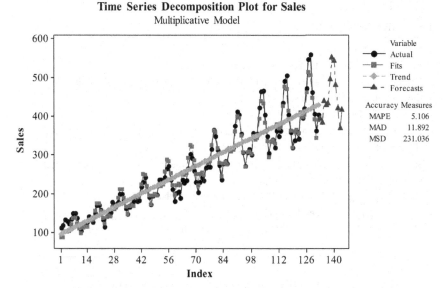

FIGURE 13.6

Decomposition model. This model adequately captures the seasonal pattern: seasonal length 12 > multiplicative model > trend plus seasonal > first observation is in seasonal period 1 > number of forecasts 12 > starting from origin 132. MAPE = mean absolute percentage error; MAD = Mean Absolute Deviation; MSD =Mean Squared Deviation.

is to fit a moving average model to the time series with the same interval and periodicity (i.e., days, weeks, months, quarters, or years). In the current example, the interval is monthly sales, which has an annual seasonal pattern that repeats every twelve months. Creating a moving average model eliminates the seasonality of the original time series. When the moving average time series is subtracted from the original time series, the seasonal indices can be calculated. If the data set is quarterly, then there will be four seasonal indices. The decomposition method continues until all components have been isolated. The irregular component is the variation of sales for which the model cannot account (i.e., the model's error).

Figure 13.6 shows the decomposition model is a good fit to historical sales and the extrapolated forecast exhibits a pattern like the original time series. The mean absolute percent error is 5% (rounded), which indicates that 95% of the sales variation is explained by the model.

Demand management drives global supply chain planning. Problems with demand estimation, whether from forecasting models or consensus models, cause misalignment of scarce resources and process issue of many types throughout the supply chain. Customer satisfaction and operational

TABLE 13.8

Time Series Decomposition

1. Start with a time series.
2. Time series = Trend + Cycle + Seasonality + Irregular
3. Calculate a new time series using a moving average model having the same order as the seasonality of the time series to create (A).
4. (A) Time Series = Trend + Cycle
5. Determine the seasonal indices. Deseasonalize the original time series to create (B).
6. (B) Time Series = Trend + Cycle + Irregular
7. Subtract (A) from (B) to obtain the irregular component to identify outliers that may need to be adjusted.

   2. $T_{\text{Original Time Series}}$ = Trend + Cycle + Seasonal + Irregular
   4. $T_{\text{Trend and Cycle Only}}$ = Trend + Cycle
   5. $T_{\text{Deseasonalized Time Series}}$ = Trend + Cycle + + Irregular
   7. $T_{\text{Irregular Component}}$ = + Irregular

productivity are reduced by inaccurate demand because capacity planning is incorrect and schedules are missed. Forecasts need to be strategically aligned at all levels, and a consensus forecast must be developed by the sales and operations planning team. To the extent that forecasts are necessary, it is important to measure and continually improve their accuracy. With digitization, organizations should emphasize customer relationships and developing systems to gather customer demand automatically through digitization methods. This will provide visibility to demand across the global supply chain using POS data and technologies.

Strategic forecasts are made at long time horizons to ensure capacity is available to produce products or services in the future. They also identify whether there is a future need for a new facility, enhancements of current locations, or facilities need to be relocated. These future needs may be regional, national, or global, and may be either temporary or permanent. Strategic capacity planning is important to an organization because a failure to adequately plan for the necessary capacity will result in lower sales, higher supply chain costs, and longer lead times.

Supply chain capacity planning also supports expansion into existing and new markets. Important components of the planning process are estimates of facility capacity, location, available equipment, materials, and needed employee skills. Design and available capacities are estimated using strategic forecasts period-by-period, over the forecasting time horizon, for each location in the supply chain. They are calculated using the expected throughputs across the supply chain's participants. Allowances are made that reduce the design capacities to available capacities. Available capacity is estimated at an aggregated level, by quarter and month, to ensure it is available where it is needed to meet forecasted demand. Business unit forecasts are made by year and broken into quarters and months by facility. At a facility level, forecasts are broken into months and weeks by product group. Capacity is planned on an aggregated basis for each facility and for the processes within them. Supply chain productivity is directly tied to how well capacity is utilized by its participants to meet external customer demand. Digitization is enabling creative ways to effectively make capacity available across supply chains.

Table 13.9 list other ideas to increase available capacity to meet demand using the tools, methods, and concepts discussed in this book. Implementation of these ideas may depend on preceding improvement actions. Efficiently matching available resources to demand through accurate forecasting and scheduling methods ensures a system is not idle or producing the wrong products, services, or information. Scheduling should be managed to the system's bottleneck, which must be matched to the takt time to prevent a buildup of excess WIP inventory. Excess inventory wastes capacity that could have been used to produce other products or left idle. Increasing scheduling flexibility using methods such as mixed-model scheduling enables systems to respond dynamically to variations in external demand and optimizes capacity. Transfer batches using unit-flow also optimize capacity. In other words, scheduling rules impact available capacity.

Supply chain capacity is increased by accurate forecasting as well as product and service design modifications that impact supporting processes by reductions of components or process steps with standardization. There are other strategies to match capacity to demand. Higher process yields using Lean, Six Sigma, and total productive maintenance increase available capacity because scrap and rework are reduced and production does not need to be replaced. Some facility layouts are more efficient than others for bringing together people, equipment, and materials to reduce waiting and unnecessary movement. Highly efficient layouts increase capacity over less efficient ones. The more highly cross-trained people are, the better they can match resources to meet customer demand. The same concept applies to the selection of equipment. To the extent that organizations can deploy multipurpose and simple machines, the greater the organization's operational flexibility will be. Finally, an organization can work with other organizations to plan and allocate capacity across a global

TABLE 13.9

Ideas to Increase Capacity

Idea
1. Match resources to demand through effective demand management.
2. Work with customers to level load demand.
3. Use price and promotional policies to level load demand.
4. Enable customers to self-service.
5. Hire temporary or part-time workers.
6. Use overtime to handle demand.
7. Overlap work shifts.
8. Lease facilities.
9. Lease equipment.
10. Modify product design.
11. Modify process design.
12. Modify the facility layout.
13. Move to mixed-model production strategies.
14. Use transfer-batch processing.
15. Change the service discipline and its type (e.g., first come, first serve).
16. Improve quality.
17. Reduce operational cycle time or process lead time.
18. Increase equipment and worker availability.
19. Use single-minute exchange of dies to reduce setup time and cost.
20. Transfer lessons learned across the supply chain.
21. Increase the skill flexibility of workers through cross-training.
22. Deploy simple and standardized redundant equipment that can be utilized at different rates or levels at a bottleneck.
23. Create virtual capacity using technology and agreements and alliances.
24. Outsource non-core operations.
25. Insource related work to core operations.

supply chain through a strategy of outsourcing and insourcing of work to improve asset utilization efficiencies and productivity.

Another effective strategy to efficiently meet customer demand without large investments in infrastructure is to employ virtual capacity by leveraging IT solutions across supply chain participants at high resource activation. Virtual capacity implies capacity can be created using technology deployed within processes to help manage resources efficiently. Virtual capacity is also integrated using agreements, contracts, and other alliances. Examples include joint ventures, partnerships, sales of non-core assets, the sharing of information and resources, as well as modifications to organizational structures such as decentralized management. These enable supply chains to increase capacity by building non-core and redundant infra-structure with other participants and avoid large capital expenditures. This increases flexibility, and capacity can be matched to demand more easily.

Asset utilization will also be higher with virtualization of capacity because flow can be balanced across a dispersed network. In some systems, such as global call centers, activation and utilization rates may exceed 98% using technology to move calls to facilities around the world based on volume and time of day or week. Bottlenecks and capacity-constrained resources are virtualized by redundancies in people and systems. As an example, geographically dispersed call centers can transfer incoming and outgoing calls immediately from those without available capacity to oth-ers with capacity. Virtual capacity is also enabled through partnerships that reduce investment and operation costs. This flexibility enables sup-ply chains to easily enter and leave markets without high costs. In effect, technology, information, collaboration, and new organizational systems replace physical facilities and objects.

The extraordinarily high productivity and operational capability of today's global supply chains is enabled by the rapidly evolving evolution of IT systems discussed in Chapter 8, which enables information to be col-lected, analyzed, and used to change a process based on software rules and algorithms such as those that control scheduling. As an example, sched-uling algorithms enable changes in the production sequences based on changes to a system's status to reduce lead time to meet customer service targets while optimizing capacity. Scheduling rules and algorithms were discussed in Chapter 6. In summary, developments in IT can eliminate manual interventions and intermediaries, and it provides information status and reporting, enables adaptable sequencing and scheduling, helps coordinate work across the global supply chain, enables rules for asset sharing amongst participants, and promotes the production of differenti-ated products and services.

INVENTORY

Inventory requires a significant investment by an organization. High inventory investment if not matched to sales negatively impacts an organi-zation by reducing its return-on-asset utilization, however, and if excessive or obsolete it may not be useable. The inventory turnover ratio measures how much inventory is on hand to support sales. It is defined as the average inventory investment necessary to support the COGS. In many organizations, inventory investment represents a significant proportion of the COGS (i.e., ~5% to 20% of COGS or more). This is for several reasons such as the types of industry and process design (e.g., batch versus continuous flow), process issues, and poor planning.

Inventory turnover directly relates to a product's lead time, its expected demand, and the required service levels. Organizations periodically take actions to reduce inventory levels by applying improvement projects. But how far inventory can be reduced depends on the ability to reduce lead time and mange demand. In fact, benchmark statistics show inventory turnover ratios vary across diverse industries in a range of one to one hundred or higher. These ratios depend on the type of industry and process, but also on the effectiveness of inventory management. As an example, in organizations that have many different products and limited capacity (e.g., consumer products), inventory will be created and stored in distribution centers. When an organization produces many different products, it is difficult to reduce economic production lot sizes without applying significant process engineering redesign through technology, although Lean significantly helps (e.g., single-minute exchange of dies and many other effective methods). Inventory management practices also vary based on the underlying process design. There are make-to-order, assemble-to-order, and make-to-stock systems. Inventory investment strategies are different for each one. Make-to-order and assemble-to-order processes will not have a large finished goods inventory compared to make-to-stock systems. Make-to-stock systems have high finished goods inventory levels because of the number of products which need to be produced in advance of demand because of limited available production capacity. In contrast, investment in raw material and WIP inventories is usually higher in make-to-order and assemble-to-order systems if system throughputs are low. It is important that organizations understand what is necessary to manage and optimize inventory investment to efficiently allocate investment resources.

Inventory models use lead time, expected demand, and service levels to calculate an optimum inventory quantity. This quantity is the amount of inventory an organization should have available for an item at a specific location to satisfy customer demand and meet the required service level. A model could also be used to re-calculate inventory investment by simulating changes in lead time or demand. This helps identify improvement projects to reduce lead time and better manage demand, including forecasting models. But, an organization may be constrained as to how best to achieve in practice the calculated optimum inventory quantities. Constraints are associated with product and process designs, quality and other issues, inventory management policies such as economic order quantities, supplier issues, and other constraints. There may also be legacy inventory investment that impacts inventory turnover targets. Legacy is a significant quantity of excess and obsolete inventory from prior years. It is caused by purchasing or producing too much inventory in advance, poor forecasting, and other issues. It may not be possible to immediately use or dispose of legacy inventory, but organizations should develop plans to reduce excess and obsolete through write-offs, selling at a discount, or sending materials back to suppliers. In addition, the causes of excess and obsolete inventory should be eliminated by systematically reducing lead times and demand variation using Lean, Six Sigma, and supply chain best practices.

Inventory investment problems can be exacerbated by where a product is in its life cycle. As an example, in the introduction phase of a product, demand forecasts may be in error. In fact, actual demand for some new products may not occur, resulting in obsolete inventory. If demand is higher than forecasted, there may not be enough inventory to satisfy customer demand, and sales will be lower than forecast. When a product enters its growth phase, there is increasing competitive pressure on sales. Higher operational efficiencies and effective inventory management are required to maintain profit margins. Even moderate amounts of excess or obsolete inventory can significantly reduce a product's profitability at this point in its life cycle. Differentiation of a product into several design variants also complicates inventory management. This occurs if a design has been slightly modified to satisfy different market segments and these design variants are be inventoried separately. A common example is packaging differences between similar products that are sold to different market segments or major customers. Finally, in a product's maturity and decline phases, demand may decline and become sporadic, resulting in a mismatch between inventory availability based on forecasting models and actual customer demand. These issues increase excess and obsolete inventory.

Inventory accumulates value as it progressively moves through a process. As an example, WIP inventories are valued using accumulated material cost and direct labor as well as allocated overhead costs. Inventory is an investment of available capacity and is built because a process cannot produce on demand. It could also be built for anticipated future interruptions caused by labor issues, plant closures, or interruption to supply. Because inventory is an asset with monetary value, it must be accurately accounted for to ensure correct financial reporting. It must be protected from damage, spoilage, and pilferage to prevent loss of value.

Organizations control inventory using inventory models that are incorporated into IT systems. These systems manage the receipt and shipments of materials as well as inventory status. The most common inventory model is a perpetual inventory model, which records receipt and shipment transactions for all items as they occur. These transactions may not be 100% accurate because in some organizations materials receipt and product shipment files are separate and they may not be synchronized until they are periodically refreshed. This refreshment cycle varies. If all transactions are in the same system, the inventory status will be up to date. If they are in different systems, there will be a mismatch of inventory status. This is important from a process perspective because additional inventory may be ordered or shipments may be backordered if inventory records are not synchronized. The periodic review model is a second common inventory model. Using this model, receipts and shipments are periodically adjusted, which means there will always be a mismatch between receipts and shipments until the next review point when they are balanced. There are many other types of inventory models having pros and cons that influence effective inventory management.

Inventory valuation also varies by organization. Some organizations use a first in, first out (FIFO) valuation method in which materials are used in the order in which they are purchased for use. A FIFO valuation system matches the flow of materials through a system. The COGS valuation method reflects a net calculation of beginning inventory plus purchases minus ending inventory. The last in, first out (LIFO) valuation method calculates the COGS based on the cost of the most recently purchased materials. Inventory valuation using a LIFO method varies depending if the perpetual or periodic review inventory management systems are used as the inventory model. If material costs are increasing over time, the LIFO method may be more useful to an organization because its COGS sold will be higher, effectively lowering income taxes. Another inventory valuation method is the average cost valuation method. In this method, inventory value is calculated as the current inventory investment divided by the current inventory quantity.

Fraudulent inventory valuation practices may occur if an organization does not have the financial and operational controls necessary to ensure receipts, shipments, and other inventory transactions are accurately recorded during day-to-day operational activities. An organization can distort its financial performance by not correctly entering receipt, shipment, or inventory transaction information or by delaying their entry into the various systems that manage these transactions. Process breakdowns such as these distort estimates of income, asset level, and cash flow. Inventory valuation problems also occur from a variety of other process issues. These are found and eliminated using frequent cycle counting audits.

Inventory has useful purposes. It maintains the independence of internal operations by serving as a buffer for both internal and external demand variation. Inventory also provides production scheduling flexibility, maintains the independence of supplier deliveries, and ensures that economic order quantities and lot sizing targets are met in practice. Maintaining adequate inventory levels to ensure operational independence is critical for maintaining a process takt time. This is particularly true at a system's bottleneck to keep it utilized. Recall that a bottleneck resource must be kept operating to maintain process throughput at the takt time rate. Regardless of the reasons for inventory, systematic reductions in investment can be made using projects that reduce lead time or demand variation.

Each inventory type has a service-level target. Raw materials and WIP normally have high service levels because a process depends on their availability. In contrast, finished goods service levels vary by a product's annual demand and its gross margin. Low-volume products having a low gross margin will normally have lower service levels than products with a high annual demand and gross margin. Raw material and WIP inventories use a service target that is expressed in units, whereas a finished goods service target can be expressed in units, lines, or orders. It should be noted that units must be used in the calculation for safety-stock calculations. A line item is one product with an associated quantity. Orders consist of one or more line items, and each line item has an associated quantity. Organizations will use all three service-level metrics depending on the discussion. External customers speak in terms of order fill, logistics speaks in terms of line fill, and inventory managers speak in terms of unit fill.

A service target should be very carefully defined and calculated to ensure an organization can fulfill orders to meet customer requirements. Once a service-level target has been set for each inventory classification, or for specific items within a classification, inventory safety-stock calculations are made to ensure product availability at the service-level target. Available implies that the probability of not running out of a product during its replenishment lead time or the reorder point lead time equals its service level. If the per-unit service level target is 95%, the probability of not running out of a product will be 95%. One way to think of this is that, for every 100 units ordered, five will be backordered if the per-unit service level is 95%.

This situation is complicated by the fact that not every order contains the product in question, and different orders may require different quantities of a product. For this reason, order fill, although correlated to per-unit fill, will usually have a lower actual service level than unit fill. This situation is common where orders consist of several high-volume products that drive higher per-unit fill rates of an order despite the fact that lower-volume products may be missing from the same order. In fact, the per-unit fill rate in these situations could be 99%, but the order fill rate, as measured by the "order being 100% complete," could be less than 50%. For this reason, as mentioned earlier, organizations often use three service-level metrics to measure fill rates. Inventory service-level targets are set on a per-unit basis because to do otherwise would require conducting simulations based on the order profiles. In simulations, an order distribution, as represented by the products that make up an order, is modeled and service targets are set on individual products to ensure they were available to fill orders 95% of the time. Inventory levels are then set based on an order fill rather than a per-unit fill statistic.

INVENTORY MODELS

Developing inventory models provides an analyst with a better understanding of how an inventory system operates based on the underlying structure and parameterization of the model. In its simplest form, a model is a representation of system inputs and outputs, as well as descriptions of the internal operations of the process. Inventory modeling offers several advantages such as creating an ability to compress the time scale of the system's operational performance and conduct what-if analyses offline or separately from the system being modeled. But there are also some disadvantages. Models are not 100% accurate, and complex models are time-consuming to create and interpret. For this reason, the modeling approach should be standardized. Modeling also requires setting parameters and decision rules that mimic how the process works. Parameters are quantitatively linked to a system's model in a probabilistic sense, in that random inputs are transformed, based on their underlying probability distribution at an operational level, into an output or event. In addition, a model's initial starting and ending states as well as simulation duration must be set. Statistical tests are used to verify the accuracy of the model.

The perpetual inventory model (PIM) is used to monitor inventory status day to day in a perpetual manner. A common PIM model is shown in Figure 13.7. At the beginning of an order cycle T, an economic order quantity Q_1 is ordered from a supplier. This quantity Q_1 is expected to be linearly depleted during the order cycle T. During the order cycle, the depletion rate may be higher or less than the original forecast for the item. If demand is higher than expected, the reorder point quantity will be reached earlier in the order cycle, causing the PIM system to release

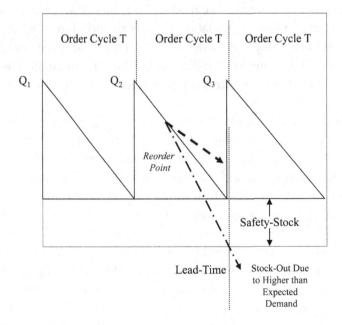

FIGURE 13.7
Perpetual inventory model (PIM).

an order earlier than planned in the original forecast. The reorder point quantity is calculated by multiplying the reorder point lead time by the average expected daily demand d and comparing the calculated quantity against the current on-hand inventory quantity with the safety-stock quantity netted out of the calculation. If the current inventory is equal to or less than a reorder point quantity, then another economic order quantity Q_2 is placed by the MRPII system. Using this model, it can be seen that an optimum inventory quantity may vary during an order cycle, but its expected value is ½ Q_1 + the safety-stock quantity, assuming a linear depletion rate proportional to forecasted demand. A qualitative depiction of a safety-stock quantity is shown in Figure 13.7, and an algorithm is shown in Figure 13.8 with supporting definitions.

Figure 13.9 is a generalized depiction of how an optimum inventory quantity for an item is impacted by its lead time and demand variation. When building the PIM inventory model, inventory quantities, their associated standard costs, and other information such as lead time, demand variation, location, supplier, and product type can be aggregated across an entire inventory population. Once aggregated, sensitivity analyses can be conducted using the PIM inventory model to identify where projects should be deployed to reduce lead time and demand variation and therefore inventory investment. The model also shows that, for any lead time and demand variation combination, there is an optimum inventory quantity for an item. Using this model, the actual on-hand inventory quantity of an item can be compared to its calculated optimum quantity to determine whether there is an excess or a shortage of inventory relative to the unit service-level target.

Figure 13.8 shows the PIM inventory model's algorithm. This algorithm will show where additions and reductions in inventory investment are possible. Steps 1 and 2 calculate an optimum inventory quantity. Additional modeling assumptions, such as safety-stock calculations, are also shown in Figure 13.8. As an example, it shows how the total standard deviation (σ_t) is calculated using lead time and demand. The formula shows that safety stock will always be required unless the variation of lead time and demand are both zero. Figure 13.8 also defines the terms used in the PIM model. In step 3, excess inventory is calculated by subtracting an optimum from the average on-hand inventory quantity. If the resultant number is positive, there is too much inventory for an item and its location, and its quantity should be reduced from its current level while still meeting the service target. However, there may be several complicating factors that

Step

1. Safety Stock = Service Constant$_k$ $\times \sigma_t$

2. Inventory$_{Optimum}$ = Inventory $_{Average\ Demand\ During\ Order\ Cycle}$ + Safety Stock

3. Excess Inventory = Inventory$_{Actual}$ - Inventory$_{Optimum}$

4. If step 3 is positive, decrease inventory.

5. If step 3 is negative, add inventory.

6. Excess inventory is calculated for every item and its location.

7. The excess inventory quantities are aggregated to the product and business unit levels using Excel pivot tables.

8. Extended standard cost is calculated for every item and its location.

9. Sensitivity analyses are conducted to evaluate the impact of potential lead-time forecasting error reductions on inventory investment.

10. This enables customer service targets to be achieved with optimum (minimum) inventory investment allowing strategic plans to be developed based on actual system capability (i.e., internal benchmarking).

1. Total Standard Deviation (σ_t):   Combined lead-time and demand variation.

2. Average Lead Time (LT):   The reorder point lead-time in days.

3. Variation of Demand (σ^2_d):   Variation of monthly demand in units.

4. Squared Average Demand (D^2):   The squared average monthly demand in units.

5. Variation of Lead Time (σ^2_{LT}):   Variation of the reorder point lead-time.

$$\text{Total Standard Deviation } (\sigma_t) = \sqrt{[\text{Average Lead-Time (LT)} \times \text{Variation of Demand}(\sigma^2_d)] + [(\text{Squared Average Demand } (D^2) \times \text{Variation of Lead-Time } (\sigma^2_{LT})]}$$

FIGURE 13.8
Perpetual inventory model (PIM) algorithm.

prevent an organization from achieving a calculated optimum inventory quantity. These may include large lot sizes representing multiples of lead time, various operational issues, and obsolete inventory that prevents the immediate reduction of an item's inventory quantity. The purpose of this analysis is to identify items with too much or too little inventory. A particularly useful attribute of this analysis is that optimum inventory investment can be aggregated upward, item by item, through the population to identify significant amounts of excess or obsolete inventory. This provides

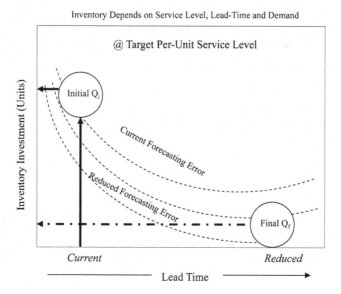

Inventory Depends on Service Level, Lead-Time and Demand

@ Target Per-Unit Service Level

Initial Q$_i$

Current Forecasting Error

Reduced Forecasting Error

Final Q$_f$

Inventory Investment (Units)

Current

Reduced

Lead Time

FIGURE 13.9
Graphical view of the perpetual inventory model (PIM).

a financial justification to deploy improvement projects to reduce the causes of high inventory investment.

Development of a useful analytical model requires that an organization build into its assumptions relevant characteristics of a system. As an example, every item in an inventory population must be described, at a minimum, by criteria such as t lead time, demand variation, and relevant demographics such as product family, facility, customer, supplier, and similar descriptive factors that are important to an efficient aggregation of business benefits.

Inventory is impacted by product demand patterns. Irregular demand patterns will require more inventory than predictable patterns that can be forecasted more accurately. Because the unit standard deviation of demand of a product (or item) is an important input in a safety-stock calculation, it is important to ensure it is estimated correctly. There are several ways to filter out the impact of irregular demand components. These range from statistically identifying outliers to truncating a time series using only observations from the most recent portion of its historical demand pattern. This assumes there is less variation in latter portions of a time series.

Lead time is another important input in an inventory model. Process issues will increase lead time. Examples include late deliveries, poor quality,

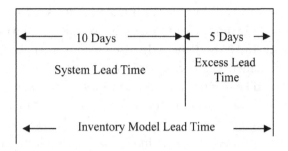

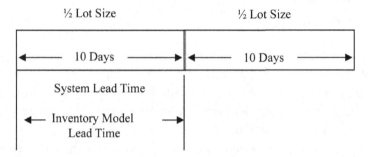

FIGURE 13.10
Impact of lead time and lot size on the model. Top: The model uses lead time to calculate inventory investment. The lead time must reflect actual on-time delivery performance to ensure adequate safety stock. Bottom: Minimum buys and large lot sizes force inventory levels higher.

and large lot sizes. Figure 13.10 shows the system lead time is 10 days versus an actual lead time of 15 days. It is important that a correct lead-time estimate is used to calculate an item's optimum inventory quantity. Minimum lot sizes also have a significant impact on inventory investment. As an example, if the actual system lead time is 10 days but the minimum lot size is 20 days, then the average inventory in this situation will be ½ × 20 days versus ½ × 10 days, or 10 days versus 5 days. The reorder quantity for the item will be calculated using the actual lead time of 10 days. It is evident that a larger lot size requires an adjustment to properly calculate an optimum inventory quantity. Other adjustments may also be necessary to make an inventory model useful for analysis and improvement purposes.

A PIM inventory model can be used in its current form, with minor adjustments, when modeling finished goods inventories. It is may also be relatively easy to apply to WIP inventories if material flows are not complicated. Regardless of the model, lead times must be calculated based on a system's critical path and its bottleneck. In assemble-to-order and make-to-order (sometimes called engineer-to-order) production systems, the process network should be mapped and its lead times carefully calculated to estimate the impact of a system's bottleneck on the order-to-cash lead time of the process. If a bottleneck is not managed well, WIP inventory will build up within a process or one or more operations within process may be starved for WIP inventory.

CYCLE COUNTING

Cycle counting is used to count inventory and verify its actual value against the stated book value. Although there are variations of cycle-counting methods, their purpose is to understand how materials and information move through an inventory system and other supporting systems. Cycle counting provides several benefits. The first is timely detection of process issues causing inventory record errors. Frequently reviewing inventory accounts provides a higher likelihood for finding errors and their root causes. Frequent cycle counting may also eliminate a need to shut down a facility if audit results show a high degree of inaccuracy. Another advantage is an ability to continually improve inventory accuracy.

There are several underlying reasons for poor inventory accuracy and hence poor investment choices. The first is a lack of work standardization and employee training, which results in inaccurate inventory counts or misplaced inventory. If employees are not properly trained to cycle count, the inventory records will not be current and accurate. Because inventory management decisions are made using information such as on-hand inventory quantities, inventory locations, and other relevant information, inaccuracies cause operational inefficiencies and inaccurate inventory. Also, if not properly protected, inventory can be damaged, spoiled, or stolen.

Cycle counting is really a system consisting of people, tools, and methods. There are proven ways to conduct audits properly. The first step is to map all material and information transactions, including roles and responsibilities. Second, policies and procedures need to be refreshed to reflect the efficient design of the cycle-counting system. Then employees must be trained to effectively support the new auditing system. If done properly, as the system is tested, the stated book values or quantities of inventoried items by location will align to the inventory transaction records. To the extent inaccuracies are found during audits, their resolution will need to be tracked so they can be eliminated through root cause identification and removal.

There are several proven methods to make a cycle-counting system more efficient and accurate. Leaning out the process is very effective. A process that is simplified and standardized, with inventory stored in standard-sized containers (i.e., Kanban containers) and in easy-to-see locations will require less inventory. A second strategy is to count inventory for an item when the tracking system shows it is depleted. If there is little or no inventory at a storage location, then cycle counting will be quick and accurate; if there is significantly more inventory than shown in the system, this indicates an opportunity for improvement. A third strategy that requires investment is to reduce the complexity of a product's design by simplifying its bill of material. The concept is that fewer items in inventory means fewer items need to be part of a cycle-counting system. These strategies will help reduce the cycle-counting time and resources while also improving accuracy of the system.

The consideration is how inventoried items should be selected for cycle counting. There are three common methods. The first is to zone count the items. In this method, all items are counted in a designated work area. The advantage of this method is that items not expected to be in the work area will be found by the audit. In effect, this is a 100% count of all the items within a selected zone. A second method is to statistically sample items using a sampling plan. There are several versions of statistical sampling that can be applied to cycle counting. One is the ABC classification based on item volume or value. A second is simple random sampling of the population. A third method is minimum variance stratification, in which an inventory population is broken into several strata. Each stratum has a minimum variance relative to any other stratification of the population. In other words, an optimum stratification occurs when the strata sample sizes are totaled and the total is less than any other stratification applied to that population. Minimum variance stratification is the most efficient of all the cycle-counting methods based on statistical analysis. It can produce a significant resource savings of more than 50% and provides an expected inventory book value and a confidence interval.

EXCESS AND OBSOLETE INVENTORY

Organizations have differing definitions for excess and obsolete (E&O) inventory. One common definition for excess inventory is or a multiple of lead time or days' supply on hand. As an example, if an item can be replenished in 30 days and there is a 90-day supply, then the excess inventory (neglecting safety stock) is a 60-day supply. Obsolete inventory cannot be sold at its normal selling price. In fact, it is usually sold at a very large discount from standard cost, if it can be sold at all. It should be written off the balance sheet if it is not saleable. High volume and popular products seldom have excess inventory because they are sold quickly, but low-volume and infrequently produced products quickly become problematic if not properly managed (e.g., with forecasting accuracy and cycle-count audits).

Common causes for E&O inventory are new products that do not sell because of inaccurate marketing or sales forecasts. In Chapter 3 we discussed that it takes a methodological approach to accurately estimate demand for a new product. Organizational issues may also contribute to E&O inventory. This occurs when new product forecasts are manipulated. These practices reduce operational efficiency because capacity is allocated to non-saleable products and cash flow is reduced when inventory is built but not sold. Forecasting error also impacts established products.

Another contributor to E&O inventory is purchasing materials and components or producing them internally hem in lot sizes that are multiple of lead times. Transaction errors for ordering raw materials and components comprise another contributor to E&O inventory. These errors occur for a variety of reasons including ordering, shipping, and inventory control. Breakdowns in cycle-counting systems also contribute. Long product lead times are especially problematic when a product's design changes and older inventory is not used quickly. An example is packaging obsolescence. Finally, inventory may become damaged as it moves through a system, and perishable products can become obsolete when their shelf-life expires.

The disposal of E&O inventory is a coordinated effort to attain the highest possible price. Disposal activities also require coordination with several organizational teams, including marketing and sales, finance, materials, and logistics. Although an item may appear obsolete, another team may still need it for various reasons (e.g., spare parts, testing, or to satisfy long-term contracts). The strategy of disposal is to attempt to sell

E&O product using discounts from the normal selling price if current sales are not eroded. A third strategy is to sell the items in other markets or countries, or at or below their standard cost to customers or back to suppliers. Finally, E&O material could be sold for scrap or donated to charity to reduce taxes. It should be noted that any sales price that is below an item's standard cost requires a write-off to a balance sheet.

Some methods to implement these disposal strategies include using the current sales force to sell the material, advertising in various industry media, or using auctions (in person or on the Internet) to dispose of the E&O material. The ability of the E&O disposal team to sell the E&O material mitigates the E&O problem to an extent, but prevention of the problem is the best course of action for an organization.

How can an organization prevent or minimize the occurrence of E&O inventory? A cross-functional team associated with these issues can be created with the authority to take action to eliminate the root causes for the E&O inventory problem. A common issue is product or component proliferation. Proliferation causes a higher frequency of expediting inventory and material handling. A proven way to minimize proliferation is to periodically review product offerings. The goal should be outsourcing or discontinuing products with low profit margins. This profitability analysis should include a careful review of a product's profit and loss statement because low profitability may be due to factors unrelated to inventory management, such as sales adjustments or high standard cost, which can be improved. Marketing is usually a major contributor to a proliferation problem because their goal is to provide broad product offerings. Design engineering is a second major contributor to proliferation problems. Product designs should be simple with the minimum number of components using the design-for-manufacturing methods discussed in Chapter 4.

SALES AND OPERATIONS PLANNING

Competitive organizations use a sales and operating planning (S&OP) team to manage variations in demand and supply across a supply chain. The S&OP team uses several performance metrics to manage supply and demand. These have been discussed in previous chapters and include asset utilization efficiencies, invested capital, forecasting accuracy, scheduling changes, metadata accuracy, end-to-end order-to-cash lead time, on-time delivery to customers, supplier on-time delivery, and many others. In most situations, an S&OP team can navigate and negotiate across functional silos to improve process workflows. In summary, initiating an S&OP process is an effective and efficient way to coordinate complicated and constantly changing demand and supply information within a supply chain.

At any point in time, there are several pressing issues around the management of demand and supply. The S&OP team coordinates and manages the resolution of these issues. These include the loss or gain of major customers, management of seasonal or promotional demand patterns, and increasing inventory levels in anticipation of work stoppages. There are many other risks and concerns that may impact an organization's supply chain. The S&OP also manages resources such as inventory, equipment, labor, and available capacity. Properly structured, an S&OP team will have the authority to coordinate operational changes as need to balance demand and supply.

Organizations develop three- to five-year strategic plans to estimate demand and supply across the global supply chain. These planning and coordination activities are done at various forecasting time horizons, geographical locations throughout the supply chain, as well as its various product families or groups. Once the goals are aligned, all participants create their own plans to ensure operational plans are executed to meet annual operational goals. Some goals may require reductions in lead time, demand management, yield improvements, and capital expenditures or reengineering. Monthly or quarterly reviews are held to ensure all levels of an organization and supply chain participants meet their annual operations plan. Adjustments, including recovery and risk-mitigation plans, are also created. As an organization works through its annual operating plan during the year, all lessons learned regarding what has worked or has not worked should be incorporated into the next year's plan. This will enable the organization to develop more of an execution culture in which goals and objectives are consistently met regardless of external factors impacting the organization.

Key financial and operational metrics should meet the annual plan's goals if the combined activities of the S&OP team are successful. In other words, revenue from product sales, cash flow targets, and operational budgets should be at planned levels that approach 100% of annual operating plan goals. Another indicator of an effective S&OP process is that the master production schedule and actual shipments to customers balance each other relative to the original plan (i.e., the organization delivers products on schedule without having to process backorders). Backorders require longer order-to-deliver cycle times and higher transaction costs. When schedules or shipments are missed, the reasons need to be investigated and actions taken to ensure root causes are eliminated from the process. An effective S&OP process also ensures schedule changes occur within a product's lead time or frozen time fence. Production schedules should also be accurate and realistic. This means that processes should be standardized and available when needed for production. Work schedules should not be changed except on very rare occasions. Supply chain metadata should also be accurate and governed.

The accuracy of supply and demand metadata and actual data should be frequently reviewed because decisions regarding the efficient allocation of resources requires accuracy. If forecasting accuracy is poor, demand will be poorly estimated, causing inaccurate production schedules, inventory buildup, or errors in production (e.g., a product may be produced at a wrong location). On the supply side, lot sizes, lead times, and other measures directly impact an organization's internal or supplier schedules. Problems in these areas result in longer order-to-delivery cycle times and higher transaction costs. To resolve these issues, S&OP participants must be empowered to make supply and demand decisions at a product-family level or even lower to ensure a fast response to disruptions of the supply chain.

There are several indications an S&OP process is not properly working. As an example, if product forecasts are not based on an S&OP consensus, there may be differing demand estimates across the organization or supply chain participants. In this situation, several different estimates for demand may exist. These create an imbalance between demand and supply if teams second-guess each other. This can occur in several different ways. In one scenario, senior management may force an S&OP team to plan its supply using unrealistic forecasts due to external pressures to meet certain levels of sales revenue. This poor practice can seriously reduce operational efficiencies by causing production on the basis of nonexistent orders. Inventory will increase throughout a supply chain and, over time, the inventory pipeline of a supply chain may be filled with products that will not sell. After a time, customers will not accept additional inventory, even with pricing discounts. This causes a temporary suspension of internal production or supplier deliveries until the inventories are worked off over time. Another indication of a poorly performing S&OP process is excess inventory for some products or not enough inventory for others. There may be several reasons for this, such as new products that could not be sold or ordering lot sizes that are multiples of lead time.

Inventory is barometer of successful supply chain practices. An S&OP team should continually monitor its inventory investment levels and take corrective action to prevent an increase of E&O inventory. The build-up of E&O inventory usually indicates that a consensus demand forecast was not reached by an S&OP team. Another indication of a poorly performing S&OP process is capacity deterioration. Capacity deterioration can occur by building products that cannot be sold or not achieving needed operational efficiencies because of poor operational practices. Another is an arbitrary reduction of inventory at the end of the fiscal year to meet cash flow and investment goals (i.e., to avoid showing too much inventory was built). Arbitrarily reducing inventory causes lower order-fill rates and operational inefficiencies early in the next fiscal year because internal production must be increased to meet expected demand that was not met by low inventory levels. Excessively long lead times are another indication of breakdowns in the S&OP process. Reducing lead times dramatically improves the ability of a supply chain to dynamically respond to changes in customer demand.

Relative to the S&OP team's membership, the finance team is focused on revenue, cash flow, and budgetary targets needed to execute the annual operating plan. Variations to the annual operating financial plan require an S&OP team to adjust its demand and supply planning to meet financial goals. A financial forecast is one of several versions of a forecast that may exist in an organization. It is allocated linearly down through to the product group level and a finally to a forecast at an individual item or location level. It is also converted to a unit forecast using an item's standard cost. Initially, marketing and sales may have different forecast estimates based on the information they obtain from customers and the sales force. The differences between what finance has forecast versus forecasting estimates by the marketing and sales organizations must be reconciled by the S&OP team. A reconciliation process should have occurred during the strategic planning process. At the strategic planning level, forecast variations between finance, marketing, and sales are reconciled. If there are gaps, then planned promotions and increased sales activities are created to increase demand and close the gaps prior to starting the new fiscal year. In summary, a major function of the S&OP team is to reconcile financial, sales, and marketing forecasts to obtain a consensus forecast or "one number" for an organization. This may require additional promotional and sales efforts, but it is important that the S&OP financial forecast, based on strategic goals from the annual operating plan, is met at a product group level so supply is matched to demand.

Key marketing team activities include the introduction of new products, expansion of current markets, or development of new markets and customers. It is very important that marketing use statistically based market research tools and methods to develop forecasts for new products. These are inputs to an organization's sales plan and directly impact its supply chain. New product forecasts should be very carefully built by marketing and evaluated by the S&OP team. Miscalculations can significantly increase E&O inventory investment. Some organizations assign the cost of the E&O inventory to marketing's budget as an effective way to ensure marketing is held accountable. New product forecast accuracy is especially important for industries in which new products are the basis for an organization's revenue growth and profit. As an example, in high technology industries, the first company to get to market with a product or service often obtains a sizable market share and maintains this market share even after competitors later enter the same market. Marketing also impacts the degree of design obsolescence as it changes product packaging and other features of products and services. If the changes are not properly phased into a supply chain, through the S&OP team, the result may be that products or services become obsolete more quickly.

The sales team focuses on the revenue and gross margin on current product sales as well as product returns and other adjustments to sales. Failure to meet the original sales forecasts creates a situation in which the organization cannot achieve revenue and other financial goals. The information from field sales is critical for estimating demand at a product group level. Also, because sales are points of contact with customers, valuable information can be obtained that will help an S&OP team more efficiently manage supply to meet demand. Organizations should not use ad hoc or informal methods to obtain sales information. This may result in missed opportunities to manage supply and demand effectively.

Design engineering responsibilities to the S&OP team include resolving issues for new product development, design revisions to current products or services, bill-of-material issues, and warranty claims. Issues in these areas will delay the time to market of new products, increase the standard cost of products and services, and may have negative impacts on quality. They also directly impact sales forecasts for new products and the supply of current products. Bill-of-material and warranty issues may also impact an organization's operational costs. Chapter 4 discussed how product design and marketing drive the eventual cost of production and distribution over product life cycles. The more complex the design of a product or service, the more difficult it is for an S&OP team to manage supply and demand. Also, when design errors are found after release to production, any changes that need to be made will increase returned goods, warranty, and other costs.

The procurement team is responsible for the purchase of raw materials, components, and other resources needed to produce products and services. Key procurement activities are acquisition cost management, management of supplier lead times, new product launch lead times, and strategies for sourcing materials. In some organizations, procurement may also manage scheduling and inventory systems. Otherwise these systems are managed by materials planning or manufacturing. In addition, procurement is concerned with supplier development, optimum inventory levels, reducing order expediting and premium freight costs, studying new sourcing opportunities, and consolidating supply sources where possible, as well as insourcing or outsourcing activities. Finally, procurement works with design engineering to standardize product and service designs and their purchased components. As part of the S&OP team, procurement is responsible for managing major portions of an organization's supply chain.

The production team is responsible for creating and managing available capacity to meet production schedules, as well as resolving production scheduling and quality issues, material throughput, new product and process design issues impacting production, and supplier issues that impact production. It is important that production be provided with the resources and information needed to successfully produce an organization's products or services. The representatives of manufacturing or operations have major responsibilities on the S&OP team.

The production activity control team may be a separate team or a part of procurement or operations. Key activities include the maintenance of customer fill rates to meet service levels, management of lead times with procurement and suppliers, management of inventory, and improvements to forecast accuracy in collaboration with the forecasting team, which may reside within the finance, marketing, or the materials team. Additional responsibilities nclude managing unplanned orders and material controls systems, managing order backlogs, ensuring materials are available to production, and certifying that supporting metadata are accurate.

Distribution is focused on achieving customer fill rates and service levels, inventory investment goals, lead times by product class and inventory type, balancing inventory levels across distribution centers to improve inventory turns, reducing unplanned orders for products and service parts, working to eliminate excess and obsolete, managing labor expenses and overtime, ensuring orders are shipped on time and accurate, eliminating damaged products, reducing emergency orders, and reducing order redeployment and backorders. Additional responsibilities are an efficient transfer of materials across the supply chain.

GLOBAL SUPPLY CHAIN ISSUES

Process issues occur for many reasons, a number of which are influenced by the complexity of geographical dispersed locations and participants. Table 13.10 lists common global supply chain issues with their description. Poor line-item availability causes unfulfilled orders, higher transaction costs, and lower customer satisfaction. A line item is a product, component, material, or an associated service having a quantity. An order consists of one or more line items. If customer orders do not have all their line items in the right quantity and defect-free, then order fulfillment is less than 100%. A backorder is created when a line item is not shipped as part of an original order. This requires another shipment at a later time, increasing order handling and shipment costs. There are several reasons for backorders. Customer complaints occur if an order does not arrive on time and as promised.

Schedule changes occur if products or services are not ordered within their standard lead times, if orders are displaced from an established schedule, or if other causes interrupt production and fulfillment. This causes expediting of processes and degradation of operational efficiency. Although schedule changes can occur because of unforeseen circumstances, chronic rescheduling should be investigated and the root causes eliminated. Typical reasons for overtime include unplanned orders, schedule changes, and poor process yields, among other reasons. High inventory levels occur because of low inventory turnover causing higher inventory carrying costs which impacts investment. Low inventory turnover causes include long lead times, inaccurate forecasting, or other issues. Low cash flow is caused by long order-to-cash lead times and the causes of them such as quality issues, internal billing errors, customer payment policies,

TABLE 13.10

Global Supply Chain Issues

Issue	Description
1. Poor Line Item Availability	A "line" is one product and its associated quantity. An order can consist of one or more-line items. When product is not available to fill customer orders the line item availability is less than 100%.
2. Backorders	A backorder is created when a product is not shipped to a customer as part of the original order or a service is not provided. This situation requires the product be shipped later resulting in incremental handling and shipment costs.
3. Customer Complaints	Customer complaints occur if 100% of an order does not arrive on-time, defect free and at the agreed upon cost.
4. Schedule Changes	Schedules for products or services should not be changed within their lead time unless circumstances have changed since materials have been ordered and system capacity has been reserved to produce the product or service. Although schedule changes occur, and external causes eliminated from the process.
5. Unplanned Overtime	Chronic problems causing unplanned overtime expenses should be investigated and their causes eliminated from the process. Typical reasons include unplanned orders, schedule changes and poor process yields.
6. Unplanned inventory Carrying Costs	High inventory carrying costs should be investigated and their causes eliminated. The causes are either related to demand or lead time management e.g. large lot size and poor quality increase lead time and required safety stock or capacity.
7. Low Cash Flow	Low cash flow is caused by long order to cash lead times. Reasons include quality issues, internal billing errors and customer payment policies and other issues.
8. High Product Transfer Costs and Premium Freight	When materials or information are moved unnecessarily and especially between locations lead time and costs increases requiring more inventory or capacity.
9. Low Inventory Turns, Excess and Obsolete Inventory	Low inventory turns are caused by high levels of current inventory as well as excess and legacy obsolete inventory. High inventory or any type is caused by poor demand estimation and long lead times.
10. Damaged Product	Product can be damaged because of poor packaging, poor handling, environmental conditions and many other reasons. Chronic damage problems should be investigated, and their internal and external causes eliminated.

and other issues. Incremental transaction costs related to labor and transportation increase if materials or information are moved unnecessarily across a supply chain. Sometimes this may be needed from a strategic perspective when people, equipment, or materials are at either a central or decentralized location. Low inventory turnover is also caused by high levels of E&O inventory. Obsolete inventory is caused when it is no longer in demand because of design changes, changes in customer preferences, or demand was low. Materials can also be damaged, and information can be lost or corrupted because of poor packaging, poor handling, or environmental conditions. Chronic damage problems should be investigated and their root causes eliminated.

OUTSOURCING AND INSOURCING

Given the extent of globalization, the available technology, and the ease of creating virtual teams, new outsourcing and insourcing solutions have been created over the past several decades. Outsourcing and insourcing work is not simply sending it out or bringing it back into an organization. It is a set of activities that determine where and how work should be done, and by whom and under what conditions to increase its value-add content. The concept of what an organization "is" and "does" is under constant review. Outsourcing and insourcing have grown to more than the sum of the work being moved around the world. As an example, a manufacturer might insource some work activities that reduce the order-to-cash lead time to gain sales or reduce cost. Or perhaps it needs to increase customer satisfaction and revenue by expanding current product and service offerings by purchasing from competitors. These decisions are made from an end-to-end supply chain perspective to add value for all participants

Table 13.11 lists reasons why organizations outsource or insource work. Outsourcing work to increase capacity is a major benefit. Insourcing is sometimes needed to utilize in-house capacity more effectively. Organizations should be careful to insource only value-add work aligned with a core competency. Insourcing extraneous work into a process that is not designed for it causes operational inefficiencies. A classic example is when high and low technology is mixed, with the result that quality problems occur in the high technology operations and high unit costs occur in the lower technology operations. The result is overpriced or

TABLE 13.11

Reasons to Outsource and Insource

Reason	Outsourcing	Insourcing
1. Increase Capacity	Expand current labor and equipment capacity at low cost and risk.	Increase utilization of current capacity using labor and equipment having similar skills and capabilities as insourced work.
2. Obtain New Technology	Avoid the cost and risks of developing new technologies especial those which are not aligned with core technology.	Purchase or license new technology which is been fully developed by another organization to reduce cost and lead-time and ensure quality targets are met.
3. Reduce Financial And Market Risks	Allocate financial resources to core processes and current marketing activities.	Bring in work which external organizations cannot do at the cost, lead-time and quality levels required.
4. Reduce Supply Chain Lead Time	Move supply activities closer to markets to reduce lead-time and cost.	Bring in work that reduces supply chain lead time. Don't send work across the supply chain unless it is virtualized.
5. Focus On Core Processes	Outsource non-core processes to focus organizational resources on core activities important to drive sales growth.	Outsource non-core processes and insource core process work to improve volume efficiencies.
6. Expand Into New Markets	Partner with organizations in other markets to expand market share, reduce risk and cost.	Bring in work that is not currently done but uses common labor skills and equipment.
7. Improve Operational Efficiency And Reduce Cost	Work with external organizations which have a competitive labor or capital cost advantage.	Bring in work that increases increase volume and level load schedules.
8. Satisfy Country Rules, Regulations And Laws	Work with organizations having a favored regulatory position within their country such as licenses or permits.	Bring in work that cannot not be outsourced due to country rules, regulations and laws.
9. Obtain Cultural Expertise Relative To Market Segmentation.	Work with organizations to obtain design and marketing expertise relative to cultural norms and behavior.	Bring in design and marketing experts from other countries to create new products and markets.
10. Environmentally Challenging Operations	Work with organizations to deploy challenging operations which can only de done in certain regions of the world i.e. dry, wet, hot, or cold.	Bring in work which requires special handling equipment or skills.

underperforming products or services. The historical solution is to separate processes supporting different technologies unless they can be efficiently combined to maintain efficiencies regardless of the work being done. If insourced work reinforces core competencies and is properly integrated, there should not be process issues.

A second reason for outsourcing or insourcing work is to obtain new and unique technology. When outsourcing work, it might be more efficient to let other organizations that have advanced technology do portions of the work that your organization cannot or will not do. But proper contractual and other controls need to be in place to ensure the technology remains available, performance and costs are stable, and it cannot be used without permission. For insourcing, organizations can license technology from other organizations with similar assumptions. Minimizing financial risk or obtaining scarce materials are other benefits. The remainder of benefits include increasing operational synergies; reducing order-to-cash lead times in the supply chain; moving work closer to its markets to reduce lead time and cost; aligning resources to processes that are strategically important to drive sales growth, improve volume efficiencies, and expand into new markets; satisfying local country rules, regulations and laws; working with organizations that have a favored regulatory position such as licenses or permits; obtaining cultural expertise; accessing design and marketing expertise; or deploying challenging operations that can only be done in certain regions of the world. These include work that must be done under dry, wet, hot, or cold conditions or requires special handling equipment or skills.

Table 13.12 shows strategies used to create new relationships for outsourcing or insourcing work across a supply chain. These apply to the management of both intangible and tangible assets such as fixed assets, facilities and equipment, information, product, services, and people. These span a range of options from the outright sale of a business or process to the licensing of new technology and methods for sharing information. Regardless of the supply chain participant relationships, it is important that evaluations of outsourcing and insourcing are made using predetermined decision criteria and a risk analysis.

Table 13.13 provides key criteria that can help evaluate the feasibility for outsourcing or insourcing between organizations and locations. This list can be expanded or reduced depending on needs. In addition to ranking the relative importance of each evaluative factor, the methods necessary

TABLE 13.12

Outsourcing and Insourcing Scenarios

Strategy	Intangible Assets & Intellectual Property	Fixed Assets & Facilities	Equipment	Labor
Sale of Core Business	✓	✓	✓	✓
Sales Non-Core Business	✓	✓	✓	✓
Joint Venture	✓	✓	✓	✓
Partnership	✓	✓	✓	✓
Licensee Relationship	✓	✓	✓	✓
Share Information	✓	✓	✓	✓
Share Resources	✓	✓	✓	✓
Supplier Relationship	✓	✓	✓	✓
Contractor Relationship	✓	✓	✓	✓

Almost anything can be outsourced or insourced

to collect and analyze data for each criterion should be established and a model built for each combination of criterion levels to evaluate decisions.

SUMMARY

The development of an effective and efficient global supply chain having processes that are adaptable and flexible and contain high-value content is difficult, but this is a necessary component for competitiveness and increasing productivity. It requires creating a strategic vision of how global supply chain capacity is matched to localized demand. This requires analysis and justifications for where and when work is done as well as by whom and how it is done. Supply chain participants need to develop the right types of relationships to maximize productivity. They must continually rationalize asset utilization, transportation modes, and insourcing and outsourcing

TABLE 13.13

Outsourcing and Insourcing Criteria

Category	Evaluation Criteria	Relevancy		
		Low	Medium	High
Cultural	Cultural Norms			
	Cultural values			
Demographic	Population size			
	Population density			
	Age distribution			
	Education and skills			
	Language			
	Religious tolerance			
Economic	Economic stability			
	Available infrastructure			
	Available capital			
	Available equipment			
	Available labor			
	Available suppliers			
	Available customers			
Political	Legal system			
	Regulatory system			
	Taxation policies			
	Internal stability			
	Geopolitical stability			

strategies. The goal is to dynamically increase the percentage of value-add work across the supply chain for all participants. This requires products and services be optimally designed and supporting processes be adaptable and easily reconfigurable to meet changing customer needs.

Important characteristics of successful global supply chains include high collaboration between all participants, a high multi-cultural presence, adherence to global operational standards, high product availability, low costs, low order-to-delivery lead times, high transaction accuracy, and high asset availability and flexibility. High collaboration is enabled by virtual meetings, e-mail, and other communication systems. This helps identify where assets should be positioned across the supply chain to increase return on assets. Virtual project teams reflect local demographics and supplier networks. Adherence to global design and operational standards relative to packing, fulfillment, and logistics ensures products and services consistently meet customer requirements across diverse regions. Standards help simplify product and service designs and enable them to be used in different countries. Cost is also lowered.

Inventory provides a view into supply chain efficiency relative the use of assets. High inventory levels are a barometer for many types of process issues. It hides them. It does have several useful purposes. It preserves the independence of internal operations by serving as a buffer for both internal and external demand variation, provides production scheduling flexibility, maintains independence of supplier deliveries, and ensures that economic order quantities and lot-sizing targets are met in practice. Maintaining adequate inventory levels to ensure operational independence is critical for upholding a process takt time. This is particularly true at a system's bottleneck, which should be utilized at all times to maintain process throughput at the takt time rate. Regardless of the reasons for inventory, systematic reductions in investment can be made using projects that reduce lead time or demand variation.

Competitive organizations use a S&OP team to manage variations in demand and supply across a supply chain. This team coordinates all capacity resources including inventory to meet demand on the system. The S&OP team uses several performance metrics to manage supply and demand. These have been discussed in previous chapters and include asset utilization efficiencies, invested capital, forecasting accuracy, scheduling changes, metadata accuracy, end-to-end order-to-cash lead time, on-time delivery to customers, supplier on-time delivery, and many others. In most situations, an S&OP team can navigate and negotiate across functional silos to improve process workflows. In summary, initiating an S&OP process is an effective and efficient way to coordinate complicated and constantly changing demand and supply information within a supply chain. Supply chain process improvement projects will usually flow form the S&OP team actions.

14

Sustaining Strategies

OVERVIEW

Organizations deploy many initiatives. Some are successful and become that organization's way of doing things, whereas others fail. What makes an initiative successful? How are they sustained? Technology, tools, and methods alone cannot guarantee that a change initiative will be useful for increasing productivity and customer experience. An organization's culture or way of doing things should always be considered when deploying initiatives. This does not imply that poor work habits or non-competitive processes cannot be changed. But it does imply that there are effective ways to change them as opposed to other ways that severely impede change. In Chapter 2 we discussed the success attributes for effective change. In this final chapter we discuss ways to ensure we institutionalize changes that work.

Institutionalization requires leadership support to practice new behaviors. This will not be difficult if an operational initiative increases productivity and customer experience. With leadership support, the project portfolio and other resources are integrated into the strategic operating plan. These will provide the needed support to expand or create new competencies. Based on the lessons learned, paradigms will have shifted and the old way of working will be changed. The new tools, methods, and concepts are also assimilated. Leadership engagement is critical for success, and they must also practice these new behaviors. The organization will need to continually see their value for sustainability.

Sustaining change starts when we realize that the current state for the way things are done needs to be different. The teams that are brought together to envision the future state create a common vison for moving the organization forward. This is how they modify work processes and transition plans to develop new ways to work. From this work, productivity, customer experience, and other benefits are gained that increase competitiveness. In this final stage, the beneficial ways to work are expanded across an organization, validated, and institutionalized for sustainability. As we move to practice new behaviors, we also need to identify the resisting forces that impede doing things differently. Four topics are useful for sustainability. These are resistance analysis, stakeholder analysis from a sustainability perspective, roles, and responsibilities or RACI (Responsible, Accountable, Informed, and Consulted), and communications. These were discussed in Chapter 2 and examples were provided.

GLOBAL STANDARDS

An important part of sustainability are internal and external standards. When a process is changed, the new process must be auditable. An example is the auditing requirements of the International Standard Organization (ISO) and other certifying organizations. Change is not complete without ensuring process consistency and auditability. Standards form a basis for evaluation criteria that competitive organizations jointly use, as an industry, to regulate public products and services. They also impact suppliers, customers, and society. Global and local standards exist for almost every product and service sold today. Design teams and other functions such as testing, marketing, and finance should help create the standards that control how products and services are designed, produced, tested, and sold. The advantage of industry standards is that they are well written by competitors forming committees based on extensive industry experience. They are a consensus of the industry's best practices for designing, producing, and testing. But, depending on how they are written, they can promote or inhibit competition. Some are written to exclude new market entrants. Internal proprietary information will not be included in industry standards. Normally, internal standards will exceed industry standards because this is how organizations compete, i.e., on performance advantages relative to competitors. Highly adaptable organizations can also meet regional variations of a standard to satisfy localized preferences. In summary, it is important that organizations support the creation and updating of their industry's standards for the benefit of everyone.

Figure 14.1 provides a partial listing of global organizations that actively create and manage standards. It is a long list because of the importance of the work. Each country will have unique industrial standards by industry. In fact, within a single industry there may be several standards organizations that focus on different areas such as testing. Although standards help support competitive practices, they can also be manipulated to favor one country or organization relative to others if the committees creating them

Some International Standards Organizations:

- International Organization for Standardization (ISO)
- American Society of Testing and Materials (ASTM) International World Wide Web Consortium (W3C)
- Institute for Reference Materials and Measurements (European Union)
- **Many others ......**

Some United States Standards Organizations

- American National Standards Institute (ANSI)
- National Institute of Standards and Technology (NIST)
- Society of Automotive Engineers
- American Society of Testing and Materials (ASTM)
- **Many others...**

A Partial Listing of Standards Organizations by Country

- Australia: Standards of Australia (SA)
- Canada: Standards Council of Canada (SCC)
- China: Standards Administration of China (SAC)
- India: Bureau of Indian Standards (BIS)
- Israel: The Standards Institution of Israel (SII)
- Japan: Japan Industrial Standards Committee (JISC)
- Republic of Korea: Korean Agency for Technology and Standards (KATS)
- Singapore: Standards, Productivity, and Innovation Board (SPRING SG)
- Taiwan (Republic of China): The Bureau of Standards, Metrology, and Inspection (BSMI)
- United Kingdom: British Standards Institution (BSI)
- **Many others by their country ...**

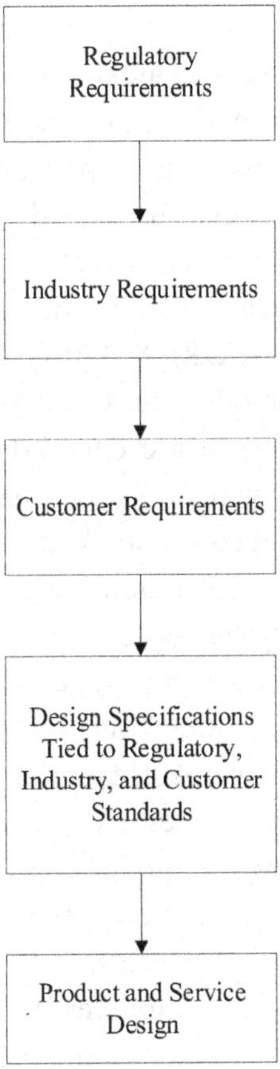

Regulatory Requirements → Industry Requirements → Customer Requirements → Design Specifications Tied to Regulatory, Industry, and Customer Standards → Product and Service Design

FIGURE 14.1
Common standards organizations.

are not fully representative of an industry. Large countries or groups of regional countries can minimize external competition by creating standards with a very narrow scope and requiring performance that competitive products or services cannot achieve. In an absence of political influence, there is a general tendency for cooperation in standards development. International standards organizations act as umbrella organizations that facilitate global commercial activities. As a result, global supply chains must simultaneously satisfy diverse types of standards to successfully operate across the world.

To the right of the standards listing in Figure 14.1 is a hierarchal listing that shows a sequence of steps for how standards influence deign and operations. Products and services need to satisfy diverse stakeholder groups. These include governmental regulatory requirements, industry standards, specific customer performance requirements, and internal design standards. Understanding and meeting or exceeding relevant standards helps organizations increase their competitiveness.

Global standards influence commerce across several industries and numerous organizations. Normally they are integrated into an industry framework that encompass different standards. A few will be described in this chapter. The first is the Supply Chain Operations Reference Model® (SCOR). SCOR is a trademark of the Supply Chain Council. The SCOR model breaks a supply chain into five components or process workflows. These are demand and supply planning; sourcing strategies; the transformation processes that vary by industry and include processes such as make-to-stock, make-to-order, assemble-to-order, and engineer-to-order; the warehousing and delivery of products; and the reverse logistical functions needed to process returns. These are further broken down into specific sub-processes. Standards have been developed for each of these as well as lower-level operations and work tasks. The goals of the SCOR model are to value stream map (VSM) the supply chain and value flow map (VFM) its processes and analyze all operations to compare their actual performance to the model's best-in-class performance benchmarks. The SCOR model provides operational definitions, expected performance metrics, and best-in-class tools, methods, and systems for its members to use for their supply chain improvements. This enables them to adapt processes to improve performance. Some metrics of the SCOR model include perfect order fulfillment, order fulfillment cycle time, system flexibility, lead times, and other performance metrics that are predictors of best-in-class global supply chain performance. Many of these are the same as those discussed in Chapter 13.

An interesting feature of the SCOR model is that it uses a generic modeling technique to fit any supply chain but then allows subsequent modifications to supply and demand, warehousing, and related supply chain processes. The modeling approach also applies specific standards to describe key supply chain operations. As an example, in the sourcing component, S_1 is source stocked product, S_2 is source make-to-order products, and S_3 is source engineer-to-order. Using this approach, each part of a global supply chain can be integrated into the SCOR model process by process. The analysis can be further decomposed into operations and work tasks. As an example, S_1 or source stocked product can be discomposed into operational tasks, such as $S_{1.1}$ or schedule product deliveries, $S_{1.2}$ or receive product, $S_{1.3}$ or verify product, and S_4 or authorize supplier payment. Each of these has a best-practice standard. The SCOR model is an example of a very well thought out and proactive standardization model that is highly flexible and adaptable as well as useful for improving global supply chain design and performance.

The International Standards Organization (ISO) is a benchmark against which manufacturing organizations are compared and evaluated across the world. There are many ISO standards that apply to diverse industries and functions in each industry. There also higher-level standards that provide guidance for how organizations approach standardization for consistent performance and most recently to improve performance and maintain process standardization. As an example, ISO 9000 was created to provide a framework of minimum quality system requirements. Associated with ISO 9000 are standards that document basic quality system requirements. These include document control, control of records, internal quality audits, non-conforming material control and disposition, corrective and preventive action systems.

As a follow up to ISO 9000, ISO 9001 was developed for organizations to demonstrate that they meet customer's contractual requirements. A criticism of the ISO 9001 system is that it is not proactive for helping improve quality systems, rather it is an auditing and status-quo evaluation method. In response to this criticism, the ISO organization developed ISO 9004. ISO 9004 is used to demonstrate the potential for process improvement. Strict adherence to agreed upon ISO standards is critical to being able to sell products and services because it is the basis on which global industries and organizations evaluate performance and conformance to standards.

Every country utilizes financial accounting standards, which can vary from country to country. In the United Sates, the Financial Accounting

Foundation (FAF) and its governing board of trustees is responsible for guiding the Financial Accounting Standards Board (FASB) and the Governmental Accounting Standards Board (GASB). These three entities are supported by constituencies including accountants, audited organizations, governmental agencies, and any other interested stakeholders. Figure 14.2 describes the basic elements of these relationships.

FASB and its associated organizations develop accounting standards and procedures that are helpful for collection, analysis, and management of financial information within the United States. In a manner like SCOR and ISO, FASB helps standardize work, but specifically work related to accounting and finance. The objectives of the FAF are to ensure that its

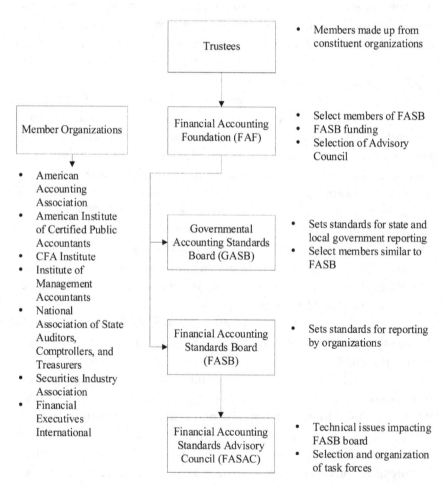

FIGURE 14.2
Financial accounting standards.

standards are fair and neutral so not to harm its stakeholders or the public. A cost to benefit analysis of newly developed standards is an important responsibility of FAF, so its standards are not unfair.

The Sarbanes-Oxley Act of 2002 was enacted by the U.S. Congress because of issues with public accounting and financial audits. The most prevalent issue was a conflict of interest between organization being audited and their independent auditors. Sarbanes-Oxley forces the chief executive officers of organizations to guarantee accurate disclosure in their financial statements. The common theme is accurate disclosure and independence of financial reporting. There are criminal penalties for falsifying financial records.

Specifically, Sarbanes-Oxley creates an oversight board (Title I) that sets registration with board, auditing, and quality control and independence standards and rules. Auditor independence (Title II) prohibits services outside of the scope of auditor practice and conflicts of interest. Title III guides the responsibilities of organizations regarding improper auditor influence. Transactions involving management and major stockholders and disclosure of the auditing committee's financial experts are described in Title IV. Statements of conflict of interest and the treatment of security analysts by registered securities associations is controlled by Title V. The balance of requirements include appropriation of resources (Title VI), various commissioned reports (Title VII), criminal penalties for altering documents (Title VIIII), criminal penalties for mail and wire fraud (Tilt IX), signing of corporate tax returns (Title X), and increased criminal penalties for tampering with records (Title XI). Auditing of financial reporting models have been updated to take into consideration the Sarbanes-Oxley Act of 2002. This Act provides an excellent basis on which to design accounting and financial control systems and their processes.

The standards of the Occupational Safety and Health Administration (OSHA) require reporting of incidents of worker injury and death and the elimination of their causes. OSHA standards are extensive and cover all known materials and situations that could harm employees. The six major OSHA standards include hazardous communication relative to hazardous chemicals in the workplace, including material fact sheets and standards; emergency action planning controls the actions employees must take in situations involving fire or other emergencies; fire safety requires employers to have a fire-prevention plan and standards in place at all locations; exit route planning requires that employers have exit routes and standards; all walking and working surfaces such as stairways, ladders, and other surfaces must be safely maintained; finally, medical and first aid requirements are required to be met in anticipation of expected incidents. These standards ensure that workers understand the materials and conditions in which they work, and the actions needed to prevent accidents, injuries, and deaths.

The standards developed, disseminated, and maintained by the Federal Drug Administration (FDA) are extensive and apply to products and services that impact the health of individuals in the United States. As an example, for medical devices, some requirements include pre-inspections, such as the application of good manufacturing practice (GMP) guidelines, directed device inspection, comprehensive device inspection, pre-approval device inspection, sterile devices. The regulations surrounding medical device manufacturing ensure organizations employ GMPs to develop and manufacture products or provide any associated thorough evaluation of performance data, clinical trials, and process audits.

The Automotive Industry Action Group (AIAG) develops standards for the design, manufacture, and production of automotive products. AIAG standards help suppliers and customers design, test, and manufacture products using best-in-class tools and methods. AIAG standards provide forms, checklists, templates, tools, and methods that ensure all information necessary to produce and validate performance is available to suppliers, customers, and other supply chain stakeholders. The AIAG standard is a phased methodology applied to a new product as it moves through the concept phase, the product and process design phases, the product validation phase, and finally into full-scale production. In parallel, quality assurance systems monitor performance to continually improve the design and production processes. It should also be noted that the tools and methods must be used in sequence, so the successful completion of a prior phase enables moving into the next phase.

Inputs to the AIAG planning phase include gathering the voice of the customer, marketing strategy, as well as previous product and process data from similar designs including testing information. The output of the planning phase is a preliminary bill of material (BOM), a design failure mode and effects analysis (DFMEA), a preliminary process flow, a list of special product features and functions, and related characteristics. These are used to create prototypes and to build a preliminary quality assurance plan. To the extent there are similar products in production, it is useful to review their performance to identify potential weaknesses in the new design. The DFMEA is also useful for looking for potential weaknesses in a new product. Design documentation will be updated when the team evaluates alternative designs and tests prototype versions of the final design.

The inputs into the product design phase are the outputs from the planning phase. In this phase, the team builds prototypes and develops documentation describing the new design using product drawings, performance specifications, and testing evaluations. A preliminary quality control plan is also created. The documentation reflects all current knowledge of the new design. The outputs of this phase include final DFMEA manufacturing recommendations, performance specifications, prototypes, engineering drawings, finalization of new equipment and testing requirements, special product characteristic lists, and a quality control plan finalized for design requirements. Design reviews are held throughout the product design phase with stakeholders, including sales, marketing, finance, manufacturing, quality assurance, and others.

The outputs from the product design phase become inputs to the process design phase. The process design team works concurrently with the design team to begin creating the supporting manufacturing process. Packaging standards and specifications, process flow charts, equipment layouts, process instructions including testing and auditing procedures, measurement systems analyses, preliminary capability studies, and a process failure mode and effects analysis (PFMEA) are developed. The next phase will control scale-up.

Customer requirements are tested and verified in the product and process validation phase. The outputs include a production trial using all specified materials, components, procedures, and measurement systems under production conditions. These include preliminary process capability studies, production part approvals by the customer, production validation testing, packaging evaluations, the production control plan, and the quality planning sign-off with management reporting. Once a new product has been qualified through the AIAG phases, it matures and goes through the classic product life cycle described in Figure 3.7. During these phases, the goal is to create products and supporting processes that meet all customer and stakeholder requirements.

The Malcolm Baldrige quality award was developed as an incentive for organizations in the United States to improve quality. The process starts with a self-assessment of organizational performance according to several criteria. The first criterion is leadership, which includes fiscal accountability, auditor independence, and strategic plans to increase productivity. The second category is an evaluation of strategic planning and its tactical linkage and execution, including its resource allocation with key performance measures indicative of success. The third category includes customer and market evaluations measured by gathering and analyzing the voice of the customer; it also includes customer relationship-building and retention statistics. Measurement, analysis, and knowledge management are the evaluation criteria of the fourth category, which is focused on ensuring data are effectively collected and managed across the organization to manage and improve financial and operational performance. In the fifth category, the hire and promotion of employees, the organization of work, and employee training and development are evaluated. Its sixth category focuses on identifying core processes that create value, and this information is used to understand how an organization reduces costs and improves productivity. The seventh category focuses on results such as customer satisfaction, market share, and financial performance. The self-assessment is just the first step of a Malcolm Baldrige evaluation process. After an organization calculates the benchmark score against the seven evaluation criteria, they have an option to ask for a formal assessment by Malcolm Baldrige auditors. In this evaluation process, independent auditors use detailed criteria and checklists to evaluate the organization. Recommendations are also provided to help the organization improve its quality system and operational performance.

METRICS DASHBOARDS

Sustainability depends on real change and the integration of those changes into the way work is done for consistency and auditability. Reporting of ongoing performance is a necessary requirement for effective change. Dashboards provide the reporting information to visualize performance and to convey information to users in rich ways that enable people to quickly grasp the meaning of the underlying information. They enable effective decision making using deep analysis of big databases. An advantage is that they are also prebuilt and can be refreshed using new information. This enhances collaboration between teams because information is current and actionable. If done properly, there will also be an ability to gain deeper insights into the underlying data by drilling down to lower levels of detail. Dashboards are tied to information technology platforms and supporting applications; this centralization provides a single source of truth and reporting governance. Other advantages are governance, a reduction in multiple reporting, time savings, and risk is reduced while accountability is increased.

There are different types of reporting dashboards. Some are targeted toward management to enable action; some are highly analytical to allow insight. Management dashboards are designed to provide information for decision making, whereas analytic dashboards bring together many variables and are designed for analysis of trends and other patterns. Design of a metrics dashboard specifically for measuring sustainability starts with the questions that need to be answered. These lead to the relevant metrics that will be gathered. After this, the metadata to support the metrics are identified and designed into the dashboard. Metadata organization also includes formulas and transformations of data or metrics. Productivity is an example of an important formula using several pieces of data. There are also several levels of dashboards used by different audiences. The overriding goal is to ensure metrics are important to the stakeholder audience, as well as being timely and actionable.

To take a Lean initiative example, lead time, yield, value-added contribution, inventory levels, and other measures are important, along with financial measures. Each initiative has specific metrics that are used for measuring success. As the dashboard audiences move up from an operational level to various leadership levels, metrics are combined to provide a single, 360-degree view of the business with drill-down capability as questions need to be answered for leadership. As an example, financial metrics can be combined to produce a productivity metric or economic value-added metric. The goals are always clarity, ease of understanding, and easy decision making based on models and business rules, and actionability.

Organizations create enormous amounts of data that need to be organized for easy consumption by employees, customers, suppliers, and other stakeholders. Reporting is a critical activity that pulls relevant data from disparate information technology systems and organizes it into formats relevant to different audiences that are easy to communicate and understand. This facilitates decisive action. In recent years, the concept of metrics dashboards has been created to bring together several reporting formats because decisions depend on more than one source of information. These types of systems are usually automated using the platforms and software applications discussed in Chapters 8 and 10. Recall that some of these were business process management tools and methods, including business process modeling and analysis, business intelligence, and business activity monitoring. There are also different software platforms and algorithms such as RPA that help create dashboards by accessing disconnected sources of data. If properly designed, reporting dashboards are useful for answering questions that rely on a meaningful display of information for easy interpretation.

Operational dashboards can also be considered from the perspective of differing levels of sophistication. The level 1 basic dashboard provides only metrics status information without intelligence. The level 2 dashboard provides users with recommended actions. Real-time process control or, for management dashboards, decision making is enabled in the most advanced dashboards at level 3. Process industries have used level 3 dashboards for several decades with sensors and advanced algorithms of various types. In the past few decades, these advanced systems were modified for discrete parts manufacturing and service systems using a business process management suite approach.

Finally, an important consideration for creating any dashboard is to ask the right questions. These should be aligned and consistent with the purpose of the dashboard, i.e., why is it needed and by whom? The next step is to identify the relevant metrics and their definitions, data sources, and owners. The metrics should also be actionable so that metadata lineage across the applications and down to lower actionable metrics are useful for root-cause analysis. A generic metrics dashboard is shown in Figure 14.3. The concept is that multiple views of a process are integrated with actionable information useful for improving performance. After the dashboard has been designed, the team finalizes the supporting process relative to its robotic process automation algorithms and other tools and methods that measure and monitor performance and enable root-cause analysis. Control points are created in the process and cross-referenced to the dashboard's metrics algorithms.

SUMMARY

To ensure sustainability, organizational promoters must be aligned to support initiatives. It is important that communications of what was accomplished, how these actions supported strategic goals, and what can be expected in the future are provided to the organization's

Data	Region ▾									
	Inventory by Region				Sales by Region				Inventory by Region	Total Sales by Region
Quarter ▾	East	North	South	West	East	North	South	West		
Q1	$ 370,000	$ 350,000	$ 735,200	$ 600,000	$ 3,700,000	$ 3,300,000	$ 3,676,000	$ 3,785,000	$ 2,055,200	$ 14,461,000
Q2	$ 260,001	$ 278,900	$ 408,000	$ 251,900	$ 2,243,000	$ 2,202,000	$ 2,008,000	$ 2,519,000	$ 1,198,801	$ 8,972,000
Q3	$ 223,205	$ 195,250	$ 360,000	$ 124,100	$ 1,013,000	$ 1,109,000	$ 1,129,000	$ 1,241,000	$ 902,555	$ 4,492,000
Q4	$ 780,000	$ 1,562,000	$ 600,000	$ 695,000	$ 8,012,000	$ 7,810,000	$ 8,001,000	$ 7,821,000	$ 3,637,000	$ 31,644,000
Total	$ 1,633,206	$ 2,386,150	$ 2,103,200	$ 1,671,000	$ 14,968,000	$ 14,421,000	$ 14,814,000	$ 15,366,000	$ 7,793,556	$ 59,569,000

FIGURE 14.3
Creating, analyzing, and interpreting metrics dashboards.

many stakeholders. Employees also need to practice the new behaviors. Therefore, leadership support is important. Training in the new concepts and ways to do the work are important to ensure people are comfortable with the changes. Rewards and recognition incentives must be updated to institutionalize the changes to reinforce the preferred behaviors. This requires polices, processes, and roles and responsibilities that are easy to understand. As we promote reinforcing behaviors, we also must avoid those behaviors that work against the changes. People should also know what to expect when using new tools and methods. There are advantages and disadvantages with any initiative. In other words, one initiative may be preferred over another for certain types of issues. No matter what, the new ways of working need to align with the organization's strategic direction. There should not be conflicting priorities with other initiatives.

Improving the value content of a global supply chain requires understanding diverse tools, methods and concepts, and their interrelationships in the context of strategic goals. As an example, Figure 14.4 integrates

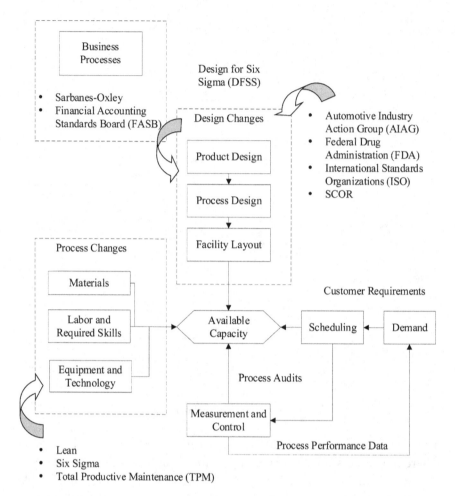

FIGURE 14.4
Control – integrating process improvements.

several the initiatives discussed in this book into a single framework. Each organization within this framework must develop effective and efficient processes through its supply chain to increase customer satisfaction and productivity. Competitive organizations manage these assets and processes for higher productivity than competitors. This is their basis for superior performance.

Organizations simultaneously must meet the requirements of several standards systems for auditability when changing products, services, and other work processes. It is important to work with international and national organizations to create these standards and to develop products and services that exceed them to remain competitive. The effectiveness of sustaining improvements is measured against internal and external standards relative to consistency and audibility.

Metrics dashboards help monitor and control the improved processes. They also link higher-level metrics to lower level metrics that are timely and actionable. Ideally, if an organization's processes are well documented, then they can be organized into a framework or model showing how the metrics and metadata are related and impact each other. The Dupont financial model discussed in Chapter 7 is an example of how financial and operational metrics should be organized to show the underlying dependencies. Dashboards have evolved to the point that they are supported on many device platforms such as mobile devices and available from cloud infrastructure from anywhere and at any time. They are also increasingly collaborative and intuitive tools. This promotes rapid decision making. Dashboard reporting uses 360-degree views of financial, customer, and operational performance data created through many sources, including the IoT. This ensures that reporting is always up to date. It should be noted that there are different types of dashboards that differ in sophistication.

Conclusion

This book was written for process improvement experts, consultants, and other people interested in improving global operations. It discussed useful tools and methods that are proven to improve customer satisfaction and productivity. It incorporated practical information to integrate the tools, methods, and concepts necessary to improve productivity from the "voice of" back into an organization's front-end sales and back-end fulfillment operations. It brought together leading-edge tools, methods, and concepts that provide process improvement experts and others a practical reference for improving their organization's quality, productivity, customer service, and other operations.

The major topics we discussed included alignment of strategy to the design of supporting systems to meet customer expectations, enhance their experience, and manage capacity and improve performance. Customers now expect a seamless experience when using products and services. The fourteen chapters in this book were carefully designed to show relationships between innovative tools and methods for deploying initiatives such as Lean and Six Sigma to increase operational productivity. The goal was to take a fresh approach for implementing operational excellence by considering the latest trends of digitalization, automation, and virtualization. It introduced and integrated from an operational perspective several leading-edge topics. These included customer experience, design thinking, Big Data, information technology (IT) ecosystems, and other initiatives to improve global supply chain productivity.

The interrelationships between Big Data and traditional data gathering methods were discussed relative to IT ecosystems. Supporting systems across diverse industries are virtual, and data move through many IT platforms and applications to support manufacturing and service processes. Understanding the ways that virtual work is now done also requires an understanding of how metadata is defined, traced through applications, and governed. Operations are now digitized and rely on automation, artificial intelligence, and related methods such as robotic process automation to do work efficiently and cost effectively. Global virtual teams are now a common way to work. This is especially true for the supporting back-office operations. All the important topics from the first edition have also been refreshed.

In the last few decades, several accelerating trends have changed the way in which we view the management of operations. Digitization has been a huge transformational force connecting IT systems and devices around the world. Work products are now, to a large extent, more informational than material. Teams collaborate globally through video conferencing of various types. Productivity and quality are also higher. Expectations around customer experience have become increasingly personal and seamless. Enhanced operational capabilities are continually evolving to support these disruptive changes. The expansion of the Internet with increasingly large capacity makes information readily available to much of the world. As a result, operations are focused on enabling innovative ways to offer highly customized products and services to customers globally. These trends contribute to the creation of new production systems that enable organizations to dominate, not necessarily by virtue of their size, but on core competencies in niche and newly created markets.

Automation is also being introduced through the IoT and other applications to increase productivity. The IoT is composed of interconnected smart devices and sensors. These can be accessed to aid information exchange and operational management. Operations are also being positively impacted from use of artificial intelligence to aid decision making and reduce mundane work tasks such as building reports or searching for information. In addition to artificial intelligence, RPA is a growing field that automates routine work. Most organizations are increasing this capability.

Globalization has also forced organizations to rethink operational strategy and capabilities. This book discussed how to align operational strategy to execute business goals, how to design systems to meet customer experience expectations, and how to improve performance to increase competitiveness. The emphasis was on improving operational efficiency, customer experience, and productivity through discussion of key enabling initiatives such as Lean, Six Sigma, Design, and Supply Excellence, as well as other methods. In Chapter 7, we discussed productivity to show how to measure the success of initiatives and their projects. Practical examples and applications were presented for manufacturing, service, and supporting operational systems. These demonstrated that processes can be substantially improved through the right strategic alignment and method application.

Competitive organizations focus on the usefulness of actions and their impact. These adaptable organizations do not resist change, instead embracing it with a willingness to learn and apply new thinking to solve problems. They have a strong motivation to change behaviors because experience teaches that competitiveness comes from leading rather than from following. Change is about building relationships and consensus with collaborative teams empowered to apply best practices to improve operational performance. Numerous cultural studies indicate that successful change initiatives have key success factors. These included identification of financial and operational performance gaps to make a business case for change. It is easier to gain support for an initiative that directly increases productivity and customer satisfaction. The specific initiative should also be aligned to the organization's business strategy. In other words, initiatives should be resourced based on strategic considerations and anticipated business benefits. Initiatives also need the formal support of leadership.

Organizations sometimes struggle with questions of where and how best to add value to gain competitive advantage. Sometimes they have competitive advantages based on favorable labor rates, laws and regulations that accelerate value creation, or efficient infrastructures that facilitate commerce. There are compensating strategies that can be used to increase relative competitiveness. These may include technology, effective use of capital and other resources, and using best-in-class organizational design and workforce management methods. Initiatives provide the new tools and methods, and they must be strategically aligned and provide benefits relative to the committed resources. If they do not create observable business benefits, they will fall into disuse. For this reason, it is important to measure the cumulative benefits of an initiative by type, impact, and other criteria relevant to the organization's goals. Operational improvements change processes to close gaps and provide benefits through new technology, tools, and methods that change the way work is performed.

At one time, organizational size and available capital could ensure market share. This enabled organizations to adapt slowly to changing market conditions. Market dominance used to be determined by the ability of large organizations to set industry standards and deploy capital-intensive barriers that prevented new entrants. Prior to the advent of globalization, an organization's operational strategy was relatively simple, and it was determined by the organization's available technology, its logistical systems, and competitive threats on a regional or, at worst, a national level. In today's world, competition is fierce. In fact, in some situations, smaller organizations dominate their market by neutralizing larger and historically more entrenched organizations. Effective execution requires doing the right things efficiently and according to schedule to achieve strategic and tactical goals and objectives. Competition leaves little room for poor strategic execution.

Customer interactions are increasingly more personal and engaging. Smart devices and social media enable customers to interact to a much higher degree with suppliers. Many transactions are initiated using mobile devices, and the decision to purchase is often immediate. The supporting systems around the purchase therefore need to be immediate (e.g., confirmation of purchase, order status, delivery estimates, and returns, as necessary). Operational systems are being adapted to service remote customers. Examples include automation, self-service inquiries, chat bots, and other software that directly engage customers to answer inquiries immediately. Customers can also access service agents because many work remotely and across the world to provide immediate service for inquiries. This provides real-time customer support. Customers can also be trained to use products and services through videos and self-service training.

Understanding the customer experience helps identify new products and services as well as ideas to improve current ones. VOC information is gathered from many sources, called listening posts, which are relatively new (e.g., social media). Listening modes have differing cost and time commitments and produce differing levels of information. For these reasons, they need to be carefully planned, piloted, and fine-tuned. Improvement projects identified from gathering the VOC should be selected and aligned to solve customer issues. Sometimes several projects may be needed to favorably impact overall customer experience. As an example, improvements in product availability, pricing accuracy, location, and other areas may be needed to improve a net promoter score (NPS).

Translating the VOC through an organization can identify exciting new solutions to old problems or completely redefine older problems in terms of new paradigms and solutions. This translation also enables organizations to align the gathering, analysis, and translation of the VOC into meaningful internal metrics and targets to identify performance gaps. New or modified products and services are created to close gaps to increase productivity and global competitiveness. This is done in a systematic way using standardized tools and methods. These changes are then aligned to production, supply chain, and other processes using translation tools and methods.

Quality function deployment (QFD) is an important translation tool discussed in Chapter 3. QFD the structured methodology used to map "critical-to" (CT)-customer requirements into design specifications (i.e., KPOVs or Ys). QFD is also used to analyze the relative performance of KPOVs to targets and current performance to identify gaps and to facilitate internal and external benchmarking. Customer experience mapping is another method used to translate customer feedback through the processes customers use to purchase and use products and services. This approach is different from obtaining customer feedback using surrogates such as sales and marketing personnel or third parties. Chapter 3's topics formed a basis for the subsequent discussions on increasing design and operational efficiencies.

Chapter 4 discussed product and service design. Design is a competitive differentiator that creates demand for products and services and influences total life cycle costs. The more complex a design, the higher the total cost. High complexity increases lead times and reduces overall quality of a product and its supporting systems. The best designs use concurrent engineering to manage the design process within a Design for Six Sigma (DFSS), Design Thinking (DT), or Agile framework. They also use design for manufacturing (DFM) to design products and services that are easy to produce for customers and employees.

Process design directly aligns to a product or service design. For this reason, process engineering works closely with a design team using concurrent engineering methods. Once a new process is designed and its steps are documented, its dynamic relationships can be modeled for optimization. The modeling approach varies depending on the process, ranging from evaluating process layouts using a whiteboard to utilizing highly mathematical analyses. The information gained from process modeling helps reduce process variation and ensures the design intent is met.

There are numerous case studies about organizations that have successfully applied Lean tools and methods. There is a sequence for creating an effective Lean deployment. It may take several years to stabilize a supply chain, although immediate cost savings, reductions in lead time, and higher quality levels can be seen even from limited application of key Lean methods. But the full benefits like pull scheduling and low inventory require foundational work be implemented as was shown in Figure 6-12. This includes establishing metrics to measure operational improvements for on-time delivery (schedule attainment), increasing value-add time to total time, increasing the throughput (order-to-cash cycle), enabling faster machine or job changeovers (especially at bottleneck resources), increasing machine uptime (available time), improving the quality of work (reductions in scrap, rework, warranty claims, and returns), using less floor space through process simplification and changes to layouts, lowering inventory levels to expose operational problems, improving supplier on-time delivery, and lowering overall system cost. Other foundational work requires implementation of a takt time to create a baseline from which waste can be systematically eliminated from a process, process simplification and standardization, mistake-proofing, bottleneck management, transfer batching, and mixed-model scheduling, as well as others. It is important that an organization determine the best scheduling rules and algorithms to manage their processes. These scheduling systems could be manual or automated based on the process. Scheduling will always be easier if the workflow has been configured optimally and Lean tools and methods are applied to simplify and standardize operations. Finally, we discussed useful methods for reducing process waste. These included the eight wastes, 5-Why analysis, 5-S, total productive maintenance (TPM), and mistake-proofing.

In Chapter 7, we discussed productivity. Increasing productivity is methodical process that requires doing the right things (effectiveness) in a strategic sense and doing these things in the right way (efficiency). Financial analysis identifies projects that improve productivity and are aligned to strategy. Once projects are identified, they need to be prioritized to balance resource commitments. Then the right initiatives with their tools and methods should be aligned to improvement projects. Every project should also be documented using project charters. This enhances communication across an organization and its stakeholders. Finally, all the projects driving productivity should be coordinated through a leadership forum (e.g., a steering committee to ensure periodic reviews and recommendations are provided to the project teams). This process also helps prioritize resource commitments.

Chapter 8 was a new chapter focused on the importance of IT in operations management. Regardless of the industry, IT integrates various systems consisting of machines, people, materials, and information. Creating an IT ecosystem that supports adaptable and flexible processes enables organizations to compete globally in diverse markets. IT ecosystems are very complex, having hundreds or even thousands of software applications supported by IT platforms with thousands of metadata fields. These need to be formally governed through a council. Clear roles and responsibilities are needed as well as an understanding of the metadata flowing from source to consuming systems. These systems and their metadata need owners and supporting governance processes. IT ecosystems may also have redundant systems if an organization has acquired other organizations having their own IT ecosystems.

Operations also benefits through direct IT automation across the ecosystem as well as focused RPA. Over the past few decades, advanced software applications have been designed to automatically navigate these ecosystems to collect and organize the enormous amount of data so it is useful for reporting, providing insights, and making decisions. RPA can be applied to mature and stable processes having high volumes or large batch sizes for which the business rules for doing work are logical. A RPA algorithm or macro mimics a highly manual process used to produce the work, but at lower cost and with higher quality. This includes automated access to metadata in other applications to copy, delete, or modify it to build reports, models, invoices, and other work products.

Organizations need to create IT ecosystem strategies for operations as well as global supply chains. Ecosystems contain hundreds or thousands of applications with multiple formats of metadata. Those focused on data domains (e.g., marketing, sales, finance, and production) would be a subset of the larger ecosystem and contain focused applications. Ecosystems may not be formally organized. Some may also be closed except to participants who have defined points of access. Open ecosystems are usually associated with e-commerce platforms. Supporting back-end operational systems in those applications need to adapt both to open ecosystems if they exist as well as to closed systems within their organization. Strategies should be developed to coordinate use of a platform and its applications to ensure operational efficiencies are maintained for participant satisfaction. This approach often leads to unique ecosystem designs where subgroups of participants work together to share information, work products such as analytics, algorithms, and reports with the hosting organization that provides platform governance.

Hosted ecosystems are also supported by a variety of third-party applications that provide information or a vehicle to create work products. Key roles include the hosting organization, suppliers, consumers, and experts of various applications. Data are easily shared by all participants based on data and business rules through cloud platforms and portals. Normalization of data is straightforward using metadata governance and rules. The second level of the ecosystems is the production of discrete workloads for data domains by their participants. This enables participants to contribute information to the work product. The highest level of the ecosystem are the user interfaces or portals that control access to the metadata, rules, and work products. These are organized by participant groups. Supporting the ecosystem are engineers and analysts who conceive new applications and coordinate the use of current applications through analytics, algorithms, functions, and features. These roles include discipline experts associated with coding, data domain experts, and application developers who improve the value of current applications or create new ones. This leads to the question of which organization owns the customer experience. Strategy is important. Customer satisfaction and the efficiency of internal operations, both IT and supporting systems, need to be governed across the supply chains to ensure excellent customer experience and productivity.

Agile project management is an effective methodology for coordinating and managing IT projects. It promotes the gathering of customer use stories and requirements by displaying them visually. This helps the Agile scrum team organize work tasks with discrete features and functions tied to user stories. These can be executed in a scrum sprint. At the end of a sprint, a working solution is reviewed by the business owner, customers, and stakeholders. Software development productivity will be higher and lead time will be reduced using Agile methodology.

Chapter 9 discussed the most common tools and methods used in the Six Sigma program from a management perspective. Quality management and improvement are also critical for improving an organization's competitiveness. It is important to align quality assurance and control activities with the concurrent engineering team to ensure products and services are designed to have high capability to meet customer requirements under a variety of actual use conditions. A quality program should be integrated to include continuous improvement as well as Six Sigma breakthrough tools and methods. All associates should be trained in basic quality tools, methods, and concepts to continuously improve their process. But sometimes it is important to use the rigorous Six Sigma methodology to achieve significant performance.

Chapter 10 discussed how Big Data is impacting operations. Big Data is a collection of very large and complex databases that defy previous management and processing methods. These have large volumes, large velocities, and a large variety of data formats, and the amount of available data has grown exponentially. Differing data formats (e.g., numbers, text, pictures, videos, voice, etc.) require enormous amounts of computer storage, server speed, and specialized analytical software to access, process, and interpret them. As a result, Big Data analytics ecosystems have evolved to include users, hardware devices, specialized software, storage arrays, private or public clouds, a variety of data sources, and conditioning and analytical software to enable access to the large databases. Big Data also affects classic process improvement tools and methods such as those used by Six Sigma practitioners. These methods rely on statistical sampling and small samples. In contrast, Big Data analytics usually counts 100% of a database's records and uses modified methods to analyze patterns and relationships between the variables.

Metadata are data fields where data are created, reviewed, updated, and deleted. Organizational systems have thousands of metadata fields. Some metadata is more important than others because it is used by several IT applications and processes. As an example, customer profiles are used for quoting, order, delivery, and invoicing. Metadata is associated with data domains, each having unique processes and owners. Because of this core metadata must be shared, information governance is important to ensure consistent definitions and use.

Data security is also an operational concern because data gathering and management devices are dispersed through a global supply chain (i.e., the IoT). Most organizations have policies, procedures, and processes designed to ensure secure data creation, review, updating, and deletion, depending on roles and responsibilities, but some are more effective than others, as evidenced by periodic data breaches. The General Data Protection Regulation (GDPR) was created by the European Union (EU) to control the security of personal data. Personal data are defined as information associated with an identified individual, who is called a data subject in the GDPR. The GDPR applies to personal data stored in IT systems located either within the EU or personal data of EU citizens stored and used in non-EU systems. Potential penalties for non-compliance are 2–4% of an organization's annual revenue.

Even very productive organizations should step back periodically to assign a team or bring in consultants to review how work is done and how it could be redesigned to focus more on customers or to be digitized or automated. Operational assessments are a proven strategy for increasing productivity. They are also used to evaluate changes to policies, process, roles, and responsibilities that impede productivity. Chapter 11 discussed the planning and execution of assessments as well as the methods for analyzing the information that is gathered. Although requiring an up-front commitment of time and resources, a well-done assessment creates a diverse project portfolio. The portfolio identifies opportunities for increasing business benefits and how to align them to strategy. In other words, whereas available reporting shows known performance gaps, operational assessments identify additional opportunities for improvement. These are incremental to current operational planning. The resulting impactful projects can be deployed either across an organization to start a new initiative or focused on a single function such as manufacturing or distribution and then expanded over time. Chapter 11 integrated many of the tools and methods from previous chapters into an assessment strategy. Rigorous analysis to prove that productivity opportunities exist above what is already in planning by the organization. Operational assessments identify these opportunities by creating project charters for major processes including production, the front office and supply chain that are supported by financial and operational analysis.

In addition to analytical identification of productivity opportunities, Chapter 11 discussed the advantages of value flow mapping of major processes to identify process improvement opportunities. The advantage of creating value flow maps is that the information gained by "walking a process" provides information beyond that available from existing management reports. This is especially true for rework loops and the "hidden factory," a term used to describe all of the undocumented and non-value-add process activities that take place within an organization. An organization is unaware of these activities, hence the term "hidden factory."

A major goal of operational assessments is the creation of project charters with site teams using interviews, reports, and process evaluations. The right tools and methods can be used to identify the root causes for a process issues or, if the solutions are known, execute them. As the charters are executed, the work needs to be balanced with available resources to avoid an overload on a few processes. After completing the assessment, the collected data are analyzed, and the operational impact is calculated for return on investment and other financial and operational analyses. Operational assessments should also be used on a continuing basis to improve organizational productivity.

Chapter 12 discussed virtual teams. This is another discussion of how people are now working. Teams are formed for different purposes. They differ in goals, duration, and form. Organizations are organized around work teams. This is a formal construct with a leader and reporting hierarchy. Everyone is part of a work team. Roles and responsibilities are clearly documented, and performance is evaluated according to this documentation. The team lead will often make decisions and allocate work to team members. Some work teams are self-managing to varying degrees. Teams are collocated, virtual, or a combination of both. They may also be geographically dispersed. Management teams resemble work teams in that they are formal, but their members are leaders for lower-level work teams normally organized by functional role. At times, organizations will bring together focused teams to complete focused goals on a high-priority basis. These teams need formal project charters to identity scope, goals, team members, sponsorship, resources, a schedule, and other relevant information. The charter is needed to avoid ambiguity of effort. These teams may also be highly cross-functional, depending on scope.

Recent studies report significant productivity increases from remote working, and the capability and opportunities to work remotely and still relate to others are growing. Prior to forming a virtual project team, there are several important considerations, including building trust, maintaining connections between team members, managing work, and eliminating barriers for doing remote work. It is important to build trust between remote workers and central teams, and policies and procedures for the teams to work together need to be well documented.

Few teams are immediately successful. All teams move through a maturation process discussed earlier in this chapter. There are several potential barriers to high performance. Teams need rules of engagement and norms that govern how they will work. A project charter is a good start, but meetings must be facilitated to enable good decision-making based on a full consideration of topics and result in fact-based action. Full consideration implies that all members participate in meeting discussions and that the team is diverse with respect to ideas to avoid groupthink. Facilitation also minimizes team conflicts and promotes mutual trust. Transparency is crucial for effective teams.

Chapter 12 also discussed project management. Projects have associated risks that must be identified, eliminated, mitigated, or managed, depending on their likelihood of occurrence and impact. Effective project management organizes people and resources to ensure activities remain on schedule and within budget at minimal project risk. Using a Gantt chart to organize activities is important to show the sequence of activities and the work tasks that must be completed on the critical path to reduce the time for project completion. In addition to estimating work task duration, the milestone schedule is estimated to enable periodic stakeholder reviews. Project status is communicated to the right audience, in the right format and with the appropriate frequency.

Project management requires an attention to detail to enable a project manager to keep a project on schedule and within budget. Understanding details and using the methods discussed in this chapter will help team leaders manage projects when conditions change. These methods are incorporated into project management software. Software enables a team to create simulations of a project's activities and work tasks to analyze the impact of adding resources on the critical path. Alternatively, if a project's activities are delayed, resources can be reallocated to the delayed activities to maintain the schedule. This is also useful if a project can be completed ahead of schedule, with the incremental resource cost offset by incremental revenue obtained through the early completion. In summary, project management is a complicated series of activities requiring specialized tools and methods. Effective project management requires an attention to detail at a work task level, but also at a higher level to keep the overall project schedule in view and achieve the schedule, target cost, and other benefits required by the project's charter.

Supply chains continue to undergo rapid evolution. Operational capabilities are increasing in ways that were not possible only a few years ago. Some organizations now deliver products or services on the same day they are ordered based on digitization and advanced inventory models. Energy efficiency and sustainability are also a focus of ethical supply chains. These trends have already been operative in manufacturing and other operations for several years. Global supply chains have unique IT platforms and applications that integrate with the supply chain participants through cloud infrastructure. Previously discussed trends such as customer experience, Big Data, and the other initiatives directly impact global supply chains. RPA and the IoT applications are everywhere. Machine learning and artificial intelligence are being applied across supply chains, just as they are in manufacturing and services. Cybersecurity has never been more important because of remote access to sensitive data. Operational changes are being pushed by digital transformations.

Even with all of these changes, the foundations for supply chain operations and improvement remain the same. These are meeting service-level agreements with enough capacity while reducing lead times and operational cost. Supply chains are becoming more complicated with different transportation modes, changes in laws and regulations, and competition from different directions. The focus is on enabling the workforce, and the emphasis on effective project management and team virtualization are competitive differentiators. Understanding where value is created and reconfiguration of supply chain design are key differentiators in an era of global supply chain digitization and competition.

The development of an effective and efficient global supply chain having processes that are adaptable, flexible, and contain high value content is difficult, but this is required for competitiveness and increasing productivity. To achieve this requires creating a strategic vision of how global supply chain capacity is matched to localized demand. This requires analysis and justifications for where and when work is done as well as by whom and how it is done. Supply chain participants need to develop the right types of relationships to maximize productivity. They must also continually rationalize asset utilization, transportation modes, and insourcing and outsourcing strategies. The goal is to dynamically increase the percentage of value-add work across the supply chain for all participants. This requires products and services be optimally designed and supporting processes be adaptable and easily reconfigurable to meet changing customer needs.

The last chapter discussed sustainability of initiatives and change programs as well as standardization of the new way of working. To ensure sustainability, organizational promoters for sustainability must be aligned to support initiatives. It is important that communication of what was accomplished, how it supports strategic goals, and what can be expected in the future are important. Employees need to practice the new behaviors. Therefore, leadership support is important. Management will allow workers to behave as they have been enabled. Training in the new concepts and ways to do the work are important to ensure people are comfortable with the changes. Rewards and recognition incentives must be updated to institutionalize the changes and to reinforce the preferred behaviors. This requires policies, processes, roles, and responsibilities be easy to understand. As we promote reinforcing behaviors, we also need to avoid those behaviors that work against the changes.

Regardless of the initiatives an organization deploys to increase productivity and remain competitive, its products, services, and supporting processes must meet the requirements of several standard systems. It is important to align and prioritize these and other initiatives with the organization's business strategy. Figure 14.4 integrates most of the initiatives discussed in this book into a single view. Each organization must develop effective and efficient processes through its supply chain to increase customer satisfaction and productivity. Improving the value content of a global supply chain requires understanding diverse tools, methods, and concepts as well as their interrelationships in the context of strategic goals. Competitive organizations manage assets and processes at very high efficiency and have higher productivity and shareholder economic value added than competitors. This is the basis of their superior performance.

It is important to work with international and national organizations to create standards and to develop products and services that exceed those standards. The effectiveness of sustaining improvements is measured against internal and external standards. Metrics dashboards help monitor and control improved processes. They also link higher-level metrics to lower-level measures that lead to actionable ideas. Ideally, if an organization's processes are well documented, then they can be organized into a quantitative framework or model showing how all the components are related and impact each other. The DuPont financial model discussed in Chapter 7 is an example of how financial and operational metrics should be organized to show the underlying dependencies. Understanding financial and operational models of processes so that improvement actions can be taken will improve productivity and shareholder economic value added.

The focus of this book was on increasing customer satisfaction and productivity through effective operations management. The tools, methods, and concepts can be applied to any process, including front-office services, manufacturing, and other production environments, as well as global supply chains. Diverse industries can improve productivity and shareholder value by aligning initiatives and projects that improve performance with operational strategy. Because we live in a highly competitive world, organizations need to identify their value-adding core competencies and create processes that also increase customer satisfaction. These should be designed and managed to further increase the value content for all supply chain participants.

The key concepts of this book are translating the voice of the customer to create products, services, and supporting systems that enhance the customer experience by making it seamless and intuitive. Effective translation now requires operational systems be adaptable to change through digitization, automation, and virtualization. These increase productivity and competitiveness, and enhance the customer experience.

Index

Printed in the United States
by Baker & Taylor Publisher Services

Printed in the United States
by Baker & Taylor Publisher Services